doubt with all the disadvantages that normally accompany structural change usually produced by accelerated growth. But we might also conclude that France's massive wealth did not help her to overcome the 'artificial' wealth (as Accarias de Sérionne would have called it) of England. Once more, I am inclined to sing the praises of the *artificial*. If I am not mistaken, England lived under a situation of greater strain than France, for years on end. But it was this strain which shaped the genius of Albion. And we should not forget that circumstances too played a part in this long duel. If reactionary and conservative Europe had not served England and laboured on her behalf, the victory over revolutionary and imperial France might have been put back for years. If the Napoleonic Wars had not distracted France from world trade, England would not have found it so easy to impose her rule on the globe.

5

For and Against Europe:
the Rest of the World

LET US NOW TURN AWAY from the quarrelling giants of the European world-economy – Britain, France and their allies, accomplices and rivals – and try to look more closely at the rest of the world, which for the purposes of this chapter will mean:
– the Americas – slowly but surely becoming 'Europeanized';
– Black Africa – which has perhaps been too hastily dismissed as 'primitive';
– the great expanse of eastern Europe, the self-contained world-economy represented by Muscovy (or indeed by modern Russia until the reign of Peter the Great);
– Islam, its splendour now in decline;
– and lastly a world in itself, the Far East.[1]

While we might have preferred to see this 'non-Europe'[2] on its own terms, it cannot properly be understood, even before the eighteenth century, except in terms of the mighty shadow cast over it by western Europe. Already all the world's problems were beginning to be seen in a Eurocentric perspective; and from this standpoint, limited and misleading though it might be, it is quite possible to describe *America* as a near-total success for Europe; *Africa* as a more promising success than it first appeared; the parallel cases of *Russia* and the *Ottoman Empire* – contradictory yet analogous – as areas of slowly-maturing success, gradual but inevitable; and the *Far East* – from the shores of the Red Sea, Abyssinia and South Africa to the East Indies, China and Japan – as a questionable success, more apparent than real: Europe's presence might be visible there in a thousand details, but that is only because we are looking for it – from a misleadingly privileged position what is more. (If the little continent of Europe were to be cut loose to float among the seas and land-masses of Asia, it would vanish from sight. In the eighteenth century, Europe had not yet acquired that overwhelming industrial superiority which would, for a while, eliminate the disparity.)

It was from all over the world, at any rate, that Europe was now drawing a substantial part of her strength and substance. And it was this extra share which enabled Europeans to reach superhuman heights in tackling the tasks encountered on the path to progress. Without this constant assistance, would Europe's industrial revolution – the key to her destiny – have been possible by the end of the eighteenth century? Whatever answer historians may propose for this question, it is one that must be asked.

It might also be asked whether Europe was somehow of a different human and *historical* nature from the rest of the world; and thus whether the confrontation which is the subject of this chapter, stressing contrasts and differences, will or will not help us to form a clearer judgment of Europe – that is of Europe's success. The conclusions do not in fact all tend in the same direction. For the rest of the world, as we shall see, very often went through economic experiences resembling those of Europe. Sometimes the time-lag was very slight – but it was nevertheless there, essentially as a result of Europe's coherence and effectiveness, which may after all have merely been a function of its comparatively small area. If France was, by the standards of the time, at a disadvantage compared to England because of covering a larger area, what is one to say about Asia, or Russia, or the infant Americas, or under-populated Africa, compared to the tiny but super-charged space occupied by western Europe? Europe's advantage can also, as we have seen, be explained by the particular social structures there, which encouraged capitalist accumulation on a larger scale and on a more secure footing than elsewhere – more often than not with the state's blessing. But it is also clear that if these forms of superiority, comparatively slight as they were, had not been translated into domination in every sense of the word, the European advance would not have occurred with such brilliance and rapidity, nor above all would it have produced the same consequences.

The Americas: playing for the highest stakes of all

Were the Americas Europe's 'periphery', its 'outer skin'? Both expressions are an indication of the way in which the New World, after 1492, was gradually drawn – body and soul, past, present and future – into the European sphere of action and thought,[3] the way in which it became integrated to Europe and eventually assumed its fantastic new meaning. Is not America – which Immanuel Wallerstein unhesitatingly includes in the sixteenth-century European world-economy – perhaps the true explanation of Europe's greatness? Did Europe not discover or indeed 'invent'[4] America, and has Europe not always celebrated Columbus's voyage as the greatest event in history 'since the creation'?[5]

Friedrich Lütge and Heinrich Bechtel[6] may well be right to minimize the *immediate* effect of the discovery of the New World, particularly from the standpoint of German history. But once America had made its entry to European life, it gradually altered all the deepest features of the Old World, drawing Europe's action in a new direction. Ignace Meyerson[7] following certain other writers, tells us that the individual is what he does, that he defines and reveals himself by his acts, and that 'being and doing' are one and the same: if so, I would say that America was Europe's 'doing', the achievement by which Europe most truly revealed her own nature. But it was an achievement which took so long to accomplish and to complete that its meaning can only be grasped when it is seen whole, in the fullness of its history.

America's wide open spaces: hostile but promising

If the discovery of America brought Europe little return in the short run, this was because the new continent was only partly apprehended and settled by the white man. Europe had patiently to reconstruct America in her own image before it began to correspond to her wishes. Such a labour of reconstruction was not of course accomplished overnight: in the early days, Europe indeed seemed insignificant and impotent faced with the superhuman task ahead and as yet only imperfectly perceived. In fact Europe took centuries to build a world in her own image across the Atlantic, and then only with immense variations and distortions, and after overcoming a long series of obstacles one after another.

In the first place, there were those of the natural world, that 'bites, smothers, silts, poisons and crushes',[8] and those caused by the inhuman expanse of territory stretching into the distance. 'The Spanish', complained a Frenchman in 1717, 'have [in America] kingdoms larger than the whole of Europe.'[9] They did indeed: but the extent of their dominions hindered their conquests. It had taken the conquistadors a mere thirty years to overcome the fragile Amerindian civilizations; but this victory had brought them 3 million km² at most, and even these were but imperfectly controlled. A hundred and fifty years later, in 1680, when Spanish and European expansion was coming to an end, only about half the New World had been settled – some 7 million km² out of 14 or 15 million.[10] Once the great American Indian civilizations had been subdued, the struggle would thereafter be waged against an empty landscape or against peoples still living in the Stone Age, foundations on which no conquest could be reliably based. The famous expeditions of the *Paulistas* across the wastes of South America in the sixteenth century, in search of gold, precious stones and slaves, were voyages neither of conquest nor of colonization: they left no more trace behind them than a ship does in the sea. And when in mid-sixteenth century, the Spanish arrived in southern Chile, they found nothing but a barren waste. 'Towards Atacama, near the deserted coast, you see a land without men, where there is not a bird, not a beast, nor a tree, nor any vegetation.'[11] Thus spoke Ercilla. The 'frontier', the open space to be conquered by human settlement, was forever on the horizon of American history, whether in eastern Peru or southern Chile, whether looking across the Venezuelan *llanos* or the wastes of Canada, in the Far West of the United States, the rolling plains of Argentina in the nineteenth century, or even in the Brazilian interior north-west of São Paulo in the twentieth century.[12] Distance on this scale meant wearisome travelling and exhausting and

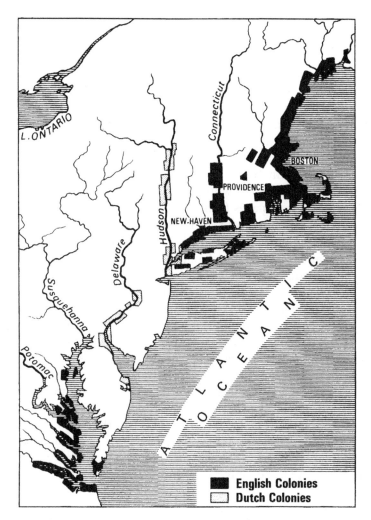

■	**English Colonies**
□	**Dutch Colonies**

39 THE ENGLISH AND DUTCH IN NORTH AMERICA IN 1660
The small colonial settlements, scattered along the coast, had not yet, by 1660, reached more than a tiny part of the territory to be colonized. The Dutch positions in New Amsterdam and on the Hudson River were handed over to the English at the Treaty of Breda in 1667. (From Rein, *Europäische Ausbreitung*, pl. XVII.)

interminable expeditions on foot. In the interior of New Spain (Mexico), voyagers travelled with a compass or astrolabe at hand, as if on the high seas.[13] Bueno da Silva and his son discovered gold in the far-off Goyaz region of Brazil in 1682; ten years later 'in 1692, the son set off for Goyaz with several companions; they were to take three years to reach the deposits'.[14]

The English colonies, still only sparsely populated, were scattered from Maine to Georgia over 2000 km, 'the same distance as from Paris to Morocco'.

In 1776, 'news of the Declaration of Independence took the same time – 29 days – to travel from Philadelphia to Charleston as it took to reach Paris from Philadelphia'.[15]

Like all natural features, the sheer size of the American continent did, it is true, work in more ways than one: it was both hindrance and opportunity, constraint and freedom. Because land was so plentiful it was cheap, while human labour was scarce. Lacking population, America could only become something if man was shackled to his task: serfdom and slavery, those ancient forms of bondage, appeared once more as if a necessity or a curse imposed by the size of the territory. At the same time, the open country offered a way of escape, a tempting prospect. The Indian who fled from his white masters had unlimited places to hide. Runaway slaves from the workshops, mines or plantations had only to make for the mountains or the impenetrable forests. It is only too easy to imagine the daunting task of the *entradas*, the expeditions sent to pursue them across the dense and trackless Brazilian forests: 'every soldier had to carry on his back weapons, powder and shot, . . . flour, drinking water, meat and fish'.[16] The *quilombo* of Palmares,[17] the republic of runaway slaves which lasted so long, covered a region perhaps the size of Portugal in the hinterland of Bahia.

As for white workers, willing or unwilling immigrants, they were bound by contract to a master who rarely treated them well. But once their term was up, they could go as pioneers to the 'new found lands'. Colonial America offered unlimited paths to 'the ends of the earth', *fines terrae*, awesome in prospect but the equivalent in their way of the 'good earth' which fulfilled the same role in the southern Siberian *taiga*; like the latter, the American frontier was a promised land, since it held out the offer of freedom. This was the major contrast with the Old World in western Europe, already 'full to bursting', where there was no frontier, no virgin lands, where the balance between subsistence and population was restored, if it had to be, only by famine or emigration.[18]

Regional or national markets

Gradually, however, the land was brought under control. Every pioneer settlement, however modest, was another position won; every town that grew was a small but undeniable victory. Every trail blazed (usually thanks to Indian lore and to food provided by the natives) marked progress, the condition of further progress, notably towards improvements in supplying the towns or towards the creation of fairs which sprang up almost everywhere. I refer not only to the internationally recognized fairs at Nombre de Dios, Porto Belo, Panama, Vera Cruz or Jalapa, on the road to Mexico City, but to the local fairs and modest markets which appeared in the middle of nowhere – the fur market at Albany in upstate New York for instance, or the wholesale markets of San Juan de los Lagos and Saltillo, in northern Mexico, which were just beginning to make their fortunes.[19]

The building of Savannah in Georgia. Frontispiece of Benjamin Martyn's book, *Reasons for establishing the colony of Georgia, 1733.* (British Library.)

When towards the end of the seventeenth century, a new breath of life surged through the Americas, the initial structuring of the economic area was almost complete. *Regional* (or even quasi-national) *markets* were taking shape within Spanish America, inside the prematurely-drawn administrative boundaries which at first enclosed half-empty spaces – later to be covered with roads, mule-trains and human settlements: such was the case of the vice-royalty of Peru (whose frontiers were larger than those of present-day Peru); of the *audiencia* of Quito (now Ecuador); or of the *audiencia* of Charcas (now Bolivia). Jean-Pierre Berthe[20] has described how, within the boundaries of the Mexican *audiencia* of New Galicia, drawn up in 1548, a regional market was constituted around the city of Guadalajara and its environs. Marcello Carmagnani's monograph on eighteenth-century Chile[21] is perhaps the best existing study of the formation of a regional or indeed 'national' market, particularly since it is situated within a general theoretical context.

Bringing the land under control was a slow process and at the close of the eighteenth century, there were still – as indeed there are today – unpopulated lands far from any road, territory to spare all over America. This explains why there have always been, and still are, so many wanderers that they have generic names – the *vadios* of Brazil, the *rotos* (ragged ones) of Chile, the *vagos* of Mexico. Mankind has never taken root in any real sense in the expanses of America. In the mid-nineteenth century, the *garimpeiros*, gold- and diamond-hunters wandering in the Brazilian *sertão*, returned to the Atlantic district of the

Ilheos south of Bahia and planted acres of cocoa bushes which can still be seen today.[22] But even farming was not enough to keep people in one spot: they would often move off, masters, men and beasts together, as if the New World had difficulty in creating and maintaining peasant communities attached to the soil like those in Europe. The typical peasant of the Brazilian interior, in the past and even today, the *caboclo*, is almost as mobile as the modern factory worker. The Argentinian *peón*, though not as mobile as the *gaucho* of the past, is still ready to travel.

So man was only partly in control over the country: wild life was still running riot in the eighteenth century – especially in the wide open spaces of North America, the land of the deer and the buffalo, of bison, bears, and animals prized for their fur, as well as of the grey squirrels now familiar in Europe – which migrated *en masse* in extraordinary journeys across rivers and lakes.[23] Cattle and horses from Europe reverted to the wild, where they bred in fantastic numbers, threatening the crops – perhaps the most picturesque form of colonization in the history of early European settlement in the New World. In large areas of New Spain, where the native population had drastically diminished, herds of livestock roamed where once humans had lived.[24]

Patterns of slavery

The everlasting problem in this boundless landscape was consequently a shortage of manpower. For emergent America required a supply of labour that was plentiful, easily controlled, cheap – ideally costing nothing at all – in order to develop the new economy. Eric Williams's pioneering study, *Capitalism and Slavery*,[25] points repeatedly to the causal links between the slavery, near-slavery, serfdom, quasi-serfdom, wage-earning and quasi-wage-earning in the New World, and the rise of capitalism in old Europe. The essence of mercantilism, he concludes, was slavery.[26] Marx had expressed the same thing in another way 'in an inspired sentence of perhaps unrivalled historical density': 'The veiled slavery of the wage-workers in Europe needed, for its pedestal, slavery pure and simple in the New World'.[27]

We are now familiar with the hardships of these American labourers, whatever the colour of their skin: such hardships are not to be laid at the door simply of the planters, the mine-owners, the moneylending merchants of the *Consulado* in Mexico City or elsewhere, the harsh officials of the Spanish Crown, the sugar- and tobacco-dealers, the slave-traders, or the grasping captains of trading vessels. All of these must carry some blame, but they were essentially middlemen, agents for other people. Las Casas accused them of being wholly responsible for the 'infernal servitude' of the Indians and wanted to refuse them the sacraments and expel them from the Church; but not once did he contest the rule of Spain – on the contrary. The king of Castile, *Apostol Mayor*, being responsible for all missionary activity, had the right to be *Imperador sobre muchos reyes*, ruler over all native sovereigns.[28] In reality the root of the evil lay back across the Atlantic, in Madrid, Seville, Cadiz, Lisbon, Bordeaux, Nantes, or Genoa, without question in Bristol, and in later years in Liverpool, London and Amsterdam. It was inherent in the reduction of a whole continent to the status of *periphery*, a result brought about by a distant force, indifferent to human sacrifice, operating by the almost mechanical logic of a world-economy. The word genocide is not too strong to describe what happened to the American Indians or the black people of Africa, but it is worth noting that white men did not survive entirely unscathed and were sometimes lucky to escape at all.

In fact one kind of servitude followed on the heels of another in the New World: the enslavement of the local Indian population led to its collapse; the servitude of white men (French *engagés* and English indentured servants) filled the gap for a while, especially in the West Indies and the English mainland colonies; and black slavery eventually created a community with the strength to put down roots and multiply, against all the odds. Lastly, mention should be made of the waves of immigration from all over Europe in the nineteenth and twentieth centuries, which swelled, as if by coincidence, just as the supply of slaves from Africa was slowing down or about to stop. The commander of a French ship once confided to me in 1935 that there was no more convenient cargo than the emigrants travelling steerage: 'they see themselves on and off the ship'.

Indian servitude could only survive where the population density and coherence of the pre-existing society were sufficient to create obedience and docility and to guarantee steady supplies of labour. In other words, it was confined to the areas of the former Aztec and Inca Empires. Elsewhere, the indigenous population collapsed on the first impact of the white conquests, whether in Brazil, where the natives fled from the coasts to the interior, or in the United States (the thirteen original colonies): 'In 1790, there were only 300 Indians left in Pennsylvania; 1500 in New York State; 1500 in Massachusetts; 10,000 in the Carolinas'.[29] In the Caribbean, invaded by the Spanish, the Dutch, the French and the English, the original inhabitants were wiped out, either by epidemics brought from Europe or for want of being found employment by the newcomers.[30]

By contrast, in the populated zones which were from the start the target of the Spanish conquest, the Indian population proved easy to regiment. Miraculously it survived the hardships of conquest and colonization: the mass murders and pitiless wars, the severing of social ties, the appropriation by force of its 'labour power', the high mortality of the portages and mines, and lastly the epidemics brought from Europe and Africa by both white and black men. Central Mexico, which had once had some 25 million inhabitants, was reduced, it is estimated, to a residual population of one million. The same 'abysmal' demographic collapse occurred in the island of Hispaniola (Haiti), in the Yucatan, in Central America, and later in Colombia.[31] A graphic illustration comes from

This scene probably depicts the mobilization of Indian labourers in front of the *senzalas* (the shanties in which the slaves lived). It is a marginal illustration on the map of the three naval battles in which the Dutch and Spanish united to fight the Portuguese on 13, 14 and 17 January 1640. Map of the Praefectura of Paraiba and Rio Grande, engraved in 1647.
B.N., Paris, Map Room, Ge CC 1339, map 133. (Photo B.N.)

Mexico, where in the early days of the conquest the Franciscans were celebrating mass on the steps of the churches, so great was the throng of the faithful; by the end of the sixteenth century, mass was being said inside the same churches, or even in mere chapels.[32] This demographic collapse was quite unprecedented, out of all proportion even to the horrors of the Black Death in fourteenth-century Europe. And yet the native population did not entirely disappear, but began to build up again from mid-seventeenth century, for the greater benefit of its Spanish masters, needless to say. The exploitation of the Indians continued with the semi-serfdom of the *encomiendas*, domestic service in the towns, and compulsory labour in the mines – referred to under the general heading of *repartimiento*, and known in Mexico as *cuatequitl* and in Ecuador, Peru, Bolivia and Colombia as *mita*, forced labour.[33]

In New Spain however, 'free' labour, that is in return for wages, was beginning to appear by the sixteenth century, the result of a crisis of some complexity. In the first place, the sharp decline of the Indian population led to large zones becoming waste lands, as deserted as parts of Europe in the fourteenth and fifteenth centuries after the Black Death. The land farmed by Indian villages shrank to a series of islands and it was in the empty space thus spontaneously vacated or wrongfully confiscated that the large estates, the *haciendas*, were established. The Indian who desired to escape from the collective duties imposed upon him by village society or from the state in its hunt for manpower, could flee to the *haciendas*, where a *de facto* serfdom came into being, and into which later wage-labourers would have to be recruited; or he could flee to the towns, where domestic service or the craft workshops would welcome him; or to the mines, not those nearest Mexico City which still used forced labour, but those further north, in the towns that sprang up in the desert from Guanajuato to San Luis de Potosi. Over 3000 mines, some of them tiny, were scattered over this area, employing a total of ten or eleven thousand workers in the sixteenth century and perhaps 70,000 in the eighteenth; the workers came from all directions, Indians, half-breeds and whites, all mingling together. The introduction in about 1554-6 of the mercury amalgam process[34] made it possible to treat inferior ores, to reduce overheads, and to increase productivity and production.

As in Europe, the mining community was a world apart; masters and men were heavy spenders, poor savers and fond of gambling. The workers received a sort of bonus – the *partido* – according to the quantity of ore they mined. Their wages were very high, by the standards of the time, but the work was terrible (dynamite was not in use before the eighteenth century) and it made for a restless, violent and sometimes cruel community, much given to drinking and feasting. Not only were there 'artificial paradises' on which one historian has wryly commented[35] but a craving for festivity and above all a persistent love of display. In the eighteenth century, such tendencies were aggravated as if prosperity had proved a poor counsellor. If a worker found himself with 300 pesos at the end of the week,[36] they were quickly spent. One man might buy himself fine clothes, cambric shirts. Another might invite 2000 guests to banquet at his expense, and squander the 40,000 pesos he had made by discovering a small mine. So this restless world wagged, in its own peculiar way.

Less dramatic and less lively indeed was the scene in the Peruvian mines, the largest in sixteenth-century America. The amalgam process reached Peru late, in 1572, but did not bring freedom. The forced labour (*mita*) continued and Potosi was still the miner's purgatory. Was the system kept going by its own success? Possibly: not until the end of the century did Potosi lose the lead it never afterwards recovered, despite a spurt of renewed activity in the eighteenth century.

In the end then, the Indian population bore the brunt of the first large-scale development of the New World by Spain: Indians worked in the mines, in agriculture – in particular growing maize, the key to survival in the Americas; they manned the mule- and llama-trains without which neither silver nor anything else could have been carried, officially from Potosi to Arica, or clandestinely from the High Andes, by Cordoba, to the Rio de la Plata (the River Plate).[37]

On the other hand, where there were only scattered tribes of Indians, European colonists had to build with their own hands: in Brazil, before the sugar plantations; in the French or English mainland colonies, or in the West Indies. Until about the 1670s, the French and the English both called very largely on the service of *engagés* (the French term) or indentured servants (the English term). Both *engagés* and servants were virtually slaves.[38] Their lot barely differed from that of the black Africans who were now beginning to arrive; like them, they had been transported across the ocean crammed into the holds of narrow ships and fed on uneatable food. Moreover when they had been brought to America at a company's expense, the company had the right to recoup its losses: the *engagés* were sold, in exactly the same way as slaves, having to suffer being inspected and looked over like cattle by their purchasers.[39] The *engagés* and indentured servants were not of course slaves for life, nor would their descendants be slaves. But this in itself hardly incited their master to treat them well, since he knew he would lose them when their contract was up (36 months in the French West Indies, four to seven years in the English colonies).

In England, as in France, every device was tried to recruit the necessary numbers of emigrants. More than 6000 contracts to serve as *engagés* have been found in the archives at La Rochelle for the period 1635-1715. Half of the recruits came from Saintonge, Poitou and Aunis, provinces whose 'wealth' was illusory. To swell the numbers of emigrants, misleading advertisements were sometimes supplemented by violence. Press gangs would swoop on certain districts of Paris.[40] Men, women and children were kidnapped into emigration in Bristol; or heavy criminal sentences were passed to increase the number of 'volunteers' for the New World who could thus save themselves from the gallows or from the galleys. Large numbers of Scottish and Irish prisoners were transported under Cromwell. Between 1717 and 1779, England dispatched 50,000 deportees[41] to the colonies; the humanitarian evangelist, John Oglethorpe, in 1732 founded the new colony of Georgia to receive the large numbers of transported debtors.[42]

White 'servitude' went on over a long period and on a large scale, as Eric Williams has pointed out, arguing that the different forms of slavery in the Americas followed on each other's heels and in a sense governed each other: as soon as one form ended, another took its place. The sequence was not absolutely automatic, but the general rule is clear enough. White slavery was called upon only when there were not enough Indians; and black slavery, the massive importation of black Africans into the New World, did not develop until the supply of both Indian labour and the white manpower imported from Europe dried up. In areas where black slaves were not employed – in the grain belt north of New York for instance – white indentured servants were still to be found until the eighteenth century. The demands of colonialism thus governed a series of changes, for economic rather than racial reasons: they had nothing 'to do with the colour of the labourer'.[43] White 'slaves' gradually disappeared because they had the drawback of being on fixed contracts – and they may have cost more to keep too, in terms of diet.

Once the *engagés* and indentured servants were released from their contracts, they might clear and farm small-holdings devoted to tobacco, indigo, coffee or cotton. But subsequently, they often lost out to the big plantations developed for the all-conquering sugar industry, a costly and therefore capitalist enterprise which required a large labour force and expensive plant, in other words fixed capital. And under the heading of fixed capital came black slaves. The big sugar plantations drove out the small-holdings which, ironically, had helped them to start up: on land which had been cleared and cultivated by the small farmer, it was easier to establish plantations. Exactly the same process could be seen at work in the 1930s in the pioneer districts of São Paulo state in Brazil, where temporary small farms were preparing the way for the huge coffee-growing *fazendas* which would eventually take over.

During the sixteenth and seventeenth centuries, as larger farms (proportionally) appeared, the numbers of black slaves essential to such enterprises increased. After the dramatic drop in the Indian population, the economic process which drew African populations to America began to operate of its own accord: 'money, not passions, passions of wickedness and goodness, spun the plot'.[44] Stronger than the Indian (it was said that one black slave could do the work of four Indians), more docile and dependent since he was cut off from his community of origin, the black slave was bought and sold as merchandise, or even ordered in advance. The slave-trade made it possible to set up sugar plantations gigantic for the time – going to the very limits of distance in view of the problem of carting the cane, which had to be taken to the mill for processing as soon as it was cut, or it would rot.[45] On these huge plantations, the work was essentially regular, repetitive and unskilled, with only a handful of jobs for technicians or skilled workers.

The docility, permanence and physical strength of the black work-force made it the cheapest, most efficient and before long the most sought-after labour. If in Virginia and Maryland tobacco-growing, originally practised by white smallholders, expanded rapidly between 1663 and 1699[46] – when exports increased sixfold – it was because black labour was replacing white. At the same time, and it comes as no surprise, a semi-feudal aristocracy was becoming established – cultured, sophisticated but also oppressive. Once tobacco was grown on a large scale for export, like wheat in Sicily or Poland, or sugar in the Brazilian Nordeste and the West Indies, it created a similar social order as the same causes produced similar results.

But black slaves were used for many other tasks. Gold extraction in Brazil, which began in the last years of the seventeenth century, was the result of the massive incorporation into the *Minas Geraes*, the Goyaz and the *sertão* of Bahia, of thousands of black slaves. And if black slaves were not on the whole sent to

An engraving illustrating J.-B. Debret's *Voyage pittoresque et historique au Bresil* (1834). The author provides a commentary on pp. 78-9: this slave dealer's shop in Val Longo street in Rio de Janeiro was a 'veritable warehouse' where black slaves arriving from the African coast were brought by their owners. The dealer, sitting in the armchair, is discussing the purchase of a child with a *Mineiro* (owner of the Geraes Mines). The attic behind bars at the back of the room served as a dormitory for the slaves who climbed a ladder to reach it. There were no windows apart from a few loopholes. 'This', writes Debret 'is the Bazaar in which men are bought and sold.' (Photo B.N., Paris.)

the silver mines of the Andes or northern New Spain, it was for the good reason that after the long journey to the interior they cost more than on the Atlantic coast – and not only, as is sometimes claimed, because the cold in the mountains (real enough) made it impossible for them to perform the hard labour required in the mines.

The different kinds of slave-labour in America were in fact more interchangeable than has been thought. Indians could be used as gold-panners, as happened near Quito. And we can dismiss as nonsense the idea that white men could not live as manual labourers in the tropics (as Adam Smith among many others believed).[47] The *engagés* and servants certainly worked with their hands in the seventeenth century. German settlers established themselves a hundred years ago in Seafort, Jamaica and are living and working there still. The Panama canal was dug by Italian navvies. And cane-cutting in the tropical part of northern Australia is done entirely by white labourers. Similarly in the southern United States, white manual labour has taken over to a large extent as black people have moved north to the cold climate of the big cities, Chicago, Detroit or New York, without any particular detriment to their health. So if climate (although it certainly should not be ignored) is not the only explanation of the distribution and settlement of populations in the New World, then clearly we must turn for further enlightenment to history: not only to the complex history of European exploitation, but also to the powerful past of the pre-Columbian civilizations, the Aztecs and the Incas, which left on American soil indelible traces of Indian culture. In the end, history allowed an Indian America, an African America and a white America to survive to the present day: they may have intermingled but not to any great extent, since they can still be unmistakably distinguished from one another.

When the colonies worked for Europe

How many times has it been said that America had to recreate Europe across the sea? This is true only in part, but sufficiently so for one not to take literally Alberto Flores Galindo's view[48] that no European interpretation of any American phenomenon can be entertained. By and large, America was obliged to travel, as best she could and on her own account, through the long stages of Europe's history – without necessarily respecting either the same order or the original models, it is true. The experiences of Europe – Antiquity, the Middle Ages, the Renaissance, the Reformation[49] – can be detected in America, although not clearly distinguished. I still have a very strong visual recollection of the pioneer zones of twentieth-century America, which provide a clearer picture than any learned disquisition could give of what it must have been like when the forests were cleared in thirteenth-century Europe. Similarly, certain features of the earliest European towns in the New World, with their patriarchal dynasties, conjure up for the historian a vision of classical antiquity – part true, part false perhaps, but unforgettable. And I admit to being fascinated by the history of these American towns which sprang up even *before* the countryside was settled, or at much the same time. They make it possible to imagine in a new light that crucial burst of urban growth in eleventh- and twelfth-century Europe – which most medievalists have persisted (rather oddly to my mind) in regarding as the slowly-maturing fruit of agricultural (rather than commercial or urban) advance.

How sensible is it to see such things as mere echoes, when in fact Europe was firmly controlling overseas development and making all the rules? Since every colonial power was determined to hold on to its own share of America without yielding an inch (forcing upon it the 'colonial pact' or the *exclusif*) transatlantic societies would have found it very difficult to detach themselves from the remote control and ever-present model of Europe – a mother which kept her offspring firmly attached to her apron strings and had moments of distraction only in the early days, during the dark hours of the first modest settlements. England and Spain allowed their original American colonies to develop more or less under their own steam. Then when their progeny had grown and prospered, they were taken in hand and brought under metropolitan control: the institutions of the mother country were both the instruments and beneficiaries of 'centralizing' policies.

Such centralization was both natural and the more willingly accepted since it was indispensable if the infant colonies were to be defended against attack from other European colonial powers. For rivalry remained keen among those who had shared out the New World and endless conflicts were waged along the landward frontiers as well as along the interminable American coastline.

A further reason for the ready acceptance of centralization was that it maintained the rule of the white minority within the colony, a minority still attached to the beliefs, thought, language and way of life of what was already regarded as the 'Old World' back in Europe. Although small in numbers, the landed aristocracy which settled the central valley of Chile in the eighteenth century was effective, active and dominant – 'the 200 or so families'[50] of the country. The plutocracy of Potosí in 1692 consisted of a mere handful of persons 'dressed in cloth of gold and silver, for no other costume would be good enough for them'.[51] Their households were unbelievably luxurious. How many wealthy merchants were there in Boston on the eve of the American Revolution, in 1774? What enabled such tiny communities to survive was probably the passivity of the workers in the first place, but they also depended on the complicity of an all-embracing social order which it was in Europe's interests to maintain at all costs.

It is true that these societies might vary in their degree of docility or of dependence on the mother country. But disobedience – when it occurred – did nothing to alter their way of life or the internal ordering and functioning of the colony, itself inseparable from the order and functioning which have formed the backbone of all European societies, past and present. The least subservient and the least easy to control of these societies were those outside the major intercontinental trade routes, those whose 'mediocre economy ... was not governed by one dominant product',[52] by some monoculture controlled from the other side of the Atlantic.[53] These neglected societies and economies, receiving little investment and few orders, remaining poor and comparatively undisturbed, were pushed towards self-sufficiency. Such for example were the pastoral regions of Peru on the slopes of the Andes, above the Amazon rain-forests; the Venezuelan *llanos*, where the *encomenderos* did not allow themselves to be dictated to by the authoritarian government in Caracas; or the valley of the São Francisco, the 'sheep-river' in the Brazilian interior, home of half-wild flocks, where the feudal landowner Garcia de Rezende was said to possess an area as big as France under

Louis XIV (but virtually uninhabited). The same would have been true of any remote town so isolated in the great open spaces of America that it was virtually obliged – even if it had no urge for independence – to govern itself. In the late seventeenth century and even in the eighteenth, São Paulo, the old capital of the first *bandeirantes*,[54] was still an example of such involuntary independence. 'The Portuguese', wrote Accarias de Sérionne in 1766, 'have few settlements in the Brazilian interior; the city of São Paulo is the one they regard as the most important ... This city is more than a twelve-hour journey inland.'[55] 'It is a sort of Republic', wrote Coreal, 'originally composed of all kinds of godless and lawless men.'[56] The *Paulistas* considered themselves to be a free race: an apter description of the town would have been a hornet's nest: its inhabitants scoured the roads of the interior and if they took supplies to the mining camps, they also raided the Indian villages of the Jesuit foundations along the Paraña, even venturing into Peru and Amazonia (1659).[57]

Nevertheless, there were docile and obedient economies in plenty. How could tobacco-growing Virginia or sugar-growing Jamaica have rebelled, when they depended on sales to the English market and on credit from London banks? Before the American colonies could gain their independence, a number of conditions not easily united had to be fulfilled. What was more, the right moment had to be chosen, as would be demonstrated by the first great anti-European revolution, that of England's American colonies in 1774.

Rebel colonies also needed sufficient strength of their own to enable the colonial order to be maintained and developed without the assistance of the mother-country. And this order was under constant threat. The planters of Jamaica lived in terror of a slave uprising; the Brazilian interior had its 'republics' of runaway slaves; Indian 'bravos'[58] threatened the vital communications of the isthmus of Panama; in southern Chile, the Araucanians were a threat until far into the nineteenth century; in Louisiana, an Indian rising in 1709 required the dispatch of a small French expeditionary force.[59]

When the colonies worked against Europe

But could the 'colonial pact' be maintained in circumstances of the most glaring inequality? The colonies only existed to serve the wealth, prestige and strength of their mother-countries. Their trade and indeed their entire life was under constant surveillance. Thomas Jefferson, the future President of the United States, baldly described the plantations of Virginia as 'a species of property annexed to certain mercantile houses in London'.[60] Another grievance was the near-critical shortage of currency: England was constantly besieged with complaints on this score from her American colonies. No steps were taken to remedy the situation: the mother-country intended to maintain a positive trade balance with the colonies and therefore to extract currency from them, not to dispatch it to them.[61] So however boundless the patience of these subordinate countries, such a regime might not have lasted long if all the rules and regulations had been scrupulously observed; if distance – to mention only the long sea voyage across the Atlantic – had not created a measure of freedom; and if smuggling – ubiquitous and unstoppable – had not appeared to oil the wheels of commerce.

The result was a certain *laissez-aller*, a relaxation of discipline, so that certain habits and expedients crept in, at first unobtrusively, which it was afterwards difficult to forbid. Thus there were no effective customs posts; and the colonial administration saw itself as being there not to carry out to the letter instructions from home, but to accommodate local and private interests. Moreover, the expansion of trade helped the American economies to acquire their own sources of currency, to see to it that some of the bullion from the American mines, whether by fraud or simply by market forces, remained behind instead of sailing to Europe. 'Before 1785, it was normal to find the Church in Mexico contracting with the peasants to receive tithes in silver'[62] – a significant detail. And credit, a sign of advanced development, had a role to play even in the distant Brazilian interior. It is true that there the presence of gold made all the difference: the *Conselho* of Vila Rica wrote to the king on 7 May 1751 that many miners 'clearly still owe the money for the slaves they own, so that the man who looks rich from outside is really poor, while many who live poorly are actually rich'.[63] The owner of a gold-panning concession would be operating thanks to advance payments made to him by merchants, funds which he would have used in particular to buy slaves. The same development appeared in the silver-mining countries. From D.A. Brading's fascinating book on eighteenth-century New Spain, seen largely from the vantage-point of Guanajuato, the biggest mining town of the time in America or indeed the world, one has the impression that credit could take any of a multitude of forms, combining or mingling them, destroying one combination and inventing another, *ad infinitum*.

The clear lesson of all this is that a by no means negligible accumulation of capital on the part of local merchants was taking place. In Spanish America, there were even such rich Creole merchants that it was said at the end of the eighteenth century that Spain was 'the colony of its colonies'. Was this merely a figure of speech or does it betray Spanish resentment against people who did not know their place? At any rate, during every independence crisis, one finds plenty of evidence of bitter conflicts and animosity between the merchants settled in the New World and the capitalists back home. Such was the case in Boston, in Buenos Aires where local merchants wanted to break off dealings with the wholesalers in Cadiz, and in the Brazilian towns where hostility to Portuguese merchants turned to hatred. In Rio de Janeiro, where murder and theft were commonplace, the Portuguese merchant with rings on his fingers, ostentatiously dining off silver plate, was a hated figure: any stick was good enough to beat him with – failing all else savage ridicule, depicting him as a clumsy and odious figure of fun, perhaps a cuckolded husband. A fascinating study in social psychology could be made of those who were known throughout Spanish America as the *chapetones* or *gachupines* – the recent arrivals from Spain, inexperienced, presumptuous and very often with a fortune secured in advance. They arrived to reinforce the small groups already on the spot who had succeeded in capturing the key places in commerce. The whole of Mexico for instance was under the thumb of merchants originally from the Basque provinces or from the mountains behind Santander. These merchant dynasties brought out from Spain nephews, cousins or neighbours from their home villages, and recruited assistants, successors and sons-in-law. The newcomers romped home in the 'marriage stakes'. In 1810, Father Miguel Hidalgo y Costilla, the Mexican revolutionary priest who, like many other people, would have liked to put an end to this *gachupina* immigration, accused them of being 'unnatural men ... The force behind all their toil is sordid avarice ... They are Catholics through policy, their true God is money', *Su Dios es el dinero*.[64]

The conflict over industry

In industry as in commerce, the conflict between colonies and mother country had roots reaching far back. As early as the end of the sixteenth century, a long crisis hit Latin America and probably the whole of the continent.[65] European capitalism was going through a difficult patch to say the least; so during the seventeenth century, the 'American end' had to find its own salvation. The emergent regional markets extended their trade links: the Brazilians moved steadily out towards the Andes; Chile supplied grain to Peru; ships from Boston brought flour, timber and Newfoundland cod to the Caribbean, and so on. Local industries sprang up. In Quito in 1692, there were 'manufactories of serge and canvas ... coarse fabrics ... which serve to clothe the people. These are sold in Peru and Chile, and even in the Tierra Firme and Panama, by way of Guayaquil which is Quito's port [on the Pacific]. And they are also transported overland to Popayan'.[66] Similar expansion in textile production occurred in New Granada at Socorro,[67] in the Peruvian province of Cuzco, in the Indian provinces of southern Mexico at La Puebla;[68] and in the interior of what would later be Argentina, notably in Mendoza where, reports Bishop Lizarraga, 'the Indians who have been brought up among us make a thread as fine as the finest Biscay thread'.[69] Many other transformation industries of agricultural or animal products developed: soap and tallow candles were manufactured everywhere, and everywhere too leather was processed.[70]

Having been established it seems during the difficult years of the seventeenth century, at a time when much of America was being 'feudalized' as the great *haciendas* appeared, would this elementary industry lead to greater things when the economic climate improved? For this to occur, Europe would have had to surrender its monopoly on manufacture – and this was very far from what Europe had in mind. Lord Chatham is supposed to have said: 'If America so much as considers making a stocking or a horseshoe nail, she shall feel the full

An embroidery workshop in Peru. The workers are women of mixed race. Madrid, Palacio Real, Libro Trujillo del Peru. (Photo Mas.)

weight of British might'.[71] Such a remark, if it really was made, reveals something of Britain's intentions, but also of her ignorance of realities across the Atlantic: the New World was quite prepared to manufacture the things it needed.

In short, the whole of America, as it matured, developed its own reciprocal arrangements and devised its own expedients. Spanish America in particular found in the smuggling networks a measure of freedom and a source of profit. The Manila galleon, as everyone knew, was a means of snatching American silver out of the clutches of Spain or indeed Europe, for the benefit of far-off China and the capitalists of the *Consulado* in Mexico City. What was more, up to the end of the eighteenth century, by far the lion's share of the silver coins and ingots was going not to the king of Spain (now no more than a poor relation) but to private merchants - including the merchants of the New World.

The English colonies choose liberty

The general unrest in the New World first surfaced in the English colonies in America. 'Insurrection' is perhaps too strong a word for the Boston Tea Party when, on 16 December 1774, a number of rebels disguised as Indians boarded three ships owned by the India Company standing at anchor in Boston harbour, and threw their cargo of tea into the sea. But this minor incident marked the beginning of the break between the colonies - the future United States - and England.

The conflict undoubtedly had its origins in the economic progress of the eighteenth century which brought increased prosperity to the English colonies along with the rest of America - possibly more so since they were in the thick of internal and external trade.

The earliest sign of such prosperity was the constant stream of immigrants - English workmen, Irish peasants, Scots - many of the latter in fact from Ulster and having taken ship in Belfast. In the five years preceding 1774, 152 ships left Irish ports carrying '44,000 passengers'.[72] And there was a wave of German colonists too: between 1720 and 1730, they virtually 'Germanized ... Pennsylvania'[73] where the Quakers were soon in a minority compared to Germans and Irish Catholics. German immigration increased even more after independence, since many German mercenaries in the British Army decided to settle in America.

This immigration amounted to 'a trade in human beings'.[74] In 1781, 'one major dealer boasted of having himself, before the war, imported 40,000 Europeans: "Palatines", Swabians, some Alsatians. They emigrated through Holland'.[75] But it was above all the Irish who were the object of a traffic akin in all but name to the slave trade, and which did not cease with independence, indeed the contrary.

> The import trade [sic] from Ireland [explains a report in 1783], which was suspended during the war, has been resumed with large profits for those engaged in it. [One boat has landed] 350 men, women and children, no sooner arrived than immediately hired. [The procedure is a simple one]: a [ship's] captain puts his conditions to the emigrants in Dublin or some other Irish port. Those who can pay for their passage - usually about 100 or 80 [*livres tournois*] - arrive in America free to take any engagement that suits them. Those who cannot pay are carried at the expense of the shipowner, who in order to recoup his money, advertises on arrival that he has imported artisans, labourers and domestic servants and that he has agreed with them on his own[76] account to hire their services for a period normally of 3, 4 or 5 years for men and women and 6 or 7 years for children. The most recently imported have been hired for the sum of 150 or 300,[77] delivered over to the captain, depending on sex, age

and strength. Their masters have only to feed, clothe and lodge them. When their service is up, they are given a suit of clothes, and a shovel and they are absolutely free. Fifteen or sixteen thousand are expected for the next winter, mostly Irish. The Dublin magistrates have great difficulty preventing emigration. And the entrepreneurs are beginning to look to Germany.[78]

As a result, there became established a form of migration 'running from the [Atlantic] coasts to the mountains and even further westwards ... A single dwelling serves for all until one has been built for each [family]'. The newcomers, as soon as they had made some money, 'come to Philadelphia to pay the price of the land' assigned them, which was usually offered for sale by the government of the colony (later the state government). The colonists 'very often ... resell these plots and go elsewhere in search of uncultivated land which they again sell once they have worked it. Many labourers have thus cleared up to six different sites'.[79] This document from the end of the eighteenth century provides a good picture of what had already become the well-established phenomenon of the 'frontier', attracting immigrants eager to make their fortunes once they had served out their contracts. The Scots in particular ventured into the great forests and lived in the Indian style, moving all the time from one clearing to another. Behind them, less adventurous immigrants, often Germans, stayed to farm the reclaimed land.[80]

This human tide, flowing towards the lands and forests of the West, both accompanied and stimulated a general economic advance. Observers felt they were watching a biological explosion: the Americans, they said 'have as many children as they can. Widows with a large family are sure to remarry'.[81] The high birth rate swelled the population figures as a whole. At this rate, even the regions north of Philadelphia gradually ceased to be inhabited by settlers of exclusively English stock. And since the Scots, Irish, Germans or Dutch felt only indifference or hostility to England, this ethnic mixture, beginning early and increasing quickly, no doubt hastened the break with the mother country. In October 1810, the newly-arrived French consul in New York tried, as he had been instructed by Paris,[82] to define 'the present state of mind of the inhabitants of the State and their real feelings towards France'. His reply is interesting:

> It is not by the populous city where I live [New York at the time had 80,000 inhabitants] that one should judge: its inhabitants, who are for the most part foreigners and made up of every nation except Americans so to speak, have in general no mind for anything but business. New York might be described as a permanent fair in which two-thirds of the population is always being replaced; where huge business deals are being made, almost always with fictitious capital, and where luxury has reached alarming heights. So trade rarely has a sound foundation: the frequent bankruptcies – often of men of great fortune – cause little stir; what is more, a bankrupt rarely meets anything but the greatest indulgence from his creditors, as if each man hoped to acquire a right to reciprocal tolerance. It is in the countryside and in the inland towns that one must look for the American population of New York State.

As for the human transformations brought about by the 'melting-pot', were these not felt by the entire 'American' population (still quite small at this time – 3 million in about 1774) to be foreign intrusions, as massive in comparative terms as those of the late nineteenth century?

All the same, this phenomenon was more marked in the northern colonies (New England, Massachusetts, Connecticut, Rhode Island, New Hampshire, New York, New Jersey, Delaware and Pennsylvania) than in the southern colonies (Virginia, Maryland, North and South Carolina and Georgia) which were the scene of a completely different society of plantation owners and black slaves. Even today, if one visits Jefferson's magnificent mansion at Monticello, deep in Virginia, one can see parallels between this and the *Casas Grandes* of Brazil or the Great Houses of Jamaica, with the difference that most of the slaves' quarters are here in the basement of the huge building which seems to press down on them with all its weight. Much of what Gilberto Freyre has written about the plantations and the towns of the Brazilian Nordeste could be applied to the American Deep South. But despite their similarities of situation, these two experiences remain distinct in human terms. They are separated by everything that divides Portugal from England – differences of culture, mentality, religion, sexual habits. The amours between the lords of the *engenhos* and their slaves were conducted openly, as Gilberto Freyre reports, whereas Jefferson's long-standing passion for one of his young slave-girls was a closely-guarded secret.[83]

This distinction between North and South was a strongly marked structural feature which would influence the history of the future United States from the start. In 1781, an observer wrote of New Hampshire: 'One does not see here as one does in the southern states, the owner of 1000 slaves and eight or ten thousand acres lording it over his more modest neighbour'.[84] A year later, another writer wrote in the same vein: 'In the South, there is greater wealth of a smaller number; in the North there is more public prosperity and individual happiness, a happy mediocrity, a larger population'.[85] This is perhaps simplifying the picture unduly, and Franklin Jameson has introduced some nuances to it.[86] Even in New England, although they were extremely rare since the aristocracy was mainly city-dwelling, some large estates did exist. In New York State, 'manors' covered a total of 2½ million acres and the Van Rensselaer manor for instance, about a hundred miles from the Hudson River, measured 24 miles by 28, that is two-thirds the size of the entire colony of Rhode Island (which was admittedly very small). The big estates were even bigger in the southern colonies, even in Pennsylvania and more so in Maryland and Virginia, where the Fairfaxes owned a property of 6 million acres. In North Carolina, Lord Granville's estate alone was the equivalent of one-third the area of the colony. It is clear that the southern states, but also some of the northern ones lent themselves to an aristocratic regime, sometimes concealed, sometimes undisguised, amounting to a 'transplant' of the social system from the old country, of which primogeniture

Boston in 1801. View of State Street and Old State House: brick-built houses, carriages in the street, European fashions. Painting by James B. Marston, Massachusetts Historical Society, Boston. (Photo I.P.S.)

was the corner-stone. At the same time, since small properties found corners for themselves in between the big estates, either in the North where the relief made the land unsuitable for large-scale agriculture, or in the West where virgin forest had to be cleared to make way for the plough, the unequal division of the land, in an economy overwhelmingly dominated by agriculture, did not prevent the establishment of a fairly stable social balance, from which the privileged bene-fited most – that is until the revolution, which destroyed many landed families who took England's side, and which was followed by a wave of expropriations, sales and developments, conducted 'in a quiet, sober Anglo-Saxon way'.[87]

So the agrarian regime was more complicated than a simple North–South contrast might suggest. Of the 500,000 black slaves in the thirteen colonies, 200,000 were in Virginia, 100,000 in South Carolina, 70 or 80 thousand in Maryland, about the same in North Carolina, perhaps 25,000 in New York State, 10,000 in New Jersey, 6000 in Connecticut, 6000 in Pennsylvania, 4000 in Rhode Island, 5000 in Massachusetts.[88] In Boston in 1770, there were 'over 500 carriages and it was a sign of magnificence to have a Negro coachman'.[89] Curiously, it was in the state with most slaves – Virginia – that the aristocracy was most favourable to the Whigs, that is to the revolution, whose success it probably ensured.

It seems that the contradiction between demanding freedom for white settlers from English rule and continuing to acquiesce in black slavery did not yet unduly trouble anyone. In 1763, an English parson preaching to a congregation in Virginia assured his listeners that he did them 'no more than justice in bearing witness, that in no part of the world were slaves ever better treated than, in general, they are in the colonies'.[90] One need not regard this as gospel truth. In any case, the real situation of the slaves, even in the southern plantations, could vary greatly from one place to another and it may well be that, being better integrated into the Spanish or Portuguese American settlements, black slaves were actually happier there, or less unhappy, at any rate in some regions.[91]

Competition and rivalry in trade

The thirteen colonies taken together formed an essentially agricultural unit: in 1789, 'the number of workers employed in agriculture is at least nine out of ten in the United States as a whole and the value of the capital invested in agriculture several times as great as that in all the other branches of industry put together'.[92] But despite the prime importance of land, of pioneering and of crop cultivation, the colonies were in fact driven to rebellion primarily by the growing maritime and mercantile activity of the northern regions, especially New England. While commerce was not the dominant economic activity, it was nonetheless the determining one. Adam Smith (who understood the American colonies he had never seen in his life better than the industrial revolution taking place under his nose at home) perhaps came nearest to the essential causes of the American rebellion, the events and repercussions of which he followed closely: *The Wealth of Nations* was published in 1776, two years after the Boston Tea Party. Adam Smith's interpretation is contained in one little sentence. Duly praising the British government as being so much more generous towards its colonies than other European powers, he points out that 'the liberty of the English colonists to manage their own affairs their own way is complete' – but he is obliged to add a qualification: 'in everything except their foreign trade'.[93] Quite an exception – and one which caused both direct and indirect damage to the whole economy of the colonies, forcing them to go through London for everything, to depend on London credit and above all to stay inside the trading straitjacket of the British 'Empire'. But New England, with its key ports, Plymouth and Boston, which had quickly sensed the possibilities offered by trade, could only consent to such restriction grudgingly, or by cheating and evading the controls. 'American' trade was far too lively and too spontaneous not to seize the freedom it was not granted; but such expedients could never be more than half-satisfactory.

New England had been rebuilt[94] between 1620 and 1640 by Puritans expelled from Stuart England whose ambition was to found a closed society, free from the sins, injustices and inequalities of this world. But the land was poor and the sea offered its services: a small trading community became established there almost from the start – perhaps because the northern English colonies were closest to and most conveniently situated for trade with the old country? Or perhaps because the coast of Acadia, the mouth of the St Lawrence and the banks of Newfoundland were a nearby source of providential food from the sea? The New England settlers 'made most money' from fishing: 'Without delving into the entrails of the earth which they leave to the Spanish and Portuguese, they get [this money] from the fish which they carry to the latter'.[95] Further assets were the sailors who became expert in this hardy enterprise, and the ships which had to be built to carry it out. In New England in 1782, the fishing industry accounted for 600 vessels and 5000 men.

But the New Englanders were not satisfied with this activity on their door-step. 'They were known [and this in itself is revealing] as the Dutchmen of America.... It was said that American ships operated even more economically than those of the Dutch. This quality and the low prices of their goods made them unbeatable freighters.' They had indeed organized to their own advantage coastal shipping between the central and southern colonies and distributed over a wide radius their products: grain, tobacco, rice and indigo. They took it upon themselves to supply the English, French, Dutch and Danish West Indies: they shipped out fish, salt mackerel, cod, whale oil, horses, salt beef, and also timber, barrel-staves, planks, even what we should call pre-fabricated houses, 'ready-made, and a carpenter travelled with the load to supervise the construction'.[96] The ships returned carrying sugar, molasses and rum – but also silver coins since they could make contact in the West Indian ports or those of the mainland with the circulation of Spanish American silver. It was no doubt the success of this trade expansion in the south which increased the trading strength of the northern colonies and stimulated the development of their industry: shipbuilding, coarse woollen and cotton textiles, ironmongery, rum distilleries, iron bars, cast iron, pig-iron.

What was more, the merchants and dealers of the northern ports – including New York and Philadelphia – had extended their voyages to the entire North Atlantic, to islands like Madeira, to the African coast, the Barbary Coast, Portugal, Spain, France and of course England. They were even shipping dried fish, grain and flour to the Mediterranean. It is true that this extension of trade on a world scale, creating triangular patterns of traffic, by no means by-passed England. Although American ships were sailing directly to Amsterdam, London was almost always the apex of one of these triangles; it was to London that American trade brought its payments from the various centres in Europe; and from London that it obtained its credit. A considerable share of American profits thus remained there, for the balance between England and her colonies favoured the former. 'By means of purchases and commission', remarked an observer in 1770, before the colonial rebellion, 'all the money of these establishments [the

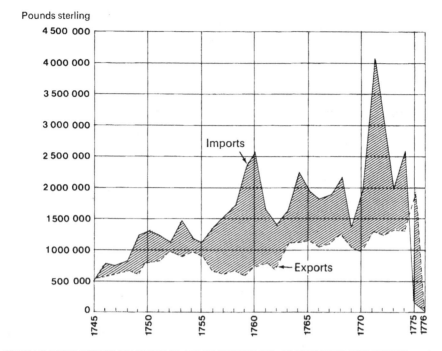

Pounds sterling

40 BRITAIN'S POSITIVE TRADE BALANCE WITH HER AMERICAN COLONIES
Their trade deficit forced the colonies, in order to restore their foreign balance, to engage in
'triangular' trade, with centres in Africa (the slave trade), the West Indies and Europe, including
the Mediterranean. (From H.U. Faulkner, *American Economic History*, 1943, p. 123.)

colonies] goes to England, and all the wealth they have left is in paper [money].'[97]
All the same, America undoubtedly appeared as a rival from the start and her
growing prosperity dented Britain's own prosperity and worried the great merchant houses of London – hence a number of irritating but ineffective measures
of retaliation. As a shrewd witness noted in 1766:

> England now passes pointless laws to hinder and confine the industry of her
> colonists: she palliates the evil but does not remedy it ... [she] is losing to this
> trade, that of economy and re-export, customs duties, warehousing charges
> and commission and a share of labour in her ports. And in the case of direct
> returns to the colonies, which is today the general habit, is the result not that
> the shippers, especially those of Boston and Philadelphia whose shipping
> numbers over 1500 vessels, are supplying not only their own colonies, but also
> the other English colonies with European merchandise loaded in foreign ports?
> And this cannot be done without causing great prejudice both to England's
> commerce and to her finances.[98]

There were of course other quarrels between the colonies and the Old
Country; and the occupation by the British of French Canada in 1762, sanctioned
the following year by the Treaty of Paris, may have precipitated events by
providing the English colonies with security on their northern frontier. They no

longer required protection. In 1763, both victorious England and defeated France reacted in what (to our eyes at least) is an unexpected fashion. Rather than Canada (which they had captured from the French) or Florida (which Spain ceded to them) the English would have preferred possession of the sugar island of Saint-Domingue (Santo Domingo). But the Jamaican planters disagreed, refusing to share with anyone else the English sugar market, which they had always monopolized. Their protests, combined with France's desire to hang on to Saint-Domingue, queen of the sugar islands, meant that the 'few acres of snow' as Voltaire called Canada, fell to England. But irrefutable evidence survives of England's coveting Saint-Domingue. When war broke out again with France in 1793, the English wasted six years launching costly and profitless expeditions to take the island: 'The secret of England's impotence for the first six years of the war [1793-9] may be said to lie in these two fatal words: St Domingo'.[99]

The ink was no sooner dry on the Treaty of Paris of 1763 at any rate, before tension began to mount between the colonies and England. The Old Country wanted to bring the colonies to heel, to make them bear part of the huge expense of the late war. The colonies went so far in 1765 as to boycott English goods, which was nothing less than *lèse-majesté*.[100] This was sufficiently evident for the Dutch bankers in October 1768 to fear 'that if there is trouble between England and her colonies, the result may be bankruptcies of which this country [Holland] might well suffer the effects'.[101] Accarias de Sérionne was already envisaging the rise of an 'American' Empire in 1766: 'New England is more to be feared than Old England' he wrote, 'as regards the loss of the Spanish Colonies'. And this would be an empire 'independent of Europe',[102] an empire, as he wrote a few years later, in 1771, which 'would in the very near future be threatening the prosperity above all of England, Spain, France, Portugal and Holland'.[103] In other words, the first signs were beginning to appear of the United States' subsequent domination of the European world-economy. And this, surprisingly enough, is what the French plenipotentiary in Georgetown explicitly states, thirty years later it is true, in a letter of 27 Brumaire, Year X (18 October 1801):

> I think that England now finds herself in relation to the United States in a position altogether similar to the situation which brought the great power [i.e. England] face to face with Holland at the end of the seventeenth century, when the latter, worn out with expenses and debts, saw her commercial influence pass into the hands of a rival which was taking its first steps so to speak in commerce.[104]

The exploitation of America by Spain and Portugal

In the other America, Latin America, we shall find quite different realities and a very different history. Not that there are no similarities at all, but what happened in the North was certainly not repeated mirror-fashion in the South. Northern and southern Europe reproduced their own contrasts and differences across the Atlantic. There were also considerable time-lags: the English colonies became independent in 1783, the Latin American colonies not earlier than 1822 and 1824 – and even then the liberation of Latin America was no more than a fiction since colonial rule was replaced by English domination lasting more or less until 1940; after which the United States moved in. In short the North was characterized by strength, activity, independence and individual initiative; the South by inertia, servitude, the heavy hand of the colonial powers, and all the constraints inherent to the condition of any 'periphery'.

Such divergence was obviously the result of different structures, of different experiences and inheritances. The situation is clear enough, but it cannot be adequately expressed in terms of the convenient distinction textbooks used to make between 'settler colonies' and 'exploited colonies'. How could there be settler colonies where there was not also exploitation, or 'exploited' colonies where there were not also settlers? More appropriate perhaps than exploitation would be the term *marginalization*: the condition, within a world-economy, of being condemned to serve others, of being told what to do by the all-commanding international division of labour. For this was indeed the allotted role of Latin America (unlike North America) – both before and after the gaining of political independence.

Spanish America reconsidered

Spanish America gained its independence belatedly and very slowly. The process of liberation began in Buenos Aires in 1810, and since dependence on Spain would only be replaced by a new dependence, on English capital, the end of Spain's rule only became visible in 1824-5,[105] the years which mark the beginning of massive investment in South America by the City of London. (Brazil attained independence without too much upheaval: on 7 September 1822, Pedro I proclaimed the country's independence from Portugal, at Ypiranga near São Paulo, and in December of the same year he took the title of emperor of Brazil. The separation – John VI, the new emperor's father was still ruling in Lisbon – was an extremely complex process in detail, connected with spheres of influence in both European and American politics.[106] But we shall do no more here than record its peaceful outcome.)

In Spanish America on the other hand, independence was a long-drawn-out drama. We shall be less concerned with this for the moment though, than with the history leading up to a break which had international repercussions more

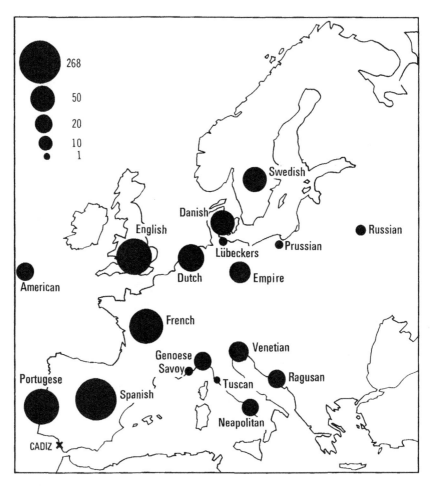

41 EUROPE HASTENS TO EXPLOIT SPANISH AMERICA
The number and origin of the ships entering the bay of Cadiz in 1784. (Data from
Archives Nationales, Paris, A.E., BIII, 349.)

important than those of Brazil's separation from Portugal. From the start,
Spanish America had inevitably been a decisive element in world history, whereas
Brazil, once it had ceased to be a major gold producer in the nineteenth century,
mattered much less to Europe.

Even in the early days, Spain had been incapable of exploiting unaided the
'colossal'[107] market of the New World. Even when marshalling all her strength
and all her men, all the oil and wine of Andalusia and the cloth from her
industrial towns, Spain, a still-archaic power, had proved unequal to the task. In
any case in the expansionist eighteenth century, no European 'nation' alone
would have been able to meet the demand. As Le Pottier de la Hestroy explained

in 1700, 'consumption in the West Indies of the goods which they must necessarily fetch from Europe, being very considerable, [is far beyond] our powers [i.e. those of France] however many manufactories we set up at home'.[108] As a result, Spain had to appeal to the rest of Europe, particularly since her own industry had begun to decline by the end of the sixteenth century; and Europe hastened to seize the opportunity. Indeed the Spanish colonies were exploited by other European countries more than by Spain, of which Ernst Ludwig Carl said in 1725 that she was 'hardly more than an entrepôt for Foreigners'[109] – perhaps a go-between would be more accurate. The Spanish laws against the 'transportation' of silver, the principal resource of America, were certainly strict and yet 'this coing [i.e. Spanish coin] is to be seen throughout Europe', as Charles II of England remarked in November 1676.[110]

Twenty years earlier, Father Antonio Vieira, a Portuguese Jesuit, had exclaimed in a sermon delivered at Belem in Brazil: 'The Spanish extract the silver from the mines, and transport it, and it is the foreigners who have all the benefit'. Of what use was all this precious metal, he asked; it was never used to relieve the poor, 'only to help swell and inflate even more the men who order these peoples about'.[111]

If the strict Spanish laws were to no avail, it was of course because of smuggling: fraud, corruption, cheating and jiggery-pokery were by no means confined to the trade and economy of America but they were magnified in this huge arena: they had the entire Atlantic Ocean and the southern seas as their sphere of action. Philip II himself refers to some apparently innocent ships which sailed in 1583, 'claiming to carry wines to the Canary Islands, [but which] in reality made for the Indies, very profitably according to report'.[112] An entire ship could be laden in Seville with goods for the West Indies 'without the officers even being aware of it!'[113] And before long the Dutch, French, English and Italians of all origins, especially the Genoese, were illegally loading cargoes aboard the official fleets for the Indies, without difficulty. In 1704, 'the Consulate [of Seville] admitted that Spanish interests accounted for only a sixth of the cargoes of the fleets and galleons',[114] whereas in theory only Spanish nationals were permitted to engage in this trade.[115]

On the other side of the ocean, in the 'Indies of Castile', smuggling was equally indefatigable. In 1692, a Spanish traveller reported that 'the King's Treasure which leaves Lima is worth at least 24 million pieces of eight [a year],[116] but before it can get from Lima to Panama, Porto Belo or Havana ... the Corregidors, the Excisemen, the Customs officers and so on, all possessed of healthy appetites, have each taken a share'.[117] The galleons themselves, which combined the role of warship and merchantman, provided the opportunity for regular fraud by insiders. And smuggling by outsiders increased in the seventeenth and eighteenth centuries. Alongside the existing colonial systems, flexible and effective counter-systems grew up. Such for instance were the voyages of the Saint-Malo sailors along the coasts of the south Atlantic: they had probably already begun before the War of the Spanish Succession, and they continued after it ended in 1713. A Spanish fleet is supposed to have driven them out in 1718,[118] but they were back in 1720,[119] and again in 1722.[120] Another example is the shipping out of the non-Spanish ports in America, along the interminable and poorly-patrolled coastline of the continent. The Dutch practised this trade (known as trading 'at pikestaff's length') out of St Eustace and Curaçao (which had belonged to them since 1632); the English did it from Jamaica; the French from Saint-Domingue and their other possessions in the West Indies. And the daring group of Scots who landed by force and not without trouble on the isthmus of Darien in 1699, were hoping to do the same thing, with the intention, by settling 'on the coast of the mainland itself', to undercut the English and Dutch whose bases were further away.[121] The mariners of North America were equally ready to take part: in the 1780s, their whalers, on the pretext of standing off the coast of Peru, were in fact shamelessly importing contraband goods which local merchants naturally welcomed with open arms, since they could buy them cheap and sell them at the 'official' price which had not dropped.[122]

But for smuggling on the grand scale, there was nothing to beat the contraband traffic which diverted silver from the Spanish mines of Potosi to the Portuguese colony of Brazil. The favoured route was down the Rio de la Plata after 1580.[123] After the separation of the two Crowns in 1640, the Portuguese persevered in this trade and for a long time held an ideal base in the little enclave of Colonia do Sacramento, in what is now Uruguay (occupied in 1680). The Spanish had to lay siege to it and eventually captured it in 1762.[124]

Needless to say, smuggling could never have prospered without the complicity of local merchants and corruption among the customs officials. If it developed on a massive scale, it was, as Accarias de Sérionne said, because 'the immense profit of this commerce enabled it to bear at once the great risks and the costs of corruption'.[125] In the same vein, speaking of the governorships in America which were up for sale in 1685, an anonymous writer declared roundly that 'these are always tacit licences to allow the importing of foreign goods'[126] – a suggestion confirmed by the case, back in 1629–30 in Lima, of the honourable *Oidor de la Audiencia*, appointed as judge for smuggling offences, who was hoarding forbidden goods in his own house and although caught red-handed, nevertheless continued his career as a respectable *oidor*.[127]

Of course, to listen to the apologists of smuggling, it was entirely in the public interest. 'The Spaniards in America', explains a Frenchman in 1699, 'to whom their own galleons bring less than half the goods they require, were pleased that foreigners [in this case usually French] brought the goods instead.'[128] The former used 'every expedient' to further this illicit commerce, with the result that 'over 200 [vessels] are carrying on in the sight of all Europe and of the Spanish themselves a commerce which is forbidden on pain of the strictest penalties'. A French report of 1707 even reveals that 'the cargoes of the [French] ships the *Triomphant*, the *Gaspard* and the *Duc de la Force*, ... had been sold before they set sail, to merchants in Vera Cruz'.[129] It is true that there was at the time some collaboration between Louis XIV's France and a Spain uncertain of her future under Philip V.

Smuggling was ever-present; but the scale varied according to the period. On the basis of some plausible calculations, one has the *impression* at least that it was exceeding in volume the normal (official) trade of Spanish America by 1619, if not earlier – a state of affairs which lasted until the 1760s or so, that is over a hundred years.[130] But this is only a hypothesis, as yet untested. The answer probably lies in the archives of other European countries as well as in the Spanish documents, if someone is prepared to tackle this research.

The Spanish Empire taken in hand again

In the end, the Spanish government did react to these irregularities. Slowly and with difficulty, matters were taken in hand, but towards the last years of the eighteenth century, the restoration of order was pursued energetically and in 'revolutionary fashion'. Let me point out straight away that due attention has not always been paid to the administrative measures taken on this score by the Spanish authorities – the *intendants* were not simply the establishment in America of a French institution, a sort of cultural transfer: they also corresponded to the deliberate intention of the government in Madrid to break the power of the Creole aristocracies who traditionally held the commanding positions in America. Similarly, the suppression of the Society of Jesus in 1767 proved to be the beginning of a 'military' regime, one of force and authority to replace what had been a kind of moral order. For their greater misfortune, those states which later gained their independence inherited this military regime. Here too, a transformation, almost a revolution was taking place. Should credit for this be given to the Bourbon dynasty, which had brought to Spain from France the principles of a centralized monarchy and an arsenal of merchantilist measures? Or was it rather that Spain was already moved by a strong desire for change, a desire which was shortly to sweep through the whole of Europe during the Age of Enlightenment? Claudio Sanchez Albornoz[131] even goes so far as to say that the Bourbon monarchy was not responsible for Spain's transformation – rather the Spanish desire for change opened the door of the kingdom to a French dynasty.

By 1713, the attention of the reformers was naturally turning to the area where Spain had most at stake, her last chance – the New World. Could Spain hold on to what she had created on the other side of the Atlantic? France, whose ships had prowled with ease along the American coasts, had not given up her ambitions either on the borders of the south Atlantic or in the territories of New Spain. In Law's time, after all, the French government had considered using Louisiana as a base from which to venture into nearby Spanish territory. A Spanish writer gloomily prophesied in November 1720: 'We shall have the misfortune of seeing the kingdom of New Spain divided and falling into the hands of the French, if God does not send some remedy'.[132] The threat from England, though less visible, was even more serious, if only because of the double concession made at the Treaty of Utrecht in 1713, of the *asiento* and the licensed voyage: this gave the English South Sea Company the means of combining the advantages of both licit and illicit smuggling.[133]

But all was not yet lost. The government set to work and in 1714 set up on the French model a ministry of the Navy and the Indies; in the same year a Honduras Company was also created; in 1728 a Caracas Company, destined to thrive; in 1740 a Havana Company;[134] in 1717-18, the *Casa de la contratación*, the mechanism for the Seville monopoly, was transferred to Cadiz, along with the *Consejo de Indias*: in other words Cadiz, for so long Seville's rival, at last became the single port for the Indies traffic. It is true that these chartered companies were not a success; in 1756, their monopolies had to be rescinded.[135] Even so, this failure probably did help free trade to develop outside the 'cumbersome system of fleets',[136] which proved unequal to the task of *regularly* servicing the economies of the New World. The 1735 reform which established the voyages of registered shipping[137] was not immediately effective, since the *registros* found it hard to rid themselves of the habit of sailing in convoy. But 'in about 1764 ... communications between Spain and the New World began to operate on a regular footing'.[138] Monthly packets sailed between Cadiz, Havana and Puerto Rico, and at two-monthly intervals to the Rio de la Plata. Finally the decree of 12 October 1778 declared trade free between America and 13 (later 14) Spanish ports.[139] Trade between Spain and the New World took a substantial upturn and inevitably Spain's hold over her possessions abroad increased.

Another important measure was the creation in 1776 of the viceroyalty in Buenos Aires: this reduced smuggling along the Rio de la Plata. Over the whole of Spanish America, while smuggling no doubt increased in absolute terms, it went into *relative* decline with the general upswing in trade (by the 1790s, contraband was accounting for no more than a third of the value of official trade). Active patrols were introduced, which led to some picturesque or indeed comical incidents. In 1777, it was suddenly discovered that the island of Orna off the coast of Maracaibo had been secretly occupied by the Dutch, and that the governor they had put in had become the regular protector of 'all the malefactors, criminals and smugglers from Spain and other nations who take refuge in this spot'.[140]

But smuggling at the expense of a healthy economy was not as serious a threat as it had been in the previous century to the solidity of the Spanish Empire. The renovated system was even able to withstand two severe trials: the Tupac Amaru rising in Peru in 1780[141] and that of the *Comunidades* in Venezuela in 1781, both massive rebellions provoked in part by the 'Bourbon modernization'. The Tupac Amaru rising, which caused such upheaval in Peruvian society, concerned all the complex currents stirring among the Indians, the half-breeds and the Creoles. But this widespread movement, an extraordinary indicator of

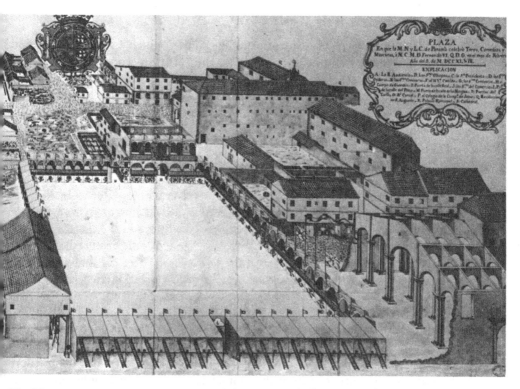

The *Plaza Mayor* in Panama in 1748. Around this square, which is typical of Spanish American towns, with its *Audiencia*, cathedral and *Cabildo*, stands have been prepared for some public holiday with bullfights, plays and masquerades. Watercolour, Archivo General de Indias, Seville. (Photo Mas.)

what was stirring in the depths of that society, was over in barely five months: the destruction of churches, workshops and *haciendas* did not last and the insurrection was finally crushed by Indian auxiliaries armed and trained by the Spanish.

Like all progress everywhere, progress in America brought the destruction of old orders. The Bourbons deliberately chose not to observe long-standing privileges. Alongside the old *consulados*[142] of Mexico City and Lima, other *consulados* were created as rivals of their predecessors and neighbours: the *consulado* of Vera Cruz was thus established as a counterbalance to the ancient powers of the *consulado* of Mexico City. The simultaneous arrival of manufactured goods from Europe (chiefly from England and Spain) swamped local markets, and their high quality and low price brought about the progressive destruction of local industries. Trade circuits were also changing, sometimes favouring local trade, sometimes discriminating against it. Peru for instance[143] on being deprived of the mining areas of the High Andes (which were in 1776 attached to the viceroyalty of Buenos Aires) lost a valuable annex which by its demand for foodstuffs and textiles had helped to balance the Peruvian economy. New Spain is another example: great upheaval was caused there by the terrible famines of 1785 and 1786[144] and order (or at least a semblance of order) could only be restored if the ruling classes (Creoles and *gachupinas*) would consent to sink their passionate and complex differences.

The treasure of treasures

The destiny of Spanish and Portuguese America as a whole (later to be known collectively as Latin America) clearly depended on the fortunes of an even greater area, that is the total European world-economy of which South America was no more than a peripheral and closely controlled zone. Would it ever be able to break out of its bonds? Yes and no – on the whole, no. There are many reasons, the most important being that neither Brazil nor Spanish America, while they did have some ships and even some sailors, were naval powers. (This was not the case in the United States, whose sailors were really the 'founding fathers' of the new country.) Another reason is that Spanish America, even before the eighteenth century but especially during that crucial period, was in double thrall – to the Iberian powers, Portugal and Spain, but also to the rest of Europe (and most of all to England). The English colonies had had to break only one chain, that binding them to England, to achieve their freedom. South America, on the contrary, having freed itself of the shackles binding it to the colonial powers, was still not independent of Europe. It had rid itself of only one of the two masters who had for so long watched over and exploited it. Could Europe be expected to give up the gold and silver of America? Even before the revolutions that led to independence, the European powers were poised for action: each was on the alert for the succession which could confidently be expected. The English occupied Buenos Aires in 1807, but could not hold on to it; the French invaded Portugal in 1807 and Spain in 1808; thus precipitating the emancipation of the Spanish colonies – but without gaining anything from it for themselves.

Was such haste or greed justified? Was the prize real or a mirage? Was America still at the beginning of the nineteenth century the 'treasure of treasures', as Nicole Bousquet has described it? To answer such a question, one needs some figures: the estimated G.N.P. of Spanish America and Brazil, and the surplus available to send to Europe, since this surplus was the treasure in question.

The only credible figures (and they concern only New Spain) are those provided in 1810 by the secretary to the *consulado* of Vera Cruz, Jośe Maria Quiros.[145] And even these give only the *physical output* of New Spain (in millions of pesos and round figures): agriculture: 138.8; manufacturing: 61; minerals: 28; total: 227.8 (so mining output, surprisingly, represents only 12.29 per cent of the whole). But how can we estimate G.N.P. from physical output? In the first place, we should add the vast amount accounted for by contraband; then there is the considerable item of services: since Mexico had few navigable rivers, the chief form of transport was the mule-train – inconvenient and terribly expensive. All the same, G.N.P. can hardly have been more than 400 million pesos. And since it is usually accepted that the mineral output of New Spain was the equivalent of that of the rest of Spanish America put together, are we justified in suggesting that the G.N.P. of the whole (16 million inhabitants) would have been double that of Mexico, that is 800 million pesos at most? Next, Brazilian G.N.P., if J.A. Coatsworth's figures for Brazil in 1800[146] can be accepted, was a little under half that of Mexico, or about 180 million pesos. So 'Latin' America as a whole might have had a total G.N.P. of getting on for 1000 million pesos.

Uncertain though these figures may be, they do at least allow us to draw one conclusion: that per capita income was low: 66.6 pesos for the 6 million Mexicans, 50 pesos for the 16 million inhabitants of the whole of Spanish America; less than 60 in Brazil which had a population of slightly over 3 million. And in 1800, according to the figures accepted by Coatsworth,[147] per capita income in Mexico was only 44% of that in the United States, which must therefore have been (according to my own calculations, since Coatsworth gives them in 1950 dollars) 151 pesos or dollars of the time (the two currencies were equivalent). This is not a totally absurd figure, even compared to Alice Hanson Jones's results in a study of the three most advanced of the North American colonies: somewhere between 200 and 336 dollars.[148] The per capita income of the *most privileged* colony of the South, Mexico, was only 33% or so of that of the privileged northern colonies. With the passage of time, the gap grew even wider: by 1860 this figure had dropped to 4%.

But our problem here is not only to work out the living standards of the population of Latin America, but to calculate the amount by which exports from America to Europe exceeded imports from Europe. The *official* figures for the year 1785[149] record exports to Spain of 43.88 million pesos in bullion, plus 19.41 million in goods, a total of 63.3 million (of which gold and silver accounted for 69.33% and goods, though rising sharply, only 27.6%). Exports in the other direction, from Spain to America were worth 38.3 million pesos, so the difference was 25 million. Let us for the moment simply take this figure on trust, though some doubt surrounds it. If we add to this the corresponding figure for Brazil (25% of the total, or 6.25 million) we reach a further total of 30 or 31 million pesos, or 3% of the G.N.P. of the whole of Spanish America but this figure (since it is based on the official records) must be regarded as a *lower limit*, since it leaves out contraband which we know was considerable. If we convert these 30 million pesos into pounds sterling (5 pesos = £1) the 'treasure' Europe was taking out of America was of the order of at least £6 million. This was of course an enormous sum; by way of comparison, in about 1785, the whole of Europe, including England, was obtaining £1,300,000 from India.[150]

So Latin America (about 19 million inhabitants) was sending back to Europe every year four or five times as much as India (about 100 million inhabitants).

millions of pesos

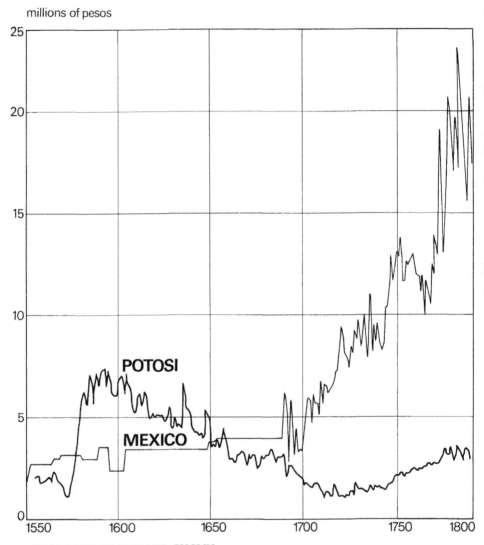

42 TWO AMERICAN SILVER CYCLES
The curve for Potosi is from M. Moreyra Paz-Soldan's article in *Historia*, IX, 1945; the curve for the Mexican mint comes from W. Howe, *The Mining Guild of New Spain, 1770-1821*, 1949, pp. 453 ff. The first American silver boom occurred in Potosi. But the Mexican mining boom at the end of the eighteenth century reached previously unparalleled heights.

This would certainly make it the greatest treasure-store in the world – and in the popular imagination American treasure swelled to truly fabulous proportions. A French agent wrote in 1806, at a time when the revolutionary and Napoleonic Wars had led to the stockpiling of mined metals on the spot, for fear of sending them by sea:

> If what I have heard is correct, there are over a hundred million piastres in gold and silver ingots lying in the vaults of the mints of the Three Viceroyalties

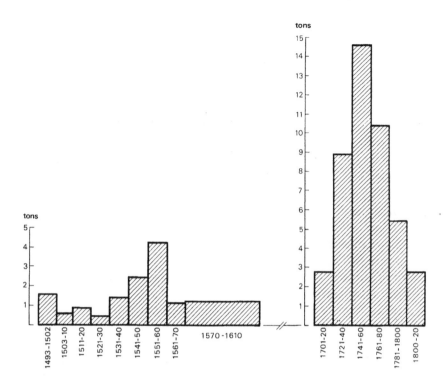

43 TWO AMERICAN GOLD CYCLES
A 'Spanish' cycle (gold from the West Indies, New Spain, New Granada and Peru) gave way to a 'Portuguese' cycle (gold from Brazil). The first brought about 170 tons of gold to Europe over a period of 120 years; the second 442 tons, that is three times as much over a similar period. These figures, calculated in annual averages and in tons are not a hundred per cent reliable. One thing only is certain: the overwhelming superiority of the Brazilian cycle. (Spanish figures from Pierre Chaunu, *Conquête et exploitation des Nouveaux Mondes*, 1969, pp. 301 ff.; Portuguese figures from F. Mauro, *Études économiques sur l'expansion portugaise*, 1970, p. 177.)

of Peru, Santa Fe [Bogota] and Mexico, not forgetting the enormous amount of capital shared out among the owners of the mines ... The capitalist merchants have been obliged by the war to keep back their shipments. [Smuggling] has been able to handle [only] a certain proportion of the circulation of this silver.[151]

England was tempted by such booty, but hesitated for fear of upsetting matters in Brazil, where the king of Portugal had taken refuge in 1808, and Spain which an English army under Wellington was slowly and with difficulty liberating. As a result, the break-up of the Spanish Empire took place in slow motion. But the outcome was inevitable: from the day that Spain, as she industrialized, began to take her colonies in hand again and to become more than a mere intermediary between America and Europe, 'the fall of the empire was at hand, for it was in the interests of no other nation that it should remain Spanish'. In particular of course, it was not in the interests of the nation now towering above the others, the nation which had long temporized, but with France beaten and the American revolutions out of the way, no longer had any cause for prudence. 1825 saw a rush by English capitalists to invest in the markets and mining enterprises in the new (ex-Spanish and ex-Portuguese) states of America.

There was logic behind this: the other countries of Europe had been industrializing in Britain's wake and, like Britain, had sheltered behind protective tariff barriers. European trade was thus stifling for lack of air.[152] Hence the need to look to overseas markets. It was a competition in which Britain was well placed, particularly since she had used the most reliable and the most direct method, that of financial contacts. From now on, bound hand and foot to the City of London, Latin America would remain on the periphery of the European world-economy: even the United States, after their constitution in 1787, despite all their initial advantages, had had great difficulty extricating themselves from a similar position. The ups and downs of American fortunes were now registered by the prices quoted for their loans on the London Stock Exchange (and to a lesser extent on the Paris Bourse).[153]

The 'treasure of treasures' though, to return to this question, while still apparently surviving into the nineteenth century, seems to have diminished considerably. One sign of this is that all 'South American loans' were quoted below par. And the fact that the slump in the European economy (1817-51) began very early in South America (in 1810), that this peripheral crisis brought immense upheaval, and that Mexican G. N. P. declined from 1810 until the 1860s, gives further indication of the depressing history of Spanish America during the first half of the nineteenth century. The 'treasures' of America were being eaten up or squandered, for the wars of independence were ruinous. To give but one example, the mining population of Mexico was torn apart, providing the revolution with its agents, torturers and victims. Abandoned mines were flooded when the pumping stopped, in particular the largest mines, famous only shortly before for their high yields. When extraction did not come to a complete standstill, there was a bottleneck at the crushing stage; more particularly the mercury essential for the amalgam process was obtainable only at excessive prices if at all. The Spanish regime had always maintained a supply of comparatively cheap mercury, since it was brought in by the public authorities. In the early days of independence, the only mines still working were usually small enterprises drained by sloping tunnels instead of pumps.

Finally South America was the scene of the first mistakes made by 'developed' countries about the technology suitable for transfer to 'under-developed' countries. We have for example a report written on 20 June 1826 by the French consul in Mexico City concerning an English venture:

> Dazzled by the prodigies they have acomplished at home by means of the
> steam engine, they believed it could render similar services here. The steam
> engines were therefore brought from England, together with wagons for trans-

porting them, nothing was forgotten: except roads for the wagons to travel along. The principal highway in Mexico, the best and most frequented, is the one leading from Vera Cruz to the capital. Your Excellency will be able to judge the state of this road when I say that ten mules have to be harnessed to a carriage holding four persons if they intend to travel ten or twelve leagues a day. It was along this road that the English wagons had to cross the Cordillera: so each of the wagons required no less than twenty mules. Each mule travelled six leagues a day and cost ten francs. Bad this road might be, but it was at least a road; they had to leave it to approach the mines, there were nothing but tracks to follow. Some entrepreneurs, discouraged by the obstacles, have left their machines temporarily in store in Santa Fe, Encerro, Xalappa or Peroti; others, more intrepid, have at great expense built paths which have carried their machines to the mines; but once they arrived, there was no coal to start them up; where there was wood, this was used; but it is scarce on the plateau of Mexico, and the richest mines, those of Guanajuato for instance, are more than thirty hours away from a forest. The English miners were quite amazed to encounter these obstacles which had been pointed out by M. Von Humboldt twenty years ago.[154]

Such for many years were the conditions productive of poor business and low quotations on the London Stock Exchange. But since speculation will always find takers, shares in the Mexican mines, on account of their popularity in public opinion, made huge fortunes for some capitalists before they collapsed. The English government also succeeded in selling to the Mexican state the war *matériel* used by Wellington on the field at Waterloo – some small compensation!

Neither feudalism nor capitalism?

In concluding this section, it is difficult to avoid mention of the intense and highly abstract discussions which have taken place about the forms of society and economy found in the American continent, and whether they are reproductions or altered versions of the models found in the Old World. Historians have sought to define them in terms of concepts familiar to Europe and to produce a model which might bring them together in some kind of unity. The attempt is not a very promising one: some people have talked of feudalism, others of capitalism; the would-be wise have opted for a transitional model sufficiently elastic to satisfy everybody, accepting both feudalism and its variants as well as signs heralding the arrival of capitalism; the truly wise, like B.H. Slicher Van Bath,[155] reject both terms and prefer to start from a completely clean sheet.

In any case, how can one seriously propose a single model of society for the whole of America? Any such thing would immediately have to admit a number of exceptions. Not only do social systems differ from country to country, but they may coexist, mingling elements impossible to classify under any of the suggested headings. The American continent was essentially a *peripheral zone* in our terminology, with the single exception (and there was still some doubt even about this one in the late eighteenth century) of the United States, which became a politically-constituted unit in 1787. But it was a periphery made up like a mosaic with a hundred different colours: modern, archaic, primitive, or curious mixtures of all these.

I have made sufficient mention of New England[156] and the other English colonies to say no more than a few words about them here. Were these capitalist societies? That would be going too far. In 1789, they were with some exceptions, still predominantly agricultural economies; and to the south, as one approached Chesapeake Bay, one would have found regular slave-owning societies. It is certainly true that once peace returned in 1783, an unprecedented wave of enterprise swept through the young States: every kind of industry sprang into existence at once: the domestic system, workshops, manufactories, but also cotton factories using new machines from England; banks and numerous trading companies were created. All the same, in practice, although there were banks, the money in circulation consisted less of hard cash than of drastically devalued banknotes issued by the States, or of clipped foreign coins. Moreover, when the war ended, the fleet – the instrument of independence and greatness – had to be rebuilt. In 1774, it had been divided between coastal shipping and long-haul trade: 5200 vessels (250,000 tons) in the first category; 1400 in the second (210,000 tons). The two branches were approximately equivalent: but while coastal shipping had been 'all-American', the long-distance ships had been English, and these had to be replaced – providing plenty of work for the shipyards of Philadelphia. What was more, England had succeeded in regaining her dominant position in American trade by 1783. So the real capitalism was still in London, the centre of the world: the United States had only a second-best version of capitalism, quite a sturdy one admittedly and one which was to develop during England's absorption in the Revolutionary and Napoleonic Wars (1793–1815), but this spectacular growth was not yet enough to take them into the first rank.

Elsewhere in America, the only signs of capitalism I can detect were in isolated spots, confined to individuals or investments more closely integrated into European capitalism than to any local network. This was even true of Brazil, which had moved further in this direction than Spanish America, but which effectively consisted of a few cities: Recife, Bahia and Rio de Janeiro, which had a 'colony' of its own in its vast hinterland. Similarly in the nineteenth century, Buenos Aires, with the vast Argentine pampas stretching away to the Andes behind it, would be a striking example of the all-devouring city, capitalist after a fashion, dominating, organizing and attracting to it the wagon-trains of the interior and ships from all over the world.

Alongside these islands of merchant capitalism, is it too fanciful to identify patches of 'feudalism' here and there? German Arciniegas[157] argues that in the seventeenth century great tracts of the Spanish New World partly abandoned by Europe were subject to 'refeudalization'. I am willing to accept that the Venezuelan *llanos* or parts of the Brazilian interior were subject to a seigniorial

An 'industrial village' in New England. (New York State Historical Association, Cooperstown.)

regime, but this can hardly be described as 'feudal' unless one simply means an autarkic or near-autarkic system, of the type Gunder Frank refers to: 'a closed system only weakly linked with the world beyond'.[158]

It is no easier to draw clear conclusions from a study of land tenure. In Spanish America, three forms of ownership co-existed: the plantations, the *haciendas* and the *encomiendas*. We have already discussed the plantations:[159] this was capitalism after a fashion, but only in the person of the planter or the merchants who gave him financial backing. The *haciendas* were large estates, chiefly created in the seventeenth century during the 'refeudalization' of the New World – which operated to the advantage of the landowners, the *hacendados* and, no less, that of the Church.[160] These great estates were partly self-support-ing, and partly in contact with the market. In some areas, Central America for instance, they remained largely self-sufficient; but the estates belonging to the Jesuits – often enormous in area and better known to us than the rest because of their archives – were divided between a natural subsistence economy and an exchange economy based on money. The fact that the accounts of the *haciendas* were kept in money does not rule out the possibility that the wages they refer to may have been paid only at the end of the year – in which case the peasant would not receive any coin, since payments in kind already received might have cancelled out or even exceeded the sum due to him.[161] Similar situations certainly occurred in Europe.

The *encomiendas* in theory at least take us closer to 'feudalism', although these concessions of Indian villages to Spanish citizens took the form of 'livings' rather than 'fiefs'. In theory these were temporary concessions entitling the *encomendero* to the dues paid by the Indians, but not to the outright ownership of the land or the right to dispose of the labour force. But that is only the position on paper: the *encomenderos* often broke the rules. A report in 1553 for instance[162] criticizes both unscrupulous masters who sell their Indians 'under cover of selling an *estancia* or some livestock', and 'frivolous or prevaricating *oidores*' who shut their eyes to this practice. The proximity of local authorities limited such infringements, but the further one went from the large cities[163] the less possible it became to exert control. The *encomendero* as one element in the colonial command structure, was only theoretically in the service of the Spanish authorities, on the same terms as officers of the Crown. In practice, *encomenderos* were tending to shake off this constraint and a crisis in the *encomienda* system began in 1544 with the revolt of the Pizarro brothers in Peru. It was to continue for long years, for conflict between *encomenderos* and officials of the Crown was inevitable. The officials – the *corregidores* and *oidores* of the *audiencias*, the colonial assemblies modelled on the *audiencias* in Spain – could hardly be other than opposed, most of the time, to landowners who, if left to themselves, would quickly have created or recreated a feudal regime. Much, though not all, of the activity of Spanish America, as George Friederici has suggested[164] rapidly turned it into a classic instance of bureaucracy and officialdom. This is hard to reconcile with the standard image of feudalism, just as the lord of the *engenho* in Bahia and his slaves cannot be easily assimilated to a properly capitalist model.

Should we conclude that neither feudalism nor capitalism had crossed the Atlantic? America as a whole could be seen as a collection, a miscellany of different societies and economies. At the lowest level came the semi-closed economies, however we choose to label them; immediately above these, the partially-open economies, if such there were; and lastly, at the highest levels, came the mines, the plantations, some (not all) of the major grazing concerns, and wholesale trade. Capitalism was at most no more than one of the higher echelons of commercial life: its representatives were the *aviadores* of the mining towns, the privileged merchants of the *consulados*, the merchants of Vera Cruz (constantly at odds with those of Mexico City), the merchants who could indulge themselves behind the facade of the metropolitan-based companies, the merchants of Lima, the merchants of Recife (by contrast with the 'seigniorial' city of Olinda) or those of the lower town of Bahia as opposed to those of the upper town. But with all these men of business, we are really still caught in the mesh of the European world-economy which cast its net over the whole of America; we

The Dutch colony on the Cape of Good Hope. (Drawing, J. Rach, 1762. Atlas van Stolk.)

are not in the presence of national forms of capitalism, but within a system extending across the globe and controlled from its nerve centre in Europe.

In Eric Williams's view[165] Europe's superiority (by which he means her approaching industrial revolution and which I would extend to include British world supremacy and the emergence of an even more powerful form of merchant capitalism) can be directly explained by her exploitation of the New World, in particular by the fresh stimulus imparted to the European economy by the regular profits from the plantations and above all, he says, from the sugar plantations worked by black slaves. The same thesis, simplified further, is advanced by Luigi Borelli,[166] who attributes the modernity of the Atlantic and European economy entirely to sugar and therefore to America, where sugar, capitalism and slavery are all combined. But can it really be argued that America, including the gold and silver mines, was the sole source of European greatness? Surely not, any more than it can be argued that India is the single explanation of European supremacy, although Indian historians can certainly maintain today, with convincing arguments on their side, that the English industrial revolution drew much sustenance from the exploitation of their country.

Black Africa: collaborator as well as victim?

I should like now to concentrate on the heartland of Black Africa, leaving aside the countries of the Maghreb – a 'White Africa' contained within the orbit of Islam; leaving aside too, with less obvious justification perhaps, the eastern part of Africa, from the Red Sea and the coast of Abyssinia to the southern tip of the continent.

This southernmost tip of Africa was, in the eighteenth century, still only semi-inhabited. The Cape Colony, founded in 1657 by the Dutch, although its 15,000 inhabitants made it the largest European colony on the continent, was no more than a stopping-point on the way to the Indies, strictly serving the *Oost Indische Compagnie*,[167] which remained fiercely watchful over this strategic position. As for the long east coast of Africa, looking out on the Indian Ocean, it belonged to the Indian world-economy for which it had been at once an important route and a *peripheral* zone, well before the arrival of the Portuguese in 1498.[168] The long interlude of Portuguese commercial activity did of course bring many changes. It was indeed along this coast that Vasco da Gama sailed, after rounding the Cape, as he headed north towards India, putting in at Mozambique, Mombasa and Malindi; from the latter port the Gujerati pilot, Ibn Majib, guided him without too much difficulty, thanks to the monsoon, straight to Calicut. So the coast of Africa was a valuable route both on the way to and from the Indies: its ports enabled the crews to take on fresh provisions, to repair their ships and sometimes to wait for the right time to put to sea when, late in the season, it was dangerous to sail back round the Cape of Good Hope.

There was for a long time, another attraction on the Contra Costa:[169] the existence of gold-panning deep in the vast state of Monomotapa.[170] The gold was exported through the port of Sofala south of the Zambezi delta. The small conurbation long dominated by the town of Kilwa, to the north, became a centre for Portuguese enterprise. Force was effectively applied in 1505, and the situation was well in hand by 1513. Since the gold could only be brought to the coast in exchange for goods, whether grain from Malindi or more often cotton from India, the Portuguese had to use the fabrics of Gujerat for the purpose, and quickly learnt to do so. But this profitable traffic did not last long: Monomotapa was riven by constant wars; gold became scarce and meantime Portuguese control was slipping. Arab merchants were regaining the upper hand in Zanzibar and Kilwa, where they picked up slaves to be re-sold in Arabia, Persia and India.[171] The Portuguese did manage to hold on to Mozambique where they maintained a sort of presence. Towards the end of the eighteenth century, they were said to be exporting several thousand slaves from here every year, and the French even took part in this trade, between 1787 and 1793, in order to obtain manpower for the Ile de France (Mauritius) and the Ile Bourbon (Réunion).[172]

But we can on the whole accept the pessimistic conclusion reached in a memorandum addressed to the Russian government on 18 October 1774, concerning this long coastline. 'It is a long while since the river of Sofala or any of the adjacent streams rolled any gold down with their waters.' The ports of Malindi and Mombasa north of Mozambique were all but deserted and the few Portuguese families still residing there were 'more barbarians than civilized'; their trade consisted of 'the dispatch to Europe of a few degenerate Negroes, most of whom are good for nothing'.[173] The message thus conveyed to the Russian government, which was looking for international outlets, was that this was not a promising spot. So we shall not lose a great deal by leaving aside the 'Indian' side of southern Africa; its great days were by now over.

The western half of Africa

Things were very different on the Atlantic coastline of Africa, from Morocco to Portuguese Angola. Europeans had, as early as the fifteenth century, prospected these mostly unhealthy shores and made contact with local populations. Was it lack of curiosity which stopped them bothering to explore the interior, as has often been said? They certainly did not find in Black Africa terrain as well prepared[174] as that of the Aztec and Inca Empires in America, where Europeans could appear to the many subjugated peoples in the guise of liberators,[175] and where they could eventually base their rule on well-ordered societies which were comparatively easy to exploit.

In Africa, Portuguese and other European explorers had found near the coast only a scatter of tribes, or weak states on which it was impossible to build. The more solid states, such as the Congo[176] or Monomotapa, lay inland, protected both by the continental landmass and by the coastal belt of societies whose political organization was minimal or feeble. Perhaps too, the tropical diseases so prevalent in coastal areas were another obstacle. But this may not be entirely the case, since the Europeans overcame similar obstacles in the tropical regions of America. A more serious reason may be that the African interior was protected by its comparatively dense settlement and by the resilience of societies which, unlike those of the pre-Columbian Americans, were acquainted with iron metallurgy and often harboured warlike populations.

The Europeans did not in any case have much incentive to venture far from the sea, since within easy reach of the coast were ivory, wax, Senegal gum, malaguetta, gold dust and the highly profitable merchandise of black slaves. And at the beginning at any rate, these goods could be obtained in exchange for mere trifles: glass beads, brightly-coloured fabrics, a little wine, a skin of rum, one of the rifles known as 'trading' guns, and the copper bracelets known as *manillas*, 'a rather strange ornament' which the African 'puts on his leg just above the ankle ... or on the arm just above the elbow'.[177] In 1582, the black people of the Congo were being paid by the Portuguese 'with old iron, nails and so on, which they prize more highly than gold coins'.[178] All in all, these were suppliers and customers whom it was easy to dupe, easy-going, sometimes lazy, 'taking each day as it comes'. But 'as a rule, the crops produced by these people are so meagre that the European captains who go there to buy men are obliged to bring from Europe or America enough provisions to feed the slaves who will be their cargo'.[179] In short, the Europeans were confronted everywhere with still primitive economies. For them André Thevet's terse comment in 1575: money 'is not in use there', said it all.[180]

But what is money after all? The African economies had their own currencies, that is to say 'a means of exchange and a standard of recognized value', whether these were pieces of cloth, blocks of salt, livestock or, in the seventeenth century, imported iron bars.[181] Dismissing such currency as 'primitive' in no way authorizes us to conclude forthwith that African economies were lacking in energy or that they would never be roused to activity before the nineteenth century and the repercussions of the industrial and commercial revolution in Europe. In mid-eighteenth century for instance, these backward regions were after all sending *possibly as many as 50,000* black slaves every year to the trading ports (whereas Spain in the sixteenth century could drum up only about 1000 emigrants a year in Seville,[182] and the immigrants to New England between 1630 and 1640[183] numbered on average about 2000 a year). What was more, the raids which produced this human merchandise did not even interrupt the rhythm of everyday life, since the thousands of slaves, harnessed together by leather collars round their necks, were dispatched to the Atlantic with their numerous slave-drivers during the dry season, when there was no work in agriculture.[184]

The regular consignments of slaves, year in, year out, point inescapably to the existence of a fairly vigorous economy – a conclusion repealed with varying degrees of emphasis by the authors of several recent studies of Africa. The comings and goings of the slave-ships are not therefore sufficient in themselves to explain the slave trade, which must also be analysed in the African context. 'Just as the slave trade was a sub-system of the Atlantic economy', writes Philip Curtin, 'it was also a sub-system of a broader pattern of West African society, attitudes, religion, professional standards, self-identity, and much else.'[185] Africa's share of rights and responsibilities in this matter should be acknowledged.

Black Africa: isolated yet accessible

Black Africa consists of a great triangle between three equally large masses: the Sahara to the north, the Indian Ocean to the east, and the Atlantic to the west. As already indicated, we shall not here consider the east coast. As for the wastes of the Sahara and the shores of the Atlantic, these were endless hostile fronts from which foreigners (whoever they were, whatever the period, whatever the circumstances) could approach the very gates of Black Africa and, with unfailing regularity, find their way in. Was this so surprising, since the black continent was after all inhabited by peasants who had turned their backs both on the sea

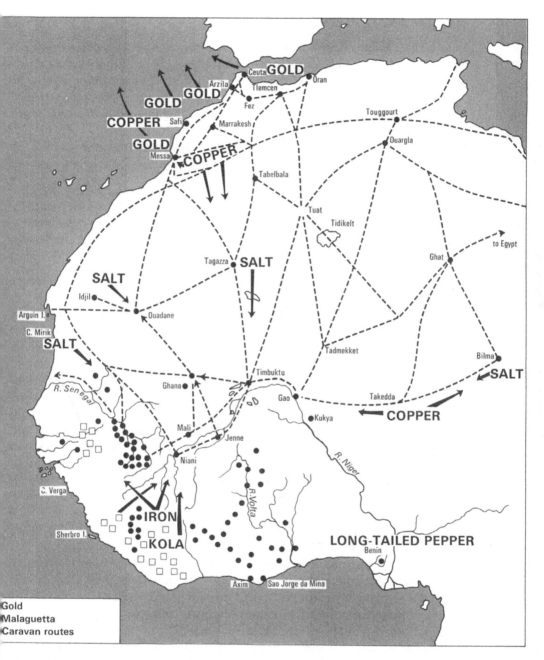

44 THE PORTUGUESE CONQUEST OF THE COAST OF AFRICA (FIFTEENTH AND SIXTEENTH CENTURIES)

By the sixteenth century, the maritime routes were outpacing the ancient roads across the Sahara. The gold which used to travel to the Mediterranean was now being diverted towards the coast. To the various sources of wealth exploited by the Portuguese, we should of course add that of black slaves. (From V. Magalhães Godinho, *L'Économie de l'Empire portugais aux XVᵉ et XVIᵉ siècles*, 1969.)

and on the Sahara desert which 'functioned in many respects like the sea'?[186] Curiously, no black explorers ever undertook any of the voyages across either the desert or the ocean which lay on their doorstep. On the Atlantic coast, the only shipping was from one side to the other of the mouth of the Congo river.[187] To the African, the Atlantic was, like the Sahara, an impenetrable obstacle much more than a mere frontier.

To West Africans, the white men were *murdele*, men from the sea.[188] Even today, traditional accounts tell of the black people's surprise at their appearance:

> They saw a great boat appear on the wide sea. This boat had white wings, flashing like knives. White men came out of the water and spoke words no one could understand. Our ancestors were afraid, they said these were *Vumbi*, ghosts of the dead. They drove them back to the sea, with flights of arrows. But the *Vumbi* spat fire with a noise of thunder. . . .[189]

In these first encounters, the blacks did not even imagine that the whites lived or had any existence outside their boats.

On the Atlantic coasts of Africa, the European ship met neither resistance nor surveillance. It had complete freedom of manoeuvre, could travel wherever it wished, trade wherever it pleased, compensating for failure in one place by success in the next a few days later, or simply going from strength to strength. The Europeans even introduced trading 'to Africa from Africa', the equivalent of 'the country trade' in the Far East, though on a much smaller scale. The forts built along the coast made solid operational bases, and the nearby islands could be used as look-out posts: hence the settlements in Madeira, the Canaries and the curious island of São Tomé in the Gulf of Guinea, the island of sugar and slaves which was developed on a prodigious scale in the sixteenth century – no doubt because the west winds and the southern trades met at this point, so that shipping could leave in either direction, westwards to America or eastwards to nearby Africa.

If I am not much mistaken, the same process occurred along the edge of the Sahara. Islam's camel-trains were as free to choose their entry-points as Europe's ships. Ghana, Mali and the Empire of Gao were gateways apparently linked to the commercial exploitation of ivory, gold dust and slaves. And the day this traffic was surprised from the rear by the arrival of the Portuguese in the Gulf of Guinea, the ancient political structures began to crumble. Timbuktu was captured in 1591 in a raid by Moroccan adventurers.[190]

Once more we can observe the profound identity of action between Islam's imperialism and that of the West. Here were two aggressive slave-trading civilizations, to whom Black Africa paid the price for her weakness and lack of vigilance. It is true that the invader appeared at her door carrying unfamiliar offerings guaranteed to fascinate potential customers. Greed played a part in the tragedy: 'thieves and men without conscience come in the night to carry off [the sons of our nobles and vassals]', said the king of the Congo, 'goaded by the desire to possess the goods and merchandise of Portugal, for which they hunger'.[191] 'They will sell each other', wrote Garcia de Resende in 1554, 'and there are many merchants who specialize in this and deceive them and hand them over to the slave-traders.'[192] The Italian Gio Antonio Cavazzi, who lived in Africa from 1654 to 1667, noted that 'for a coral necklace or a little wine, the Congolese would sell their own parents, their own children, or their brothers and sisters, swearing to the purchasers that these were household slaves'.[193] It cannot be denied that greed was a motive, nor that the Europeans deliberately encouraged it. The Portuguese, who liked to use costume as a badge of rank, introduced the same love of *vestir* to the Africans under their influence. Perhaps this was not without ulterior motive, since a Portuguese in Sofala in 1667 even proposed that the ordinary black people who unashamedly went naked, should be *obliged* to wear loin-cloths: then 'all the cloth of India would not be enough to meet the needs of even half the blacks'.[194] Any and every means were indeed used to impose trading, including the practice of paying in advance: in cases of non-repayment, a creditor had the right to seize the goods and finally the person of the defaulter. Straightforward violence was also widely used; whenever it met no resistance, profits broke all records. In 1643, a witness reported that he was 'absolutely certain that this kingdom [Angola, where the hunt for slaves was at its height] has enabled some men to grow even richer than in the East Indies'.[195]

It has to be said that if there was a traffic in human beings in Africa, it was undoubtedly because the Europeans desired and dictated it. But it is also true that Africa had already developed this bad habit long before the Europeans arrived, sending slaves to Islam, the Mediterranean and the Indian Ocean. Slavery was endemic in Africa, part of the structure of everyday life, within a social framework we can only wish we knew better. Even the patience of the historian accustomed to fragmentary documentation, even the bold hypotheses of the comparatist, or the ingenuity of a Marian Malowist[196] are insufficient to recreate this society. Too many questions remain unanswered: what role did the towns play in relation to the clusters of villages? What was the place of craft working and long-distance trade? What was the role of the state? Besides, there cannot have been a single model of society. Slavery came in different guises in different societies: there were court slaves, slaves incorporated into princely armies, domestic and household slaves, slaves working on the land, in industry, as couriers and intermediaries and even as traders. Recruitment was both internal, drawing on the local population (if delinquency in the West led to the galleys, here it led to a death sentence or slavery) and external, following wars or raids against neighbouring peoples, as in the days of ancient Rome. In the long run, these wars and raids became something of an industry. Was there perhaps a risk that the batch of slaves resulting from a war might be too numerous, too difficult to feed and keep, and thus superfluous to needs? By selling them on the foreign market, Africa may have been getting rid of a surplus of hungry mouths.

Slavery in Islam. The slave market in Zabid, in the Yemen, thirteenth century. From an illustration of the Maqamats 635/1237, of al Hariri. B.N., Paris, Ms. ar. 5847. (Photo B.N.)

The slave trade developed out of all recognition in response to demand from America, and had repercussions throughout the black continent. It played a dual role between interior and coast: weakening and sapping the strength of the inland states such as Monomotapa and the Congo; encouraging by contrast a host of little states near the coast, which acted as go-betweens supplying European merchants with slaves and merchandise, just as the successive empires of the Niger had acted as go-betweens for Islam, providing North Africa and the Mediterranean with gold dust and slaves. The same thing had happened in tenth-century Europe, when the zone along the Elbe had been a collecting point for slavs (slaves) to be dispatched to the countries of Islam. And had not the Crimean Tartars in the sixteenth century provided Istanbul with the Russian slaves it requested?[197]

From the coast to the interior

By such processes Black Africa was more thoroughly enslaved than the history books of the past might suggest. Europe sent its roots deep into the heart of the continent, far beyond the coastal bases, the island lookouts, the moored ships rotting away at anchor, the well-known slaving ports or the forts (the first and most famous of which was São Jorge da Mina which the Portuguese built on the coast of Guinea in 1454). These forts, first the Portuguese and later the Dutch, British or French, though so costly to maintain, gave protection against possible attacks either from the blacks or from rival Europeans. For whites engaged in similar trading operations attacked each other on every occasion, seized each other's forts, and waged an active if not very rewarding war of their own on the fringes of major conflicts. They could only unite against a common enemy: for instance the English Royal Africa Company and the French *Compagnie du Sénégal* (later absorbed into the French Indies Company in 1718) could reach a measure of agreement in their hostility to the privateers and 'interlopers', English or not, that is against any merchants trading outside the big companies. The latter, including the Dutch V.O.C, were admittedly in a sorry state, unable to keep up their fortresses and garrisons without grants from the government; in the end they abandoned many of their claims and let things slide.

Trade was taken inland from the coast in light boats which were rowed up the rivers to the upstream ports and to the fairs where European traders met African caravans. The natural intermediaries for this traffic were for many years the mixed-race descendants of the Portuguese, half-black and half-white, who had become 'children of the land' and whose services were much sought after. Later, both the English and the French decided to go upstream themselves and settle in the interior. 'Captain Agis [an Englishman] is not at present in Bintam', noted Father Labat. 'The English employ him to do their trading up-river; he is an enterprising man, and has been seen on the Faleme river, a day's journey from Fort St Stephen of Caynoura.'[198] In the latter part of the eighteenth century, when the English Royal Company gave up most of its activities and Fort St James at the mouth of the Gambia river was abandoned, European trade fell once more into the hands of native middlemen; black oarsmen, who were cheaper than white labour, went upstream with European goods and returned with African commodities, including ebony often destined for a privateer's ship. The blacks had become the subsidiary masters of trade.

This development is curiously reminiscent of the early pattern followed in trade by the Portuguese, who had been the first Europeans to penetrate Africa just as they had the Far East. The earliest *lançados*[199] had been Portuguese; and so were the merchants on the island of São Tomé, who were very soon operating an Africa-with-Africa trade from the Gulf of Guinea to Angola, as merchants one day and pirates the next. At the end of the sixteenth century, there were in San Salvador, the capital of the Congo, over a hundred Portuguese merchants and about a thousand adventurers of the same nationality. Then the expansion slowed down, as subordinate roles were handed over to African middlemen and commission agents, notably the Mandingos, who were known by the generic name of *mercadores*; and to subordinate assistants, both black and mixed race, known as *pombeiros*. The latter, whoever the master they worked for, exploited their African brothers even more cruelly than the whites had.[200]

The three-cornered traffic and its terms of trade

Everyone knows where the slave trade led: to the Middle Passage, the terrible Atlantic crossing endured by the slaves crammed into the crowded holds of the trading-ships. But this voyage was only one element in the three-cornered operation in which every ship setting sail from the African coast was engaged, whether under the Portuguese, Dutch, French or English flag. An English ship might for instance land its slaves in Jamaica, return to England carrying sugar, coffee, indigo, and cotton, then set out for Africa again. The pattern was the same, *mutatis mutandis*, for all the ships in the slave trade. At every corner of the triangle a fresh profit was made, and the total return of the voyage was the sum of these profits.

Ships leaving Liverpool or Nantes would be carrying substantially the same cargoes: many textiles of course – including Indian cottons and striped taffetas – copper utensils, pewter plates and pots, iron bars, knives in leather sheaths, hats, glass trinkets, fake crystal, gunpowder, pistols, 'trading guns', and spirits. This is in fact literally the manifest of the cargo a French banker loaded on to his three-hundred tonner, *Le Prince de Conty*, before she sailed from Nantes, France's leading slave-trading port, in April 1704.[201] At this late date, the list would hardly have differed in Liverpool or Amsterdam. The Portuguese always took care not to carry either firearms or spirits to Africa, but their successors no longer displayed such scruples – or such prudence.

As European demand began to rise sharply, the African market had in the end to offer a degree of elasticity to accommodate the increased supply of European goods. This was what happened in Senegambia, a curious region between desert and ocean, on which Philip Curtin has written a remarkable new study[202] laying particular emphasis on the African economy itself, on the volume of trade despite the difficulty of transport, on the high attendance at markets and fairs, on the vigorous growth of the towns which necessarily demanded surpluses, and on the so-called primitive systems of currency which nonetheless proved quite effective.

As time went by, African buyers became more selective about European goods, no longer blindly buying everything. If Senegambia continued to buy iron bars or even iron scrap, it was because unlike other African regions, it had no metal industry; if some other region (or rather sub-region) bought quantities of textiles, it was because local weaving capacity was insufficient, and so on. Finally

- and here comes the surprise - faced with Europe's still-voracious demands, Africa in the end reacted according to the classic rules of economics: by putting up her prices.

I

THE TERMS OF TRADE OF SENEGAMBIA

1680	100	The terms of trade are obtained by relating the indices of exports and imports (to be precise E/I × 100)
1780	475	
1830	1031	

The benefit to African exporters multiplied about 10 times over the period. Even allowing for a large margin of error, the rise is striking.

II

SENEGAMBIA'S EXPORTS

(by commodity, as a percentage of total exports)

	1680	1730	1780	1830
gold	5.0	7.0	0.2	3.0
gum	8.1	9.4	12.0	71.8
hides	8.5	—	—	8.1
ivory	12.4	4.0	0.2	2.8
slaves	55.3	64.3	86.5	1.9
wax	10.8	14.5	1.1	9.9
peanuts	—	—	—	2.6
total	100	100	100	100

Tables from P.D. CURTIN, *Economic Change in Precolonial Africa*, 1975, pp. 336 and 337.

The evidence in support of Philip Curtin's thesis[203] comes from a study of prices and of the terms of trade, which the primitive nature of the 'currency' did not prevent him from conducting effectively. He explains that when the iron bar, the money of account in Senegambia, was quoted by an English merchant at £30, this was not in fact a price, but a *rate of exchange* between the pound sterling (one fictional currency) and the iron bar (another fictional currency). Goods, quoted in bars (and later in pounds), varied in price as can be seen from the tables below; it is therefore possible to calculate plausible totals for Senegambia's exports and imports and thus to work out approximately the terms of trade, 'an indicator enabling one to appreciate the advantage which an economy derives from its foreign trade'.[204] By comparing exports and imports, prices of goods entering and leaving the country, Curtin concludes that Senegambia was deriving increasing benefits from its foreign trade. The fact was that in order to obtain more gold, slaves and ivory, Europe had to increase supply, thus lowering the price of its merchandise in comparative terms. Having been established in Senegambia, this rule could probably be applied to the whole of Black Africa which in response to the demand from the plantations, goldmines and towns of the New World, was sending increasing consignments of slaves off with the slave traders: 900,000 in the sixteenth century, 3,750,000 in the seventeenth, between 7 and 8 million in the eighteenth, and despite the abolition of the slave trade in 1815, 4 million in the nineteenth century.[205] If one remembers the modest means employed and the primitive nature of the transport of the time, the slave trade really broke all the records.

The impact of European demand led to increasing specialization in Senegambia, as first one then another commodity dominated the market: in the early seventeenth century it was hides; then until the nineteenth century, slaves; later, gum; and later again, peanuts. (A comparison could be made with the 'cycles' of colonial Brazil: dyewoods, sugar, gold.)

The end of the slave trade

Such trading strength, once it had been achieved, explains why traffic did not come to an end overnight when the slave trade was officially abolished, on the proposal of the English, at the Congress of Vienna in 1815. According to an English traveller in 1817,[206] Rio de Janeiro, Bahia and above all Cuba became the new centres for a 'traffic in human beings' which continued to thrive. Was Havana the most prosperous of these reception stations? Seven slave ships entered the harbour there at one time – four of them French. But it was the Portuguese and the Spanish who took over the best part of what remained of the trade, taking advantage of the drop in purchases and prices occasioned in Africa by the withdrawal of the English (£2 to £5 per slave, whereas the price was £100 in Havana and twice as much in Florida or New Orleans because of the difficulties of smuggling). The fall was only temporary, but our English traveller was very indignant at such profits being made from a traffic voluntarily renounced by his own country to the greater gain of the Spanish and Portuguese. The latter, he argued, taking advantage of the low price they were paying for slaves, would have 'the means to sell cheaper than we can in foreign markets, not only sugar and coffee but all tropical products'. At the time, many Englishmen would have shared the sentiments of the outraged Portuguese who in 1814 claimed that it was 'both the interest and the duty of the great continental powers formally to refuse their assent to the insidious proposal of England that the Slave Trade be declared contrary to the rights of man'![207]

Did these wholesale transportations in the end disturb the fundamental balance of the black societies of Angola, the Congo and the regions on the Gulf of Guinea? To answer this question one would have to know the size of the population before the arrival of the first Europeans. But it seems to me that in the last analysis such huge totals were only made possible by the extraordinary demographic vitality of the African population. And if as may be the case, the population actually continued to increase in spite of the slave trade, the entire question would have to be looked at afresh.

(I do not mean, by saying this, in any way to diminish the blame or responsibility attaching to Europe, as regards the African population. If such had been my aim, I would have pointed to the gifts which, intentionally or unintentionally, Europe took to Africa: maize, manioc, American beans, sweet potatoes, pineapples, guavas, coconuts, citrus fruits, tobacco, vines; domestic animals – the cat, the Muscovy duck, the turkey, the goose, the pigeon. Not to mention the impact of Christianity which was often welcomed as being a way of acquiring the strength of the white man's God. And one could go even further: whatever the rights and wrongs of the past, black America now exists – is it to be so lightly dismissed?)

The Russian world-economy – a world apart

The world-economy centred on Europe[208] did not extend to the whole of the old continent. Beyond Poland, there was always the remote and marginal world of Muscovy.[209] On this point it is impossible to disagree with Immanuel Wallerstein who unhesitatingly places it outside the western sphere, outside 'European Europe', at least until the beginning of the personal reign of Peter the Great in 1689.[210] The same could be said of the Balkans, where for centuries the Turkish conquest had smothered and subdued a Christian civilization – and of the rest of the Osmanli Empire in Asia and Africa, where huge areas existed in autonomy or near-autonomy.

Vis-à-vis Russia and the Turkish Empire, Europe exerted her monetary superiority, the attractions and temptations of her technology and merchandise, and her strength. But whereas in Muscovy European influence spread almost naturally, as the huge country gradually swung towards the West, the Turkish Empire remained obstinately aloof from Europe's destructive intrusion, or at any rate put up resistance to it. Only force, exhaustion and the passage of time would eventually wear down its visceral hostility to the West.

The return of the Russian economy to quasi-autonomy

Muscovy had never been completely closed to the European world-economy,[211] even before 1555 when the Russians took Narva, the little Estonian port on the Baltic, or before 1553, when English merchants first settled in Archangel. But opening a window on to the Baltic, 'whose waters are worth their weight in gold',[212] allowing the new English Muscovy Company to push open a door in Archangel (even if this door was closed early in the season every year by the winter ice) meant directly accepting European intrusion. At Narva, which had soon been taken over by the Dutch, shipping from all over Europe crowded into the little harbour before scattering again to a variety of European ports.

The so-called Livonian War however ended disastrously for the Russians: they were only too glad to sign an armistice on 5 August 1583 with the Swedes, who had entered Narva.[213] The Russians now lost their only access to the Baltic, keeping only the inconvenient port of Archangel on the White Sea. This blow put an end to any further opening up of Russia to Europe. But the new masters of Narva did not forbid the passage of goods being imported or exported by Russian merchants.[214] So trade with Europe continued, either via Narva, or via Reval and Riga[215] and the trade balance in Russia's favour was made good with gold and silver. The purchasers of Russian grain and hemp, particularly the Dutch, usually brought to settle their account bags of money each containing 400 to 1000 *riksdalers*.[216] 2755 bags arrived in Riga in 1650; 2145 in 1651; 2012 in 1652. In 1683, trade via Riga ended in a Russian trade surplus of 823,928 *riksdalers*.

In these circumstances, if Russia remained somewhat inward-looking, it was for a number of reasons: her unmanageable size, her still sparse population, her limited interest in the West, and the difficult and ever-renewed attempt to establish an internal equilibrium – and not so much because Russia was cut off from Europe or hostile to trade with the rest of Europe. The Russian experience was not unlike that of Japan, but with this major difference that Japan had in 1638 taken the political decision to cut herself off from the world economy, whereas Russia was the victim neither of her own deliberate action, nor of some categorical exclusion on the part of the outside world. It was simply that Russia tended to manage her affairs on the margins of the rest of Europe, as an autonomous world-economy with its own communications network. If M.V. Fechner is correct, the centre of gravity of Russian trade and the Russian economy in the sixteenth century lay closer to the south and east than it did to the north and west, that is to Europe.[217]

At the beginning of the sixteenth century, Russia's principal foreign market was Turkey. Contact was made through the valley of the Don and the Sea of Azov, where goods were transferred exclusively to Ottoman ships: the Black Sea was at the time a jealously guarded Turkish lake. The horseback courier service between the Crimea and Moscow is clear evidence that there was regular and substantial traffic along this route. Towards mid-century, the occupation of the lower reaches of the Volga (by the capture of Kazan in 1552 and of Astrakhan in 1556) opened up further the road to the south, although the Volga flowed through still-unpacified regions, making the land route difficult and the river route dangerous: every time one set foot ashore one was running a risk. But the Russian merchants organized river convoys which were large enough to defend themselves if necessary.

From now on, Kazan and particularly Astrakhan became turntables for

The port of Archangel in the seventeenth century. B.N., Paris, Cabinet des Estampes. (Photo B.N.)

Russian trade with the steppes of the Lower Volga and, above all, with Central Asia, China and nearby Iran. Merchants travelled to Kasvin, Shiraz and the island of Hormuz (which it took three months to reach from Moscow). A Russian fleet, built at Astrakhan in the latter part of the sixteenth century, was active on the Caspian Sea. Other trade routes ran to Tashkent, Samarkand and Bukhara and even as far as Tobol'sk – in those days the gateway to the Siberian East.

This trade with the South and East, although we have no figures for it, must have been greater in volume than trade to and from Europe. The Russians exported untanned skins, furs, ironware, coarse fabrics, wrought iron, arms, wax, honey and other foodstuffs, besides re-exporting European goods: Flemish and English cloth, paper, glass and metals. Back in return came spices (especially pepper) and silks from China and India, all of which passed through Iran; Persian velvets and brocades; sugar, dried fruits, pearls and gold ornaments from Turkey; cheap cottons from Central Asia. All this exchange activity was controlled, protected and sometimes even developed by the state.

To go by the few available figures, which relate to the state monopolies (thus only to a certain proportion of all exchange, and that not necessarily the greatest) trade with the East brought Russia a positive balance and on the whole acted as a stimulus to the economy. Whereas the West took from Russia only raw materials, sending in exchange manufactured articles and currency (which had its importance, it is true), the East bought manufactured goods from Russia and provided in return dyestuffs for Russian industry, some luxury goods admittedly, but also cheap silks and cottons for the popular market.

A strong state

Whether deliberately or not, Muscovy had chosen the East rather than the West. Was this the reason for Russia's economic backwardness? Or did Russia, by postponing contact with European capitalism, avoid the unenviable fate of nearby Poland, whose economic structures were reshaped by European demand, where fortune had singled out Gdansk (the 'eye of Poland') and where the great noblemen and magnates had become all-powerful, while the state's authority diminished and the development of the towns was held back?

In Russia on the contrary, the state was like a great rock in the middle of the sea: omnipotent, strongly-policed, the authority of the Russian state extended everywhere, to the towns (whose air did not 'make a man free'[218] as in the West), to the conservative Orthodox Church, to the peasant masses who belonged to the Tsar before they belonged to their overlord, or even to the boyars themselves, who had been brought to heel, whether they were hereditary nobles or the holders of *pomestye* (the livings granted for services rendered to the sovereign, and which may remind the reader of the *encomiendas* of Spanish America or the Turkish *sipahiniks*). In addition, the state had taken control of essential commodity trades, holding a monopoly in salt, potassium, spirits, beer, hydromel, furs, tobacco and later coffee. The grain market operated well at national level, but the export of grain was subject to permission from the Tsar, who often used it as a form of pressure to further his territorial conquests.[219] It was the Tsar too who arranged for the official caravans which, from 1653 onwards, left at what were supposed to be three-yearly intervals for Peking, carrying precious furs and returning with gold, silk, damask, porcelain and later tea. For the sale of alcohol and beer which were subject to state monopoly, special taverns were opened, 'which are known in the Russian language as *kobaks*, and which are exclusively the property of the Tsar ... except in the part of the Ukraine inhabited by Cossaks'. He derived a large annual income from them, perhaps a million roubles, and 'since the Russian nation is accustomed to strong liquor, and since soldiers and workers receive half their pay in bread or flour and the other half in cash, [they] spend the second half in the taverns so that all the coin circulating in Russia ends up in His Imperial Majesty's coffers'.[220]

Everyone took liberties, admittedly, with state property. Fraud was 'unlimited'; 'boyars and other private individuals contrive to sell clandestinely tobacco from Circassia and the Ukraine where it grows in great quantities'. And what can one say about the black market in vodka which operated at all levels of society? Smuggling on the grandest scale, which the authorities were powerless to prevent, concerned Siberian pelts and furs which were reaching nearby China in such quantities that the official caravans sent to Peking were soon unable to do business. In 1720, 'they cut off the head' of 'Prince Gagarin, former governor of Siberia, for having amassed so much wealth that so far they have only sold [the] furniture and merchandise [he owned in] Siberia and China, and there are still several houses full of unsold goods, not to mention precious stones, gold and silver, said to be worth over 3 million roubles'.[221]

But fraud, smuggling and breaking the law were not peculiar to Russia, and however widespread they may have been, they did not greatly impede the Tsar's arbitrary rule. We are very far removed from the political climate of the West, as can be seen from that peculiarly Russian institution, the *gosti*,[222] great merchants whom long-distance trade here as elsewhere had enriched, but who were firmly attached to the state. There were twenty or thirty of them in the service of the Tsar, endowed both with enormous privileges and enormous responsibilities. The *gosti* were required by turns to levy taxes, to collect customs duties in Astrakhan and Archangel, to sell furs and other goods belonging to the treasury, to handle foreign trade on the state's behalf, in particular the sale of commodities under state monopoly, and to supervise the management of the Mint and of the 'ministerial' department of Siberia. They were answerable for all these duties with their lives and personal property.[223] In return, their individual fortunes were sometimes colossal. In the reign of Boris Godunov (1598–1605) the *annual* wages of a worker have been estimated at 5 roubles. The Strogonov family – the richest of all the Russian merchants it is true, having made their fortune from usury, the salt trade, mining, industry, the conquest of Siberia, the fur trade and the acquisition of large colonial estates in the Perm region east of the Volga in the sixteenth century – advanced to the Tsar during the two Polish wars of 1632–4 and 1654–6[224] the sum of 412,056 roubles. And they had already, in the early days of Michael Romanov's reign, provided him with massive quantities of grain, salt, precious stones and money in the form of loans or extraordinary taxes.[225] As the owners of land, serfs, paid workers and household slaves, the *gosti* thus formed the very pinnacle of society, making up a very particular 'guild'.[226] There were two other guilds consisting of merchants of the second and third category, who also enjoyed certain privileges. The functions of the *gosti* declined however with the reign of Peter the Great.

It is clear then, that by contrast with what happened in Poland, the jealous and sharp-eyed authority of the Tsar in the end succeeded in preserving an autonomous trading system covering the whole of Russia and contributing to the country's economic development. And just as in the West, the great wholesale merchants did not specialize. One of the richest *gosti*, Gregor Nikitnikov, handled not only sales of salt, fish, cloth and silk, but also had businesses in Moscow, a share in the trade down the Volga, owned boats at Nizhniy–Novgorod (now Gorkiy) and had dealings in exports via Archangel; at one time he was negotiating with Ivan Strogonov for the purchase of a hereditary estate, a *votchyna*, for the fabulous price of 90,000 roubles. A certain Voronin owned more than 30 shops in the *radjs*[227] of Moscow; the merchant Shorin transported goods from Archangel to Moscow, from Moscow to Nizhniy-Novgorod and the Lower Volga; together with a partner, he bought up 100,000 poods of salt in a single purchase.[228] And these great wholesalers also went into the retail trade in Moscow to which they systematically transferred the surpluses and wealth of the provinces.[229]

The yoke of serfdom in Russia: an ever-increasing burden

In Russia as elsewhere, state and society went hand in hand. A strong state corresponded to a tightly controlled society, condemned to produce the surpluses from which the state and the upper class lived – for without the latter the Tsar would have been unable to control unaided the great mass of peasants who represented the essential source of royal income.

Every Russian folk tale has four or five main characters – the Peasant, the Landlord, the Prince, the Artisan and the Merchant (the two last-named usually being, in Russia, peasants who had gone up in the world but who remained socially and in the eyes of the law peasants still, subject to the constraints of the seigniorial society). And this was a regime becoming more and more oppressive: from the fourteenth century the lot of the peasants grew steadily worse from the Elbe to the Volga.

But Russia did not follow the usual pattern. In Poland, Hungary and Bohemia, the 'second serfdom' was established to the advantage of the nobles and magnates who stood between the peasants and the market and who controlled supplies to the towns, that is when the latter were not purely and simply their personal property. In Russia, the leading role was taken by the state: everything was governed by the state's needs and undertakings and by the heavy weight of the past: three centuries of fighting against the Tartars of the Golden Horde was even more effective than the Hundred Years' War which had given rise to the authoritarian monarchy of a Charles VII or a Louis XI. The solution adopted by Ivan the Terrible (1544–84) who founded and shaped modern Muscovy, was the displacement and if necessary suppression of the old aristocracy and, in order to have an army and an administration obedient to his desires, the creation of a new service nobility, the *pomechtchiki* to whom were granted for life the lands confiscated from or abandoned by the old nobility, or the virgin lands in the southern steppes which the new 'nobleman' would have to bring under cultivation with the aid of a few peasants or slaves. For slavery persisted among the Russian peasants longer than is sometimes thought. As in early colonial America, the problem was the supply of labour, which was scarce, rather than land, which was plentiful.

And this was what in the end led to serfdom and extended it. The Tsar had brought his nobility to heel – but the nobility had to live. If its peasants deserted it to colonize the newly-conquered lands, how was it to survive?

Seigniorial property,[230] previously based on a regime of free tenants, was transformed in the fifteenth century with the appearance of the *domain*, an estate which the landlord farmed himself, as in the West, and which was established at the expense of peasant holdings. The movement began among the lay nobility and spread to monastery-owned estates and those of the state. The domain sometimes employed slave-labour, more often that of indebted peasants who voluntarily enslaved themselves to pay off their debts. The system tended increasingly to demand payment of dues in the form of labour from the free tenant, and compulsory labour increased in the sixteenth century. But the peasants always had the possibility of flight – to Siberia after the late sixteenth century or better still to the black earth lands of the south. Their constant movements had become an endemic problem, as they persisted in changing masters or making for the virgin lands of the 'frontier' or perhaps trying their luck at craftworking, peddling or small shopkeeping.

This was all perfectly legal: according to the code of 1497, during the week of the feast of St George (25 November) when the year's heavy labour was over, every peasant was entitled to leave his master, provided he paid whatever he owed him. Other feast-days were also the signal to move on: Lent, Shrove Tuesday, Easter, Christmas, the feast of St Peter. Landlords used every means at their disposal to halt such flights, including corporal punishment or increasing the indemnities payable. But once a peasant had taken to the road, how could he be brought back to the fold?

Such peasant mobility threatened the foundations of seigniorial society, whereas it was the policy of the state to shore up this society, turning it into an instrument adapted to serve the crown: every subject had his place in an order which laid down the duty of one and all to the prince. The latter had therefore to call a halt to the escapades of the peasants. For a start, the feast of St George was declared the only legal day for departures. Then in 1580, an edict by Ivan IV suspended all freedom of movement 'temporarily' until further notice. The temporary ban was to last – especially since peasant flight continued despite further ukases (24 November 1597 and 28 November 1601), culminating in the code of 1649 which, in theory at any rate, marked the point of no return. This ukase declared illegal, once and for all, any movement by the peasant without the consent of his landlord, and abolished the old rules which granted runaway peasants the right not to be brought back to their masters, once a certain interval had elapsed (originally five years, later fifteen). This time no interval was specified: however long he had been away, a fugitive could be forced to return to his former landlord, along with his wife, children and worldly goods.

Such a development was only possible to the extent that the Tsar whole-heartedly took the side of the nobility. Peter the Great's ambitions – to develop a fleet, an army and an administration – required the reduction of the whole of Russian society, noble and peasant alike, to obedience. The priority accorded to the needs of the state explains why, unlike his Polish opposite number, the Russian peasant although in theory reduced to total serfdom in 1649, was in fact subject to *obrok* (dues payable in money or in kind, and to the state as much as to the landlord) rather more than to *barchina*[231] or forced labour. Where this did exist, even in the worst periods of serfdom, in the eighteenth century, it never exceeded three days a week. The payment of dues in cash clearly implies the existence of a market to which the peasant always had access. Indeed it is the market which explains the development of direct farming by the landlord of his domain (he wanted to sell its product) and no less the development of the Russian state, which depended on income from taxation. Depending which way one looks at it, one could equally well say either that the early appearance of a market economy in Russia was consequent upon the opening up of the peasant economy, or that it was the condition of such opening. In the process, Russia's foreign trade with Europe (which some people would no doubt dismiss as comparatively insignificant compared to the huge domestic market) had a part to play since it was Russia's positive balance with the West which injected into the Russian economy the minimal monetary circulation – silver from Europe or China – without which market activity would scarcely have been conceivable, certainly not at the level reached in practice.

The market and rural society

This basic freedom – access to the market – explains many contradictions. On one hand, the status of the peasant clearly deteriorated: in the age of Peter the Great and Catherine II, the serf had become a slave, 'a thing' (in the words of the Tsar Alexander I), a chattel which his master could sell when he pleased; the peasant was powerless in the face of seigniorial justice which might sentence him to deportation or imprisonment; moreover, he was liable for military service, could be enlisted as a sailor in the navy or merchant fleet, or drafted to work in the manufactories. This was indeed why so many peasant revolts erupted, to be regularly suppressed in bloodshed and torture. The Pugachev rebellion (1774-5) was only the most dramatic episode in this stormy history. On the other hand, it is quite possible that, as Le Play later thought,[232] the living standard of Russian peasants was comparable to that of many peasants in the West – in some cases at least, since one might find on the same estate serfs living in near-comfort alongside destitute peasants. And seigniorial justice was not equally harsh every-where.

It is also true that there were loopholes: serfdom allowed odd little pockets of freedom. Russian serfs frequently obtained permission to engage either full-

The Volga between Novgorod and Tver

or part-time in artisan trades, in which event they could sell the product of their work. When the princess Dashkov was in 1796 exiled by Paul I to a village in the northern region of Novgorod province, she asked her son where this village was and to whom it belonged. He made enquiries without success. 'At last by good fortune, a peasant from this village was found in Moscow: he had brought with him [to sell of course] a load of nails of his own making.'[233] Or a peasant could often obtain from his master a passport entitling him to ply some industrial or commercial trade far from the estate; and all without ceasing to be a serf, even after making his fortune, that is without ceasing to pay dues – at a rate proportionate to his wealth.

Some serfs became, with their master's blessing, pedlars, travelling salesmen, shopkeepers in the suburbs or in the town centres, or carriers. Every winter, millions of peasants hauled goods accumulated during the fine season into town on sledges. If by misfortune the snowfall was inadequate, as happened in 1789 and 1790, making it impossible to use sledges, the city markets remained empty and famine followed.[234] In summer, the rivers were thronged with boatmen. And from transporting goods to trading in them was but a short step. When conducting his survey of Russia, the naturalist and anthropologist Pierre Simon

Pallas stopped in 1768 at Vyshniy Volochek near Tver (now Kalinin) 'a large village, almost a small town. It owes its increase in size to the canal joining the Tvertsa to the Msta. This link [between the] Volga and Lake Ladoga is the reason why almost all the peasants of this region have turned to commerce: so that farming has virtually been abandoned'; the village had become a town, 'the local capital of the region of this name'.[235]

Furthermore, the ancient tradition of the rural craftsmen who worked for the market - the *kustari* who had all but abandoned agriculture by the sixteenth century - developed to an extraordinary degree between 1750 and 1850. This huge craft production far outweighed that of domestic outworking by peasants for city manufacturers.[236] The serfs were even able to take part in the rapid and wide expansion of manufactories encouraged by the state during and after the reign of Peter the Great: in 1725 there were 233 manufactories in Russia; by 1796 when Catherine II died, there were 3360, not counting mines and ironworks.[237] These figures admittedly include some very small undertakings besides large-scale enterprises. But they undoubtedly represent a remarkable increase. Most of the non-mining industrial expansion took place around Moscow. North-east of the capital for instance, in the village of Ivanovo (the property of the Shere-metev family), the local peasants who had traditionally been weavers eventually opened no less than 49 manufactories of printed fabrics (first linens, then cotton) in 1803. Their profits were fantastic and Ivanovo became the major Russian textile centre.[238]

No less spectacular were the fortunes made by certain serfs in wholesale trade. This was a profession in which there were comparatively few bourgeois - something peculiar to Russia.[239] As a result, peasants hastened to take it up and prospered - sometimes against the law but also with the protection of their landlords. Speaking in the name of the Russian government in the middle of the eighteenth century, Count Munnich stated that for a century, 'in spite of all the prohibitions, the peasants have constantly been engaging in trade, investing considerable sums of money in it', so that the growth and 'present prosperity' of wholesale trade 'are due to the competence, hard work and investment of these peasants'.[240]

For these *nouveaux riches* who remained serfs in the eyes of the law, the drama, or perhaps one should say the comedy, began when they tried to buy their freedom. Their master was usually reluctant to cooperate, perhaps because it was in his interest to continue to collect substantial rents, perhaps because his vanity was tickled by keeping these millionaires under his command, or because he wanted to raise their emancipation money to preposterous heights. The serf for his part, in an effort to release himself at least cost, took great pains to conceal the size of his fortune and frequently succeeded. In 1795 for instance, Count Sheremetyev demanded as the price for the freedom of Gratchev, the great textile manufacturer of Ivanovo, the exorbitant sum of 135,000 roubles, plus the factory, land and serfs owned by Gratchev - apparently almost the whole of his fortune. In fact, Gratchev had secreted away large amounts of capital under the names of merchants acting for him. Even after buying his liberty at so dear a price, he remained one of the barons of the textile industry.[241]

Such huge fortunes were of course acquired only by a minority. But the presence of innumerable peasants in small- and medium-scale trade was nevertheless a feature of the very special climate of serfdom in Russia. Whether well-to-do or miserable, the serf class was not imprisoned within village self-sufficiency; it remained in contact with the country's economy and found ways of surviving and making a livelihood. Moreover, between 1721 and 1790, the population doubled, a sure sign of vitality. What was more, the number of 'state peasants' gradually increased to the point at which it embraced half the rural population, and these state peasants were comparatively free, often being subject to no more than notional authority.

In the end, Mother Russia was absorbing into her bloodstream not only silver from the West but also a kind of capitalism. The innovations the latter brought with it were not necessarily earnest of progress; but under their weight the old regime began to crumble. Wage-labour made a very early appearance and developed in the towns, in transport, and even in the countryside for urgent seasonal tasks like haymaking and harvest. The workers who hired themselves out were often ruined peasants setting out to seek a living as farmhands or labourers; artisans who had lost all their money and continued to work in the *posad*, the worker's district, but now on the payroll of a more fortunate neighbour; or poor men who were hired as sailors, boatmen, hauliers (there were 400,000 *burlaki* on the Volga alone).[242] Labour markets came into existence, in Nizhniy Novgorod for example – a sign of the future fortune of this remarkable centre. The mines and manufactories needed not only serfs, but also wage-labourers who were given a bonus on being hired – at the risk of seeing the newly-engaged workman slip quietly out of town.

But the picture should be presented neither in too favourable nor in too gloomy a light. We are speaking in all cases of a population accustomed to privation, to surviving in harsh conditions. Perhaps the most telling image is that of the Russian soldier who was, we are told, 'really easy to feed ... He carries a little tin box, and has a small flask of vinegar, a few drops of which he pours into his drinking water; if he comes across a piece of garlic, he eats it with flour mixed with water. He can withstand hunger better than any other man, and when meat is given out to the troops he regards this largesse as a treat'.[243] When the army stores had run out of food, the Tsar had only to declare a day of fasting and crisis was averted.

A small-town society

A national market took shape early in Russia, one broadly based on the produce from noble or ecclesiastical estates and the surpluses of peasant farms. But this profusion of rural productivity was perhaps counterbalanced by the mediocrity of the towns. These were essentially small towns rather than cities, not only in size, but because they had not developed to any great extent the true functions of a city. 'Russia is one big village.'[244]: such was the impression of European travellers, correspondingly surprised by the abundance of the Russian market economy – which was however still at an elementary stage. It had its origins in the villages and included the small towns – which were themselves barely distinguishable from the surrounding countryside. The peasants had invaded the suburbs, taking over the bulk of artisan activity there, and even in the town they had set up an incredible number of small artisan shops. The German traveller J.P. Kilburger remarked in 1674 that 'there are more shops in Moscow than in Amsterdam or in an entire German principality'. But they were all tiny: a dozen of them would easily have fitted into the average Dutch shop. Sometimes two, three or four shopkeepers shared the same premises, so that 'the vendor can scarcely turn round amid his goods'.[245]

These shops, arranged according to their specialities, would run into two rows along a *radj* (literally 'row'). The word *souk* would not be an inappropriate translation since these districts with their close-packed shops were more reminiscent of Muslim towns than of the specialized streets of a western medieval town. In Pskov, 107 icon-makers had their shops in the *ikonnyi ryad*.[246] In Moscow, the site of what is now Red Square was 'covered with shops, as are all the streets around; every trade has its own street and district, so that the silk merchants do not mix with the cloth or canvas merchants, nor the goldsmiths with the saddlers, shoemakers, tailors, furriers and other artisans ... and there is one street where they sell nothing but Images of their Saints'.[247] One step further took the visitor to the larger shops, the *ambari*, which were in fact wholesale stores but also engaged in the retail trade. Moscow also had its markets and even specialized markets – including fleamarkets, where barbers operated in the open air among the old clothes, or meat and fish markets of which a German traveller insisted that 'you can smell them before you see them ... The stink is so strong that foreigners have to hold their noses'.[248] Only the Russians themselves do not seem to notice it, he claimed.

Apart from these small-scale market activities, there was also long-distance trade. This had inevitably developed on a national scale because of the diversity of the Russian regions, some of which were short of grain, others of wood or salt. Certain imported goods, or furs, crossed the country from end to end. Fairs rather than towns were the true generators of this trade, which made the fortunes of the *gosti* and later of other great merchants. There were probably between three and four thousand fairs in the eighteenth century[249] – that is ten or twelve

The *piroshki* seller (*piroshki* were little meat pies very popular in Russia). Engraving by K.A. Zelencov, eighteenth century, from *The Cries of Petersburg*. (Photo Alexandra Skarzynska.)

times the number of towns (in 1720 apparently there were only 273 towns). Some of the fairs, like those of Champagne, had the function of linking regions as distant from each other as Italy from Flanders. Among the major fairs[250] was Archangel in the far north; further south was the very lively fair, 'one of the most considerable in the Empire',[251] of Sol'vychegodsk; there was Irbit, on the road from Tobol'sk to Siberia; Makaryev, the early version of the great fair of Nizhniy Novgorod which really came into its own only in the nineteenth century; Briansk, between Moscow and Kiev; Tikhvin, on the approaches of Lake Ladoga, on the way to the Baltic and Sweden. These are by no means to be dismissed as archaic means of trading, since the age of fairs lasted until the eighteenth century in the West as well. But the problem about Russia is the comparative insignificance of the towns compared to the fairs.

Another sign of the lack of urban maturity was the absence of a modern system of credit; hence the reign of usury in both town and countryside on unimaginably harsh terms: at the slightest default, everything fell forfeit, including human life and liberty. For 'anything could be lent ... money, food, clothing, raw materials, seed-corn'; and anything could be pawned, shop, workshop, booth, wooden cabin, garden, field, plot, even the pipes from a salt pit. Incredible rates of interest were commonplace: when a Russian merchant lent money to a fellow countryman in Stockholm in 1690, the interest was 120 per cent over nine months, or more than 13 per cent per month.[252] In the Levant, where usury was commonly practised between Jewish or Muslim moneylenders and Christian borrowers, interest rates were no more than 5 per cent a month – modest by comparison. In Moscow, usury was the high road to capital accumulation. And the rate of return specified in the agreement mattered less than the acquisition of the goods pledged – property, workshops, hydraulic pumps. This was another reason why the interest rate was so high and the time limits so strict: everything was calculated to make the agreement impossible to keep, so that at the end of the day, the pound of flesh could be seized without hope of remission.

A world-economy – but what kind of world-economy?

Mighty Russia, for all its surviving archaisms, was unquestionably a world-economy in itself. Viewed from its centre, Moscow, it possessed not only vigour but also a certain power of command. The axis running north-south along the Volga was a crucial dividing line, just as the capitalist backbone of fourteenth-century Europe had run from Venice to Bruges. And if we imagine a map of France magnified to the scale of Russia, Archangel would be Dunkirk; St Petersburg, Rouen; Moscow, Paris; Nizhniy Novgorod, Lyon; and Astrakhan, Marseille. Later in 1794, the southern terminus would have moved to Odessa.

An expanding world-economy, pushing its conquests into the almost trackless peripheries, Muscovy was an immense unit, and it is this immensity which places it in the first rank among the economic monsters. Foreign observers were not mistaken when they regularly stressed this fundamental question of dimensions. Russia is so vast, wrote one of them, that at the height of summer 'at one end of the Empire the daylight lasts only 16 hours, while at the other it lasts for 23'.[253] It is so vast, with its reputed 500,000 square leagues, writes another,[254] 'that all the inhabitants [of the world] could easily fit [into it]'.[255] But, he adds, they would probably 'be unable to find enough to live on'.

In such surroundings, journeys became interminable, inhuman undertakings. Distance bedevilled and complicated every aspect of life. Transactions took years to complete. The official caravans leaving Moscow for Peking took three years to make the round trip. In the course of their long journey, they had to cross the Gobi Desert – at least 4000 versts (about 4000 km).[256] One merchant who had done the trip several times, assured two Jesuit fathers inquiring about it in 1692 that it was no worse than crossing Persia or Turkey[257] – as if that was not bad enough! In 1576, an Italian observer remarked of the realm of Shah Abbas,[258] *che si camina quatro mesi continui nel suo stato*, that it took four months to cross it. The journey from Moscow to Peking took even longer: as far as Lake Baikal, sledges were used, after that horses and camel trains; and one had to reckon with the inevitable halts and the harsh necessity of stopovers lasting the entire winter.

The same problems affected the north-south route from the White Sea to the Caspian. It is true that in 1555, a party of English merchants had succeeded in travelling from Archangel to the Iranian border. But the long-nourished plan to capture the Indian Ocean spice trade from the rear by crossing the 'Russian isthmus' north to south, took little account of the real problems of such an endeavour. Yet even in 1703, the news (probably premature) of the recapture of Narva by the Russians,[259] was inspiring much excitement in London: what could be simpler than to use this port as a starting-point for crossing Russia to the Indian Ocean, and thus beating the Dutch to it? But the English failed on several occasions to carry out the venture. In the 1740s, they did succeed in establishing themselves on the shores of the Caspian, but the indispensable permission of the Tsar, which had been granted in 1732, was withdrawn in 1746.[260]

Distance, which was the underlying reality of the Russian world-economy, and indeed gave it its shape, also had the advantage of protecting it against foreign invasion. Distance also encouraged the diversification of production and a more or less hierarchical division of labour between one zone and another. The claims of Russia to be a world-economy are also supported by the existence of its peripheral zones: the south and the Black Sea;[261] or the endless wastes of Siberia stretching eastwards to Asia. The Siberian case is a fascinating one, so let us take it as an example.

The invention of Siberia

If Europe 'invented America', Russia had to 'invent' Siberia. In both cases the 'inventors' were overwhelmed by the scale of the task. Europe in the early sixteenth century was however at the height of her powers, and America was firmly linked to the old continent by prime transport routes across the Atlantic. Sixteenth-century Russia by contrast was still short of resources and of people, and the sea-passage between Siberia and Russia, although at one time exploited by Novgorod, was not a convenient one: this was a sub-polar route leading to the wide estuary of the Ob, blocked by ice every year for months on end. The Tsarist government eventually closed the route entirely for fear that it would make contraband in Siberian furs too easy.[262] So Siberia was linked to the Russian 'hexagon' only by the long overland routes, to which fortunately the Urals did not prove too great an obstacle.

It was only in 1583 that communication by these routes, although initiated long before, became a reality with the expedition led by the Cossack Yermak on behalf of the brothers Strogonov, merchants and manufacturers who had received from Ivan IV large land concessions beyond the Urals, 'with the right to install cannon and arquebuses there'.[263] This was the start of a comparatively rapid conquest (100,000 km² a year).[264] Within a century, in their pursuit of furs, the Russians had moved progressively from the valleys of the Ob, the Yenisey, and the Lena, and had reached the banks of the Amur on the outposts of China (1689). The Kamchatka peninsula was taken between 1695 and 1700; Alaska, across the Bering Strait which was discovered in 1728, saw its first Russian settlements in the 1740s.[265] Towards the end of the eighteenth century, a report mentions the presence of two hundred Cossacks on the American mainland, roaming the country and trying 'to accustom the Americans to pay tribute' – tribute as in Siberia, consisting of sable and fox furs. And, it adds, 'the vexations and cruelties which the Cossacks exercise in the Kamchatka will no doubt soon be introduced to America'.[266]

The Russian advance had on the whole preferred to concentrate on the area stopping short of the Siberian forests, moving into the southern steppes where the frontier became established in about 1730 from the banks of the Irtys, a tributary of the Ob, as far as the Altay range. This was truly a *limes*, a continuous frontier held by the Cossacks, unlike the less systematic occupation of Siberia as a whole with its scatter of wooden fortresses (*ostrugi*). And this key frontier maintained its 1750 shape until the reign of Nicholas I (1825–55).[267]

Siberia then was a vast expanse of the unknown, originally conquered by a few unprompted expeditions and individual ventures, a process carried on independently of official intentions or schemes which would make an appearance only later. There was even a term to denote these early obscure pioneers: the *promyslenniki* – hunters, fishers, graziers, trappers, artisans and peasants, 'axe in hand, bag of seed-corn over shoulder'.[268] Not to mention genuine adventurers, who were feared and made unwelcome: or religious dissidents, merchants of other nationalities and, from the end of the seventeenth century, deported prisoners. The number of immigrants was derisory in relation to the great wastes of Siberia – 2000 a year at most on average; this was barely enough to establish scattered settlements of peasants, who possessed the priceless advantage of being virtually free, along the southern borders of the forests (silver birch forests here, by contrast with the dark conifer forests of the north). On these light soils, the swing-plough with beechwood ploughshare was adequate to cultivate a few fields of rye.[269]

The Russian settlers naturally chose the most fertile regions and the banks of fish-filled rivers, pushing the indigenous population back towards the deserts of the southern steppes or the deep forests of the north: to the south were the Turco-Tartars, from the Kirghizes on the shores of the Caspian to Mongolian peoples such as the amazing and warlike Buriats of Irkutsk province where a fort was built in defence against them in 1662; to the north were the Samoyeds, the Tunguses and the Yakuts.[270] The south was a world of merchant caravans and tent-dwelling nomads who grazed their flocks over immense stretches of the steppes; the north a world of log cabins in forest clearings, where the fur-trappers had to use compasses to find their way.[271] European travellers inclined to amateur ethnography have left many observations about these unfortunate peoples driven back into hostile natural surroundings:

> The Tunguses of the Ona valley [notes Gmelin the elder] almost all speak the Russian language, and wear Russian dress but it is easy to tell them by their height and the patterns they draw on their faces. Their clothing is of the

simplest, they never wash, and when they go into a tavern, they have to bring their own glasses: they would never be given any. Apart from the marks by which they can be distinguished from Russians, it is also very easy to recognize them by their smell.[272]

By the end of the eighteenth century, Siberia probably had a population of a little under 600,000, counting the native peoples who were easily dominated because of their poverty and small numbers, and who might even be incorporated into the small detachments of troops guarding the forts. They were frequently used for heavy labour: hauling barges, transport, mining. And they also provided the outposts with fur, game or goods from the south. The few Mongol or Tartar slaves – who were usually sold on the market in Astrakhan[273] – or those who were sold in the Siberian markets of Tobol'sk or Tomsk, were insignificant in number. There was nothing here comparable to what was happening in the slave-plantations of America or even in some parts of Russia.

Transport was crucial and never an easy matter. The rivers, running from south to north, were ice-bound for months on end, and the thawing of the ice in spring could be terrifying; portages for flat-bottomed boats (*strugi*) made it possible in summer to cross from one valley to another at key watersheds, where towns sometimes grew up, at first on a modest scale, like the towns built by Europeans in the American interior. Despite the intense cold, the winter was comparatively favourable for travelling since sledges could be used. The *Gazette de France* for 4 April 1772 records, passing on a dispatch from St Petersburg, that 'there have arrived by the latest sleds a considerable quantity of gold and silver ingots from the Siberian mines [probably from Nerchinsk] and the Altay mountains'.[274]

Confronted with the slow formation of Siberia, the Russian state had time gradually to take precautions, to instal controls and post detachments of Cossacks and active if prevaricating officials. The assertion of control over Siberia was given concrete expression in 1637 by the creation in Moscow of a Siberian department (*prikaz*) – a sort of ministry for Siberian affairs to handle the 'colony', not so very different in its attributions from the *Consejo de Indias* or the *Casa de la Contratación* in Seville. Its role was at once to organize the administration of Siberia and to collect such merchandise as was the object of state monopoly. This did not mean precious metals, since mining was a later development. The mines of auriferous silver at Nerchinsk were not discovered until 1691: they were first worked by Greek entrepreneurs and did not yield their first silver until 1704 or their first gold until 1752.[275] So for many years deliveries from Siberia consisted simply of fantastic quantities of furs, known as 'soft gold', strictly controlled by the state: trappers, whether indigenous or Russian, and merchants had to pay tribute or taxes in furs, and these were collected and re-sold by the *prikaz*, either in China or in Europe. But not only was the state often obliged to pay its agents in the same currency (keeping only the best pelts for itself), it was also unable to keep an eye on the entire output of the trappers. Siberian furs were being smuggled out of the country and sold in Gdansk or Venice at cheaper prices than in Moscow. And it was even easier of course to smuggle them into China, which was a major purchaser of furs – sea-otter and sable particularly. Between 1689 and 1727, fifty caravans of Russian merchants left for Peking – only a dozen of them on official business.[276]

For the Russian hold over Siberia was far from complete. As late as 1770, according to a contemporary (a Polish exile whose adventures would later take him to Madagascar), 'it is even part of the policy of the Russian government to close its eyes to such infringements [i.e. smuggling]: it would be too dangerous to arouse the Siberians to revolt. The slightest trouble would make the inhabitants rise up in arms, and if things reached this pass, Siberia would be quite lost to Russia'.[277] Benyowski was exaggerating, and in any case Siberia would never be able to escape the Russian grip: it was imprisoned by its primitive level of development, revealed by the low prices in its new towns, the near-autarky of many of its regions and what was in some ways the artificial character of its long-distance trade, which nevertheless locked it into a chain of obligations.

For the fact was that however slow or long-drawn-out, these exchanges formed a system of interdependence. The great Siberian fairs – Tobol'sk, Omsk, Tomsk, Krasnoyarsk, Yeniseysk, Irkutsk, Kyakhta – were all connected. The Russian merchant leaving Moscow for Siberia would stop first at Makaryev and Irbit, then at all the Siberian posts, sometimes making return journeys (between Irkutsk and Kyakhta for instance). The round trip could last four and a half years with some long halts; at Tobol'sk, 'the caravans of the Kalmucks and Burkaskis ... stay all winter'.[278] Into such places would crowd men and draft animals, with sleds to which both dog and reindeer teams were harnessed, unless there was a strong wind, when a sail was hoisted and the animals ran behind the 'ship' as it sailed along under its own power. These staging-post towns with their shops were places of congregation and amusement. The press of stall-keepers was so 'thick on the market-place of Tobol'sk that it was hard to push a way through'.[279] Irkutsk possessed numerous taverns where travellers systematically drank all night long.

The towns and fairs of Siberia were thus hosts to a twofold network of commerce: long-distance trade in which Russian or European goods were exchanged for those of China or even India and Persia; and the sale of local products (above all furs) in exchange for the supplies necessary to all these settlements lost in the wastes of Siberia – meat, fish, flour and the sacrosanct vodka which had rapidly conquered northern Asia (it was the only thing that made exile bearable). The further east and north one went, of course, the wider the range of prices. At Ilimsk, well beyond Irkutsk, capital of the province of the same name, a kind of fur market was held with certain western goods being handed over in exchange. In 1770, a merchant could make a profit of 200 per cent on such goods and double his profit again by selling the furs in China. Out here, a pound of gunshot was worth three roubles, a pound of tobacco, one and

A meeting of Russian and Chinese merchants at the house of the 'burgomaster' (*gorodnitski*) of Kyakhta, the town where the Russo-Chinese fairs were held. After C. de Rechberg, *Peuples de la Russie*, Paris-St Petersburg, 1812, vol. I. (Photo B.N.)

a half; ten pounds of butter cost six roubles, a keg of eau-de-vie of eighteen pints, fifty roubles; forty pounds of flour, five roubles. In return, a sable pelt was worth only one rouble, a black fox fur, three; a bearskin, half a rouble; fifty grey squirrel pelts, one rouble; a hundred white rabbit pelts, one rouble; twenty-four ermine pelts, one rouble – and so on. It is easy to see who got rich at these prices.[280] On the Chinese frontier, a beaver pelt was 'valued at exchange at 80 to 100 roubles'.[281]

On the other hand without the lure of gain, what merchant would ever have ventured out into these infernal regions, where there were no roads, where there was danger from wild beasts and no less from human marauders, where horses dropped dead in harness, where the last frosts were in June and the first began again in August,[282] where wooden sledges easily broke and might be caught and buried in lethal snowstorms? If horses went off what was literally the beaten track, they might plunge into soft snow up to their necks. To make matters worse, after the 1730s North American furs began to compete with the 'soft gold'

Plan of the town of Astrakhan in 1754.
Atlas maritime, III, 1764. B.N., Paris,
Ge. FF 4965. (Photo B.N.)

of Siberia, where a cycle was coming to an end, or at any rate deteriorating. It was now that the mining cycle began, as dams, mill-wheels, hammers, forges and furnaces were built. But northern Asia, an imperfect version of America, had no black slaves or Indian peoples to draw on. The only available manpower here was Russian or Siberian, and this was in reality forced rather than voluntary labour. During the first fifty years of the nineteenth century, there was an extraordinary and fantastic gold rush, of which haunting images have survived: the frantic searches for gold up the Siberian rivers; the long marches through the swamps of the *taiga*; the recruitment of workers from among deportees and peasants for the four summer months. The workers were rounded up and supervised and were no sooner freed than they spent all their money on drink; they had no choice, after surviving the winter as best they could, but to answer the recruiters' call again in the spring, to receive the signing-on bonuses and the rations required for the long trek back to the mine.[283]

Inferiorities and weaknesses

Russian expansion was not uniformly steady or unchallenged. It was an extraordinary achievement, but it had its vulnerable points. The weaknesses of the Russian world-economy showed up most clearly in the north and west, by comparison with the western world, as one might expect; but they were also evident in the south, from the Balkans and the Black Sea to the Pacific, as it faced the double presence of Islam and China.

Under the rule of the Manchus, China was turning out to be a politically powerful, aggressive, and victorious state. The Treaty of Nerchinsk (1689) virtually brought to a halt Russian expansion into the Amur valley. After this, Russo-Chinese relations thoroughly deteriorated and in January 1722, the Russian merchants were expelled from Peking. An improvement was brought about by the double treaty of Kyakhta (20 August and 21 October 1727) which established the frontier between Mongolia and Siberia and created a Sino-Russian fair on the frontier itself, south of Irkutsk: from now on, this would handle the bulk of trade between the two countries, although a few official caravans[284] for a while continued to reach Peking. The Chinese derived most benefit from this arrangement, since they had now banished Russian traders far from their capital to the outer edge of Mongolia, and they stepped up their conditions. From now on Chinese gold, in flakes or ingots, could be exchanged only for silver. And in 1775, the Russians in the caravan were arrested and hanged in Peking.[285] The Kyakhta fair still had some good days ahead of it, but Russian penetration into the Chinese sphere had been effectively halted.

The Russian position was rather different as regards Islam, which was weakened by political splits between the Turkish Empire, Persia and the Mogul Empire. There was no continuous political front from the Danube to Turkestan. On the other hand trading networks here were ancient, solidly-established and almost impossible to intercept or dislodge. It is an indication of Russian weakness that the merchants of India, Iran and the Balkans invaded (there is no other word for it) Russian territory: there were Indian merchants in Astrakhan and Moscow, Armenians in Moscow and Archangel. And if the latter in 1710 obtained privileges from the Tsar, or if the Tsar agreed in 1732 to grant English merchants facilities to trade with Persia through Kazan, it was because the Russians had encountered setback after setback on the Caspian.[286] Communications were only effective in this direction if they could count on local communities in the key staging-towns – starting with Astrakhan, which contained a Tartar suburb, an Armenian district, and Indian colony, and a caravanserai for 'foreigners' (which in 1652 for instance, put up two Jesuit fathers who were hoping to travel to China). Similarly, for communications with the Black Sea and the Turkish markets in the Balkans, including Istanbul, it was the Turkish merchants (often of Greek origin) and a handful of Ragusan traders, who carried the most weight.

It was indeed a Ragusan, born in Bosnia, brought up and educated in Venice, Sava Lukitch Vladislavitch Raguzinskii, newly arrived in Russia in 1703, whom Peter the Great employed for negotiations with the Balkans and later appointed to organize Siberian trade.[287] And in Siberia itself, there were Greek fur-buyers and mining entrepreneurs in the Altay region. On 20 January 1734, when the Irbit fair opened and the roads were 'thronged with horses, men and sledges . . . I saw there', a traveller reports, 'Greeks, Bukhars and Tartars of all kinds. . . .

The Greeks brought with them chiefly foreign goods purchased at Archangel, such as French wines and spirits'.[288]

Foreign superiority was even clearer to see on the European side, where the beneficiaries were Hanseatic, Swedish, Polish, English and Dutch merchants. In the eighteenth century, the Dutch were gradually being ousted; poorly served by their local correspondents, they were going bankrupt one after another, as the English took over the commanding positions: by the time of the negotiations at the end of the century, the latter were dictating their terms. In competition with foreign merchants, in Moscow and later in St Petersburg, Muscovite merchants rarely proved much of a challenge. It is surely curious that the richest merchant in Siberia in the 1730s – a man who had travelled to Peking as agent for Muscovite caravans and who later became vice-governor of Irkutsk, Lorents Lange – was probably a Dane.[289] Similarly, when after 1784 Russia began direct trading with the Black Sea, once again this was handled by foreign intermediaries – Venetians, Ragusans and Marseillais. That is not to mention the adventurers, tricksters and 'persons of ill repute', who had been active in Russian affairs since before Peter the Great. As late as April 1785, Simon Vorontsov was writing from Pisa to his brother Alexander: 'All the scoundrels in Italy, whenever they are at a loss what to do, publicly declare that they are off to Russia to make their fortunes'.[290]

The conclusion is obvious: on its far-flung frontiers the Russian giant was not firmly established. Russia's foreign trade was always manipulated by hidden hands in Peking, Istanbul, Isfahan, Leipzig, Lwow, Lübeck, Amsterdam or London. It was only within the domestic markets or at the huge fairs scattered over the country that the Russian merchant could take his revenge, by dealing in European goods imported through St Petersburg or Archangel and used as exchange currency all the way to Irkutsk and beyond.

The price of European intrusion

Peter the Great's military victories and his far-reaching reforms are said to have 'brought Russia out of the isolation in which she had hitherto lived',[291] a formula which is neither entirely false nor entirely correct. Was Muscovy not already looking towards Europe before Peter the Great? Above all, while the founding of St Petersburg, around which the Russian economy was reorganized, certainly opened a window or rather a doorway on to the Baltic and Europe, making it easier for Russians to reach the outside world, by the same token Europeans coming the other way found it easier to penetrate the Russian stronghold and by increasing their share of trade to conquer the Russian market, shaped it to suit their own purposes as far as possible.

Once more, all the means Europe ordinarily employed to further her ends were pressed into service – above all flexible credit arrangements (buying stocks in advance) and the European secret weapon, ready money. A consul in France's

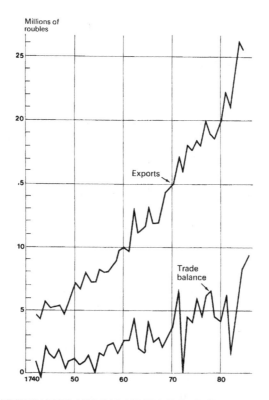

Millions of
roubles

Exports

Trade
balance

1740 50 60 70 80

45 THE POSITIVE RUSSIAN TRADE BALANCE (1742-1785)
From a document in the Moscow Central Archives (Vorontsov collection 602-1-59) which gives
the Russian trade balance overland and by sea. There were two short lived drops in the surplus,
in 1772 and 1782, probably as a result of arms purchases.

service at Elsinore on the Sound noted on 9 September 1748: 'Considerable sums
of money in Spanish pieces of eight pass through here on every English vessel
bound for St Petersburg'.[292] This was because the trade balance measured in St
Petersburg, Riga and later at Odessa (1794) always worked out in Russia's
favour – with a few exceptions, at moments when the Russian government was
engaged or about to engage in some large foreign operation. The best way to
promote trade in poorly-developed countries was to import precious metals: the
European merchants allowed the same 'haemorrhage of specie' to Russia as they
did to the Levant ports or the Indies – with the same results: the progressive
takeover of the Russian market, with the real profits being made on the return
journey by the resale or redistribution of merchandise in the West. What was
more, the manoeuvring of foreign exchange on the Amsterdam and later the
London money market,[293] meant that Russia was sometimes fobbed off with
meaningless promises.

Russia thus became accustomed to receiving the manufactured articles and luxury goods of Europe. Having been a late entrant to international trade, she would subsequently find it hard to disengage from it. Her rulers came to think that the development taking place under their eyes was their own work, and they encouraged and helped it to penetrate their country as a new structural element, seeing it as bringing advantage both to themselves and to a Russia now open to Enlightenment. But was Russia paying too high a price? That is the suggestion in a memorandum, probably from the pen of a Russian doctor, dated 19 December 1765 – an almost revolutionary document, certainly running against the received wisdom of the time. It calls upon Russia more or less to close the door to all foreign penetration. The proper models to follow, suggests the writer, are the policies of India and China (as he imagines them at any rate). 'These nations carry on much trade with the Portuguese, the French and the English, [who] buy from them all their manufactured goods and some raw materials. But neither the Indians nor the Chinese buy the slightest amount of European goods, except for watches, ironware, and a few arms.' So the Europeans are obliged to pay for their purchases with money, 'the method adopted by these nations ever since they have been known to history'.[294] The writer is of the view that Russia ought to return to the simplicity of the time of Peter the Great; since those days, alas, her nobles have become accustomed to luxury which 'has continued to increase for forty years'. The worst temptations are aboard French ships, of which there are not many, but 'the cargo [of one of them] being entirely made up of luxury goods', is generally worth ten or fifteen times that of other nations' ships. If such luxuries were to continue to be imported, they would bring about 'the desolation of agriculture and of the few factories and manufactories of the Empire'.

Is there however not a little irony in the fact that this 'nationalist' memorandum which was communicated to Alexander Voronstov, and therefore brought to the attention of the Russian government, was written in *French*? In itself it illustrates another side of the European intrusion, an acculturation which changed the way of thinking and the way of life not only of the aristocracy, but also of the Russian bourgeoisie and of the entire intelligentsia which was also contributing to build the new Russia. The philosophy of the Enlightment now spreading throughout Europe deeply penetrated Russian intellectual and ruling circles. In Paris, the engaging Princess Dashkov felt the need to exonerate herself from charges of tyranny towards her peasants. She explained in 1780 to Diderot, who had used the word 'slavery', that the greatest threat to the serf lay in the greed of 'governments and their provincial officials'. It was in the interests of the landlord on the contrary that his peasants should be rich, since they 'create his own prosperity and increase his income'.[295] Fifteen years later, she congratulated herself on the results of her management of her estate of Troitskoe near Orel: in 140 years the population had approximately doubled and no woman 'wishes to marry away from my estate'.[296]

But along with ideas, European influence also communicated fashions and undoubtedly contributed to the thorough penetration of Russia by all the luxuries condemned by the good doctor. Rich and leisured Russians became as intoxicated with European ways, with the refinements and pleasures of Paris and London, as westerners had been for centuries with the dazzling civilization of the Italian cities. Simon Vorontsov - who had himself tasted and praised the charms of the English way of life - nevertheless wrote with irritation from London on 8 April 1803: 'I hear that our gentlemen are making extravagant purchases in Paris. That fool Demidov has ordered a porcelain dinner service, every plate of which costs 16 gold louis'.[297]

When all is said and done however, there was no comparison between the Russian situation and the complete dependence of, say, Poland. When the European economy launched its assault on Russia, the latter had already embarked on a course of action which protected her domestic market and the development of her own artisan production, her own manufacturing enterprises created in the seventeenth century,[298] and her own active commerce. And Russia had even adapted very well to the 'industrial pre-revolution', that is to the general upturn in production of the eighteenth century. On state orders and with state assistance, mines, foundries, arsenals, new manufactories of silks and velvets and glassworks sprang up from Moscow to the Urals.[299] And an enormous substratum of domestic and craft industry continued to operate. On the other hand when the real industrial revolution came, in the nineteenth century, Russia was to mark time and fall further and further behind. This was far from the case in the eighteenth century when, according to J. Blum, Russian industrial development was equal and sometimes superior to that of the rest of Europe.[300]

None of this prevented Russia from - more than ever - fulfilling her role as provider of raw materials: hemp, flax, tar, ships' masts; and of foodstuffs: grain and salt fish. Sometimes it was even the case that - as in Poland - exports did not correspond to a genuine surplus. In 1775, for example, 'Russia allowed foreigners to extract her grain, although famine was devastating part of her Empire'.[301] Indeed, the same note dating from 1780 continues, 'the scarcity of specie obliges the farmer to deprive himself of necessities in order to pay taxes' (which were collected in cash). And this scarcity of coin was a burden to landowners who were obliged 'commonly to buy on one year's credit and to sell their foodstuffs for cash six months or a year before the harvest', letting their crops go for 'low prices in order to compensate for the interest on the advance'. Here as in Poland, advance payments for future harvests distorted the terms of trade.

This was the easier in that the landlords, or at any rate the richest of them, were within easy reach of the European merchants. The Russian nobles had been bidden in authoritarian manner to live in St Petersburg 'which they hate', says a report of 1720, 'because staying here ruins them, by keeping them away from their estates and their old way of life which they love above all things in the world, so that if the Tsar does not establish before his death a successor capable of maintaining what he has so auspiciously begun, his people will revert, like a torrent, to their former barbary'.[302] The prophecy was not fulfilled however,

The port of St Petersburg in 1778. Engraving after a drawing by J.B. Le Prince. (Photo Alexandra Skarzynska.)

since although the Tsar died suddenly in 1725, Russia continued to have contacts with Europe, and to sell increasing quantities of raw materials over there. On 28 January 1819, Rostopchin wrote from Paris to his friend Simon Vorontsov in London, 'Russia is an ox which they are eating and turning into stock cubes for other countries' (a metaphor which tells us incidentally that the process for evaporating beef stock to make dried extract had been discovered before Liebig (1803–73) who is usually credited with the invention).[303]

Rostopchin's imagery may be strong but he was not entirely mistaken. It should not be forgotten however that these deliveries of raw materials to Europe provided Russia with a positive trade balance and thus with a constant supply of money. And this in turn was the pre-condition for the introduction of the market into a peasant economy, an essential element in the modernization of Russia and in her powers to resist foreign invasion.

The Turkish Empire

The case of the Turkish Empire is reminiscent of Russia, but with several important differences. An early creation and from the start a vigorous one, by the fifteenth century the Ottoman Empire was an anti-Europe, a counter-Christendom. Fernand Grenard rightly saw the Turkish conquest as something very different from the barbarian invasions of the fifth century: it was 'an Asiatic and anti-European revolution'.[304] And the empire was also unquestionably from the very beginning a world-economy, one which had inherited the ancient ties between Islam and Byzantium and was firmly controlled by effective state authority. 'The *Grand Seigneur* is above the law', said the French ambassador, M. de la Haye, in 1669, 'he may have his subjects put to death without formality and often without any foundation in justice, and may seize their goods and dispose of them as he wishes'.[305] But the counterpart of this despotic power was the long-lasting *pax turcica* – a latter day *pax romana*, the envy of the West. By the same token, the Ottoman rulers were visibly capable of keeping their indispensable western interlocutors firmly in their place. Even Venice was obliged to wheel and deal to get anywhere in Istanbul, penetrating the Turkish economy so far and no further. Only when the authority of the Grand Signor declined would the Ottoman world-economy show signs of disorganization. Even the 'decadence' about which historiography has been so eloquent was 'less rapid and far-reaching than is generally thought'.[306]

The foundations of a world-economy

A fundamental condition of Turkey's autonomy was its physical area: the Ottoman Empire was of planetary dimensions. Who could fail to join the western chorus of amazement and alarm at its fabulous size? Giovanni Botero in 1591 estimated that it had 3000 miles of coastline, and noted that the distance from Tauris to Buda was 3200 miles, that from Derbent to Aden the same, and that the distance from Basra to Tlemcen was just under 4000.[307] The sultan reigned over thirty kingdoms, over the Black Sea and 'the White Sea' (the Aegean), the Red Sea and the Persian Gulf. The Habsburg Empire in its prime was even larger, but that was an empire dispersed worldwide and broken up by great oceans. The Osmanli Empire was in one piece: a jigsaw of interlocking landmasses in which potentially divisive stretches of water were held prisoner.

Lying between the frontiers traced by the long-distance international trade routes, this landmass was a complex of permanent communications and constraints, virtually a fortress and also a source of wealth. It was certainly the overland traffic which turned the Middle East into a crossroads of trade, providing the Turkish Empire with the lifeblood that made it mighty, especially after the conquest of Syria in 1516 and Egypt in 1517 which rounded off its triumphs. It is true that by this time the Middle East could no longer claim to be the centre of the world it had still been in the days of Byzantium and of the first triumphs of Islam. The Europeans had meantime benefited from the discovery of America in 1492 and of the route round the Cape in 1498. And if Europe was too preoccupied in the New World to devote herself whole-heartedly to resisting the Ottoman Empire, this was partly because a number of obstacles had providentially appeared to block Turkey's conquering advance, which failed to go beyond the regency of Algiers to capture Morocco, Gibraltar and the gateway to the Atlantic. Turkey did not achieve overall mastery of the Mediterranean, nor did she ever succeed in conquering Persia, the insurmountable barrier to the east which deprived the Ottomans of the key positions overlooking India and the Indian Ocean. C.R. Boxer suggests that the battle of Lepanto (7 October 1571) which ended Turkish control of the Mediterranean (acquired thirty years earlier by the Turkish victory at La Preveza in 1538) and the more aggressive posture of Persia under Shah Abbas were the basic reasons for the halt of the Turkish advance.[308] I agree; but neither should one underestimate the presence of the Portuguese who were running rings round Islam in the Indian Ocean: for this triumph of European maritime *technology* continued to prevent the Turkish monster from establishing any real presence outside the Persian Gulf and the Red Sea.

So the Middle East as a crossroads of trade had declined in value, but it was far from being reduced to insignificance. The precious Levant trade, so long unparalleled, was not suspended when the Turks occupied Syria in 1516 and Egypt in 1517, nor were the routes through the nearby Mediterranean by any means abandoned. The Red Sea and the Black Sea (the latter as important to Istanbul as the 'Indies' were to Spain) continued to offer their services. After 1630, pepper and spices bound for Europe seem to have been permanently diverted to the Atlantic route but their place was taken by silk, before long by coffee and drugs, and eventually by cotton and cotton textiles, both printed and plain.

Furthermore, the sheer size of the empire ensured that, given the modest level of local consumption, there would be abundant surplus production: animals for butchering, grain, hides, horses – even textiles. The Turkish Empire had also inherited the towns and great conurbations of Islam: it was scattered with merchant cities with their many crafts and trades. Indeed almost every eastern city surprised the western visitor by its noise and bustle: there was Cairo, a great parasitic growth yet at the same time a powerhouse, and a capital in its own way; Aleppo, on its marvellous site surrounded by fertile land, a town about the same size as Padua, *ma senza nessun vacuo e populatissima*, but without any empty spaces, and densely-populated;[309] even Rosetta, 'a very large town, well peopled and pleasantly constructed [with] brick houses standing [twelve feet] above the street';[310] Baghdad and its busy city centre, with 'six or seven streets

... of tradesmen's and craftsmen's shops, streets [which] are closed at nights, some by gates, others with heavy iron chains';[311] Tabriz, on the Persian border, a town 'remarkable for its size, its commerce, its multitude of inhabitants and the abundance of all the necessities of life'.[312] Edward Brown of the Royal Society described Belgrade on his visit there in 1669 as 'a large, strong, populous and great trading city'.[313] The same could be said of almost every Turkish city in Africa, Asia and the Balkans (where they were 'white cities' by contrast with the 'dark' world of the villages).[314]

How then is one to believe that all these cities, ancient and restored, or new and sometimes very close to the western pattern, could possibly have prospered in a Turkey supposedly in decline? Why should something generally considered to be a sign of progress here be thought a sign of deterioration?

An even greater misunderstanding arises from seeking to relate the Turkish Empire's economic history to the chronology of its political history. There is great uncertainty about the latter, to judge by the hesitations of Turkey's historians. One of them has argued[315] that the empire reached its political zenith in 1550, during the last years of Sulaiman the Magnificent (1521–65); another[316] no less convincingly suggests that Turkey's decline set in after 1648 (a whole century later) but this, the year of the Treaty of Westphalia and the assassination of the sultan Ibrahim I, is more of a European than a Turkish landmark. If any date is to be singled out, I should prefer to take 1683, just after the dramatic siege of Vienna (14 July – 12 November 1683), when the Grand Vizier Khan Mustapha, the unfortunate hero of the undertaking, was put to death in Belgrade on the sultan's orders.[317] But no political landmark seems entirely valid to me. Yet again, while politics clearly bears some relation to economics and vice versa, the political 'decline' of the Ottoman Empire, whenever that decline occurred, did not immediately bring about that of the economy. After all, between the sixteenth and the seventeenth century, the population of the empire grew spectacularly, almost doubling in size. In the Balkans, according to Iorjo Tadic,[318] the *pax turcica* and the demand of Istanbul created a genuine *national market*, or at the very least stimulated trade. And in the eighteenth century, there are clear signs of revival.

It was certainly at some cost to themselves that the Ottomans controlled 'not only all the Islamic Mediterranean ports (except those of Morocco) but also the ports providing outlets on the Red Sea and Persian Gulf',[319] plus the towns on the Black Sea which connected with Russian trade routes. The major axes of trade running through the empire themselves gave it a certain coherence. These axes might shift, but they remained in existence. In the fifteenth century, the major crossroads of trade was probably not so much Istanbul, the top-heavy capital which needed rebuilding, as Bursa, city of many trades, and a centre for transit and commerce. The Turkish advance into Syria and Egypt then moved the centre of the Ottoman economy towards Aleppo and Alexandria, thus setting up throughout the sixteenth century a sort of trade diversion operating against

The city and the bazaar of Ankara in the eighteenth century. Detail of painting by J.B. Van Mour, a French artist living in Istanbul between 1699 and 1737. (Rijksmuseum, Amsterdam.)

Istanbul, so that the internal balance of the empire shifted southwards. It is known that the centre moved yet again in the seventeenth century, this time to Smyrna, though this has never been satisfactorily explained. And in the eighteenth century, it seems to me, the economy was re-centred on Istanbul. Could it be that in the course of these little-known episodes, the world-economy corresponding to the Ottoman Empire had a series of different centres of gravity, depending on the period and the economic climate?

In or around 1750 at any rate, Istanbul recaptured its dominant position in the economy. The customs tariffs of the city, a list of which was passed on in 1747 to Moscow, do not in themselves prove anything about the volume of trade. But they do have the particular feature of distinguishing between merchandise 'quoted at the old tariff' and goods added in 1738 or later. The list of imported goods is interminable: numerous textiles, mirrors, panes of glass, paper, pewter, sugar, brazil-wood and campeachy wood, English ales, mercury, every kind of drug and spice, Indian indigo, coffee, etc. Among the *new* products, various other kinds of textiles are listed: cloth, silks, cottons from France, England and Holland; steel, lead, furs, calicoes, indigo from St Domingue, 'coffee from Christendom'; all in a wide range of qualities. The catalogue of outgoing products is shorter, listing the classic exports of Constantinople: buffalo hides, 'black ox' hides, morocco, shagreen, goat's hair and camel hair, wax; only a few articles were added later: fine camlets, silk and goat's hair processed for wigs'. In other words, the list of imports grew ever longer and more varied from distant countries, especially Europe which sent to Constantinople luxury articles and even products from the New World. But there were few additions to the list of exports.[320] A long French report on the Levant trade confirms this impression:

> [French] ships carry more goods to Constantinople than to all the other ports in the Levant. Their cargoes consist of cloth, spices, sweetmeats, dyestuffs and various other goods. Merchandise to the same value cannot be bought in Constantinople, because the only goods the French merchants take on there are hybrid hides, serges and plush, sheep- and goat-skins, printed cottons, a little wax, timber and shagreen. The surplus funds are transferred to other ports by means of bills of exchange which the French merchants of Smyrna, Aleppo and [Port] Said provide for the Pashas who have to make returns to the treasury of the *Grand Seigneur*.[321]

So Constantinople as well as being a major consumption centre was also a currency exchange market, on which large profits could be made; the export trade on the other hand, was as a rule livelier in the other ports of the Levant.

The scale of European penetration of the Turkish Empire

But the key question concerns the place European trade occupied within the overall volume of Turkish trade. In many cases European trade scarcely scratched the surface of the Turkish economy, or merely passed quickly through.

A halt at a caravanserai (manuscript in the Museo Correr, Cicogna collection, Venice). The Italian legend reads as follows: 'Here is an open caravanserai, with the doorway guarded by chains, with hearths and fires for the convenience of travellers. Their arms are hung up on the wall, and their horses stand below the platform inside the building. Turks of all conditions stop here, as [we would] in the taverns of Christendom'. (Photo by the museum.)

It was at grassroots level that the real economy of the Turkish Empire, an elementary but vigorous one, was to be found. Traian Stoyanovich has invented a picturesque name for it, 'the bazaar economy', that is a market economy articulated around the cities and regional fairs where exchange continued to obey traditional rules and was still, he argues, characterized by transparency and good faith. Even in the eighteenth century, credit was poorly developed, apart from usury which was ever-present even in the countryside. True, it was no longer the case that as Pierre Belon had noted in 1550, 'Everything in Turkey is exchanged for cash. So there are not so many papers, record-sheets of loans[322] or ledgers, and between neighbour and neighbour for any retail merchandise, there is no more credit accorded than if they were foreigners from Germany'.[323] But the old ways still survived to some extent, even if western merchants did make advance payments for goods to their suppliers and even if as we have seen the positive balance of their sales in Constantinople enabled them to sell in Smyrna or Aleppo bills of exchange on Constantinople. Overall, commercial life in Turkey still had some archaic features, one of which was the disconcertingly low price of everything compared with western Europe. In Tabriz in 1648, 'one could buy for a sou enough bread to feed a man for a week'.[324] According to the *Gazette of Amsterdam* of 13 December 1672, in Kaminiec which had been captured by the Turks, 'one could buy a horse for 4 rixdales and an ox for 2'.[325] Near Tocat in Asia Minor, Gardane in 1807 met 'inhabitants dressed like ancient patriarchs and equally hospitable. They hasten to offer you lodgings and food, and are most astonished if one offers them money'.[326]

The reason was that money, the sinews of western trade, usually made only fleeting appearances in the Turkish Empire. Part of it found its way to the ever-open jaws of the sultan's treasury, some was used to oil the wheels of top-level trade, and the rest drained away in massive quantities to the Indian Ocean. The West was correspondingly free to use its monetary superiority on the Levant market and even, when circumstances permitted, to deal in money itself, trading on the variable silver-gold ratio and on the preference accorded to certain coins – Spanish silver reals for instance, or the Venetian gold sequin which was always overvalued in the Levant. In 1671, the director of the Venetian *Zecca*[327] pointed out that if one bought a gold sequin in Venice for 17 Venetian lire, or an *ongharo*[328] for 16 lire, it was possible to make a profit of 17.5 per cent on the first and 12 per cent on the second by selling them in Constantinople. A few years later, the rate of profit on a sequin had risen to 20 per cent.[329] By the end of the sixteenth century, it had become a profitable business to send gold by clandestine means from Turkey to Persia.[330] And when Venice witnessed a decline in her eastern trade in the seventeenth and eighteenth centuries, she continued to mint sequins to send to the Levant as a means of ensuring the extremely profitable returns she required.

Similarly, by the end of the eighteenth century, Marseille was exporting hardly any goods to the Middle East, but instead was sending silver coins, mostly Maria-Theresa thalers minted in Milan.[331] It was the easiest way for the French port to keep its position in the Levant markets.

Did the survival of such archaic elements in the Turkish economy bring about its decline? Not as long as the domestic market remained lively and while the arms industry and shipbuilding survived alongside thriving craft production and considerable textile industries (in Chios and Bursa for instance) as well as the multitude of local weaving enterprises so small that they are lost to historical record. Charles Sonnini's astonishing voyage on the Black Sea in the late eighteenth century[332] reveals what is by any standards an extraordinary catalogue of local textiles. Moreover, if we are to believe a letter from Charles de Vergennes, the French ambassador in Constantinople (8 May 1759)[333] all the fabric im-

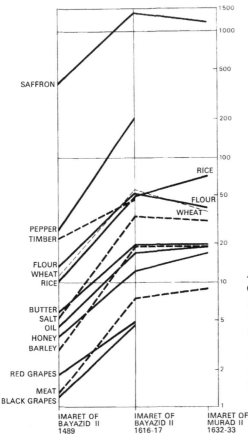

SAFFRON

RICE

FLOUR
WHEAT

PEPPER
TIMBER

FLOUR
WHEAT
RICE

BUTTER
SALT
OIL
HONEY
BARLEY

RED GRAPES

MEAT
BLACK GRAPES

1500
1000
500
200
100
50
20
10
5
2
1

IMARET OF
BAYAZID II
1489

IMARET OF
BAYAZID II
1616-17

IMARET OF
MURAD II
1632-33

46   TURKISH PRICES AND SIXTEENTH-
CENTURY INFLATION
I am indebted to Omer Lütfi Barkan for these
examples of prices which show that the price
rise of the sixteenth century extended to
Turkey. The *imarets* were religious
foundations which provided board for
students and the needy. These are nominal
prices expressed in aspers and do not take
account of devaluations of the asper.

ported from the West would clothe no more than 800,000 people; and the empire
had a population of 20 to 25 million. So there was bound to be a market for the
output of the empire's textile trades – indeed they would not be seriously
disrupted until the increase in imports from Austria and Germany at the end of
the eighteenth century. And as Omer Lütfi Barkan has explained,[334] it was really
only the flood of English textiles after the industrial revolution, in the nineteenth
century, which eventually brought about their almost total collapse.

So while the gates of the Turkish economy had long since been stormed, that
economy had still not been entirely conquered or totally marginalized, even in
the eighteenth century. The products consumed in Turkish cities mostly came
from domestic producers. Grain exporters were, as in Russia, subject to political
control. There was certainly widespread grain smuggling from the islands in the
Aegean, in which Greek sailors were profitably engaged. And a few of the
principal owners of *çiftliks* also indulged in it, but these *çiftliks*, of comparatively
recent creation, had been developed above all to supply Istanbul, not necessarily
for export; this was the case for example of the rice-producing *çiftliks* in

Pack-horses and a camel caravan on the road out of Ankara. Detail of the picture on p. 470.

Rumelia.[335] All in all, Turkish markets functioned reasonably well, relying on a long-established and still efficient transport system.

A land of caravans

The Ottoman possessions were indeed remarkable for the presence everywhere of camel caravans. Even in the Balkans, where trains of pack-horses were still used, it seems that camels had by the end of the sixteenth century invaded all the routes of the peninsula. So the 'Levant ports' seemed now to extend as far as Spalato (Split) in Dalmatia; and the Venetian *galere da mercato* instead of sailing to Syria, had only to cross the Adriatic.[336] Before the war, in 1937, there was still in Dubrovnik a vague folk-memory of these caravans as a romantic feature of the past.

A map of the caravan routes would show them running from Gibraltar to India and northern China, from Arabia and Asia Minor to Astrakhan and Kazan. Both camels and dromedaries were used. Contained within this world of caravans, indeed central to it, was the whole movement-in-space which made up the Ottoman economy.

Western travellers have often described this means of transport, the crowds of travellers herded together, the long journeys during which 'one does not find towns or inns to lodge in every night, as in England', the nights spent in the open, under 'tents when the weather permits', or in the khans and caravanserais, 'built out of charity, for the use ... of all passers-by', large and convenient buildings where lodgings were cheap. 'But [visitors] must expect nothing here generally but bare walls: as for other accommodations, of meat, drink, bed, fire, provender, with these it must be everyone's care to furnish himself'.[337] Many of the caravanserais, still standing or in ruins, can be seen in the East even today. Mapping their sites on a map as Albert Gabriel has done, is one way of reconstructing the old road networks.[338]

But although Europeans could use this form of transport for their goods and if necessary their persons, they were not permitted to take any share in its organization. The caravans were a monopoly of Islam. If western merchants went no further than Aleppo, Damascus, Cairo or Smyrna, it was largely because the caravan routes were out of their hands; the Ottoman economy itself took sole charge of this traffic so crucial to its own existence and saw that it was strictly run and supervised, frequent, and above all regular, more regular than transport by sea. The secret of independence in this sector was clearly efficiency. If it was difficult to divert Persian silk from the Mediterranean routes, if the Dutch and English failed to do so whereas the same Dutch merchants had succeeded in cornering pepper and spices, it was because silk travelled from its point of origin by caravan, whereas pepper and spices were 'sea-borne' products from the start, travelling in the holds of ships. The Ottoman economy owed its suppleness and vigour to the tireless convoys which converged from every direction on Istanbul or on Scutari, across the Bosporus; to the distant routes which wove a network round Isfahan, penetrated Persia, and reached India at Lahore; and to the caravans which set out from Cairo for Abyssinia and returned carrying precious gold dust.

Turkish waters: a well-protected sector

Turkish waters were also quite well protected from outsiders, with most sea-borne transport taking the form of coastal shipping in the seas of the Levant or the Black Sea, a sort of Turkish equivalent of the Asian 'country trade'. It is true that the coasts of the Levant had been threatened in the early days by Christian corsairs from the waters of the west Mediterranean, and the coasting trade had all but been taken over by westerners, in particular by fifty or sixty French ships. But by the end of the eighteenth century, western piracy was less of a threat and the coastal trade had, it seems, been won back from western ships, perhaps because the galleys in the Ottoman fleet had by then long been replaced by sailing vessels, and because the fleet had taken to cruising the Aegean.[339] In December 1787, Captan Pasha sailed into Istanbul with a squadron of battered ships, in poor condition but carrying 25 million piastres taken on board in Egypt.[340] In the past, tribute from Egypt had often been transported overland to Constanti-

nople for security reasons. Was this the beginning of a real change? Between
1784 and 1788, according to French observers, that is several years after the
battle of Chesme, the Turkish fleet nevertheless included 25 vessels 'with more
than 60 guns', one of which, a huge 74-gunner, had 'just been built by French
engineers'.[341] Even though this mighty vessel was manned by a crew of 600,
among whom 'there were no more than eight experienced seamen, the rest
[being] men who had never seen the sea', the fleet did manage to move about
and on the whole to accomplish what was asked of it.

As for the Black Sea, it may not have been fully exploited by ships from
Istanbul, but it long remained – and this was what mattered – closed to 'Latin'
ships. In 1609, the ban was reiterated after an English expedition got as far as
Trebizond. Historians who accuse the Turkish government of negligence and
disregard would do well to remember that the Black Sea, so crucial to the
supplies of Istanbul and to the building of the Turkish fleet, remained strictly
closed to foreign shipping until the end of the eighteenth century. In March 1765,
Henry Grenville wrote in a report to the English government:

> The Turks do not share the shipping on the Black Sea with any other nation,
> and all Foreigners are excluded from it ... The Black Sea is literally the Nursing
> Mother of Constantinople and provides it with all necessities and foodstuffs
> such as Grain, Wheat, Barley, Millet, Salt, Cattle, Sheep on the hoof, Lambs,
> Hens, Eggs, fresh Apples and other Fruits, Butter, another very considerable
> article, this Butter comes in great buffalo-skin bags, it is rancid, mixed with
> Mutton fat and very bad, but the Turks ... give it ... preference over the best
> butter of England and Holland, Tallow, very cheap Candles, Wool, Cow
> Hides, Ox Hides, Buffalo Hides, both dry and salt, yellow Wax and Honey
> ... [which the Turks] use as sugar ... much Potash, Grindstones ... Hemp,
> Iron, Steel, Copper, Timber for building, Firewood, Coals ... Caviar, Fish
> dried and salted

– plus slaves, mostly provided by the Tartars. In the other direction went goods
warehoused in Istanbul: raw cotton, incense, wine, oranges, lemons, dried fruits
from the Greek islands, textiles from Turkey or imported from Christendom –
all to be ferried to destinations in Russia, Persia, the Caucasus, or the Danube.
Coffee and rice however were forbidden to leave 'so that abundance shall reign
in Constantinople'.[342]

This huge market used the most rudimentary means of transport: on land
goods were carried in wooden wagons 'with no irons' (that is their wheels were
not bound with iron, so they were fragile and unable to transport heavy loads)
and they were drawn by buffaloes – much stronger than oxen but infuriatingly
slow; on sea they travelled in a thousand ships, but these were mostly small boats
with the irregular rectangular 'leg o' mutton' sails, or flimsy *caïques* which often
went down on this stormy sea with its sudden squalls. Only the ships carrying
grain or timber were three-masters with large crews, since the vessels often had
to be hauled along and when timber was being loaded, the crew had to land to

chopdown trees and make charcoal.[343] It used to be said that if only one in three of these ships returned from the Black Sea trip, the merchant would still make his profit; and that if Constantinople, a city built entirely of wood, were to burn down every year, the Black Sea would provide enough timber to rebuild it every time. 'I need hardly say', writes Grenville, 'that this is an exaggeration'.[344]

In this context, the access gained by the Russians to the Black Sea, the opening of the straits in 1774[345] and especially after 1784,[346] and the arrival of the first Venetian, French and Russian ships, were so many serious blows to the might of the Ottoman Empire and to the equilibrium of the enormous capital. But the new traffic did not become really significant until large-scale exports of Russian grain began in the early decades of the nineteenth century – one of the major events in European history, though rarely recognized as such.[347]

The situation in the Red Sea, a 'second Mediterranean' almost completely encircled by the Turkish Empire, was at once worse and better than in the Black Sea. Turkey had strengthened her hold on it in 1538-46 when she consolidated her position in Aden. Even earlier than this, realizing the commercial, strategic, political and religious importance of the Red Sea, Turkey had captured Mecca and the holy places of Islam. As a sea sacred to Muslims, and forbidden to Christians, the Red Sea would long remain, under Islamic control, the essential route for the ships carrying pepper and spices to Cairo, Alexandria and the Mediterranean. But the Dutch appear to have succeeded in about 1630 in diverting all the eastern pepper and spices bound for Europe to the route round the Cape of Good Hope. So Ottoman prosperity was hit much earlier in the Red Sea, a shipping corridor of international importance, than in the protected waters of the Black Sea.

The diversion of the spice trade did not however mean that the Red Sea was emptied of shipping. The difficult entrance at Bab el-Mandeb was regularly crossed every year by hundreds of ships and long boats (*germes*) carrying southwards rice and beans from Egypt or the European goods stored in the warehouses which the rather insouciant merchants of Cairo owned in Suez. And every year a convoy of seven or eight vessels, including the 'royal' flagship, probably sailing on the sultan's own account, carried the 400,000 piastres and the 50,000 gold sequins which normally travelled to Mocha and Aden, while a caravan from Aleppo to Suez, Mecca and beyond, transported about the same amount overland, though with a greater proportion of gold coins. According to a present-day historian, 'the Red Sea connection remained as a vital channel in the outflow of Spanish-American silver to India and further east', well after the sixteenth century.[348] So it was certainly by using the Mecca caravans that the most could be made of Venetian sequins and Spanish piastres[349] accompanying consignments of European and Mediterranean goods, chiefly cloth and coral. Even in the 1770s, the Red Sea trade, now mostly in Indian hands, was still bringing considerable supplies of gold and silver to Surat. There is no shortage of evidence for this. In 1778-9, an Indian ship brought back from Mocha 300,000 rupees in gold, 400,000 in silver and over 100,000 in pearls; another carried 500,000 in gold and silver. As a historian of the Mediterranean, I was astonished to find that at the end of the eighteenth century the position was still the same as it had been in the sixteenth: gold and silver coins – the most favoured merchandise – were continuing to reach the Indian Ocean by the shortest (and surest?) route.[350]

In the other direction, the major stimulus to trade was increasingly coffee from southern Arabia. Mocha was the centre of the coffee trade and with Jeddah became the leading port on the Red Sea. Ships arrived there carrying merchants and merchandise from all over the Far East. Spices were naturally prominent among their goods. A report of May 1770 does claim that 'drugs and spices' had 'entirely' ceased to travel through the Red Sea 'by the year 1630'.[351] All the same, ten ships a year from the Indian Ocean, from Calicut, Surat or Masulipatam, and the odd Portuguese ship out of Goa, were still arriving in Mocha with cargoes of pepper, cinnamon, nutmeg and cloves. And these spices travelled on with the increasingly large cargoes of coffee heading for Jeddah and Suez.

Should it be assumed that they went no further west? In Cairo, the centre which the French preferred to Alexandria or Rosetta, and where thirty or so French merchants were established, 'the number of merchants from the Indies', one of them reports, 'is beyond reckoning, in coffee, incense, gum, aloes of all sorts, senna and tamarind, saffron-bulbs, myrrh, ostrich plumes, fabrics of all kinds of thread and cotton, stuffs and porcelains'.[352] It is true that this list does not include spices. But with the new 'royal' commodity of coffee, the Red Sea was enjoying a fresh burst of prosperity. By way of Alexandria and Rosetta, coffee could reach Turkish and European customers more quickly than it did in the capacious hulls of the ships belonging to the Indies companies – which did however often go out of their way on the return journey to call at Mocha. As the scene of the revival of the Levant trade, a virtually free port and the queen of the coffee markets, Mocha was visited by many ships from the Indian Ocean. In spite of what today's historians and yesterday's documents say, I find it hard to believe that some pepper and spice was not still finding its way beyond Jeddah into the Mediterranean.

Suez, Egypt and the Red Sea were certainly arousing European appetites once more. In Constantinople and Cairo, there was keen rivalry between the French and the English.[353] In France, and even outside France, schemes to build a Suez canal were legion. One undated project goes into great detail:

> The workmen [who are to dig] the canal should be lodged in sheds barricaded at night for security. And so that these workers may be recognized at all times, it would be wise to clothe them all, men, women and children in uniform: red smocks, white turbans, hair cut short.[354]

The French ambassador, M. de la Haye applied to the sultan for free shipping in the Red Sea, 'and even to create settlements there'.[355] His request was turned down. But the careful and tenacious English East India Company was worried about the possible revival of the ancient Levant route and appointed an agent in Cairo in 1786.[356] In the same year, a French colonel, Edouard Dillon, left on a reconnaissance mission with a view to the possible 'opening of communications with the Greater Indies through the Red Sea and the isthmus of Suez'[357] with the blessing of the 'beys' of Egypt. Simolin, Catherine the Great's ambassador in Paris sent word of it to his monarch. 'From what I know of the emissary', he added, 'he seems a man of limited views and knowledge.' Was it all much ado about nothing? It was at any rate another hundred years before the Suez Canal was finally built (1869) and the revival of the ancient route to the Indies became a reality.

The merchants serving the Ottoman Empire

The economic empire which underpinned the Turkish Empire was defended by a multitude of merchants who thwarted and reduced penetration by westerners. France (that is Marseille) was represented in the Levant by perhaps 40 trading posts, staffed by 150 or 200 persons at most, and the same was true of the other 'nations' in the Levant ports. Everyday transactions were handled by Arab, Armenian, Jewish, Indian or Greek merchants (the latter category including besides authentic Greeks, Macedo-Rumanians, Bulgarians and Serbs) and even by Turks, though on the whole a career in commerce held little attraction for the latter. The Levant swarmed with ambulant salesmen, retailers, shopkeepers in their dark little stores, commission agents from every geographical and ethnic group and of every social status. Tax farmers, wholesalers and real businessmen, capable of lending money to governments, were not far away either. The fairs, gigantic meetings where business worth millions of piastres was transacted, channelled an uninterrupted flow of men, merchandise and beasts of burden.

In this busy domestic market, thronged with people, the western merchant had very little elbow-room. He might have his entrée to certain centres – Modon, Volos, Salonika, Istanbul, Smyrna, Aleppo, Alexandria, Cairo. But according to the ancient pattern of Levantine trade, in none of these places would the merchant from Venice, Holland, France or England come into direct contact with the eventual retailer of his goods. Westerners had to operate through middlemen, usually Jews or Armenians 'who needed an eye keeping on them'.

What was more, eastern merchants did not hand over to the Europeans the monopoly of exports of goods to the West. By the sixteenth century, the easterners had implanted colonies in the Italian Adriatic ports. In 1514, Ancona granted trading privileges to the Greeks of Vallona, the Gulf of Arta and Ianni: its *palatio della farina* became the *Fondaco dei mercanti turchi et altri musulmani*. Jewish merchants arrived at about the same time. By the end of the century, the eastern merchants had invaded Venice, Ferrara, Ancona, even

The square and fountain of Top Hane, Istanbul. (Photo B.N.)

Pesaro,[358] Naples and the fairs of the Mezzogiorno. The strangest of these were perhaps the Greek merchants and seamen, honest or dishonest, sometimes frankly pirates, who came from islands with practically no arable land and were therefore doomed to roam the world. Two centuries later, in October 1787, a Russian consul in Messina noted that 'sixty or more ... Greek ships bound for Naples, Livorno, Marseille and other Mediterranean ports' sailed through the straits every year.[359] When the long crisis of the Revolutionary and Napoleonic Wars (1793–1815) put an end to the presence of the French traders in the Levant, their place was taken by Greek merchants and seamen – a success which played a part in the approaching independence of Greece itself.

Less spectacular, but no less curious was the diaspora in the eighteenth century of these 'orthodox' merchants throughout the countries acquired by the Habsburgs under the Peace of Belgrade (1739) which moved the Austro-Hungarian border to the Sava and Danube. The Viennese government set out to colonize the newly conquered territories: the countryside was repopulated, towns sprang up though still on a modest scale, and Greek merchants moved into this virgin territory. They were carried by their own impetus beyond its frontiers and were soon to be found all over Europe, in the Leipzig fairs, using the credit facilities provided by Amsterdam, and even in Russia or indeed Siberia as we have already seen.[360]

Economic decadence, political decadence

The question now arises, were these merchants inside the Turkish Empire foreign bodies? Were they, as I am inclined to think, the artisans of the survival of the Turkish economy – or rats ready to leave the sinking ship? It is a question which brings us back to the irritating problem of the decadence of the Turkish Empire – a problem to which there is unfortunately no solution.

It is my view that one cannot properly speak of the decadence of the Turkish Empire before the first decades of the nineteenth century. If I had to suggest rather more precise dates, I would say that decline set in 1800 in the Balkans, the living heart of the empire and the zone which provided the bulk of its armies and its taxes, but was also the most threatened; in Egypt and the Levant, the downturn perhaps occurred during the first quarter of the nineteenth century; in Anatolia, in the 1830s. Such at any rate are the conclusions of a seductive and controversial article by Henri Islamoglu and Çaglar Keyder.[361] If these dates are correct, the advance into the Ottoman Empire by the European world-economy (an advance both destructive and constructive) moved progressively from the most active part of the empire, the Balkans, to the secondary regions like Egypt and the Levant, and finally to the least developed and thus least susceptible region, Anatolia.

That still does not answer the question whether the first third of the nineteenth century was also the period which hastened the political decline of the Ottoman Empire. That dangerous word *decadence*, which springs easily to the lips of Turkish specialists, contains so many different elements that it begs questions when claiming to answer them. No doubt if concerted action by Austria, Russia, Persia and, briefly, Venice had ever come to anything, Turkey might have been carved up in the same way as Poland. But Turkey was altogether a tougher proposition than the Polish republic; and she was offered a reprieve during the Revolutionary and Napoleonic Wars (although the Egyptian expedition did briefly pose a threat).

Turkey's fatal weakness, we are told, was her inability to adapt to the military technology of Europe. Such a failure only seems apparent with hindsight. Simolin,[362] Catherine the Great's ambassador at Versailles, was protesting in March 1785 against the constant stream of French officers entering Turkey – and being answered by Vergennes that these were 'means far too insignificant' to cause any alarm. A diplomatic answer no doubt, but if the Russian government was anxious, it was because it was not so sure of its superiority over the Turks as historians would have us think. Orlov's fleet did indeed in 5 July 1770 at Chesme, off the island of Chios, destroy all the Turkish frigates, which stood high out of the water and were perfect targets for the cannon balls and blazing brands fired at them.[363] But the Russian fleet was on this occasion commanded by English officers, and it proved incapable thereafter of effecting any serious landing on Turkish soil. The Ottoman artillery certainly left much to be desired, but thinking Russians, such as Simon Voronstov, realized that their own was not much better. The sickness or sicknesses that attacked Turkey came from all quarters at once: the state had lost its authority; its servants were being paid wages at the old rates, while the cost of living had gone up: they 'compensated themselves by embezzlement'; the money supply was probably inadequate – or at any rate the economy was hard to get moving. To introduce reform, while defending itself and at the same time remodelling the army and the navy, would have been a long-term task requiring massive expenditure proportionate to the dimensions of the weighty body of the empire.

The new Grand Vizier saw this very clearly in February 1783. His first decision was:

> to bring back into the bosom of the Empire the domains of the Grand Signor alienated during the last war under the reign of the sultan Mustafa. The government would derive 50 million piastres from this. But these alienated domains are at present in the hands of the greatest and wealthiest personages of the Empire who are employing all their credit to bring down the project, and the sultan lacks all firmness.[364]

This piece of information from Constantinople, passed on by the Neapolitan consul in the Hague, confirms Michel Morineau's recent remarks about the narrow base of Ottoman taxation:

> When bad times came, and the financial demands of the Ottoman Empire increased, greater fiscal pressure was exerted on the population and since the only means the people had of obtaining the piastres needed to pay their taxes was to sell goods abroad, they got rid of their products at rock-bottom prices. This is not so very different from the absurd trade balance quoted for twentieth-century China.[365]

The triumphal entry of industrialized, active and insatiable Europe, blundering as it were into this troubled world, would sound the death-knell of Ottoman greatness. Even so, we should be wary of adopting the conventional chronology and would do well to distrust contemporary declarations, since eighteenth-century Europe was already beginning to take her success rather for granted. In 1731, an author who does not deserve to be famous, wrote: 'All it would require against this Nation [the Ottoman Empire] which observes no Discipline or Order in its combats, is to pitch the right moment to drive it [out of Europe presumably] like a flock of Sheep'.[366] Twenty-five years later, the Chevalier Goudar did not even see the need for the 'right moment': 'We have only to reach agreement about the spoils of the Turk', he writes, 'and the Empire is as good as gone'[367] – an absurd claim. It was the industrial revolution which in the end got the better of an empire whose undoubted vigour was nevertheless insufficient to haul it out of its archaic ways and the legacy of its past.

The Far East – greatest of all the world-economies

The Far East[368] taken as a whole, consisted of three gigantic world-economies: Islam, overlooking the Indian Ocean from the Red Sea and the Persian Gulf, and controlling the endless chain of deserts stretching across Asia from Arabia to China; India, whose influence extended throughout the Indian Ocean, both east and west of Cape Comorin; and China, at once a great territorial power – striking deep into the heart of Asia – and a maritime force, controlling the seas and countries bordering the Pacific. And so it had been for many hundreds of years.

But between the fifteenth and eighteenth centuries, it is perhaps permissible to talk of a *single* world-economy broadly embracing all three. Did the Far East, favoured by the regularity and the usefulness for shipping of the monsoon and the trade winds, actually combine to form a coherent whole, with a series of successive dominant centres, a network of long-distance trading connections and an inter-related series of prices? This combination – gigantic, fragile and inter-mittent – is the true subject of the following pages.

One has to use the word intermittent since the relationship between these huge areas was the result of a series of pendulum movements of greater or lesser strength, either side of the centrally positioned Indian subcontinent. The swing might benefit first the East then the West, redistributing functions, power and political or economic advance. Through all these vicissitudes however, India maintained her central position: her merchants in Gujerat and on the Malabar or Coromandel coasts prevailed for centuries on end against their many com-petitors – the Arab traders of the Red Sea, the Persian merchants of the Gulf, or the Chinese merchants familiar with the Indonesian seas to which their junks were now regular visitors. But sometimes the pendulum malfunctioned or stopped working altogether: at such times the loose garment of Asia was more than usually divided into autonomous fragments.

The crucial feature in this simplified model is precisely this ebb and flow, favouring by turns the West, that is Islam; and the East, that is China. Any advance on the part of these two economies, one each side of India, might have incalculable repercussions, sometimes lasting many centuries. If the West forged ahead, ships from the Red Sea and/or the Persian Gulf would invade the Indian Ocean, crossing it from side to side, and appearing (as they did in the eighth century) off Canton (Han Fu to Arab geographers).[369] If, on the other hand, the usually home-loving Chinese ventured abroad, it meant that seamen from the

Arab-style boat photographed in Bombay harbour: boats like this are still plying between India and the Arabian coast and Red Sea. (Photo F. Quilici.)

south coast of China sailed to the East Indies, which they never lost from sight, and to the other 'Indies' east of Cape Comorin. There was nothing to prevent them from going further still.

In the thousand years or so before the fifteenth century, Far Eastern history is simply a monotonous repetition of the same events; one port would rise to prominence on the shores of the Red Sea, only to be replaced in time by one of its identical neighbours. The same thing happened along the coast of the Persian Gulf or in India, or in the islands and peninsulas of the East Indies; and maritime zones too might dominate by turns. For all the changes, however, history followed essentially the same course.

The beginning of the fifteenth century, the starting-point of this work, was marked by the revival of China under the Ming dynasty which liberated the country from the Mongols in the years after 1368, as well as by an extraordinary wave of maritime expansion, an event which has been much discussed but still remains in many respects a mystery, from its origins to its interruption in about 1435.[370] The foreign expeditions by Chinese junks, which went as far afield as Ceylon, Hormuz and even the Zendj Empire on the African coast,[371] drove back or at any rate disrupted Muslim trading. The voice of the East now spoke louder than the Centre or West. And it was at this time as I shall try to show, that the centre of gravity of this huge super-world-economy became stabilized in the East Indies, with their busy ports of Bantam, Atjeh, Malacca and – much later – Batavia and Manila.

It might seem absurd to attribute such importance to these ports in the East Indies – which were certainly not large in size. But then Troyes, Provins, Bar-sur-Aube and Lagny were also small towns in the days of the Champagne fairs; lying along a strategic communications axis commanding all traffic between Italy and Flanders, they nevertheless became the centre of a very great trading complex. Was this not exactly parallel to the position of the East Indies, a crossroads of trade with its fairs sometimes prolonged for months on end as the merchants waited for the monsoon to change direction so that they could set sail for home? Perhaps these East Indian ports even positively benefited – like the trading towns of medieval Europe – from not being strictly integrated into any very powerful political units. Despite all the kings and 'sultans' who ruled them and maintained order there, these were virtually autonomous towns: wide open to the outside world, they could orient themselves to suit the currents of trade. So whether Cornelius Houtman arrived in Bantam in 1595 by chance or calculation, he had landed unerringly at the complex heart of Far Eastern trade – hitting the jackpot first time so to speak.

All things considered, how wise is it for one historian to try to bring together in a single analysis the scattered fragments of a history still insufficiently explored by research? It is true that we still know very little about this world – though more than we used to. We can for instance challenge the traditional image (briefly revived by J.C. van Leur)[372] of Asiatic traders as high-class pedlars hawking about in their small packs tiny quantities of valuable merchandise – spices, pepper, pearls, perfumes, drugs and diamonds. The reality is rather different. Everywhere, from Egypt to Japan, we shall find genuine capitalists, wholesalers, the rentiers of trade, and their thousands of auxiliaries – the commission agents, brokers, money-changers and bankers. As for the techniques, possibilities or guarantees of exchange, any of these groups of merchants would stand comparison with its western equivalents. Both inside and outside India, Tamil[373], Bengali and Gujerati merchants formed close-knit partnerships with business and contracts passing in turn from one group to another, just as they might in Europe from the Florentines to the Lucchese, the Genoese, the South Germans or the English. There were even, in medieval times, merchant kings in Cairo, Aden and the Persian Gulf ports.[374]

Thus we are gradually becoming more and more clearly aware of 'a network of maritime traffic comparable in volume and variety to that of the Mediterra-

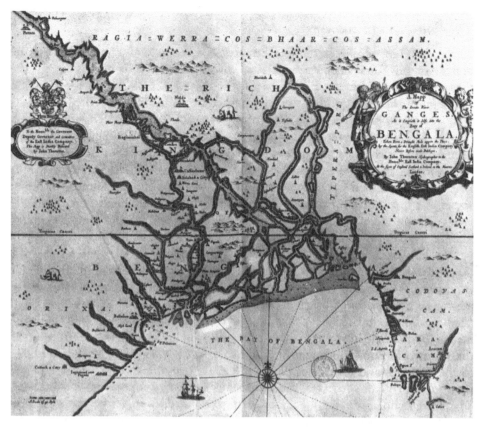

The huge Ganges delta, mapped for the East India Company by John Thornton, early eighteenth century. (Photo B.N., Paris.)

nean or of the northern and Atlantic coasts of Europe'.[375] Everything and anything could be found here: luxury goods alongside commonplace commodities, silk, spices, pepper, gold, silver, precious stones, pearls, opium, coffee, rice, indigo, cotton, saltpetre, teak (for shipbuilding), Persian horses, elephants from Ceylon, iron, steel, copper, pewter, shimmering fabrics for the rich and powerful, coarse cloth for the peasants of the spice islands or the black population of Monomotapa.[376] The 'country trade' had been in existence long before the arrival of the Europeans, since complementary products attracted and balanced each other: in the seas of the Far East they maintained a perpetual flow of trade, like that in the seas of Europe.

The fourth world-economy

Three world-economies in the Far East might already be thought a lot. But the arrival of the Europeans brought into being a fourth – conjured up by the Portuguese, the Dutch, the English, the French and others. When Vasco da Gama sailed into Calicut on 27 May 1498, he pushed open the door. But the Europeans were not yet strong enough to force their way into this unknown world which they had yet to discover (for all the sensational tales brought back by their celebrated predecessors, the first western travellers). Asia was still a *terra incognita*, another planet; even the plants and animals were different here[377] in this whole continent of different peoples, different civilizations, religions, forms of society or types of land tenure.[378] Everything was strange and new: even the rivers were not like European waterways. What was large in the West was multiplied immeasurably here. The towns of the East were vast ant hills teeming with people. How strange the westerners found these civilizations, societies and cities!

And these distant lands could only be reached after months at sea in difficult conditions. The fourth world-economy was liable to find itself out of its depth here. The possession of bases in the Middle East (which Christian forces had tried to capture during the Crusades) gave the states and traders of Islam the means to intervene in strength and as they pleased in the Indian Ocean; whereas the ships from Europe brought only derisory forces with them in their ventures to the societies and territories of Asia. So far from home, even at the time of their most brilliant successes, the Europeans never had superiority of numbers. There were no more than 10,000 Portuguese settlers in all in the sixteenth century, from Hormuz to Macao and Nagasaki.[379] For years the English were equally poorly represented, despite the scale of their early successes. There were a mere 114 English 'civilians' in Madras, in about 1700; 700 or 800 in Bombay; 1200 in Calcutta.[380] In September 1777, Mahé (a very secondary French base it is true) contained no more than 114 Europeans and 216 Sepoys.[381] In 1805, there were only '31,000 English in [the whole of] India', a tiny contingent, but one capable of ruling the entire country.[382] At the end of the eighteenth century, employees of the Dutch V.O.C. both at home and in the Far East numbered 150,000 at most.[383] Even supposing that less than half of these served overseas, the Dutch were still by far the largest group. One might add that the *strictly European* armies, in the time of Clive and Dupleix were very small.

The disproportion between the *apparent* means employed and the results of the European conquest, is striking, 'A chance happening, the merest puff of public opinion', wrote an American of French origin in 1812, 'might ... blow away English rule in India.'[384] Twenty years later, Victor Jacquemont repeated the same sentiments with emphasis: 'In the singular construction of English power in India, everything is artificial, abnormal and exceptional'.[385] The word 'artificial' is not pejorative: artifice was generally a synonym for intelligence and in this context for success. A handful of Europeans managed to impose themselves not only on India but on the whole of the Far East. By all the rules, they should not have succeeded – but they did.

India's self-inflicted conquest

In the first place, the Europeans were never acting in isolation. Thousands of slaves, servants, auxiliaries, associates and collaborators bustled around them – a hundred or a thousand times more numerous than the men who were not yet – but soon would be – the masters. The European ships engaging in the 'country trade' for instance, were manned from the start by mixed crews, largely composed of local seamen. Even those that sailed to the Philippines employed 'a few Spaniards [but] many Malays, Hindus and Filipino half-breeds'.[386] The ship carrying Father de Las Cortes from Manila to Macao in 1625, which went off course and was wrecked on the Cantonese coast, had no fewer than 37 Lascars among the crew.[387] When in July 1690 the French fleet, under Duquesne's nephew, captured the Dutch flyboat the *Montfort of Batavia* off Ceylon, among the captives figured two 'Lascaris or black slaves, who are terrible to behold. These wretches would let themselves die of hunger rather than touch anything a Christian had touched [i.e. cooked]'.[388]

Likewise, the armies which the companies eventually set afoot were composed overwhelmingly of native troops. In Batavia in 1763, for every 1000 to 1200 European soldiers 'of all nationalities', there were nine or ten thousand Malay auxiliaries, plus 2000 Chinese soldiers.[389] Whose fertile mind hit on the brilliant idea (if indeed it was a new discovery) of enlisting sepoys – thus using Indian troops to conquer India? Was it François Martin?[390] Or Dupleix? Or the English – of whom a contemporary (but he was French) wrote: 'they levied [sepoys] in imitation of M. Dupleix'?[391]

Similarly, the crucial centres of commercial enterprise were occupied by local merchants. A western businessman would find himself besieged by thousands of native brokers pressing their services on him: Moors from Egypt, the ubiquitous Armenians, Banyans, Jews from Mocha, Chinese from Canton, Amoy or Bantam, not to mention the Gujerati, the merchants from the Coromandel coast, or the Javanese – lean and hungry auxiliaries who literally encircled the Portuguese when the latter made their first expeditions to the spice islands. It was after all perfectly natural that they should. In Kandahar where his wanderlust had taken Maestre Manrique in 1641, a Hindu merchant, taking the Spanish traveller for a Portuguese, offered his services because as he explained, 'the people of your nation do not speak the language of these countries so you are sure to encounter difficulties unless you find someone to guide you'.[392] Help, collaboration, collusion, coexistence, symbiosis – all these became necessary as time went by and the local merchant, ingenious and unbelievably frugal, capable of surviving long voyages on a small ration of rice, was as indestructible as couch-grass. In Surat, the 'servants' of the English East India Company had in any case been hand in glove with the big-time moneylenders in the town virtually from the start. And how often we find English factories from Madras to Fort William, asking permission from the board of directors in London to borrow money from Indian merchants! In 1720, when the liquidity crisis resulting from the South Sea Bubble was raging in England, the East India Company borrowed the cash it needed in India – a wise move as it turned out since thanks to this decision 'the crisis passed as quickly as it had come'.[393] In 1726, when the French company began to recover, it kept well away from Surat where it owed the Banyans no less than 4 million rupees.[394]

It thus became impossible to shake off these indispensable collaborators already on the spot and busily creating wealth. Pondicherry, says a report of 1733, will never be a prosperous centre 'unless some means is found of attracting there merchants capable of trading on their own account'[395] – merchants of whatever nationality, but above all Indian. Indeed would Bombay ever have been built without the Parsees and Banyans? What would Madras have been without the Armenians? In Bengal, as elsewhere in India, the English made unlimited use of the local merchants and bankers. Only when British rule was firmly established in Bengal were the native capitalists of Calcutta brutally eliminated from the more profitable sectors (banking and foreign trade) and obliged to fall back on land, usury, tax-collecting or even, in about 1793, 'the greater part of the obligations [i.e. bonds] of the British East India Company'.[396] But at the same time in Bombay, where everything still remained to be done, the British took care not to displace the Parsee, Gujerati or Muslim merchants who continued to amass huge fortunes there in foreign trade or as owners of the port's merchant fleet – until the arrival of the steamship in the 1850s.[397] Nor, despite several attempts, did English banking ever entirely manage to eliminate the *hundi*, the bill of exchange used by the Indian *sarrafs*, the symbol of their freedom of manoeuvre and of a solid banking organization of which the British had taken advantage long before they tried to suppress it.

Gold and silver, strength or weakness?

We are often told that Europe, America, Africa and Asia were complementary. It would be equally correct to say that world trade did its best to render them complementary and often succeeded in doing so. The Far East did not on the whole welcome European products with the frenzy and appetite displayed from an early date by the West for pepper, spices or silk. Since trade balances require that one passion be compensated by another, Asia had retaliated from the days of the Roman Empire by consenting to exchange her goods only for precious metals – gold (which was preferred on the Coromandel coast) but above all silver. China and India in particular became, as I have had numerous occasions to point out, bottomless pits for the precious metals in circulation: they were sucked in, never to re-emerge. This curious but constant phenomenon accounted for the flow of bullion from West to East, which some people have seen as a weakness of Europe vis-à-vis Asia, but which I regard, as I have already said, merely as the usual method employed by Europeans, not only in Asia but elsewhere as well, even inside Europe, when they wanted to break into a particularly profitable market. In the sixteenth century, this method was to assume unprecedented proportions thanks to the discovery of America and the output of the mines of the New World.

American silver reached the Far East by three routes: through the Levant and the Persian Gulf, a route which as Indian historians have proved was still the most important as late as the seventeenth and eighteenth centuries; the route round the Cape; and the route taken by the Manila galleon. Leaving aside the very special case of Japan (which possessed its own silver mines whose output occasionally played a part in Japanese foreign trade) almost all the silver in circulation in the Far East was of European – that is American – origin. So the rupees which a European might borrow from an Indian banker or money-changer were in fact, tit for tat, made of silver imported some time previously by European trade.

As we shall see later, this influx of precious metals was vital to the movements of the most active sector of the Indian, and no doubt the Chinese economy. If the Indian boats sailing from Surat to Mocha by some mischance failed to rendez-vous with the Red Sea ships carrying gold and silver, Surat – for so long the dominant centre of Indian trade – would quickly have plunged into crisis. This being so, it is perhaps not an exaggeration to see Europe, committed to Asia only by her passion for luxury goods, as having a stranglehold in the form of silver over the economies of the Far East, and thus being in a position of strength. But whether this superiority was fully and lucidly appreciated is open to question. European merchants seeking to pursue profitable trade in Asia were themselves at the mercy of the arrival in Cadiz of the American silver fleet – always unpredictable and sometimes disappointing. The need to find at all costs the necessary specie for trading in Asia could only have been regarded as a burden. Between 1680 and 1720 in particular[398] silver was comparatively scarce, and its price on the open market exceeded the price offered by the mints. The result was a *de facto* devaluation of the key silver currencies, the pound sterling and the florin, and thus a deterioration of the terms of trade in Asia for both England and Holland.[399] Silver might give the West an advantage, but it also created difficulties and uncertainties for everyday trade.

The European assault force: merchants with a difference

The Europeans had from the start another source of superiority, one of which they were fully aware and without which their efforts would never have got off the ground: this priceless advantage was the western warship, easy to manoeuvre, capable of sailing against the wind, rigged with a range of sails, and armed with

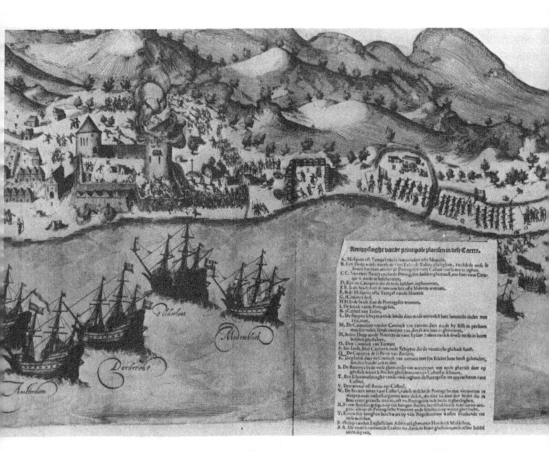

The Dutch assault on and capture of Tidore, one of the Molucca islands held by the Portuguese, in 1606. On the right of the picture, longboats are landing the attacking troops.
(Atlas von Stolk.)

cannon which were even more effective once the use of gun-ports became widespread. When, in September 1498, Vasco da Gama's fleet left the approaches to Calicut, it encountered eight large Indian vessels which had sailed to intercept it. They were all rapidly put to flight and one was captured (the other seven ran aground on a sandbank on a beach which the Portuguese vessels could not approach since the waters were too shallow for them).[400] What was more, Indian maritime customs had always been extremely pacific. There is only one known exception to this rule of non-aggression, the Empire of Chola which had in the thirteenth century built an impressive navy on the Coromandel coast, had several times occupied Ceylon, the Maldive and Laccadive islands, and had been able to cut the Indian Ocean in two at will. By the sixteenth century however, all this was in the past, and despite the presence along certain parts of the coast of pirates (who were not particularly hard to avoid) merchantmen never needed to sail in armed convoys.

The task of the Portuguese was thereby made much easier. Unable to occupy the great landmasses of the Far East, they found it a simple matter to control the seas, the medium of transport and communications. This was what mattered after all: 'If you are strong in ships', Francisco de Almeida wrote to the king in Lisbon, 'the commerce of the Indies is yours, and if you are not strong in ships, little will avail you any fortress on land.'[401] In Albuquerque's opinion, 'If once Portugal should suffer a reverse at sea, your Indian possessions have not power to hold out a day longer than the Kings of the land choose to suffer it'.[402] In the following century, the commander of the Dutch base of Hirado in Japan spoke in similar terms in 1623: '[We have] barely sufficient force to set ashore unless under the protection of the ships' cannon'.[403] And a Chinese resident in Macao remarked with regret: 'We shall know how to put [the Portuguese] at death's door as soon as they nourish any disloyal design. [But] if we move them to the open sea, by what means would we punish the evil doers and how could we ... defend ourselves against them?'[404] Thomas Roe, ambassador of the East India Company to the court of the Mogul emperor, thought the same: hence his advice to the English officials: 'Keep to this rule if you look for profit: seek it out on the seas and in peaceful trading; for there is no doubt that it would be an error to maintain garrisons and to fight in India on land'.[405]

These pronouncements, elevated almost to the status of maxims, should not be interpreted as a desire for peace, merely as the clear recognition over a period of many years that any attempt at territorial conquest would be extremely hazardous. European intrusion could nevertheless, when the occasion arose, take aggressive and brutal form. There is no shortage of examples of assault, pillage and warlike designs. In 1586, shortly before the sailing of the Invincible Armada, Francisco Sardo, the Spanish governor of the Philippines, offered his services for the conquest of China with 5000 men: later, Coen's effective approach to the islands of the East Indies, which were easier to control than the mainland, was characterized by force, colonization and strong-arm tactics.[406] And the time of territorial conquests did eventually come – rather late in the day perhaps – in the age of Dupleix, Bussy and Clive.

But before this burst of colonization, Europeans were already making the most of their overwhelming superiority both *on* sea and *from* the seaward side. When local pirates were active, Europeans could handle freight on behalf of non-European merchants fearful for their goods; they could attack or threaten to bombard a recalcitrant port; or force local vessels to pay for safe-conduct passes[407] (the Portuguese, Dutch and English all practised this form of ransom demand); they could even, in cases of conflict with a territorial power, wield the effective weapon of a blockade. During the war against Aurangzeb in 1688, conducted at the instigation of Sir Josiah Child, director of the East India Company, 'The subjects of the Mogul', Child wrote, 'cannot bear a war with the English for twelve months together, without starving and dying by the thousands for want of work to purchase rice; not singly for want of our trade,

Native pirates off the Malabar coast: they are using oars and sails, arquebuses and arrows.
Watercolour by a Portuguese artist long resident in Goa in the sixteenth century.
(Photo F. Quilici.)

but because by our war, we obstruct their trade with all the Eastern nations which is ten times as much as ours and all the European nations put together'.[408]

This text spells out admirably not only how much the English appreciated the massive strength and indeed commercial might of Mogul India, but also their determination to use all the advantages they possessed, to do business 'sword in hand', as one of the Company's servants put it.[409]

Trading posts, factories, supercargoes

The Great Indies companies were the multinationals of their age. They had to grapple not only with their 'colonial' problems but also with the state which had created and continued to support them. They were a state within – or outside – the state. They did battle with their shareholders, creating a form of capitalism at odds with traditional trading practices. They had not only to handle the capital belonging to the shareholders (who clamoured for dividends), the capital of holders of short-term bonds, and the company's circulating capital (that is liquid assets) but also to see to the maintenance of fixed capital – ships, harbours and fortresses. They had to keep an eye from a distance on several foreign markets and relate these to the possibilities and advantages of their own national market, that is to the sales at auction in London, Amsterdam and elsewhere.

Of all these difficulties, distance was the hardest to overcome – indeed the old Levant route was still used to send letters, agents, important instructions, gold and silver. In 1780, with the aid of a favourable monsoon, an Englishman even set up a record speed for the journey London-Marseille-Alexandria-Calcutta: 72 days.[410] The normal route by the Atlantic and the Cape generally took eight months each way, so that a round trip could hardly be completed in less than 18 months – that is assuming all went well and that the traveller was neither obliged to winter in port nor faced with untoward problems when rounding the Cape of Good Hope. It was this slow turn-around time of ships and goods which made it impossible for the directors in London and Amsterdam to keep control in their own hands. They were obliged to delegate powers and share them with local boards of the company, which might have to take urgent decisions on their own authority (as they did in Madras or Surat) as well as to translate the wishes of the company into action on the spot, arranging 'contracts'[411] and orders at appropriate times (six months or a year in advance), anticipating payments and collecting cargoes.

These trading units far from home had various names: trading posts, factories, settlements. The two first terms were interchangeable in everyday language, but by and large they are listed in order of descending importance. Thus the English 'factory' in Surat set up a series of 'settlements' in Goga, Broach, Baroda, Fatehpur Sikri, Lahore, Tatta, Lahribandar, Jasques, Mocha and Isfahan;[412] and the 'establishments' of the French company at Chandernagor were divided into three categories: surrounding the headquarters, Chandernagor, 'the six great trading posts (*comptoirs*) were Balasore, Patna, Cassimbazar, Dacca, Jugdia, and Chittagong; and there were mere settlements at Supur, Kerpoy, Karagola, Monghur and Serampore', the last two being 'branches where an agent without territory resided'.[413]

The 'territory' of a trading post or company headquarters proceeded from a concession by the local authorities, difficult to obtain and never granted without something in return. Taken as a whole, the system was another form of colonization – of a purely commercial nature: the Europeans settled within easy reach of the points of production and the markets, at the intersections of trade routes, using networks in existence before their arrival, thus saving themselves the trouble of creating infrastructures, and leaving to local communities the tasks of transporting the goods to the ports, organizing and financing production and handling elementary exchange.

Clinging like a parasite to a foreign body, European occupation of the East before the British conquest of India (with the exception of the Dutch successes in the special case of Indonesia) was sporadic, confined to a series of positions and strongholds. Macao, on the outskirts of Canton was no bigger than a village. Bombay, on its island, three leagues by two, had hardly space for its harbour, shipyard, barracks and houses and had it not received supplies from the neighbouring island of Salsetta, its richer inhabitants would not have been able to eat meat every day.[414] Deshima, a settlement within the port of Nagasaki, was certainly smaller than the *Ghetto Nuovissimo* in Venice. Many 'factories' were little more than fortified buildings, or glorified warehouses, where the Europeans lived a life more cut off even than that of the most closed castes in India.

There were exceptions of course: Goa on its island, Batavia, Mauritius (Ile de France) and Reunion (Bourbon). European positions in China on the other hand were even more precarious. Merchants from Europe had no permanent status in Canton, and unlimited access to the free market was refused to them (unlike in India). The companies were represented on each of their ships by travelling salesmen, who made up a sort of mobile factory, a travelling community of supercargoes. If the latter quarrelled or refused to obey the chief who had been chosen for them, problems and disappointments were to be expected.[415]

Should one therefore conclude that until the British conquest, European trading activity did no more than skim the surface of Asia; that it was confined to trading posts which made little impression on this gigantic body; that European occupation was superficial, skin-deep and of no consequence, changing neither societies nor civilizations; and that economically it concerned only the export trade, that is only a minor part of production? This is none other than the old argument about the domestic market and foreign trade raising its head again. The European trading posts in Asia were in fact no less effective than those of the Hanseatic League or the Dutch in the Baltic and North Sea, or than the Venetian and Genoese trading posts throughout the Empire of Byzantium, to take only a few examples among many. Europe sent very small groups of settlers out to Asia, where they were in a tiny minority it is true, but it was a minority in direct contact with the most advanced capitalism in the western world. These European minorities, of whom it has been said that they constituted merely 'an inherently brittle superstructure',[416] were in touch not with the masses of Asia but with other commercial minorities who dominated trade and exchange in the Far East. And it was indeed these *local* minority groups who, partly under pressure, partly of their own accord, paved the way for the European intrusion, teaching first the Portuguese, then the Dutch and English (and even the French, Danes and Swedes) the way through the labyrinth of the 'country trade'. The process had thus begun which was by the end of the eighteenth century to deliver more than 85 or 90 per cent of India's foreign trade over to the English monopoly.[417] But it was only because the accessible markets of the Far East formed a series of coherent economies linked together in a fully operational world-economy, that the merchant capitalism of Europe was able to lay siege to them and to use their own vitality to manoeuvre them to its own advantage.

How to get at the real history of the Far East?

The real object of our interest then is the subterranean history of Asia; but let me at once say that this is not easy to discover. In London, Amsterdam and Paris, there are plenty of excellent archives, but we always see the landscape of India or the East Indies filtered through the history of the big companies. There are also, in Europe, and throughout the world, many eminent Orientalists. But a specialist on Islam cannot also be an expert on China, or India, or the East Indies, or Japan. Moreover Orientalists are more likely to be linguists and cultural experts than social or economic historians.

Today this state of affairs is changing. Specialists on China, Japan, India or Islam are showing more interest than in the past in these countries' societies or political and economic structures. There are even some sociologists who think like historians.[418] Best of all, over the last twenty or thirty years, as they have pursued the identity of their countries now liberated from Europe, historians in the Far East, whose numbers are growing, have begun to catalogue the available sources; various studies now bear witness to what Lucien Febvre used to call a sense of 'problem-based history'. These historians are toilers in the vineyard of the new history and its harvest is beginning to appear in their books and in a number of excellent journals. We are on the brink of some far-reaching reappraisals.

To follow in their footsteps and tackle the whole area at once is out of the question. There is so much material (although many questions remain unanswered) that the time is simply not ripe for an overall view. I have nevertheless tried, rashly perhaps, to convey through *one* example, some idea both of the scope and of the novelty of the problems which are now coming to light. The example I have chosen is India. There are now several fundamental studies in English, and the work of an outstanding team of Indian historians is now available, since they too have fortunately published in English. In them we have excellent guides for exploring the splendours and miseries of 'medieval' India – since the convention is already well-established in India of making the Middle Ages run until the installation of the British Raj. This is the only point in their analysis that I find questionable because of the *a priori* classifications it suggests (notably a lag of several centuries behind Europe) and because it introduces to the picture the so-called problems of 'feudalism', which is described both as surviving and as deteriorating between the fifteenth and eighteenth centuries. But such criticisms are merely points of detail.

If my choice fell on India, it was not only for the reasons just mentioned; nor because Indian history is particularly easy to grasp; on the contrary, by the norms of general history, India seems to me to be a subtly deviant case, and a very complex one, politically, socially, culturally and economically. No, the reason is that India was a world-economy occupying a central position, on which everything depended: every kind of development could take root in this tolerant environment with its weaknesses. It was here that the Portuguese, the French and the English first set foot. The Dutch were the only exception: by hitching their wagon to the East Indies they won the race to obtain a monopoly. But in doing so, did they perhaps forfeit the chance of success in India – which later proved to be the foundation of any durable achievement by the other newcomers to the East, first the Muslims and later the westerners?

The villages of India

India is made up of villages – thousands and thousands of them. It is more appropriate to use the plural than the singular[419] which suggests a misleading image of 'the typical' Indian village, enclosed in its little community, surviving as an intangible, unchanging and always self-sufficient unit, throughout the eventful history of India; and which also seems to suggest that by some second miracle, 'the village' was the same throughout the huge sub-continent, despite the clear identities of different provinces (the particular features of the Deccan, for instance, 'the land of the south'). No doubt a self-sufficient village, producing its own food and clothing and entirely self-absorbed, could still be found in remote and backward regions even today. But it would be an exception.

As a rule, the village community was open to the outside world, subject to various authorities and to the markets which watched it closely, emptied it of its surpluses and forced upon it the convenience and the dangers of a money economy. This brings us close to the secret of the entire history of India: the vitality drawn up from the base to animate and nourish the great political and social corpus. In a very different context, the pattern is similar to that of the Russian economy at the same period.

Through recent studies, it is now possible to see how the machine functioned, fuelled as it was by harvests, rents and state-imposed taxes. The ubiquitous money economy was an excellent drive-belt, facilitating and increasing the number of transactions, including compulsory exchange. Credit for the creation of these circuits is only partly due to the government of the Mogul emperor. India had in fact been for centuries subject to a money economy, partly through her links with the Mediterranean world, which had since Antiquity been acquainted with money, and indeed after a fashion had invented it and exported it abroad. If we can believe L. C. Jain,[420] India already had bankers six centuries before Christ, a hundred years before the age of Pericles. The money economy had certainly penetrated Indian trade many centuries before the sultanate of Delhi.

The decisive contribution of the latter, in the fourteenth century, was a coercive administrative organization, with a hierarchy reaching down through the provincial and district authorities to the villages, which it kept under firm control. The weighty mechanisms of this state, inherited by the Mogul Empire in 1526, enabled the latter to stimulate and confiscate surplus output in the

The Mogul emperor's court: an Indian lord approaches the sovereign. (Photo B. N.)

countryside. Consequently it encouraged the maintenance and expansion of such surpluses. For the Muslim despotism of the Moguls contained a measure of 'enlightened despotism', a desire not to kill the goose that laid the golden eggs, a desire to encourage peasant 'reproduction', to extend cultivation, to substitute a profitable crop for a less profitable one, to colonize virgin land, and to increase the possibilities of irrigation by wells and reservoirs. The village was also encircled and penetrated by the network of travelling merchants, by the neighbouring market towns, even by the markets held for the barter of foodstuffs within large villages or out in the country between villages, as well as by the hungry markets of near or distant towns, and by the fairs connected with religious festivals.

To what extent then were the villages controlled from outside? This was certainly the aim of the provincial and district authorities, as it was that of the nobles, who had received from the emperor (theoretically the sole owner of the land) a share of the dues from the estates (*jagirs* or life-holdings); it was also the concern of the vigilant tax-collectors, the *zamindars*[421] who had hereditary rights to land; and of the merchants, usurers and money-changers who bought, transported and sold harvests, and who also converted taxes and dues into cash so that their product could circulate more easily. The landlord would actually live at court in Delhi, keeping up his rank, and the *jagir* was granted him for a fairly short term, usually three years. He exploited it by flying visits quite shamelessly, from a distance; like the state, he preferred to receive his dues in cash rather than in kind.[422] The conversion of crops into coin was therefore the cornerstone of the system. Not only were silver and gold both an object of and an encouragement to hoarding, they were also the indispensable mechanisms which made the whole great machine function, from its peasant base to the summit of society and the business world.[423]

The village was, in addition, controlled from within by its own hierarchy and the caste system (embracing artisans and the proletariat of untouchables). It had a vigilant leader, the village headman, and an exclusive 'aristocracy', the *khud-kashta*, a small minority of relatively wealthy or at any rate comfortably-off peasants, owners of the best land, possessors of four or five ploughs, four or five bullock or buffalo teams and in addition enjoying a favourable tax rating. These men effectively represented the famous village 'community' about which so much has been written. In exchange for their privileges and the *individual* ownership of the fields they farmed themselves with family labour, they were *collectively* responsible to the state for the payment of taxes on behalf of the whole village. Indeed they received a share of the money collected. They enjoyed similar favours regarding the colonization of virgin lands and the creation of new villages. But they were closely watched by the authorities who viewed with suspicion the development of anything like tenant-farming or share-cropping which might benefit these village elders, or even of the introduction of wage-labour (which did exist but to a minimal extent) – that is of any form of land-

An Indian bullock caravan carrying grain from 'Balaguate' (Balaghat in the province of Madhya Pradesh) to the Portuguese settlement in Goa (sixteenth century). (Photo F. Quilici.)

tenure outside the norm, the extension of which might, in the hands of fiscally privileged individuals, eventually diminish the volume of taxation.[424] As for the other peasants who did not own their fields, who came from elsewhere and might move on from time to time to another village taking their bullocks and ploughs, they were more heavily taxed than the elders.

The village also had its own artisans: wedded to their trades by the caste system, they received for their labour a share of the communal harvest, plus a plot of land to cultivate (although certain castes earned wages).[425] The reader may think this a complicated system, but what peasant regime under the sun is simple? 'While the peasant was not unfree or a serf, his status was definitely a dependent one.'[426] The share of his income confiscated by the state, by the lord of the *jagir* and other interested parties might be anything from a third to a half, or even more in fertile regions.[427] So how was such a regime possible? How could the peasant economy support it, while at the same time maintaining a degree of expansion, since seventeenth-century India, despite her growing population, continued to produce enough food for her people, increased her industrial crops and even expanded the production of her many orchards to meet a higher demand for fruit and the new fashion among landowners?[428]

Results like this must be put down to the modest living standards of the peasants and the high productivity of their agriculture.

For in 1600, rural India was farming only a portion of the available land: from the available statistics, it seems probable that in the Ganges basin for instance, only half the arable land under cultivation in the same region in 1900 was being farmed at all in the seventeenth century; in central India, the figure is between two-thirds and four-fifths; in southern India one may *conjecture* the figure was higher. So one thing is certain: almost everywhere in India between the fifteenth and the eighteenth century, only the best land was being farmed. And since there was no agricultural revolution here, since basic tools, methods and essential crops did not change until 1900, it can probably be assumed that the per capita output of the Indian peasant was higher in 1700 than 1900,[429] particularly since land as yet uncultivated, on which new villages were built, offered the peasants extra space which could support more grazing and this in turn meant more draft animals, bullocks and buffaloes for ploughing, more dairy products and more ghee (melted butter used in Indian cookery). Irfan Habib[430] has argued that in view of the two annual harvests, cereal yields in India were higher than those in Europe until the nineteenth century. But even with equivalent yields, India would still have had the advantage. In a hot climate, the needs of a labourer are fewer than in the temperate countries of Europe. The modest quantity subtracted from the harvest for the peasant's own subsistence left a larger surplus available for marketing.

A further source of the superiority of Indian agriculture, besides the two harvests a year (of rice, or of grain plus peas or chick peas, or oil-yielding plants), was the place occupied by cash-crops intended for export: indigo and cotton plants, sugar cane, opium poppies, tobacco (introduced to India in the early seventeenth century), the pepper-bush (a climbing plant which produced peppercorns between the third and the ninth years but which, contrary to popular belief, would not grow unless carefully tended).[431] Such plants brought in more than millet, rye, rice or wheat. And in the case of the indigo plant for instance, 'it is the practice among the Indians to cut it three times a year'.[432] Furthermore it required complicated industrial processes; so like sugar cane, and for similar reasons, the growing of indigo which required substantial investment, was a *capitalist* venture very widespread in India, with active cooperation by large tax-farmers, merchants, representatives of the European companies and of the Mogul government which attempted to create a state monopoly by a policy of granting exclusive tenancy agreements. The indigo most favoured by the Europeans was that grown in the Agra region, especially the first crop whose leaves were 'of a deeper purple'. Given the scale of both local and European demand, the price of indigo rose steadily.[433] In 1633, when wars were affecting the areas where it grew in the Deccan, Persian and Indian purchasers turned increasingly to the Agra indigo which consequently broke the previous record price of 50 rupees a *maund*.[434] The English and Dutch companies thereupon decided to suspend purchases. But the peasants of Agra, forewarned presumably by the merchants and 'indigo-farmers' who had the affair in hand, uprooted the plants and switched temporarily to other crops.[435] Was such adaptability a sign of capitalist efficiency, of direct communication between the peasants and the market?

None of this prevented visible poverty among the rural masses: poverty which was predictable given the general conditions of the system. What was more, the Delhi government levied in taxes a proportion of the harvest – in theory once it had been harvested, but in many regions, local administrators for the sake of convenience estimated the average yield of the land in advance and established a *fixed rate* of taxation on this basis, in kind or in cash, depending on the area under cultivation and the nature of the crop (less for barley than wheat, less for wheat than for indigo, less for indigo than for sugar cane or opium poppies).[436] This being the case, if the harvest did not come up to expectations, if there was a drought, if bullocks from the caravans or elephants from Delhi ravaged the cultivated fields, if prices rose or fell inopportunely, the burden was borne by the producer. And the peasant's life was aggravated further by debt.[437] With the complexity of land tenure systems, of ownership and taxation, depending on the province, the generosity of the local prince or on the presence of war or peace, any kind of variation could be expected – usually for the worse. On the whole, however, as long as the Mogul state remained strong, it was able to maintain the minimum level of peasant prosperity essential to its own prosperity. It was only in the eighteenth century that general decline began to affect the state, the obedience and loyalty of its officials and the security of transport.[438] Peasant revolts became endemic.

Artisans and industry

The other sufferers in India were the countless artisans present in all cities, towns and villages – some of which had been transformed into entire villages of artisans. This increase in the working population was inevitable if it is true that the seventeenth century saw a massive increase in the urban population of India, which some historians put at 20 per cent of the total: if they are right, the urban population of India was some 20 million inhabitants – roughly the equivalent of the total population of France in the seventeenth century. Even if this is an overestimate, the artisan population, augmented by an army of unskilled labourers, must still have represented millions of individuals working both for the domestic and the export market.

Rather than with the history of these countless artisans as such, Indian historians seeking to discover the situation of their country on the eve of the British conquest have been most concerned to discover the nature of India's ancestral industry, and in particular whether her industry was or was not comparable to that of Europe at the same time, whether it might have been capable on its own of engendering some kind of industrial revolution.

Industry, or rather proto-industry, encountered many obstacles in India. Some have been perhaps exaggerated and exist only in the minds of historians – in particular the trammels supposedly imposed by the caste system, which affected the whole of society, including of course the artisan population. Weberian analysis sees the caste system as preventing the advance of technology, stifling initiative among artisans and, since it confined a certain group of people to a single activity laid down once and for all, as inhibiting any new specialization or social mobility from generation to generation.

> There are good grounds [writes Irfan Habib] for throwing doubt on this entire theory.... First, the mass of ordinary or unskilled people formed a reserve from which new classes of skilled professions could be created when the need arose. Thus diamond miners in the [Carnatic] must have come from the ranks of the peasantry or agricultural labourers, for when some mines were abandoned, the miners 'went back to their village'.... More important still, over a long period economic compulsions could bring about a radical transformation in the occupational basis of a caste. A well-documented case is that of the caste of tailors in Maharashtra,[439] a section of which took to dyeing, and another to indigo-dyeing early in the eighteenth century.[440]

Some flexibility among the workforce cannot be denied. Indeed the ancient caste system had developed alongside the division of labour, since in Agra in the early seventeenth century more than a hundred different trades are recorded.[441] And the workers could move about, as in Europe, in search of profitable work. The destruction of Ahmedabad stimulated a vigorous burst of growth in the Surat textile industry, in the second quarter of the eighteenth century. And the European Indies companies attracted to the areas round their branches weavers from the various provinces who, unless subject to specific prohibitions (some castes were forbidden to travel by sea for instance) could travel about to meet demand.

Other obstacles were more serious. Europeans were often astonished at the small number and rudimentary nature of the tools used by the Indian craftsmen – 'a deficiency of tools' which, as Sonnerat explained with illustrations, meant that a sawyer took 'three days to make a plank which would take our workmen but an hour'. Who could fail to be surprised that 'the fine muslins we seek so eagerly are made on looms composed of four pieces of wood stuck in the ground'?[442] If the Indian craftsman nevertheless produced masterpieces, this was the result of extraordinary manual dexterity, further refined by extreme specialization: 'A job that one man would do in Holland here passes through four men's hands before it is finished', remarked the Dutchman Pelsaert.[443] Tools were made almost entirely of wood, unlike those of Europe which already contained a large proportion of iron even before the industrial revolution. And archaic methods prevailed: for example, the Indian version of the Persian-designed wheel for irrigation and pumping water used wooden gears, wooden cogwheels, leather bags, earthenware pots and was propelled by animal or

Native blacksmiths in sixteenth-century Goa: note the elementary technology, with hand bellows and the peculiar hammers which look as if they might also be used as axes. (Photo F. Quilici.)

human power until the nineteenth century. This was not so much for technical reasons, Irfan Habib thinks[444] (since wooden mechanisms such as those used for spinning and weaving could often be sophisticated and ingenious) as for reasons of cost: the high price of European metal machinery would not have been compensated for by the savings made on labour – which was both plentiful and cheap. *Mutatis mutandis*, this is very like the problems raised today by certain kinds of advanced technology requiring heavy capital investment but only a small labour force: the adoption of such technology by Third World countries has been both disruptive and disappointing.

Similarly, although the Indians were not well-versed in mining techniques (confining their efforts to the extraction of surface minerals only) they had succeeded, as we saw in Volume I, in producing a crucible-fired steel of exceptional quality, which was exported at high prices to Persia and elsewhere. In this respect they were ahead of European metallurgy. They worked their own metal, producing ships' anchors, fine sidearms, swords and daggers of every design, good hand guns and respectable cannon (not cast but made of welded iron bars hooped together).[445] The cannon in the arsenal of the Mogul emperor at Baterpore (between Surat and Delhi) were however, according to an Englishman who saw them in 1615, made of cast iron, 'of various calibres but generally too short and too slender'.[446] But he may have been viewing them with the eyes of a seaman used to the long-barrelled naval cannon and for all we know these early pieces may have been improved. By 1664 at any rate, Aurangzeb possessed heavy artillery pulled by massive draft teams (and which had to be moved into position well ahead of battle because it was so slow) as well as pieces of very light artillery (two horses to a gun) which regularly followed the emperor in his travels round the country.[447] By this date, European artillerymen had been replaced by Indian gunners: they may have been less skilful than the foreigners, but they had obviously made technical progress.[448] Rifles and cannon were by now in any case to be found all over India. When Tippoo Sahib, the last nawab of Mysore, was abandoned by the French in 1783, he took refuge in the mountains and conveyed his heavy artillery along impossible roads across the Ghats. (Near Mangalore, he had to hitch 40 or 50 oxen to every piece; one of the elephants pushing a gun from behind lost its footing and fell over the precipice, taking nine or ten men with it.)[449] So India was by no means hopelessly backward in technology. The Indian Mints, for example, were every bit as good as the European: 30,000 rupees were being turned out every day at the Surat Mint in 1660 for the English company alone.[450]

Lastly, there was the wonder of wonders, the naval shipyards. According to a French report, the vessels built in Surat in about 1700 were 'very good and extremely serviceable ... and it would be most advantageous [for the French Indies Company] to have some built there', even if the price was the same as in France, since the teak wood from which they were made guaranteed them a lifetime at sea of forty years, 'instead of ten, twelve or fourteen at most'.[451] During the first half of the nineteenth century, the Parsees in Bombay invested considerable sums in shipbuilding, having vessels constructed both on the spot and in other ports, especially Cochin.[452] Bengal, including Calcutta from 1760,[453] also had shipyards: 'The English have since the last war [1778-83] fitted in Bengal alone four or five hundred vessels of all sizes, built in India for them'.[454] Some of these ships could be very big: the *Surat Castle* (1791-2) 1000 tons, 12 cannon and a crew of 150; or the *Lowjee Family*, 800 tons, manned by 125 Lascars; the flagship of this fleet, the *Shampinder* (1802) ran to 1300 tons.[455] And it was indeed in India that the finest Indiamen were built, vessels of enormous size for the time, which did the China run. In eastern waters, until the coming of the steamship in mid-nineteenth century, the English in fact relied exclusively on Indian-built ships. None of them sailed for Europe: indeed English ports were forbidden to them. In 1794, the war with France and the urgent need for transport ships was responsible for the ban being lifted for a few months. But the appearance of Indian ships and sailors caused such hostile reactions in London that English merchants quickly decided not to use their services.[456]

India's remarkable textile production is so well known that I hardly need

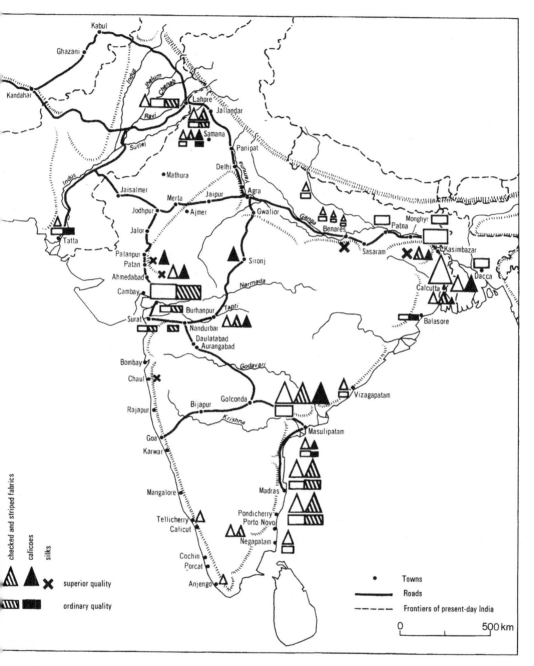

checked and striped fabrics

calicoes

silks

superior quality

ordinary quality

Towns

Roads

Frontiers of present-day India

0   500 km

47   TEXTILE ROUTES AND INDUSTRIES IN INDIA, MID-EIGHTEENTH CENTURY
Except on the Malabar coast which was rich in pepper, textile industry was to be found in every
region of India. The different symbols indicate the diversity of output and give some idea of its
volume. (Based on K.N. Chaudhuri, *The Trading World of Asia and the English East India
Company*, 1978.)

dwell on it. It possessed to the full the capacity so admired in the English cloth trade, to meet any increase in demand. It was to be found in the villages; it kept artisans busy in the towns; from Surat to the Ganges, it nourished a string of craft workshops producing for themselves or for the big export dealers; it was well entrenched in Kashmir; it was poorly represented along the Malabar coast, but had thoroughly colonized the Coromandel coast. European companies tried, in vain, to introduce western working arrangements for the weaving trade, in particular the putting-out system which I have already described at length. The clearest example occurred in Bombay,[457] where thanks to belated immigration by Indian workers from Surat and elsewhere, the attempt could be started from scratch. But the traditional Indian system of advance payments and contracts remained the rule, at least until the conquest of Bengal, when its artisans were brought under direct supervision, in the last decades of the eighteenth century.

The textile industry was hard to take over for this very reason that it was not contained within a single network as in Europe. Different sectors and circuits governed the production and marketing of raw materials; the manufacture of cotton yarn (a long operation especially if the aim was a yarn both fine and strong, to make muslin for instance); weaving; bleaching and preparation of fabrics; and printing. Processes which in Europe were vertically linked (as in thirteenth-century Florence) were here organized in separate compartments. Buyers for the companies would sometimes go to the market where the weavers sold their wares but more often, when a large order was being placed (and orders grew steadily larger)[458] it was better to strike a bargain with Indian merchants who had employees travelling through the production zones and themselves arranging contracts with the artisans. The middleman would undertake to deliver to a company servant on a specified date, at an agreed price, an agreed quantity of specified types of fabric. To the weaver he customarily made an advance payment in money, which was a kind of pledge of future purchase, enabling the worker to buy yarn and to maintain himself while he was working. When the piece of material was finished, the weaver would be paid the market price less the advance. Market prices, which were not fixed at the time of ordering, might vary according to the price of yarn or that of rice.

The merchant was thus shouldering a risk which would of course be reflected in his rate of profit. But the weaver was undoubtedly given a certain amount of leeway: he received his advance in money (not, as in Europe, in materials); and he could always resort directly to the market, something not open to the worker operating in the *Verlagssystem*. What was more, he could always default, change his place of work, even go on strike and give up the loom to return to the land or join the army. This being so, K.N. Chaudhuri finds it very difficult to explain the poverty of weavers, of which there is so much evidence. Could the reason be the antiquity of a social structure which condemned peasants and artisans to minimal remuneration? The huge increase in demand and production in the seventeenth and eighteenth centuries may have widened the range of choices for the artisan, without doing anything to alter the general low level of wages, despite the fact that production operated within a direct money economy.

On the whole this system made manufactories unnecessary, but some did exist, bringing together workers in large workshops – the *karkhanas*, which operated for their owners, the nobles or the emperor himself. The owners were not above letting these luxury goods go for export on occasion. Mandelslo (1638) speaks of a magnificent and very costly fabric of silk and cotton with gold-embroidered flowers, which the workshops had recently begun to manufacture in Ahmedabad when he was passing through, and 'which was confined to [the use of] the Emperor; nevertheless foreigners are permitted to carry it out of the country'.[459]

In fact all India processed silk and cotton, sending an incredible quantity of fabrics, from the most ordinary to the most luxurious, all over the world, since through the Europeans even America received a large share of Indian textiles. The variety of materials can be conjectured from the descriptions left by travellers and the trade lists drawn up by the European companies. Here for example, without comment, is a list taken from a French memorandum on textiles from the different provinces:

> Blue and unbleached cottons from Salem, blue guineas from Madure, bazeens from Gondelur, percales from Arni, table linens from Pondicherry, bettelles, chavonis, tarnatans, organdies, Steinkerques from the coast, cambays, nicannes, bejutapauts, papolis, korotes, brawles, boelans, lemanees, quilts, chittees, caddies, white dullees, handkerchief fabrics from Mazulipatam, sanees, muslins, terrindanis, durries [striped muslins], mulmuls, fine, embroidered in thread of gold or silver, common cottons from Patna [which were exported in such large quantities – up to 100,000 lengths – that they could be obtained 'without a contract'],[460] seersuckers [mixed silk and cotton], baftas, hummums, cossaes, four-thread weaves, common bazeens, gazas, Permacody cottons, Yanaon guineas, conjoos.[461]

And the writer of the memorandum adds that the quality could vary greatly in some types of fabric: in Dacca, which was the market for 'very fine muslins, unique of their kind ..., there are plain muslins from 200 francs for 16 ells, to 2500 francs for 8 ells'.[462] But even this impressive list pales into insignificance beside the 91 varieties of textiles Chaudhuri lists as an appendix to his book.

There can be no doubt that until the English industrial revolution, the Indian cotton industry was the foremost in the world, both in the quality and quantity of its output and the scale of its exports.

A national market

Every kind of commodity went into circulation in India, whether agricultural surpluses, raw materials or manufactured goods for export. The grain collected at village markets was conveyed by chains of local merchants, usurers and

Travelling in India in the sixteenth century: bullock-carts carrying ladies in the kingdom of Cambay; with an armed guard escort. (Photo F. Quilici.)

moneylenders, to small towns (*qasbahs*) then to the big cities through the offices of wholesalers who specialized in the transport of bulky goods – salt and grain in particular.[463] This circulation was by no means perfect: it could be surprised by sudden outbreaks of famine which the great distances between one place and another only too often turned into disaster. But was this not equally true of colonial America or even of the Old World in Europe? And in India the circulation of goods employed every conceivable means, cutting through obstacles, linking distant regions of different cultures and living standards, thus enabling every kind of merchandise to travel, the everyday and the precious (the latter covered by insurance at comparatively low premiums).[464]

On land, transport took the form of large caravans, the *kafilas* of the *banjara* merchants, protected by armed guards. These caravans, depending on the terrain, used bullock-carts, buffaloes, donkeys, dromedaries, horses, mules, goats and if necessary human porters. They suspended services during the rainy season, when their place was taken by waterways – a far less costly and often faster means of transport, but for which insurance premiums were, oddly enough, higher. Caravans were warmly welcomed everywhere; even villages gladly accommodated them.[465]

The term that springs to mind, perhaps an excessive one, is that of a *national market*: the Indian subcontinent, for all its size, had a degree of coherence in which the money economy was an important or rather essential element. This overall coherence created poles of development productive of the asymmetries indispensable to the brisk circulation of goods.

The leading role played by Surat and its region for example must surely be obvious to anyone: this was a place favoured in every sector of material life – trade, industry and exports. The port was the gateway for entry to and departure from India, linked by long-distance trade both to the flow of bullion from the Red Sea and to the distant ports of Europe and the East Indies. Another centre of increasing importance was Bengal, the wonder of India, another but bigger Egypt. A French sea captain who with some difficulty took his 600-ton ship up the Ganges to Chandernagor, rightly said of this river:

> It is the source and centre of trade in the Indies. [Commerce] can be carried on with great ease since one is not subject to the inconvenience found on the coast of Coromandel[466] ... and the country is fertile and extraordinarily populous. Besides the high quality of the merchandise made here, [it] provides grain, rice and generally everything necessary for life. This abundance attracts and always will attract a great number of traders who send vessels to every part of the Indies from the Red Sea to China. Here one can see the assembly of the nations of Europe and Asia, who differ so greatly in their national genius and their customs, reach perfect agreement or perfect disunity, depending on the self-interest which alone is their guide.[467]

More descriptions would be required of course to build up a picture of the trading geography of India in all its richness. One would have to mention in particular the 'industrial bloc' of Gujerat, the most impressive in the Far East; the contributions of Calicut, Ceylon and Madras; and the many merchants, Indian and foreign, who were prepared to embark their money or their merchandise, at considerable risk, in the freighting trade which had all the ships of Europe (except the Dutch) competing for their custom. One would also have to mention the complementary exchanges effected within India (foodstuffs but also textiles and dyes) using the waterways and overland routes, a less spectacular but perhaps even more important form of exchange for India as a whole than the export trade; it was certainly vital to the structures of the Mogul Empire.

The significance of the Mogul Empire

When in 1526, the Mogul Empire replaced the sultanate of Delhi, it took over a well-tried organization; the combination of this inheritance with a rediscovered dynamism proved to be for many years a heavy but effective machine.

Its first achievement (the pioneering work of Akbar, 1556-1605) was to persuade the two religious communities, Hindu and Muslim, to cohabit without too much conflict, although in fact the latter faith, being that of the rulers, received most honour – so much so that Europeans, seeing the countless mosques in northern and central India, long assumed Islam to be the prevalent religion in India, and Hinduism, the religion of the merchants and peasants, a sort of idolatry on the way to extinction, like paganism in Europe before the spread of Christianity. European thought did not really discover Hinduism until the late eighteenth or early nineteenth century.

The second feat of the Moguls was to acclimatize and introduce to almost the whole of India a single civilization, borrowed from neighbouring Persia and ferrying its arts, literature and sensibility. Thus the two cultures present in the country came together and it was eventually the minority culture – that of Islam – which was on the whole absorbed by the Indian masses, though only after it had itself adopted many cultural borrowings.[468] Persian remained the language of the rulers, of the upper, privileged classes: 'I will have someone write to the Rajah in the Persian tongue', a Frenchman in difficulty in Benares informed the governor of Chandernagor on 19 March 1768.[469] The administration used Hindustani, but its organization was also based on an Islamic model.

It is in the first place to the sultanate of Delhi, and then to the Mogul Empire, that responsibility must be attributed for the establishment in the provinces (*sarkars*) and the districts (*parganas*) of an ordered administration to handle the collecting of taxes and dues, but which also had the task of promoting agriculture – that is the basis of the fiscal system – as well as of developing irrigation and encouraging the spread of cash-crops for export.[470] Its activities, backed up from time to time by state subsidies and propaganda missions, were often effective.

Central to the system, housed at the heart of the empire whose existence it guaranteed and from whose resources it lived, was the terrible strength of the army. The nobles around the emperor, the *mansabdars* or *omerahs*, numbering 8000 in 1647, were the commanders of this force. Depending on their rank, they recruited dozens, hundreds or thousands of mercenaries.[471] The total size of the 'standing army' in Delhi was considerable – it would have been unthinkable in Europe: almost 200,000 horsemen, plus over 40,000 matchlockmen or gunners. Both in Delhi and in Agra, the other capital, the departure of the army on campaign left behind a deserted city, inhabited only by the Banyans.[472] If one were to calculate the total numbers dispersed in garrisons all over the empire with reinforcements along the frontiers, the answer would probably be close on a million men.[473] 'There is no little village that has not at least two horsemen and four foot soldiers',[474] detailed to keep order – and also to observe and spy on the population.

The army was itself the government, since the high offices of the regime were chiefly occupied by soldiers. The army was also the leading customer for luxury foreign fabrics, especially woollen cloth from Europe, which was not imported to make clothes in this hot climate but for 'saddlebags[475] and saddles for horses, elephants and camels, which the mighty have embroidered in embossed gold and silver, for palanquins, for gun-cases to protect them from the damp, and for the pomp of their foot soldiers'.[476] Up to 50,000 crowns' worth of cloth was being imported at this time (1724). The horses imported in large numbers from Persia or Arabia (for every cavalryman had several mounts) were themselves a luxury: the exhorbitant prices paid for them averaged four times those paid in England. At court, before the start of grand ceremonies, open 'to great and humble alike', one of the pleasures of the emperor was to have parade 'before his eyes a certain number of the finest horses in his stables', accompanied by 'a few elephants, ... their bodies well scrubbed and clean ... painted black with the exception of two broad stripes of red paint', and decorated with embroidered cloths and silver bells.[477]

The state kept by the *omerahs* was almost as grand as that of the emperor himself. Like him they possessed their own craft workshops, the *karkanahs*, manufactories whose refined products were reserved exclusively for their owners.[478] Like him, they had a passion for building. Large suites of servants and slaves accompanied them everywhere and some *omerahs* amassed fabulous hoards of gold plate and jewels.[479] It is not hard to imagine what a burden this aristocracy must have been on the Indian economy, living as it did from grants paid directly out of the imperial treasury, or from the dues paid by peasants on the *jagirs* granted to their masters by the empire, 'to maintain their rank'.

Political and non-political reasons for the fall of the Mogul Empire

The mighty imperial machinery was by the eighteenth century showing signs of wear and fatigue. There is a wide choice of dates for the beginning of what is known as the decline of the Mogul Empire: 1739, the date of the capture and terrifying sack of Delhi by the Persians; 1757, the battle of Plassey, won by the English; 1761, the second battle of Paniput, when Afghans in medieval armour triumphed over the Mahrattas armed with modern weapons, at the very moment when the latter were preparing to reconstitute the Mogul Empire for their own benefit. Historians have generally accepted with little controversy the date of 1707, the year of Aurangzeb's death, as marking the end of the great days of Mogul India. If we accept their account, the empire died from within, rather than being done to death by outsiders, whether Persians, Afghans or English.

It had been a strange empire, founded on the activities of a few thousand feudal nobles, the *omerahs* or *mansabdars*, recruited both inside and outside

India. At the end of the reign of Shah Jahan (1628-58) they were already being drawn from Persia and central Asia - in all from seventeen different sources. They were as foreign to the country they went to govern as the Oxford and Cambridge graduates who governed India in Kipling's day.

Twice a day, the *omerahs* paid their respects to the emperor. Flattery was as essential here as at the court of Versailles. 'The Emperor did not pronounce a word which was not greeted with admiration or which failed to make the principal *omerahs* throw up their hands crying *karamat* that is to say *wonders*.'[480] But what they were doing above all by such visits was reassuring themselves that the emperor was still alive and that thanks to him the empire was still standing. The briefest absence on the emperor's part, the rumour of an illness, or false reports of his death, might immediately unleash the frightening turmoil of a war of succession. Hence the determination of Aurangzeb during the last year of his long life, to make his presence known, even when he was mortally sick, to prove *coram populo* that he still existed and the empire with him. It was precisely the weakness of this authoritarian regime that it had not succeeded in making arrangements once and for all for the imperial succession. It is true that the struggle which almost always took place on such occasions was not necessarily serious. In 1658, Aurangzeb, at the end of the war of succession which marked the bloody opening of his reign, had just defeated his father and his brother Dara Shukoh. But the affliction of the vanquished was not insupportable:

> Almost all the *omerahs* were obliged to come and pay court to Aurangzeb, ... and what is almost unbelievable, not one of them had the heart to make a stir or to attempt the slightest thing on behalf of their King [i.e. the loser] who had made them what they were and who had raised them up out of the dust and perhaps even from slavery, as is quite common in this court, to bring them to richness and greatness.[481]

François Bernier, a French doctor and a contemporary of Colbert, thus reminds us that despite his long stay in Delhi his reactions and habits of mind had not changed. But the high and mighty of Delhi observed a different code of behaviour: they were guided by the precepts of a different world. For what were they but *condottieri*, like the Italians of the fifteenth century, recruiters of soldiers and knights paid for services rendered? They had to levy troops and arm them as best they could (hence the varied armour worn by Mogul troops).[482] As *condottieri*, they were too used to war not to respect its risks; they conducted it dispassionately, thinking only of their own interests. Like the warlords of Machiavelli's time, they might prolong hostilities while avoiding any decisive encounter. A glorious victory could be inconvenient: it might create jealousy towards an over-successful leader; whereas dragging out a campaign, increasing the troops and thus the payments and revenues guaranteed by the emperor, could bring nothing but gain, especially since war was not over-dangerous, largely consisting of taking up positions in front of some fortress which would be reduced to surrender by hunger; the besiegers would pitch a vast military camp the size of a town, with thousands of tents, hundreds of shops and facilities, even a certain degree of luxury. François Bernier has left us a vivid description of the astonishing cities under canvas, which were built and rebuilt along Aurangzeb's route to Kashmir in 1664 and which were inhabited by literally thousands of people. The tents were pitched in a certain order, repeated every time and the *omerahs*, as at court, came to pay their respects to the sovereign. 'Nothing is so magnificent on a dark night in the midst of the countryside as the sight of the long processions of torches threading their way between the tents, escorting all the *omerahs* to the emperor's quarters or bringing them back to their own tents.'[483]

All in all, it was an astonishing machine, rigid yet fragile. To keep it in working order required an energetic and effective ruler, as Aurangzeb perhaps was during the early part of his reign, until say 1680, the year in which he crushed the rebellion led by his own son Akbar.[484] But it also required that the country refrain from disturbing the social, political, economic and religious order which governed it. Yet this contradictory world was always stirring. It was not only the sovereign who changed – growing intolerant, suspicious, indecisive, and more bigoted than ever – but also the whole country and the army itself. Giving itself up to luxury and pleasure-seeking, the army lost its combative qualities; what was more, by over-recruiting it opened its ranks wider. The number of *jagirs* did not however increase at the same pace, and any new ones granted were often in devastated or arid regions. The general strategy of the owners of *jagirs* therefore became to seize any occasion to make a profit. In this climate of disdain for the public good, some members of the Mogul 'life aristocracy' took steps to preserve some of their wealth from the legal provisions stipulating that it revert to the emperor on their death; they even succeeded, as their counterparts were doing in the Turkish Empire at the same time, in transforming life-holdings into hereditary property. A further sign of corruption was that already by the middle of the seventeenth century, princes and princesses of the blood, ladies of the harem and nobles were engaging in trade, either directly or through merchants who lent them their names. Aurangzeb himself possessed a fleet of ships which traded in the Red Sea and the African ports.

Wealth was no longer, in the Mogul Empire, a reward for services rendered to the state. The provincial rulers, the *subahs* and *nawabs*, were showing signs of disobedience. When Aurangzeb attacked and subjugated two Muslim states of the Deccan – the kingdoms of Bijapur (1686) and Golconda (1687) – he found himself, after his victory, confronted with a sudden and widespread crisis of insubordination. Already the Mahrattas, a small tribe of poor mountain-dwellers in the western Ghats, had displayed their keen hostility towards him. The emperor completely failed to stop the raids and pillage by these extraordinary horsemen, their ranks swelled by a throng of adventurers and malcontents. Neither by force, guile nor corruption could he defeat their peasant leader Shivaji, the 'mountain rat'. The emperor's prestige suffered inordinately, parti-

The Great Mogul goes hunting, escorted by a host of nobles and servants most of whom are mounted on horses, elephants or camels, except for the foot soldiers, top right. (Photo B.N., Paris.)

cularly when in January 1664, the Mahrattas captured and sacked Surat, the wealthiest port in the Mogul Empire, the point of departure for all trade and pilgrim voyages to Mecca, the very symbol of Mogul power and rule.

For all these reasons, N.M. Pearson[485], with some justification, regards the long reign of Aurangzeb as part and parcel of the Mogul decline. He argues that the empire, faced with this domestic war of an unprecedented and persistent kind, proved unfaithful to its vocation and *raison d'être*. This may well be the case; but was this tragic war exclusively brought about, as some historians still maintain,[486] by Aurangzeb's post-1680 policies, inspired both by distrust of his blood-relations and by religious intolerance? Is this not to overestimate the influence of this 'Indian Louis XI'?[487] The Hindu reaction welled up from deep below the surface: we can see surface signs of it in the Mahrattas war, and in the triumphant heresy and determined struggles of the Sikhs,[488] but its origins are still hidden from us. Yet it is here that the explanation is probably to be sought for the deep-seated and inexorable decline of Mogul India and of its attempt to bring together two religions and two civilizations, Islam and Hinduism. Muslim civilization, with its institutions, its characteristic urban achievements and its monuments which were imitated even in the Deccan, apparently offered the spectacle of a rare success. But this success was coming to an end and India was being torn apart. It was indeed this rift which opened the way to the British conquest as Isaac Titsingh, a Dutchman who for many years represented the V.O.C. in Bengal, clearly perceived (25 March 1788): the only obstacle which the English would have found insurmountable would have been an alliance between the Muslims and the Mahrattas: 'their statesmanship is now constantly directed towards the forestalling of such an alliance'.[489]

What is certain is the length of time it took for Mogul India to collapse. The Battle of Plassey (1757) took place fifty years after the death of Aurangzeb (1707). Was this half-century of evident difficulty also a period of economic decline? If so, for whom? For the eighteenth century was of course characterized by the prosperity throughout India of European commerce. But what does this really signify?

It is actually very difficult to estimate the real economic situation of India in the eighteenth century. Some regions undoubtedly went into decline, others kept going, a few made progress. The wars which devastated the country have been compared to the suffering in Germany during the Thirty Years' War (1618–1648).[490] As comparisons go, the French Wars of Religion might provide a useful parallel, since during the struggles which split sixteenth-century France, the economic situation was on the whole quite favourable.[491] Indeed it was the survival of the economy which prolonged and maintained the war, enabling both sides, Protestants and Catholics, to pay the foreign mercenaries they constantly recruited. Were the Indian wars fuelled by a similarly benign economic situation? Perhaps: the Mahrattas were only able to launch their raids with the help of the businessmen allied to their cause, who amassed supplies and arms for them along their chosen routes. War had to pay for war.

The problem in short remains before us: it cannot be resolved without further research into statistics and price series. May I suggest, at the risk of error, that India in the latter half of the eighteenth century seems to me to have been caught up in the new revival of the economy making itself felt from Canton to the Red Sea? The fact that the European companies, the independent merchants or the 'servants' of the companies indulging in 'the country trade' were doing well and increasing the number and size of their ships, might mean either that damage was being done, or that a takeover was occurring; but all the same production in the Far East and notably in India with its central position must have followed the trend. And 'for every piece of cloth made up for shipment to Europe', as Holden Furber writes, 'hundreds of pieces had to be woven for domestic consumption'.[492] Even the African regions bordering the Indian Ocean revived under the impact of Gujerati merchants.[493] Does the pessimism expressed by historians of India about the eighteenth century simply flow from *a priori* assumptions?

At any rate, whether India's doors were opened by economic prosperity or by economic decline, she certainly put up little resistance to foreign conquest – and not only when the conqueror was British: the French, Afghans and Persians were all ready to intervene.

Was this decline confined to the highest political and economic levels, or did it also occur in the teeming life of town and village? At this elementary level, not everything stayed standing, but many structures remained intact. The English certainly did not take over a country without resources. Even after 1783, English, Dutch, Portuguese and French merchants were still doing a lot of business in Surat, although it was by now already in decline.[494] Mahé in 1787[495] was attracting the pepper trade by offering prices higher than those in the English trading-posts. The French 'country trade' handled by French nationals in the trading posts and in particular in Mauritius and Réunion, was still prosperous or at any rate holding its own. And every Frenchman seeking his fortune in the Indies rather late in the day had his own pet projects and anti-British schemes: India was still it seems a desirable prize, worth conquering.

India's decline in the nineteenth century

What is beyond doubt is the general decline of India in the nineteenth century. This was both an absolute and a relative decline, in that India proved unable to keep pace with the European industrial revolution and to imitate her English master. But was the peculiar form of capitalism in India to blame? Or perhaps the economic and social straitjacket of a low wage structure? Does the explanation lie in the difficult political situation, as the wars of the eighteenth century combined with growing intervention by Europeans, in particular by the British? Or in India's technological backwardness? Or was the crucial blow dealt belatedly by the impact, here as in Russia, of the machine revolution in Europe?

Indian capitalism unquestionably had its shortcomings. But it was part of a system which did not after all work so badly, although India was disproportionately large – ten times the size of France, twenty times the size of England. The Indian community, the national market divided against itself by geography, required a certain quantity of precious metals if the community was to live and the market to function. And the economico-socio-political system of India, harsh and even perverse though it might be, forced it to resort as we have seen to the indispensable fluidity and efficacity of the money economy. India had no precious metals of her own but she was importing enough for peasant dues in the central zone to be paid in specie as early as the fourteenth century. This was as advanced as anywhere in the world, including Europe at the time. And since the money economy could only function if it husbanded its reserves, first accumulating them then opening the sluices and creating *artificial* money in advance of harvests or payments, arranging transactions on the market or on credit; and since no economy largely based on money could function without merchants, whole-salers, shipowners, insurers, brokers, middlemen, shopkeepers and pedlars – it is clear that such a business hierarchy did exist and was fulfilling its role in India.

It is in this sense that a certain capitalism was part and parcel of the Mogul Empire. At the crucial bottlenecks, Indian businessmen and bankers controlled key positions for the accumulation and release of capital. If India, like Islam, lacked the continuity provided by the great landed families who in the West accumulated not only wealth but capital in the shape of power and influence, the caste system did on the other hand encourage and stabilize the process of mercantile and banking accumulation which was pursued with determination from generation to generation. Certain families acquired outstanding fortunes, comparable to those of the Fuggers or the Medici in the West. In Surat, there were businessmen who owned entire fleets of ships. We know of literally hundreds of important merchants affiliated to Banyan castes, and an equal number of rich or very rich Muslim merchants. In the eighteenth century, the bankers appeared to have reached the peak of their wealth. Were they (as I am inclined to think, possibly under the influence of European history) carried along by the logical evolution of an economy which was tending, as it reached maturity, to create its own high-level banking functions? Or as T. Raychaudhuri has suggested, were these businessmen driven into finance (tax-collecting, banking and usury) because European competition was tending more and more to squeeze them out of shipping and long-distance trade?[496] Both trends may have combined to make the fortune of the Jagat Sheths who, being honoured with this grand title (literally 'merchants of the world'), in 1715 substituted it for their original family names.

We know a certain amount about this family, originally from the state of Jaipur and belonging to a branch of the Marwari caste. Their fortune became immense after they had settled in Bengal, where we find them collecting taxes for the Great Mogul, lending at interest, making bank loans and running the mint at Murshidabad. One source of their fortune, according to contemporaries, was simply fixing the rate of the rupee in relation to the old coins. As money-changers, they sent huge sums by bill of exchange to the Great Mogul in Delhi. When Murshidabad was taken by a detachment of Mahratta cavalry, they lost 20 million rupees overnight, but business continued as usual. And the Jagat Sheths were by no means unique. We know of many other business families which could stand comparison with them.[497] These Bengali capitalists were to be progressively ruined after the end of the eighteenth century, it is true, but that

520 The Perspective of the World

was because of deliberate action by the British rather than any ineptitude on their own part.[498] On the west coast of India in Bombay, on the other hand, we find that in the first half of the nineteenth century a group of very rich Parsees and Gujeratis, both Muslim and Hindu, prospered in every kind of banking and mercantile activity – shipbuilding, freight, the China trade, even certain industries. One of the richest of these men, the Parsee J. Jeejeebhoy, had 30 million rupees deposited in an English bank in the town.[499] In Bombay, where the collaboration and organization of native business networks was indispensable to the English, Indian capitalism easily proved its capacity to adapt.

Does that mean to say that Indian capitalists always had their own way in India? By no means, for the merchants and bankers had never had the stage to themselves. Above them, before the structures of the British Raj, had been the despotic states of India, and not only that of the Great Mogul: the wealth of the great merchant families singled them out for exactions on behalf of the tyrants. They lived in perpetual fear of torture and dispossession.[500] However brisk the flow of money which was the lifeblood of merchant capitalism and the Indian economy, the world of the Banyans lacked the liberty, security and political tolerance which favoured the rise of capitalism in the West. But to argue on this account as some historians have done, that Indian capitalism was impotent, is taking it rather far. India was not China, where capitalism in itself, that is the accumulation of capital, was *deliberately* thwarted by the state. In India, wealthy merchants might be exposed to extortion, but there were plenty of them, and they survived. The powerful solidarity of the caste embraced and guaranteed the fortunes of the group, ensuring it the collaboration of merchants all the way from the East Indies to Moscow.

I would not therefore accuse capitalism of being responsible for India's backwardness, which is to be explained, as is always the case, by both internal and external reasons.

Among the internal causes, perhaps one should single out low wages. It is a truism to speak of the gap between Indian wages and those in Europe. In 1736, the directors of the East India Company reckoned that the wages of French workmen (and we know that these were far below those of English labour) were six times as high as wages in India.[501] Chaudhuri understandably finds it a little puzzling that highly-skilled workers, who seem to have had some freedom and means of defending themselves within the social context, should have been paid such miserable wages. But could it perhaps be argued that low wages were a structural feature, long embedded in the overall economy of India? Were they not, that is, the *sine qua non* of the flow of precious metals into India, a flow dating back to very ancient times, indeed to the Roman Empire? Is the low-wage economy not a more satisfactory explanation than unbridled thirst for gold on the part of the emperor and the privileged classes, for the cyclonic suction which seems to have drawn precious metals from the West to the East? On reaching India, gold and silver currencies automatically increased in value, compared to

An employee of the East India Company, converted to the pleasures of opium and the *dolce vita*. Indian painting by Dip Chand (late eighteenth century). Victoria and Albert Museum. (Photo by the museum.)

the very low price of human labour, which inevitably meant low prices for food and even, comparatively, for spices. This in turn would explain the powerful rebound – the penetration of western markets by Indian exports, raw materials but above all textiles, cottons and silks: they were more attractive than comparable English, French or Dutch products, not only for their quality and beauty, but because of the price difference, just as the same phenomenon is today flooding world markets with textiles from Hong Kong or Korea.

The labour of a 'foreign proletariat' was the very foundation of Europe's trade with India. Defending the principle of bullion exports in 1684, Thomas Mun had an unanswerable argument: the Indian goods which the East India Company had bought at a cost of £840,000 had been sold in Europe for

£4 million – so that they effectively brought money into England.[502] From mid-seventeenth century on, cotton textiles from India became a leading import commodity and their quantity grew rapidly. In the single year 1785–6, the English company sold in Copenhagen alone 900,000 pieces of Indian cloth.[503] K.N. Chaudhuri is however probably quite right to deduce from such statistics that there could be no incentive for technological innovations which might increase productivity, in a country where the number of artisans ran into millions, and whose output was being fought over by all nations of the world. Business was good, so why change anything? The incentive worked the other way round – providing a stimulus to the threatened industry of Europe. England's first step was to close her own frontiers for the greater part of the eighteenth century to Indian textiles, which she re-exported to Europe and America. Then she tried to capture for herself this profitable market – something that could only be achieved by making drastic reductions in manpower. It is surely no coincidence that the machine revolution began in the cotton industry.

This brings us to the second explanation for India's falling behind: an external not an internal explanation – in a word, Britain. It is not enough simply to say that the British seized India with all her resources. India was for the British an instrument thanks to which they gained access to an even larger area, coming to dominate the Asiatic super-world-economy; and it is within this enlarged framework that one can see how from an early stage India's internal balances and structures were distorted and strained to achieve aims quite foreign to her; how, in the process, India was eventually in the nineteenth century 'deindustrialized', reduced to the role of a major producer of raw materials.

It can at any rate be confidently said that eighteenth-century India was not on the brink of producing some revolutionary form of industrial capitalism. Within her own limitations, India was perfectly at ease, with a natural, strong and successful economy; her agriculture was traditional but productive and high-yielding; her industry was on an ancient pattern, but it was thriving and efficient (until 1810, Indian steel was actually of higher quality than anything produced in England, and inferior only to Swedish steel);[504] the whole country was penetrated by a well-established market economy; there were many efficient trading circuits. Last but not least, India's commercial and industrial strength was based, as one might expect, on a vigorous export trade: she was part of an economic area going well beyond her own shores.

But India did not dominate this area. I have even indicated how passive was India's attitude to this surrounding zone on which the bulk of her trade depended. And it was from outside that the threat came: as she gradually lost control of the 'country trade' routes throughout Asia, India became impoverished and slipped from her throne. The intervention of the Europeans, which had originally given a fillip to Indian exports, in the end operated against her. Ironically India's very strength was used to bring about her own destruction, by forcing open the reluctant gates of China, after 1760, to the greater profit of the English, thanks to cotton and opium. India was to suffer from the repercussions of England's newly-increased strength.

India and China: caught in a super-world-economy

After this long explanatory detour, we are now brought back to the original problem: somehow to account for the Far East as a whole, caught up as it was after 1400 in a super-world-economy – immense, impressive but fragile. This fragility has unquestionably been one of the major elements of universal history. For the Far East, structured enough to be penetrated with relative ease, but not sufficiently structured to defend itself, was asking to be invaded. The intrusion of the Europeans should not therefore be regarded as their responsibility alone; indeed they were only following in the footsteps of other invaders – those of Islam for instance.

The logical confluence of trade, the crossroads lying at the centre of this super-world-economy could hardly be elsewhere than in the East Indies. Geography placed this region on the edge of Asia, halfway between China and Japan on the one hand, and India and the countries of the Indian Ocean on the other. But if geography proposes, history disposes, and in this instance refusal or acceptance could take innumerable forms depending on the actions of the super-powers of the Far East: China and India. At times when both were prosperous, in control of themselves and simultaneously engaged in outside activities, the centre of gravity of the Far East was quite likely to lie, and to remain for a longer or shorter period, somewhere near the Malacca peninsula and the islands of Java and Sumatra. But the sleeping giants were both slow to arouse and invariably slow to act.

Only at the beginning of the Christian era, that is rather late in history, did India really recognize and start to take an interest in the East Indies. Her sailors, merchants and missionaries exploited, educated and evangelized the archipelago, successfully transferring to it her superior political, economic and religious way of life. The islands were thus converted to Hinduism.

The Chinese dragon arrived very much later in the islands, only in about the fifth century. And it failed to impose upon the states and towns by now converted to Hinduism the mark of its own civilization, which could in theory have scored triumphs here as it did in Japan, Korea and Vietnam. The Chinese presence remained confined to the spheres of politics and economics; on several occasions China foisted on to the states of the East Indies protectorates, guardianships and the obligation to send ambassadors as a sign of allegiance; but in essence, and in way of life, these states would long remain true to themselves or to their earliest conquerors. The Indian yoke weighed heavier on them than the Chinese.

Hindu expansion, followed by Chinese expansion, probably corresponded to underlying bursts of economic prosperity which must have inspired and sustained such ventures, but whose chronology, origins and agents are still unknown. Although I can claim no expertise in an area very inaccessible to non-specialists, I imagine that India by expanding eastwards was passing on the impact she had felt from the 'far West', that is the Mediterranean. Is not the connection between Europe and India, an ancient and creative one in every respect, one of the firmest structural features of ancient history? In China's case, the problem is rather different: the East Indies seem to have been for the Chinese the ultimate frontier, rarely if ever crossed. The barrier of the East Indies always proved easier to cross from west to north-east than in the other direction.

Both these expansions, first the Indian then the Chinese, at any rate made the East Indies if not a pole of attraction, then at least a busy crossroads of trade. Various outstanding periods marked the history of this region: the Krivijaya kingdom (seventh to thirteenth centuries) centred on south-east Sumatra and the town of Palembang; then the Mojopahit empire (thirteenth to fifteenth centuries), based this time on the rich rice-growing island of Java. One after the other these political units seized control of the major maritime routes, notably the crucial route through the Malacca straits. These powerful ventures into empire-building both lasted for some time – the first for five or six centuries, the second for three or four, making it possible already to talk in terms of an East Indian economy, if not of a super-world-economy of the Far East.

Probably there was no super-world-economy revolving round the East Indies until the rise of Malacca, from 1403, when the town was founded or 1409 when it began to make an impact, until its capture by Alfonso de Albuquerque on 10 August 1511.[505] It is worth looking a little more closely at this sudden but century-long success.

Malacca's hour of glory

Geography was certainly responsible for a good deal of Malacca's story.[506] The town occupies an advantageous site on the straits which bear its name, lying on the maritime channel connecting the waters of the Indian Ocean to those of the China seas on the edge of the Pacific. The narrow Malay peninsula (which good roads today enable one to cross quickly, even on a bicycle) could only be crossed in the past by beaten tracks at the latitude of the Kra isthmus. But these ran through jungles full of wild animals. Once the peninsula had been circumnavigated successfully the Malacca straits came into their own.[507]

Built on a slight eminence rising above a 'soft' and 'muddy' plain ('one spade thrust finds water')[508] and bisected by a clear running river where boats could come ashore, Malacca was a mooring and shelter rather than a true port: larger junks anchored opposite the town between the two little islands which the Portuguese christened *Ilha de Pedra* and *Ilha da Naos* (the Island of Stones and the Island of Ships), the second being 'no bigger than the square in Amsterdam where the town hall stands'.[509] However as another traveller pointed out, 'one can land at Malacca any time of year, an advantage which the ports of Goa,

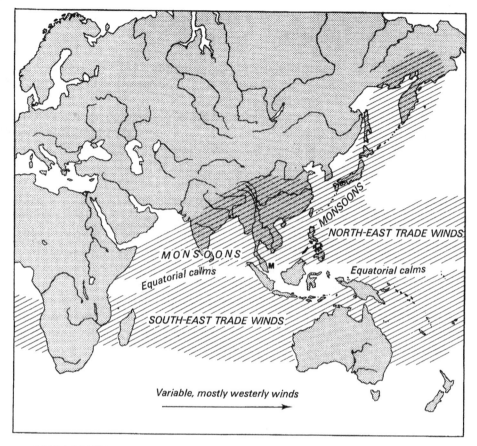

48 MALACCA'S PRIVILEGED POSITION
The band of equatorial calm moves north then south depending on the position of the sun. So
Malacca is a connection or corridor between the monsoons and the north-east and south-east
trades. (From Vidal de la Blache's *Atlas*, p. 56.)

Cochin or Surat do not offer'.[510] The only obstacles were the tidal currents in the
straits: the tide usually 'flowed eastwards and ebbed westward'.[511] As if these
advantages were not enough, Malacca stood not only at the meeting place of
two oceans but also at the intersection of two zones of atmospheric circulation,
the monsoons of the Indian Ocean to the west, and the trade winds to the south
and east. Best of all, the narrow band of equatorial calm which moves slowly
north or south depending on the position of the sun, stays for quite a long time
in the Malacca region (latitude 2°30′N) thus alternately allowing ships free
passage towards the trades or the monsoon. 'This is one of the places most
favoured by nature', exclaimed Sonnerat, 'it is perpetual springtime here.'[512]

But there were other good sites in the East Indies – the Sunda straits for
instance. The earlier fortunes of the Krivijaya and Mojopahit regimes[513] prove

that the same control could be exerted from the east coast of Sumatra and from even further east in Java. Indeed in 1522, Magellan's ships, after their leader's death in the Philippines, crossed through the Sunda Islands southwards near Timor on their homeward route, in order to catch the south-east trades. And it was by a similar route that Drake on his voyage round the world in 1580, reached the southern coast of the East Indies.

If Malacca's rise can be explained in terms of geography, history certainly made an important contribution, both at local level and at the more general level of the Asiatic economy. The newly-founded town succeeded for instance in attracting and to some extent controlling the Malay sailors who had always been fishermen, coastal traders and above all pirates. Malacca thus succeeded in ridding the straits of these corsairs, while at the same time acquiring for itself the little sailing ships, crews and even war fleets it needed. As for the large junks indispensable to long-distance trade, these could be found in Java or Pegu. It was here for instance that the sultan of Malacca (who took a great interest in and large share of the town's traffic) bought the ships with which he arranged a voyage to Mecca on his own account.

The town's rapid development soon became a problem in itself. How was it to survive? Perched on a hilly and forested peninsula, rich in tin mines but short of edible crops, Malacca's only source of food was the local catch of fish. It was therefore strictly dependent on Siam and Java, the two nearest rice-growers and exporters. Siam was an aggressive and dangerous state, and Java was still labouring under the ancient but not yet dead imperialism of the Mojopahit Empire. One or other of these states would probably have snapped up this little town that had grown up accidentally, if Malacca had not in 1409 placed itself under Chinese protection, which remained effective until the 1430s: meantime the Mojopahit Empire had collapsed, removing the threat to Malacca's existence.

The town's extraordinary fortune was also the result of a crucial combination of circumstances: the meeting of China and India – China having for thirty years or so encouraged an amazing expansionist venture by her mariners into the Java seas and the Indian Ocean, India having since an earlier date launched an even greater assault. Towards the end of the fourteenth century, under the impulsion of Muslim India and the Delhi sultanate, a wave of Indian traders and transporters, natives of Bengal, Coromandel and Gujerat had reached the East Indies, accompanied by a strong current of religious proselytism. The conversion to Islam which the Arab sailors of the seventh century had not achieved or even attempted, had become a reality centuries later, thanks to trade with India.[514] The coastal towns all went over to Islam one after another. For Malacca, which was converted in 1414, this was a golden opportunity: business and religion went hand in hand. And if the Mojopahit Empire was gradually disintegrating and ceasing to be a threat, it was precisely because the coastal towns had turned to Islam, while the interior of Java and the other islands remained faithful to Hinduism. The spread of the Muslim order only affected about a third or a

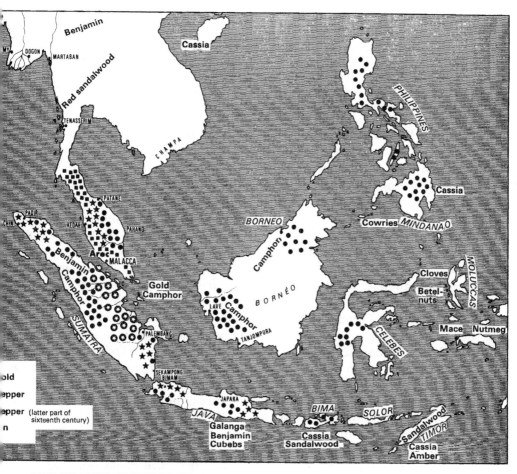

49 THE WEALTH OF THE EAST INDIES
The Portuguese from their base in Malacca rapidly surveyed the riches of the archipelago: above all pepper, fine spices and gold. This first European impact was sufficiently strong to stimulate fresh plantations and new markets, particularly for pepper. The same thing occurred on the Malabar coast in India. (From V. Magalhaēs Godhino, *op. cit.*)

quarter of the population. Some islands remained untouched by it – such as Bali, which remains today a fantastic museum of the Hindu past. And in the distant Moluccas, the conversion was incomplete: the Portuguese to their astonishment later found nominal Muslims there who were by no means hostile to Christianity.

But the rising fortune of Malacca was a direct consequence of the expansion of Indian trade. There was a good reason for this: the Indian traders had brought to Sumatra and Java an important gift – the pepper-bush. Everywhere, spreading from the points affected by contact with Malacca, a market economy began to replace what had previously been a primitive and largely self-sufficient regime.

> They took little heed of sowing or planting [writes a Portuguese chronicler of the previous history of the inhabitants of the Moluccas] ... they lived as in the first ages of humanity. In the morning they took from the sea or the forest enough to feed themselves for the whole day. Living off plunder, they derived no profit from cloves, and there was no one to buy them from them.[515]

When the Moluccas were integrated into trade networks, plantations were laid out and regular links set up between Malacca and the spice islands. A *keling* merchant (that is a Hindu merchant from the Coromandel coast) Nina Suria Deva, sent eight junks every year to the Moluccas (for cloves) and to the Banda Islands (for nutmeg). These islands, having gone over to a monoculture, depended entirely for their subsistence on the rice brought to them by the junks from Java, which even sailed out as far as the Mariana Islands deep in the Pacific.

So the Islamic invasion had created a new order. 'Sultanates' were set up in Malacca and Tidore, Ternate and later in Macassar. The most curious phenomenon of all was the establishment of a *lingua franca* necessary for doing business, based on Malay, which was commonly spoken in the headquarters of trade, Malacca. Throughout the East Indies with their 'Mediterraneans', remarked a Portuguese chronicler, 'the number of languages is so great that even neighbours do not, so to speak, understand each other. Today they use the Malay tongue, which most people speak, and it is employed throughout the islands, like Latin in Europe'. It is not surprising then that the 450 words of the vocabulary of the inhabitants of the Moluccas brought back to Europe by Magellan's expedition were in fact words of Malay.[516]

The spread of the *lingua franca* was proof of Malacca's expansionist strength. But this was really created by external factors, much as Antwerp's fortune had been in in the sixteenth century. For while the town could offer lodgings, market-places, warehouses and protective institutions, not to mention its very precious code of maritime laws, its trade was kept going by foreign ships, traders and commodities. Among these foreigners, the most numerous group was made up of Muslim traders from Gujerat and Calicut (a million Gujeratis according to Tomé Pires, 'besides four or five thousand ... seamen who came and went'); and another large group consisted of the Hindu merchants of Coromandel, the *kelings*, who had their own district, the *Campon Queling*.[517] The Gujeratis had the advantage of being as solidly established in Sumatra and Java as they were in Malacca, and of being able to control the bulk of re-exports of pepper and spices to the Mediterranean. Cambay (another name for Gujerat) could only survive, it was said, by stretching out one arm to Aden and the other to Malacca.[518] Once more, one becomes aware of India's hidden superiority: she was much more open than China to foreign contacts and had links with the trade networks of Islam as well as with the Middle East – the more so since China after 1430, for reasons which despite the fertile imagination of historians remain obscure, abandoned long-distance expeditions for good. Moreover, China was only moderately interested in spices, of which the Chinese consumed small quantities, except for pepper which they could obtain in Bantam without needing to go through Malacca.

The capture of Malacca by the little fleet commanded by Albuquerque (1400 men, 600 of whom were from the Malabar coast)[519] was inspired by the prosperity and reputation of the town, 'which was then the most famous in the Indies market'.[520] It was a brutal assault: once the bridge over the river had been stormed, the town was sacked for nine days on end. But Malacca's fortunes did not entirely come to an end on that fateful day, 10 August 1500. Albuquerque, who remained in the conquered town until January 1512, quickly re-organized it; he built an imposing fortress, and if he presented himself from Siam to the spice islands as the enemy of Muslims, he also announced that he was a friend of the Gentiles, the pagans and in fact of all merchants. After the occupation, Portuguese policy became more tolerant and conciliatory. Even Philip II as king of Portugal and lord of the Indies after 1580, pursued a watchful religious toleration in the Far East. We must not convert by force, he insisted, *Não e este modo que se deve ter uma conversão.*[521] In Portuguese-occupied Malacca, there was a Chinese bazaar as well as a mosque, though it is true that the Church of St Paul belonging to the Jesuits dominated the fortress, and from its steps one could see the sea. As Luis Filipe F.R. Thomaz has rightly remarked, 'the conquest of Malacca in August 1511 opened to the Portuguese the doors of the Java Seas and the Far East; by capturing Malacca, the victors did not merely acquire a rich town, but also control of a complex of trade routes meeting at Malacca to which the town was the key'.[522] In general, with some exceptions, they held on to these routes. Some of them were even extended when in 1555, in order to counter the mid-century crisis, the Portuguese landed at Macao opposite Canton and even reached Japan. Malacca while in their hands was the centre of communications between the Pacific, India and Europe, as Batavia later would be in the hands of the Dutch.

Before the arrival of the Dutch disturbed their Asian paradise, the Portuguese enjoyed a period of peace and prosperity, bringing profit to the king in Lisbon, to Portugal, to the pepper retailers in Europe, but also to the Portuguese adventurers in the East who often, if not always, had the semi-feudal mentality of the Spanish conquistadors in America. There were a few Turkish attacks, but they were intermittent and accomplished little. On the whole, the Portuguese profited from their quiet life. But 'by dint of travelling through these seas without hindrance, they began to neglect all kinds of precautions for their defence'.[523] So when in 1592, Lancaster's two English ships arrived by the very same route as Vasco da Gama, they had little difficulty in capturing the Portuguese vessels they encountered. And soon everything would begin to change: the Europeans would bring to the Indies their European wars and rivalries, and the reign of Malacca as a Portuguese town would be over. The Dutch took it in 1641 and immediately relegated it to a subordinate role.

The new centres of the Far East

Even before the fall of Malacca, Batavia had become the new centre of the Far Eastern trade, directing and ordering everything. Founded in 1619, it was at the height of its fortunes in 1638, when Japan barred access to the Portuguese while remaining open to ships of the V.O.C. The headquarters of the aristocracy of trade – as well as control of the vital networks of the 'country trade' – thus remained in the East Indies and would continue to do so as long as the Dutch East Indies Company retained its astute, vigilant and authoritarian supremacy, that is for over a century, with some ups and downs. In early 1662 for instance, the Dutch were expelled from Formosa, the island off the Chinese mainland and halfway to Japan where they had been settled since 1634, the date of the building of the fort at Castel Zelandia.[524] The long reign of Batavia, described earlier in this book, thus coincided broadly with the long crisis of the seventeenth century which so severely affected the European world-economy (including the New World) between approximately 1650 and 1750. But it probably did not hit the Far East so hard, since throughout India the seventeenth century was an age of prosperity, of demographic and economic expansion. Perhaps this was one of the reasons why during the European crisis Holland's economy was by far the best protected, as we have already seen, and the one which had the lion's share of what trade there was.

The new town of Batavia was certainly a striking symbol of Dutch supremacy. The two-storey town hall built in 1652 marked the centre of the town, a town criss-crossed with canals and grid-plan streets, surrounded by walls, fortified with twenty-two towers, and punctuated by four gates. Into Batavia flocked all the peoples of Asia, Europe and the Indian Ocean. Outside the walls were the Javan and Amboynan districts and a few country villas; but above all paddy-fields, sugar cane plantations, canals, and on the banks of the re-channelled river flour-mills, paper-mills, saw-mills and powder-mills, as well as sugar-mills, tile- and brickworks. Inside the town, everything was neat, clean and orderly: the market-places, warehouses, stores, butcheries, fishmarket, barracks and the *Spinhuis*, where dishonoured girls were sentenced to spin. I need not reiterate how rich, pleasure-seeking and indolent Dutch colonial society was. This wealth and love of pleasure which we have already seen in Goa, which was already to be seen in Batavia even before De Graaf's arrival in 1668, and which would later appear in identical form in Calcutta, is the unmistakable sign of outstanding success.[525]

But by the beginning of the eighteenth century, the formidable Dutch machine was beginning to break down. This is sometimes attributed to the growing corruption and unreliability of the Company's agents. But the 'servants' of the English East India Company far outdid the Dutch in this respect, yet that did not prevent the English company from moving into first place in about 1760. Was it, as one is tempted to think, because the reversal of the trend in mid-century

Macao in the early seventeenth century by Theodore de Bry. The town had been occupied by the Portuguese since 1557 and was the departure point for merchants trading with China. (Photo, B. N., Paris.)

brought increased activity, a greater volume of trade and encouraged change, upheaval and revolution? Back in Europe, there was a reshuffle of the international cards, resulting in a speedy victory for the English. In Asia, the centre of gravity of the Far East was shifting towards India, but India was only moving into first place under the rule and on behalf of England, by a process admirably described in Holden Furber's book (published as long ago as 1948).[526] The English company ('John Company') ousted its cousin ('Jan Compagnie') the V.O.C., because the latter had lost out in both Bengal and India in the 1770s and had already failed in the middle of the century to seize the first place in Canton, where China was gradually inching open the gates a little wider every day. I do not intend to suggest that John played a shrewder and more intelligent game in Canton than Jan, although this is sometimes maintained, not without some justification. But a French observer who bitterly criticized the French company, argued that in Canton in about 1752, it was the Danish and Swedish companies – the most junior and the least well equipped to succeed – who rose to the occasion best of all.[527] If the English eventually emerged on top, it was because they could combine their own forces with the formidable weight of India. Plassey (1757) did not only mark the political conquest of India, but also that of the trading 'rivieras' running along the coast of the subcontinent and extending on one side to the Red Sea and Persian Gulf and on the other to the East Indies and soon to Canton. It was entirely for the use of the country trade, in particular for the China run, that the Indian shipyards were turning out so many 'Indiamen'. According to Furber,[528] whereas in 1780 the fleet flying the English flag and carrying the country trade totalled 4000 tons, by 1790, it had risen to 25,000! The jump was not quite as big as it looks, since 1780 was a war year, the last-but-one serious confrontation between France and England, and English ships were then prudently sailing under Danish, Portuguese or Swedish flags. When the danger was past they appeared in their true colours again.

At the same time there was a rapid shift of fortunes from Batavia to Calcutta. The sudden rise of the city on the Ganges helps to explain from a distance the somnolence of the V.O.C. Calcutta grew phenomenally, in every direction, and in the greatest disorder. The count of Modave[529] a French traveller and fortune-hunter, arrived there in 1773 just as Warren Hastings' governorship was beginning. He observed both the town's exuberant growth and its lack of order. Calcutta was nothing like Batavia with its trim canals and streets. There was not even a quayside on the Ganges: 'the houses are scattered here and there on the bank, the walls of some of them are washed by the river'. Nor was there a perimeter wall. There were perhaps 500 houses at most, built by the English amid a sea of bamboo huts with thatched roofs. The streets were as muddy as jungle tracks, sometimes broad but closed at either end by barriers made of large beams. There was chaos in every direction. 'It is said to be the effect of the famous British freedom, as if freedom were incompatible with order and symmetry.'[530] Indeed, our Frenchman continues, 'it is not without astonishment mingled with a little anger that a foreigner looks on the city of Calcutta. It would have been so easy to make it one of the fairest cities in the world, simply by taking the trouble to observe a regular plan, that one cannot understand how the English could have neglected the advantages of such a fine site and left everyone complete freedom to build according to the strangest of tastes and the most extravagant dispositions'. It is true that Calcutta which had been a mere settlement in 1689, to which a fortress (Fort William) was added in 1702, was still in 1750 an insignificant town. Prévost does not even mention it. When the count of Modave observed it in 1773, by which time every possible trading population was represented there, the town was growing wildly and in the throes of a building boom. Bricks were being made in the surrounding countryside, wood was being floated down the Ganges or through the sea of Pegu; rents were reaching record levels. Calcutta already had 30,000 or so inhabitants and would have more than doubled by the end of the century. The town was growing without being responsible either for its growth or its fortune. The English behaved there without the least restraint, elbowing aside or bullying anyone who got in their way. Bombay on the other side of India was by contrast a pole of liberty, the compensation or perhaps the revenge of Indian capitalism which would score some extraordinary successes there.

Is any conclusion possible?

Long though this chapter has been, the picture it gives of 'non-Europe' is clearly far from complete.

I could have dwelt at more length on China, and in particular on the centrifugal expansion which affected the province of Fukien, a process which would only be interrupted by the departure of the Dutch from Formosa in 1662, or rather by the conquest of the island in 1683 by the Manchus, but which began again in the eighteenth century with the opening up of Canton to the many-sided trade of Europe.

I could also have devoted space to the special case of Japan which, according to Leonard Bluss's brilliant essay,[531] constructed after 1638 a world-economy for its own use and to fit its own dimensions, consisting of Korea, the Ryukyu islands, Formosa until 1683, and the Chinese junks allowed in on sufferance, together with the privileged 'vassal' trade of the Dutch.

I could have said even more about India, and made room for the analysis recently advanced by J.C. Heesterman[532] who sees as one of the main reasons for the decline of the Mogul Empire the development of urban economies which were by the eighteenth century destroying the unity of the whole.

Lastly I could have included a section on Safavid Persia, on its command economy and its role as indispensable intermediary between India, Central Asia, hostile and hated Turkey, Muscovy and distant Europe.

But even if I had been able to paint the picture in its fullness, at the risk of stretching the chapter to the proportions of a book, would we be any nearer the end of our problems and questions? Certainly not. To reach conclusions about Europe and non-Europe, that is on the world as a whole, we should need some valid measurements and figures. What I have essentially given here is a description, an outline of some of the problems and some hints at possible or perhaps probable explanations. But we have by no means solved the enigma of the relations between Europe and non-Europe. For if it can hardly be questioned that until the nineteenth century the rest of the world outweighed Europe both in population and, while the economic *ancien régime* lasted, in wealth, if it is virtually beyond question that Europe was less rich than the worlds it was exploiting, even after the fall of Napoleon when Britain's hour of glory was dawning – we still do not really know how this position of superiority was established and above all maintained – for the gap grew steadily wider.

The great service Paul Bairoch has once more rendered to historians is precisely to pose this problem in statistical terms. By so doing he does not merely agree with my position but goes well beyond it. But is he right? And am I right?

I shall not go into details and into the validity of the methods my colleague in Geneva has employed. I shall simply assume for the sake of brevity that the procedure he adopted was sufficiently scientifically valid for his results (very approximate ones, as he is the first to admit, and to warn the reader) to be taken into consideration.

The chosen indicator is per capita income, G.N.P. per inhabitant, and so as to give a meaningful picture of the respective positions of the various countries, all the levels have been calculated in dollars at 1960 US prices, so they are all presented in the same units. The results are as follows: England in 1700, between $150 and $190; the English colonies in America, the future United States in 1710, between $250 and $290; France (1781–1790), $170 to $200; India in 1800, $160 to $210 (but in 1900 between $140 and $180). These figures, which reached me as I was correcting the proofs of this book, confirmed my faith in the assertions and hypotheses I had already put forward. Nor was I surprised by the figure for Japan in 1750: $160. Only the high figure for China in 1800: $228 seems rather surprising, although it is true that this high level later declines ($170 in 1950).

But let us concentrate on what interests us most, namely the comparisons, if possible *synchronic*, between the two blocs made up of Europe-plus-the-United States and non-Europe. In 1800, western Europe reaches the figure of $213 (North America $266); not so surprising perhaps, but this figure is hardly any higher than that of the 'Third World' of the time – about $200. And that is a somewhat unexpected figure. In fact the high level reached by China ($228 in 1800, $204 in 1860) raises the average of the less favoured group. Today the figure for western Europe as measured in 1976, is $2325, whereas China – despite recent recovery – is only $369, and the Third World as a whole is at about $355, far behind the developed nations.

What emerges from Paul Bairoch's calculations is that at the time when Europe was scoring dazzling triumphs all over the globe, when her ships commanded by Cook, La Pérouse or Bougainville, were exploring the vastness of the Pacific Ocean, she was (unlike today) far from having reached a level of wealth vastly superior to living standards in the rest of the world. The combined G.N.P. of the developed countries of today (western Europe, the USSR, North America, Japan) was in 1750 only $35,000 million (1960 dollars) – whereas that of the rest of the world was $120,000 million; in 1860, the respective figures were $115,000 million as against $165,000 million; the first group only overtook the second between 1880 and 1900; in 1880 the figures were $176,000 million to $169,000 million; by 1900 they were $290,000 million to $188,000 million. But in 1976, in round figures, they were $3000 million to $1000 million.

This perspective obliges us to take a rather different view of the respective positions of Europe (plus the other privileged countries) and the rest of the world, before 1800 and after the industrial revolution, which now appears to take on tremendous significance. It seems certain that only Europe (perhaps for reasons that have more to do with her social and economic structures than with technological progress) was able to carry out the machine revolution, with England leading the way. But this revolution was not merely an instrument of development in itself. It was a weapon of domination and destruction of foreign competition. By mechanizing, European industry became capable of out-competing the traditional industry of other nations. The gap which then opened up could only grow wider as time went on. The history of the world between about 1400 and 1850–1950 is one of an ancient parity collapsing under the weight of a multisecular distortion, whose beginnings go back to the late fifteenth century. Compared with this predominant trend, everything else is secondary.

The Industrial Revolution and Growth

THE INDUSTRIAL REVOLUTION which began or rather became visible in England in the 1750s or 1760s, strikes the observer as an extremely complex process. In the first place it was the culmination of the 'industrialization' which had begun many centuries earlier. And since it is constantly being reproduced, it could be said to be still with us today. Identified in the past as the beginning of a new era, the industrial revolution is likely to influence the future for many years to come. But massive, all-pervasive and innovatory though it may have been, it does not, nor can it, tell the whole story about the modern world.

This is what I shall be doing my best to convey in the following pages, whose purpose is to define this extraordinary phenomenon and, if possible, to place it in its proper context.

Some relevant comparisons

As a first step, some definitions and in particular some preliminary comparisons may be relevant. In the first place, since its original appearance in England the industrial revolution has engendered a series of other revolutions and is evolving before our eyes, still moving on towards new horizons: the revolutions it has spawned can tell us something in retrospect about the English 'takeoff'. On the other hand, we can go back to the days before the English industrial revolution and find many instances of industrialization, something which has always been present in human societies; some of these past experiences were advanced and forward-looking, though in the end none of them came to anything. But the study of failure can sometimes be relevant to the understanding of success.

Revolution: a complicated and ambiguous term

Borrowed from the vocabulary of astronomy,[1] the word *revolution* in the sense of upheaval or overthrow of an existing society, is thought to have appeared in the English language in 1688.[2] It is in this sense, but also in the opposite sense

Honour where honour is due: the industrial revolution began with the coming of steam, the achievement of James Watt (1736-1819). This portrait by James Eckford Lauder, shows him putting the finishing touches to his steam engine in the laboratory. (Snark International.)

meaning *reconstruction*, that one should understand the convenient expression *the industrial revolution* which seems to have been coined not by Engels in 1845[3] but possibly in 1837 by the French economist Adolphe Blanqui[4] (brother of the more famous revolutionary, Auguste)– unless that is it appeared even earlier, in about 1820 in debates between various other French authors.[5] The term certainly does not seem to have been in standard use among historians until after the appearance in print in 1884 of the *Lectures on the Industrial Revolution* which the social reformer Arnold Toynbee gave in Oxford in 1880-1, and which his pupils published after his death.

Historians are often criticized for misusing the word *revolution* which, it is argued, ought to be used in the original sense, to refer only to violent and rapid change. But when one is talking about social phenomena, rapid and slow change are inseparable. For no society exists which is not constantly torn between the forces working to preserve it and the subversive forces – whether perceived as such or not – working to undermine it. Revolutionary explosions are but the sudden and short-lived volcanic eruptions of this latent and long-term conflict. In any attempt to analyse the revolutionary process, the most difficult part is always making the connection between the long and the short-term, recognizing their relationship and the links between them. The industrial revolution in England at the end of the eighteenth century is no exception. It consisted both of a rapid sequence of events and of what was clearly a very long-term process: two different rhythms were beating simultaneously.

Whether we like it or not then, we are faced with a dialectic between the long and the short-term. According to W.W. Rostow[6] for instance, the English economy 'took off' between 1783 and 1802, because a critical investment threshold had been crossed. This explanation has been challenged by Simon Kuznets whose figures tell a different story[7] but it survives in the image of the takeoff, the plane leaving the runway – that is an event precisely located in time. But before there could be any takeoff in the first place, the plane (Britain) had to be built and satisfactory conditions for the flight had to be arranged. In any case, no society is likely to be able – simply because, say, its rate of savings has gone up – to transform at a stroke 'its attitudes, institutions and techniques', as Arthur Lewis claims.[8] There will always have been some earlier experiences, stages of progress and adaptations. Phyllis Deane is right to remind us that all the innovations and even discontinuities of the late eighteenth century were, in the English case, contained within 'a historical continuum', stretching back into the past, covering the present, reaching into the future, a continuum in which breaks and discontinuities lose their identities as unique or decisive events.[9] When David Landes describes the industrial revolution as the formation of a critical mass which eventually produced a revolutionary explosion,[10] the image is an appropriate one, but it must be understood that the mass can only have been formed by the slow accumulation of all manner of necessary elements. Argue as we may, the long-term will always claim its due.

So the industrial revolution was at least twofold. It was a revolution in the ordinary sense of the word, bringing its visible changes in a sequence of short-term events, yet it was at the same time a long-term process, advancing with discreet and silent steps, sometimes barely discernible at all 'and as unlike a revolution as anything that can be imagined', according to Claude Fohlen,[11] who by contrast with Rostow, lays the emphasis on continuity.

It is hardly surprising then that even during the apparently most explosive period (let us say roughly after 1760) this vital phenomenon made very little impression on the most famous observers of the day. Adam Smith, with his example of the little Scottish pin factory, seems in retrospect to have been a rather poor witness to his age – and yet he lived until 1790. Ricardo (1772-1823) who was younger than Smith and thus has even less excuse, hardly gives any place to the machine in his theoretical writings.[12] And Jean-Baptiste Say, after describing the English 'steam chariots' in 1828, makes this short-sighted prophecy: 'Nevertheless... no machine will ever be able to perform what even the worst horses can – the service of carrying people and goods though the bustle and throng of a great city'.[13] But it is not fair to expect the great men of the age – if Say can be numbered with them – to be skilled at the art of prophecy. And it is only too easy with hindsight to accuse Marx or Weber, or even a later writer like Werner Sombart, of misunderstanding – that is of understanding differently from ourselves – the long process of industrialization. I find T.S. Ashton, usually a fair-minded writer, rather unjust in his hasty condemnation of past historians, based on a remark by Kroebner.[14]

In any case, are the historians of today – so many of whom study the industrial revolution – any more correct in their judgments? Some see the process as beginning before the seventeenth century; some regard the Glorious Revolution of 1688 as a key moment; others again see the radical transformation of England as coinciding with the broad economic revival of the later part of the eighteenth century. They can all make out a convincing case, depending on whether the accent is put on agriculture, demography, foreign trade, industrial techniques, or forms of credit. But should the industrial revolution be seen as a series of sectorial modernizations; as a sequence of stages of development; or as a phenomenon of simultaneous growth on all fronts, taking the word 'growth' in the broadest sense? If by the late eighteenth century, British growth had become irreversible, being by now as Rostow[15] puts it the 'normal condition' of Britain, it was certainly not on account of progress in some particular sector (such as the rate of savings or investment) but on the contrary as the consequence of an overall and indivisible process, the sum of the reciprocal relations of interdependence and liberation that each individual sector as it developed, sooner or later, by accident or design, had helped to create for the greater benefit of the other sectors. Can 'true' growth (or as some people would call it true development – the word does not much matter) be anything but growth which links together, irreversibly, progress on several fronts at once, creating a mutually sustaining whole which is then propelled on to greater things?

Downstream from the industrial revolution: the under-developed countries

The industrial revolution in Britain opened the door to a series of revolutions which are in its direct line of descent: some have succeeded, others have failed. It had itself been preceded by several revolutions of the same order, some of which barely got off the ground, while others were pursued quite seriously – but all of them sooner or later came to nothing. From this historical vantage-point then, one can look in two directions – towards the past or towards the present – and embark on two kinds of historical journey, each offering an approach to the subject which draws on the invaluable insights of comparative history.

If we look down the stream of history to the present, there is no great virtue in studying the example of the industrial revolutions in Europe and the United States, which followed close on the heels of the British model. But the present-day Third World, which is still undergoing industrialization, offers the historian a rare opportunity to observe something in action, something that can be seen, heard and touched. It is certainly no success story. Over the past thirty, forty or fifty years, the Third World as a whole can hardly be said to have made steady progress. Its efforts and expectations have only too often led to bitter disappointment. Can the reasons for the failure, or comparative failure of these experiments help to define *a contrario* the conditions which brought about the exceptional success of the industrial revolution in Britain?

Economists and more particularly historians will of course caution us against the procedure of extrapolating from the present in order to understand the past. They will argue, not without some truth, that 'the mimetic model, which predicated the repetition of the itinerary previously taken by the industrialized countries, has had its day'.[16] The context has completely changed and it would be impossible nowadays for the industrialization of some Third World country to follow the authoritarian state model seen in Japan or the spontaneous growth of George III's England. Agreed; but if 'the crisis in development is also a crisis in development theory' as Ignacy Sachs has said,[17] would not the process of development in itself – including the case of England in the eighteenth century – become more intelligible if we asked ourselves what has gone wrong with the theory, and why the enthusiastic planners of the 1960s so gravely underestimated the difficulties of the undertaking?

The problem, we shall immediately be told, is that a successful industrial revolution calls for a general process of growth, and therefore of overall development, which 'in the last analysis takes the shape of a process of transformation of economic, social, political and cultural institutions'.[18] The entire length and breadth of a society and economy are concerned in this process and must be capable of accompanying, sustaining and actually undergoing change. It only takes one obstacle, what we would today call a bottleneck, at one point in the process, for the whole machine to come to a standstill, for its motion to be halted or even reversed. The leaders of countries today trying to catch up with the advanced nations of the world have learnt this to their cost, and development strategy has now become as prudent as it is complex.

What advice then would a well-informed economist such as Ignacy Sachs give in these circumstances? Essentially that no *a priori* planning model be applied: no single model will do, since every economy presents a particular combination of structures which may appear to resemble each other but do so only approximately. In any given society, the planner would be well advised to take a hypothetical growth rate (say 10%), suppose it to be adopted as a target, and study one by one 'the consequences of the hypothesis'. This would mean checking one after another a number of factors: the amount of investment which would have to come out of national income; the possible types of industry with a view to potential home and foreign markets; the quantity and quality of labour required (skilled or otherwise); market supplies of the foodstuffs required to feed the workforce; the available technology (in particular from the point of view of the capital investment and the size and kind of workforce they would require); the provision of extra imports of raw materials or machine tools; the eventual effect of the new output on the balance of payments and foreign trade. If the growth rate originally posited was deliberately chosen 'at sufficiently high level to show up all the possible bottle-necks that might appear if it really were maintained as a target',[19] the checklist would indicate in which sectors insuperable obstacles might arise. It would then be possible in the second stage, to proceed to scale down, by envisaging 'variants at every level' until a more modest, but theoretically viable target was reached.[20]

The examples described in Sachs's book give a concrete idea of the principal bottle-necks encountered in the Third World today; population growth, when it cancels out the benefits of development; shortages of skilled labour; a propensity to industrialize in luxury and sometimes export sectors, because of low domestic demand for basic industrial products; and perhaps most of all, the 'agricultural barrier', the insufficiency and inelasticity of food supplies provided by an agricultural sector which has remained archaic and largely self-sufficient, and cannot expand to meet the increased consumption automatically engendered by the greater number of wage-earners; an agricultural sector which cannot always even feed its own surplus population and is thus responsible for the exodus to the towns of an unemployed proletariat; one which is lastly unable because of its poverty to swell the demand for basic industrial products. Compared with these major problems, the need for capital, the level of savings, credit arrangements and interest rates seem almost secondary. But it is surely significant that this list enumerates precisely all the obstacles which no longer existed in eighteenth-century (or indeed seventeenth-century) England.

So the prime requirement of growth is intersectorial harmony: one sector should not be allowed to block progress being made in another. This brings us back to what we sensed lying behind the concept of the *national market* – the assumption that the national market is characterized by cohesion, free circulation of goods and a certain level of per capita income. In France, a country notoriously slow to achieve economic takeoff (since the cohesion of the economy was not a reality until the railway network was complete) it might be argued that there was for a long period precisely the same kind of dichotomy which can be observed in Third World countries today: an ultra-modern, rich and advanced sector existing alongside a number of backward areas, the 'lands of darkness' as they were called by an 'entrepreneur' who in 1752 wanted to open up to trade one of these regions and its fantastic forests by rendering navigable the Vere, a small and insignificant tributary of the Aveyron.[21]

But the endogenous conditions for growth are not the only things which shape the national market. Is not the major obstacle facing today's developing nations the international economy in its existing form, and the way in which it divides and distributes tasks – something on which this book has already laid if anything too much emphasis? England successfully carried out her industrial revolution when she was at the centre of the world – when she *was* in fact the centre of the world. Today's Third World countries would like to do the same, but they are firmly on the periphery. Consequently everything conspires against them: the new technology, which they can only use under licence and which does not always correspond to the needs of their own societies; capital which they can borrow only from outside sources; shipping, which is beyond their control; even their own surpluses of raw materials, which sometimes leave them at the mercy of the purchaser. This is why the contemporary world offers such a distressing spectacle; why industrialization persistently makes a progress only in places where it has already made progress, and the gap grows ever wider between the under-developed countries and the others. It may however be the case that we are now witnessing a change in this balance of power. Since 1974, the countries producing oil and other raw materials, and the poor countries whose low wages make it possible for them to produce industrial goods at very low prices, seem to have begun to take revenge upon the highly industrialized nations. Only the history of the next few years will tell. But if the Third World is to make any progress it will somehow or other have to break down the existing international order.

Upstream from the English industrial revolution: revolutions that came to nothing

Today's failures are a salutary warning that every industrial revolution is a combination of elements, a 'family complex', a series of different factors. And it is in relation to this multiplicity of factors that the 'pre-revolutions', the movements which preceded the English revolution, are significant. In their case, there is always something missing, so that they add up to a sort of typology of failure or missed opportunity. Sometimes an invention appears in isolation, brilliant but useless, the sterile fruit of some fertile brain; no more is heard of it. Sometimes there is takeoff of a kind, perhaps as the result of a revolution in energy, or some sudden advance in agricultural or craft technology, a breakthrough in marketing or an increase in the population: there is a burst of progress, the motor seems on the point of starting – and then the whole thing comes to a halt. Is it right to lump together under the same heading this series of abortive revolutions, the reasons for which are never exactly the same? They are at least similar in their rhythm: a burst of progress followed by a collapse. Imperfect repetitions of each other though they may be, they are repetitions all the same and obvious comparisons practically suggest themselves.

My conclusion will surprise no one, certainly not an economist: no industrial revolution, indeed no advance in production or exchange in the broader sense, can be regarded as a strictly economic process. The economy cannot exist in isolation from the other sectors of human life; it depends on them, they depend on it.

Alexandrian Egypt

My first example, an ancient but intriguing one, is Ptolemaic Egypt. Perhaps this looks too like chapter one in a school textbook – but steam[22] had actually made its appearance in Alexandria between 100 and 50 BC, eighteen or nineteen hundred years before Denis Papin or James Watt. Should one dismiss as of no account the invention by the 'engineer' Hero, of the aeolipile, a sort of steam-powered turbine – a mere toy, but one which nevertheless operated a mechanism capable of opening and shutting a heavy temple door some distance away? This discovery followed in the wake of several others – the suction pump, the force pump, some early versions of the thermometer and the theodolite, various engines of war – more theoretical than practical admittedly – which depended on compressed or expelled air, or massive springs. In those distant days, Alexandria was a throbbing powerhouse of invention. Several revolutions had already taken place there during the preceding century or two – cultural, commercial and scientific: this was the age of Euclid, Ptolemy the astronomer and Eratosthenes; Dicaearchus, who seems to have lived in the city early in the third century BC, was the first geographer 'to draw a line of latitude across a map, the line running from the Straits of Gibraltar along the Taurus and the Himalayas to the Pacific Ocean'.[23]

A detailed study of the long Alexandrian episode would of course take us too far, through the extraordinary Hellenistic world resulting from Alexander's conquests, in which territorial states like Egypt and Syria replaced the earlier model, the Greek city-state. It was a transformation which in some ways brings to mind the early development of modern Europe. And it tells us something we shall find frequently repeated: that inventions tend to come in clusters, groups or series, as if they all drew strength from each other, or rather as if certain societies provided simultaneous impetus for them all.

Brilliant though it was, the Alexandrian era eventually came to an end without its inventions giving rise to a revolution in industrial production (despite their being specifically directed towards technical application: Alexandria even had a school of engineering in the third century). No doubt the explanation lies largely in the existence of slavery, which provided the ancient world with the easily-exploited workforce it required. Thus in the East, the horizontal water-wheel remained a rudimentary mechanism adapted only to the heavy tasks of grinding grain, an everyday chore, while steam was used merely to operate ingenious toys, since, as a historian of technology has written, 'no need was felt for a more powerful [source of energy] than those already known'.[24]

Hellenistic society remained indifferent to the inventions of its 'engineers'.

It might also be argued that the Roman conquest, coming as it did shortly after this age of invention, bears some responsibility. The economy and society of the Greeks had been open to the rest of the world for several centuries. Rome by contrast enclosed herself within the Mediterranean world; and by destroying Carthage, and subjugating Greece, Egypt and the East, Rome shut three doors leading to wider horizons. Would the history of the world (as Pascal suspected) have been different if Anthony and Cleopatra had won the battle of Actium in 31 BC? In other words, is an industrial revolution possible only at the heart of an *open* world-economy?

The earliest industrial revolution in Europe: horses and mills, from the eleventh to the thirteenth century

In the first volume of this book, I dwelt at some length on the changes of this period – in the use of horses, the horse-collar (an invention from eastern Europe which increased the animal's traction power); oats (which Edward Fox[25] has argued brought the centre of gravity of Europe back to the great rainswept cereal-growing plains of the north, in the days of Charlemagne and heavy cavalry); and triennial crop rotation, which was quite an agricultural revolution in itself. I also referred to water-mills and windmills, the latter new inventions, the former a revival. I can therefore afford to be brief on this subject, about which information is now increasingly available, especially since many studies of this 'first' industrial revolution have been written, including Jean Gimpel's lively and intelligent book,[26] Guy Bois's vigorous and provocative study[27] and E.M. Carus-Wilson's classic 1941 article[28] which revived[29] and gave wide currency to the term 'the first industrial revolution' to describe the widespread adoption in England of fulling-mills (about 150 between the twelfth and the thirteenth centuries) and sawmills, paper-mills, grinding-mills, etc.

'The mechanising of fulling in the Middle Ages', E.M. Carus-Wilson writes, 'was as decisive an event as the mechanisation of spinning and weaving in the eighteenth century.'[30] The large wooden paddles turned by a water-wheel and introduced to the major industry of the time – woollen cloth – to replace the feet of the fulling-workers, proved to be the instruments of a revolutionary upheaval. Most water courses near the towns, which were generally in the lowlands, did not have the motive force of the upland streams and waterfalls. Fulling-mills therefore tended to be sited in less populated areas, to which they attracted their merchant clientèle. The hitherto jealously guarded craft monopoly of the towns was thus by-passed. The towns inevitably tried to defend themselves by forbidding weavers working within the walls to have their cloth fulled outside. The authorities in Bristol in 1346 forbade 'any man to take outside this city for fulling any kind of the cloth known as raicloth on pain of losing XL d. per cloth'.[31] That did not prevent the 'mill revolution' from taking its course, both in England

This illustration from a French Bible of the thirteenth century depicts the grindstone which
Samson was condemned to turn for the Philistines under the lashes of a guard, in the form of
what was in the 1230s a modern mill, with a wealth of technical detail. The internal mechanism
is meticulously represented, showing the transmission of vertical to horizontal movement. The
wheel being turned by the man could equally well be turned by a mill race. This evidence of
respect for machinery may be compared to the words of Roger Bacon quoted below. (François
Garnier Bible, c. 1220–30, Vienna, B.N., Paris, Codex Vindobonensis 2554.)

and throughout the continent of Europe which certainly did not lag behind on this occasion.

But the point is that this revolution took place alongside a number of other revolutions: a significant agricultural revolution which pitted large numbers of peasants against forest, marsh, seashore and river, and encouraged the adoption of triennial rotation; and a simultaneous urban revolution prompted by demographic expansion – never before had towns sprung up so thickly within such easy reach of one another. A clear distinction of functions, a 'division of labour' between town and countryside, sometimes brutally felt, became the norm. The towns took over industrial activity, became the motors of accumulation and growth, and re-invented money. Trade and traffic increased. With the Champagne fairs, the new economic order of western Europe became first discernible then clearly visible. In the Mediterranean, shipping and overland routes, especially to the east were gradually reconquered by the Italian cities. The whole economic area was undergoing the expansion without which no growth would be possible.

The word *growth*, in the sense of overall development is indeed unhesitatingly used in this context by Frederic C. Lane.[32] In his view, we can undoubtedly talk of a period of 'sustained growth' in the twelfth and thirteenth centuries in, say, Florence or Venice. How could it be otherwise at a time when Italy was the very centre of the world-economy? Wilhelm Abel even maintains that the whole of western Europe was caught up in a wave of general development from the tenth to the fourteenth century, citing as evidence the fact that wages rose faster than cereal prices.

> The thirteenth and early fourteenth centuries [he writes] witnessed the first industrialization of Europe. At this time, the towns with all their commercial and craft activities were undergoing vigorous development, less perhaps because of the technical advances of the age (though these were not negligible) than as a result of the generalization of the division of labour, thanks to which work yields were increased, and it was probably this higher productivity which made it possible not only to resolve the difficult problem of providing a growing population with its essential food supplies, but even to feed it better than ever before. The only analogous occasion was during the 'second industrialization' in the nineteenth century – admittedly on a very different scale.[33]

In other words, the eleventh century saw the beginning of what was effectively a period of 'sustained growth' on the modern pattern, one which would not recur before the English industrial revolution. It is hardly surprising that the 'global development' theory seems the logical explanation. A whole series of inter-related advances were taking place in production and productivity, in agriculture, industry and commerce, as the market expanded. During this first serious awakening of Europe, there was even expansion in the 'tertiary' sector (another sign of development) with a rise in the number of lawyers, notaries, doctors and university professors.[34] We actually have some statistics about the notaries: in Milan in 1288, there were 1500 for a population of about 60,000; in Bologna, 1059 for a population of 50,000; in Verona in 1268 there were 495 for 40,000; in Florence in 1338, there were 500 for a population of 90,000 (but Florence was a special case: business was so well organized there that book-keeping methods often rendered the services of a notary unnecessary). And predictably, with the fourteenth-century recession, the number of notaries declined comparatively; although it climbed again in the eighteenth century it never again reached the heights attained in the thirteenth – no doubt because the abnormal rise in the number of notaries in medieval days was created both by the increase in economic activity and by the need for the services of clerks when the vast majority of people were illiterate.

Europe's great leap forward ended in the monster recession of the fourteenth and fifteenth centuries (roughly from 1350-1450) following the Black Death which may have been as much consequence as cause – the slowing-down of the economy, dating from the cereal crisis and famine of 1315-17,[35] *preceded* the epidemic and may have rendered its sinister work easier. So plague was not the only grim reaper of the prosperity of a previous age: this was already slowing down if not at a standstill by the time the disaster struck.

How then is one to explain Europe's greatest triumph and greatest disaster before the eighteenth century? Most probably by the dimensions of a demongraphic explosion with which agricultural production found it impossible to keep pace. Falling yields are the mark of any agriculture pushed beyond the bounds of its productive capacity, when it does not possess the methods or techniques which might compensate for the rapid exhaustion of the land. Guy Bois's study, based on the example of eastern Normandy, analyses the social aspects of this phenomenon: the underlying crisis of feudalism which broke up the old partnership between the landlord and the peasant farmer. This destructured society, shorn of its code and vulnerable to disorder and random warfare, was in search both of a new equilibrium and a new code – results not attained until the establishment of the territorial state which would be the salvation of the seigniorial regime.

Other explanations could be suggested – in particular the fragility of the countries most affected by the energy revolution represented by the new mills: northern Europe from the Seine to the Zuyder Zee, from the Low Countries to the Thames valley. New territorial states like France and England, although by now strong political units, were not yet manageable economic units: they were to be seriously affected by the crisis. What was more, in the early years of the century, with the decline of the Champagne fairs, France, having been for a brief moment the centre of European trade now found herself excluded from the circuit of profitable trading links and the first capitalist successes. The cities of the Mediterranean were soon to take over from the new northern states, and this would mark the end, for the time being, of that supreme confidence visible in Roger Bacon's extraordinary glorification of the machine:

Machines may be made by which the largest ships, with only one man steering them, will be moved faster than if they were filled with rowers; wagons may be built which will move with incredible speed and without the aid of beasts; flying machines can be constructed in which man may…beat the air with wings like a bird… Machines will make it possible to go to the bottom of seas and rivers.[36]

The age of Agricola and Leonardo da Vinci: a revolution in embryo

When after this long and painful crisis Europe began to revive again, a wave of renewed trade and vigorous growth ran along the axis linking the Netherlands and Italy, through the middle of Germany. And it was Germany, a secondary zone for trade, which led the way in industrial development: possibly because this was one way of breaking into international exchange, situated as Germany was between the two dominant poles, to the north and south. But it was above all because of the development of mining. The early revival of the German economy in the 1470s, ahead of the rest of Europe, was not the only result. The extraction of metallic ores – gold, silver, copper, tin, cobalt and iron – stimulated a whole series of innovations (the use of lead to separate out silver from copper ore for instance) as well as the creation of machinery, on a gigantic scale for the time, to pump out water from the mines and to bring up the ore. The engravings in Agricola's book provide an impressive picture of the sophisticated technology developed at this time.

It is tempting to see these achievements, which were imitated in England, as the real forerunners of the industrial revolution.[37] The expansion of mining did indeed have repercussions in every sector of the German economy of the time – in fustians, wool, the leather trade, various kinds of metallurgy, tin, wire, paper, the new arms industry and so on. Trade stimulated large-scale credit networks and big international firms like the *Magna Societas* were established.[38] The urban crafts flourished: there were 42 craft guilds in Cologne in 1496; 50 in Lübeck; 28 in Frankfurt-am-Main.[39] Transport was improved and modernized; large firms began to specialize in carrying goods. And Venice, the queen of the Levant trade, established close trading relations with High Germany, since she needed silver. The German cities unquestionably offered for over half a century the spectacle of a rapidly-expanding economy in virtually every sector.

But everything began to slow down or stop in the years around 1535 when, as John Nef's work has shown, silver from America started to compete with the output of the German mines; at about the same time, 1550, Antwerp's commercial supremacy was also being challenged. Was it not a source of inferiority for the German economy to be dependent on external powers, to have been manufactured to meet the needs of the two real centres of the European economy, Venice and Antwerp? The age of the Fuggers, when all is said and done, was the age of Antwerp.

Detail of a miniature dating from the late fifteenth century depicting the silver mine at Kutna Hora, in vertical section as was the custom. The miners are dressed in white; ladders are used for the descent and a winch for hauling to the surface. The part of the miniature not shown here shows a very modern set of equipment (the Germans led the world in mining techniques): winches operated by horse power, drainage and ventilation systems. Vienna, Oesterreiche Nationalbibliothek. (Photo by the library.)

Even more outstanding success was achieved in Italy, at about the time when Francesco Sforza came to power in Milan in 1450. It was outstanding, partly because it had been preceded by a series of exemplary revolutions. The first of these was a demographic revolution which continued until mid-sixteenth century. The second was the appearance in the early fifteenth century of the first territorial states, still small in size, but already modern in structure: it even seemed for a brief moment that Italian unity was in the air. And lastly, an agricultural revolution along capitalist lines was taking place among the canals of the great Lombardy plains. All this in a climate of scientific and technical discovery: this was the age when hundreds of Italians, sharing the enthusiasm of Leonardo da Vinci, were filling their notebooks with designs for extraordinary machines.

Milan now entered upon a singular phase in its history. Having been spared during the terrible crisis of the fourteenth and fifteenth centuries (precisely because of its agricultural productivity, according to Zangheri), the city witnessed a remarkable spurt of manufacturing activity. Woollens, cloth of gold and silver, and armour began to take the place of the fustians which had been Milan's staple industry in the early fourteenth century. The Lombard capital was caught up in a huge wave of commercial activity linking it to the fairs of Geneva and Chalon-sur-Saône, to cities like Dijon and Paris, and to the Netherlands.[40] At about the same time, the Milanese capitalists were completing their takeover of the countryside, with the reorganization of properties into large estates, the development of irrigated meadows and livestock farming, the digging of canals both for irrigation and transport, the introduction of rice as a new crop, and even in many cases the disappearance of fallow land, with continuous rotation of cereals and forage crops. It was in fact in Lombardy that 'high farming' – later to be developed in the Netherlands and transferred with celebrated results to England, first saw the light.[41]

Hence the question put by our informant and guide Renato Zangheri: why did this substantial transformation of both the industry and the countryside of Milan and Lombardy come to nothing? Why did it not lead to an industrial revolution? Neither the infant technology of the time nor the lack of energy supplies seems an adequate explanation. 'The English industrial revolution was not based on any scientific or technical progress not already available in the sixteenth century.'[42] Carlo Poni was astonished to discover the sophistication of the hydraulic machines used in Italy to throw, spin and mill silk, with several mechanical processes and rows of spindles all turned by a single water-wheeel.[43] Lynn White has argued that even before Leonardo da Vinci, Europe had already invented the whole range of mechanical devices which would actually be developed during the next four hundred years, that is until electrical energy, as and when the need was felt for them.[44] As he puts it: 'a new device merely opens a door; it does not compel anyone to enter'.[45] Quite so. But why did the exceptional conditions which were combined in fifteenth-century Milan fail to create any

FILATOIO DA AQVA. .I.

Early machines in Italy: here are two designs for a *filatoio* for producing *organzine* (thrown silk) on the Bolognese model, one dating from 1607 (on the left), the other from 1833. *Organzine* is a double, triple or quadruple thread of thrown silk used as a warp. The first silk-mill to be set up in England in 1716–17, ' a true factory, the first in England', was copied by the English after two years of industrial espionage in Italy. An almost identical model had been working since the early seventeenth century in Bologna, the city of its invention (cf. the work of C. Poni). Totally mechanized – the workers had only to watch it and reconnect the threads that broke – the machine was made up of an internal turning mechanism, the *lanterna* (bottom left) activated by a water-wheel, and surrounded by a fixed frame (top left) holding a very large number of spindles, bobbins and winders. If mechanization had been the only cause of the industrial revolution, Italy would have got there first. On the right is a *filatoio* of 1833. From P. Negri, *Manuale practico per la stima delle case et degli opisizi idrauliti*, Bologna, 1833.

such need or demand? Why did the Milanese revolution crumble instead of thrive?

The available historical data does not really provide enough evidence to answer this question. We are reduced to conjecture. In the first place, Milan did not have access to any large national market. And the profits from land did not outlast the first wave of speculation. The prosperity of the first industrial entrepreneurs, if we are to believe Gino Barbieri[46] and Gemma Miani, was only on a small scale, creating a sort of modest capitalist class. But how strong an argument is that? After all, the first cotton magnates often had very humble beginnings. Was it not rather Milan's misfortune to be so close to Venice, yet so far from sharing Venice's dominant position? And not to be a port, with access to the Mediterranean and the international export trade, free to experiment and take risks? Is the failure of Milan's 'industrial revolution' perhaps proof that an industrial revolution, as a total phenomenon, cannot be built up entirely from within, simply by the harmonious development of the various sectors of the economy; that it must also be based on command of external markets – the *sine qua non* of success? In the fifteenth century, as we have seen, this commanding position was occupied by Venice, and to some extent (for Spanish trade) by Genoa.

John U. Nef and the first British industrial revolution, 1560-1640

The industrial expansion which took place in England between 1540 and 1640 was much more clear-cut and thorough-going than the early experiences either of Italy or Germany. In mid-sixteenth century, the British Isles were still, industrially speaking, far behind Italy, Spain and the Netherlands, Germany and France. A hundred years later, the situation had been miraculously reversed and the speed of the transformation had been so fast that there is no parallel before the equivalent wave of change in the late eighteenth and early nineteenth century, in other words, *the* industrial revolution. By the eve of the Civil War (1642) England had become the leading industrial nation in Europe and was to remain so. It is this 'first industrial revolution' to which John U. Nef drew attention in his article which caused a sensation when it was originally published in 1934 and has lost none of its analytic force today.[47]

But why did this happen in England, when all the major innovations of the period – I am thinking for example of the blast furnaces, the various apparatus used for underground mining: tunnels, ventilation systems, pumps and winding gear – were all borrowings, demonstrated to the English by German miners hired for the purpose? Why England, when it was the craftsmen and workers of more technically advanced countries – Germany, the Netherlands, but also Italy (for glass) and France (wool and silk textiles) – who contributed the necessary techniques and skills for the establishment of a series of industries quite new to Britain – paper-mills, powder-mills, glass, mirrors, cannon-founding, alum and copperas (green vitriol), sugar refining, saltpetre, and so on?

The remarkable thing is that when these industries did arrive, England should have developed them on a scale hitherto unknown: the growing size of firms, the dimensions of the buildings, the rising numbers of workers, soon running into tens or even hundreds, the comparatively high level of investment which was reaching thousands of pounds, whereas the *annual* wage of a worker was only about £5 – all these were completely new and indicate how extraordinary was the expansion of English industry in this period.

On the other hand, the decisive feature of this revolution – a completely home-grown one so to speak – was the increasing dependence on coal, which had become a major element in the English economy. Not as it happened by deliberate choice, but in order to meet a visible deficiency. Wood had become increasingly scarce in England and was costing high prices by mid-sixteenth century; scarcity and expense dictated the move to coal. Similarly, the sluggish flow of most English rivers, which had to be raised by dams and diverted by canals to work overshot wheels, made hydraulic energy much more expensive here than in continental Europe and would eventually provide an incentive to research into the power of steam, or so John Nef suggests.

So England, unlike France or the Netherlands, went in for coal-mining on a grand scale, beginning with the Newcastle coalfields and the many local seams. Mines which had previously been worked open-cast by a part-time rural labour force now began to operate continuously; pits were dug up to 40 or 100 metres deep. From about 35,000 tons in 1560, output had risen to 200,000 tons by the beginning of the seventeenth century.[48] Wagons running on rails carried the coal from the pithead to the docks: specialized ships, in ever-increasing numbers were taking it all over England and even to Europe, by the end of the century. Coal was already being regarded as a form of national wealth:

> England's a perfect world, hath Indies too,
> Correct your maps, Newcastle is Peru

as an English poet put it in 1650.[49] The replacement of charcoal by coal not only made it possible to heat domestic interiors – bringing a sinister pall of smoke to London; it also affected industry which had however to learn to adapt to the new fuel and devise new expedients, in particular to protect the matter being processed from the sulphurous fumes of the burning coals. One way and another, coal was introduced to glassmaking, to breweries, brick-works, alum manufacture, sugar refineries and the industrial evaporation of sea-salt. In every case, this meant a concentration of the workforce and inevitably of capital. Manufacturing industry was born; with it came the great workshops and their alarming din which sometimes proceeded uninterrupted day and night, and their throngs of workers who, in a world used to artisans, were remarkable both for their large numbers and as a rule for their lack of skill. One of the farmers of the 'alum houses' built during the reign of James I on the Yorkshire coast and each employing about sixty workers, explained in 1619 that the manufacture of alum was a 'distracted worke in severall places, and of sundry partes not possible to bee performed by anie one man nor by a fewe. But by a multitude of the baser sort of whom the most part are idle, careless and false in their labour'.[50]

One of the earliest pictures (1750) of an English 'railway': this one was built by Ralph Allen (1694–1764) and operated by gravity, carrying blocks of stone from the hills above Bath down to the wharves on the river Avon which ran through the town. In the background can be seen Prior Park, the luxurious dwelling of Allen himself. Fashionable ladies and gentlemen have come to admire the sight. (Mary Evans Picture Library.)

Technically then, with larger factories and the widespread use of coal, England was certainly innovating in the industrial sector. But what really gave the impetus to industry and probably to innovation as well, was the substantial enlargement of the domestic market, for two complementary reasons. The first was rapid population growth – estimated at 60% in the course of the sixteenth century.[51] At the same time there was a large rise in agricultural incomes, which turned many peasants into consumers of industrial products. To meet demand from the growing population and especially from the visibly-expanding towns, agricultural output was increased in several ways – by the reclamation of land, by enclosures at the expense of commons and grazing, by crop specialization – but without any truly revolutionary measures to increase productivity or the fertility of the soil. These would only begin to appear after 1640 and then only very gradually until 1690.[52] Agricultural output thus began to lag somewhat behind demographic expansion as is proved by an agricultural price rise much greater overall than the industrial price rise.[53] The result was a visible increase in prosperity in the countryside. This was the age of the 'great rebuilding' as rural dwellings were restored, improved and enlarged, as upper storeys replaced attics, windows were glazed, chimneys were built for burning domestic coal. Inventories compiled after death tell us of a new-found affluence reflected in furniture, linen, hangings, pewter vessels. This domestic demand undoubtedly stimulated industry, trade and imports.

Promising though it appeared, this lively burst of industrialization did not carry all before it. Some important sectors continued to lag behind.

In metallurgy for instance, the blast furnace on the modern German model, a heavy user of fuel, by no means ousted all the bloomeries, old-fashioned furnaces some of which were still in operation in 1650 – and in any case even the blast furnaces continued to burn charcoal. Only in 1709 did the first coke-fuelled blast furnace appear – and this remained unique of its kind for another forty years. Several explanations have been suggested for this by T. S. Ashton and others, but Charles Hyde's conclusion in his recent book[54] seems to me to be irrefutable: if coke only replaced charcoal in about 1750, it was simply because until then production costs favoured the latter.[55] What was more, even after the adoption of coke, English metallurgy long remained inferior, both in quality and quantity to that of Russia, Sweden or France.[56] And while light metal industries (cutlery, nail-making, tools, etc.) grew steadily from mid-sixteenth century, they were using imported Swedish steel.

Another backward sector was the cloth industry, now faced with a long crisis in foreign demand which made it necessary to undergo some painful adjustments while output remained virtually stationary from 1560 to the end of the seventeenth century.[57] Still largely a rural cottage industry, cloth production was increasingly brought within the putting-out system. Whereas in the sixteenth century this industry alone had been responsible for 90% of English exports, and the figure was still 75% in 1660, by the end of the century it had fallen to only 50%.[58]

But these problems cannot explain the stagnation that set in in England after the 1640s: while the economy did not decline, neither did it progress. The population had stopped rising, agriculture was producing more and better quality crops; it was investing for the future – but rural incomes had fallen with prices; industry was ticking over but no longer innovating, at least not until 1680 or so.[59] If this standstill had been confined to England, one might perhaps have put it down to the effects of the Civil War which began in 1642 and brought considerable disruption; or one could point to the still inadequate nature of the national market, or England's comparatively poor position in the European world-economy, in which Holland was still the dominant economic power. But England was by no means alone in this experience – one that was undoubtedly shared by all the north European countries which had been progressing alongside her and were now simultaneously retreating. The 'seventeenth-century crisis' might strike at different times, but it left its mark everywhere.

To return to England however, John U. Nef's own diagnosis is that while the industrial advance certainly slowed down there after 1642, it did not collapse; there was no slipping backward either.[60] What may in fact have happened, and we shall return to this point apropos E. L. Jones's analysis, was that the seventeenth-century crisis, like all periods of demographic slowdown, brought some increase in per capita incomes and a transformation of agriculture, which had repercussions on industry too. By taking Nef's arguments further, we might say that the English industrial revolution of the eighteenth century had already begun in the sixteenth and was simply making progress by stages. It is an explanation from which some lessons may be drawn.

But could not the same be said of the whole of Europe, where since at least the eleventh century, a series of linked and in a sense cumulative transformations had been experienced? Every region in turn sooner or later underwent a burst of pre-industrial growth, with the accompanying features one could expect, particularly in agriculture. Industrialization was in a sense endemic throughout the continent. Outstanding and important as Britain's role was in this story, Britain was by no means the sole initiator and inventor of the industrial revolution accomplished on her soil. This explains why that revolution had scarcely appeared, let alone achieved its decisive successes, before it was spreading unopposed to nearby Europe, where it scored a series of comparatively easy triumphs, encountering none of the obstacles which so many under-developed countries have met in the twentieth century.

The industrial revolution in Britain, sector by sector

Britain's success after 1750 is the dazzling burst of light on which all else converges. But we should guard against illusion: this display of fireworks brings us to the heart of our difficulties, as R.M. Hartwell has explained in his challenging book, *The Industrial Revolution and Economic Growth* (1971) – a book which is in fact the sum of all the other books on the topic, a platform from which the writer speaks through the ideas of every other writer, leading us into a huge museum where a series of the most varied and discordant pictures have been placed carefully side by side on the wall. The choice is up to us. Who would not be bewildered by the hundredth debate on this subject?

It is true – and in a way reassuring – that at a conference of specialists on the industrial revolution arranged by the journal *Past and Present* in April 1960[61] agreement turned out to be impossible. And consensus proved equally elusive at the Lyon colloquium of 1970[62] on the same topic, where Pierre Vilar[63] perhaps put his finger on the problem when he confessed frankly that having studied the industrial revolution which transformed Catalonia so rapidly in the eighteenth and nineteenth centuries, he had been unable to come up with any model that entirely satisfied him. The problem was brought no nearer solution when at the same conference the expression *industrial revolution* was replaced by *industrialization*, a more neutral term but in the end equally complex. 'I admit that I am still completely in the dark about what industrialization means', said Jacques Bertin on this occasion. 'Does it mean railways? cotton? coal? metals? gas-lighting? white bread?'[64] I would reply that the list is if anything too short: industrialization, like the industrial revolution, means everything – society, economy, political structures, public opinion, and the rest. The most ambitious kind of history cannot embrace it, certainly not in any simple, all-purpose, peremptory definition. In other words, the industrial revolution which was to throw first Britain then the whole world into upheaval, was never at any stage in its career a neatly-definable phenomenon, a combination of given problems occurring in a given area at a given time.

This is why I do not really accept – though I am obliged in turn to adopt it – the approach which tries to explain the industrial revolution sector by sector. Faced with what looks like an inextricable mass of difficulties, historians have indeed proceeded by Cartesian methods, dividing to understand. They have identified a series of headings – agriculture, demography, technology, commerce, transport, etc. – all of which did indeed undergo major change; but the danger of this approach is of making them look like separate stages, affected one after another and thus forming a flight of steps towards growth. This fragmented model comes straight from the most traditional kind of political economy. It is perhaps to be regretted that the advocates of retrospective economics have not designed another model better suited to guide the steps of historical research, that they have not defined another set of indicators, landmarks and quotients which would tell us how the different sectors operated *in relation to each other synchronically*, whether they furthered each other's progress or on the contrary acted as brakes or bottlenecks for rival sectors. If we could take a series of synchronic sections at acceptable chronological intervals, we might conceivably be able to form a more accurate perception of the development of industrial growth. But this requires agreement beforehand between historians on an appropriate research model, which could then be applied to different places and different periods.

Until then we can only continue to use the classifications which have stood the test of time in a number of remarkable studies, too numerous for all of them to be listed. Within the 'industrial revolution' as a whole, they have identified a series of individual revolutions – in agriculture, demography, inland transport, technology, trade and industry. Our first step will be to try to trace these changes from which no sector was actually immune. It may seem a little tedious to follow such a well-worn path of exposition, but there are times when it is necessary.

British agriculture – a crucial factor

Agriculture usually heads the list and rightly so. But of all the problems confronting us, this is by far the most taxing. For we are faced here with a long, seemingly never-ending process, not one revolution but a series of revolutions, changes, developments, breaks and revivals forming a chain down the ages. If we were to trace it from end to end, we could easily go back to the thirteenth century and the first attempts at liming and marling the soil, experiments with different strains of wheat or oats, or the simplest forms of crop rotation. Our task however is neither to find the source nor to plot the course of this river, but to examine how it flows into the sea; we do not want to study all the ramifications of the rural history of Britain, simply to assess its contribution to the great ocean of the industrial revolution. Was agriculture an integral part of this mighty achievement?

To ask this question is to be exposed to a thousand contradictory replies. Some historians would answer yes, some no, and some would hesitate to pronounce either way. M. W. Flinn writes: 'It must remain extremely doubtful whether the agricultural developments themselves would be sufficient to have played more than a modest part in stimulating an industrial revolution'.[65] More generally, H. J. Habbakuk argues that 'This increase in agricultural output is not to be regarded as a pre-condition of growth, if only because it normally accompanied rather than preceded the acceleration of growth';[66] while Paul Bairoch, who is anxious to identify and rank the strategic variables of the English industrial revolution, argues that the takeoff in agriculture was 'the major pump-priming factor', the trigger for everything else.[67] E.L. Jones is even more categorical: from a comparative study of the history of the countries which succeeded in industrializing, he suggests that the primary condition of success was to have 'agricultural output rising faster than the population'.[68] The 'critical period' in Britain, he argues was between 1650 and 1750.

This thesis runs counter to those arguments which essentially define the agricultural revolution in terms of mechanical improvements and therefore regard it as following rather than preceding the cotton revolution or even the railway revolution. It is certainly the case that industrial and mechanized equipment played only a negligible part in agricultural life until the middle of the nineteenth century. The seed-drill described by Jethro Tull in 1733[69] for instance was only sparingly used even in progressive east Norfolk, the home of Townshend and Coke; elsewhere it appeared only in the nineteenth century.[70] The horse-powered threshing machine, invented in Scotland in about 1780, followed after some delay by the steam engine, certainly did not spread very fast. Similarly the triangular or Rotherham plough[71] which made it possible for one man to plough with only two horses (as distinct from the rectangular plough drawn by six or eight oxen with a driver and a ploughman) though patented in 1731, was not used very much before 1870.[72] It has even been calculated that new crops

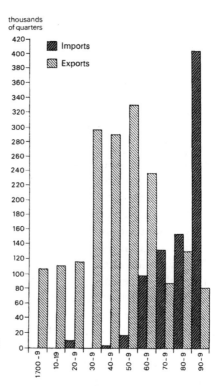

thousands
of quarters

■ Imports

▨ Exports

50 BRITISH IMPORTS AND EXPORTS OF GRAIN AND FLOUR

By and large, England consumed her own grain until about 1760; between 1730 and 1765 she was exporting on a considerable scale for the time (2% of total output in 1750, that is 330,000 quarters out of a total production of 15 million); imports began in 1760 and went on rising although output was 19 million quarters in 1800 and 25 by 1820. (From P. Mathias, *The First Industrial Nation*, 1969, p. 70.)

such as the famous turnip which moved from kitchen garden to field in the seventeenth century, multiplied at the rate of only about a thousand plants a year from its point of introduction. And until 1830 the flail, sickle and scythe remained the basic implements on English farms.[73] So it must be said that the progress in English agriculture *before the industrial revolution*, of which there is incontrovertible evidence[74] – came not so much from machines or wonder crops as from new methods of land use; new timetables for ploughing; new forms of crop rotation which eliminated fallow and encouraged grazing, a useful source of fertilizer and therefore a remedy for soil exhaustion; attention to new strains of crops; selective breeding of sheep and cattle; specialized farming for higher yields – all with results which varied according to region, to natural conditions and to the constraints of the market which were never the same in two places. The resulting system was what would in the nineteenth century be called *high farming*, 'an extremely difficult art' as a later observer was to write, 'based on long observation'. It consisted of:

enclosed fields, divided by frequent ploughing, fertilized with abundant, good-quality manure and sowed in turn with plants that either exhaust or enrich the soil, without leaving any fallow ... by alternating cereals, plants with tap roots which derive their sustenance from a great depth and give nothing to the soil, and herbaceous plants with creeping roots which enrich the soil and draw sustenance from the surface.[75]

This transformation, which would prove to be a vital one, took place after 1650, at a time when demographic pressure had eased, when the population was increasing only slowly if at all (possibly as a result of conscious efforts to postpone the age of marriage). Whatever the reason, demographic pressure was not as great. Is it not paradoxical therefore that it was precisely at this moment when demand was lower and the price of grain was falling that both output and productivity increased and that innovation spread? This apparent paradox can be quite easily explained however in the light of E.L. Jones's analysis.[76] Demand for cereals remained virtually the same, but with the expansion of the towns and the phenomenal growth of London, demand for meat went up; animal farming became more profitable than arable and therefore tended to take its place. Consequently, farmers went over to forage crops already in existence such as clover, sainfoin, turnips, and to new methods of crop rotation. The key to the paradox is that the massive expansion of livestock, both intended and achieved, had as its side-effect an increase in the quantity of manure, which in turn sent up the yields of cereals like wheat and barley included in the normal rotation. Thus there occurred what Jones calls 'a virtuous circle' (by contrast with a vicious circle) according to which the low price of cereals encouraged farmers to concentrate on livestock, therefore to plant more forage crops; which brought about a rapid rise in the head of livestock especially sheep, and this in turn improved cereal yields. English grain output increased automatically, effortlessly so to speak, to the point of exceeding home demand. Hence the fall in the price of cereals which were increasingly exported until 1760. E.A. Wrigley has calculated that the rise in agricultural *productivity* between 1650 and 1750 was at least 13%.[77]

But high farming had a further consequence. Since forage crops do best on light and sandy soils, these became the most productive land in England. Land previously regarded as poor, fit only for grazing sheep, was put under crops. Heavy clayey soils by contrast, previously regarded as the richest for cereal-growing, and unsuitable for forage crops, were hit by the low prices created by higher yields in rival regions. They went out of cultivation and complaints began to be heard. In the Midlands in the 1680s, a call went up for nothing less than a law to stop the land improvements in the south of England: in Buckinghamshire, the owners of clayey soils in the vale of Aylesbury demanded that clover be a prohibited crop.[78]

Various regions discriminated against by neighbouring success tried livestock instead, especially draft animals or, if they were near London dairy farming. But it was more frequent for agricultural decline to be compensated for by an increase in artisan production. This explains why the years after 1650, when John U. Nef detects a slowing-down in the *large-scale* industry which had developed over the previous century, saw vigorous expansion in *cottage industry*, within the ancient but still effective framework of the putting-out system. In the late seventeenth and early eighteenth centuries, lace-making developed in east

A brickworks in the English countryside. The smoke pouring from chimneys like these was already being accused of polluting the air in the eighteenth century. (Photo Batsford.)

Devon, and to an even greater extent in the counties of Bedford, Buckingham and Northampton; straw-plaiting for hats spread from Hertfordshire to Bedfordshire; nailing was making headway in the countryside round Birmingham; there was paper-making in the Mendips where there were over 200 paper-mills in 1712, many of them in old cornmills; and hosiery in the counties of Leicestershire, Derbyshire and Nottingham.[79]

The 'seventeenth-century crisis' in England thus corresponded to a fairly slow and uneven development of the countryside, which nevertheless favoured the coming industrial revolution on two counts: it encouraged the establishment of a high-yield agriculture which would be capable, by holding grain back from export, of meeting the sudden demographic explosion after the 1750s: and in the poorer regions it was responsible for the rise of cottage industries with a proletariat more or less accustomed to craft working, in short a 'trained and malleable' workforce, ready to meet the demand from large-scale urban industry when this appeared in the late eighteenth century. It was on this reserve labour force that the industrial revolution would draw, rather than on the strictly agricultural workforce which maintained its previous levels, contrary to assumptions made by commentators from Marx to the present day.

If things happened very differently on the European continent, it was probably because the very original development of English agriculture was conceivable only within a context of large land holdings: a large estate for those days was about 200 acres. For such estates to become commonplace, the tenacious seigniorial regime had to be destroyed and adapted, and the archaic relationships between tenant and landlord transformed – something that had long been accomplished in England by the time the industrial revolution occurred. The big landowner[80] had become a *rentier*, who regarded his estate as a sign of social status, but also as a going concern, which it was in his interest to rent out to efficient tenant-farmers (traditionally, the landowner even made good the losses of the tenant in a bad year). A prosperous estate, farmed out at a good rent, moreover guaranteed its owner easy credit, perhaps for investment elsewhere, for landowners were frequently also industrial or mining entrepreneurs. As for the farmer, he was assured of his leasehold by convention, if not by law; he could thus safely invest money in the farm[81] and run it by the rules of the market and capitalist management. The major feature of this new order was the rise of the farmer, a genuine entrepreneur. Farmers are 'truly respectable people', said a French observer. 'Although they put their hands to the plough, in their farm or lodging, they are equal to the bourgeoisie of the towns.'[82] This was in 1819, but even three-quarters of a century earlier in 1745, a visiting Frenchman described the English farmer as a peasant 'who enjoys an abundance of all the commodities of life'; his farmhand 'takes tea before taking up the plough'. He was equally impressed by the 'countryman who wears a frock-coat in winter', with a wife and daughter so elegantly dressed that they might be mistaken for 'shepherdesses in a novel',[83] an impression certainly not contradicted by a nice little engraving of the seventeenth century, claiming to represent a 'paisants woman' riding to market on horseback, with a basket of eggs at her side, but shod and hatted like a woman of property.

The French observer, Maurice Rubichon, struck by the contrast between the rural landscape in England and France, described the British agricultural system at length. The landed gentry – two or three families in each of the 10,000 parishes of England, he estimated[84] – owned roughly a third of the parish's land, divided up into large farms worked by tenant farmers; another third was owned by yeoman, small (or not so small) independent proprietors, while the peasants had little plots and the right to the use of the common land which made up the last third of the cultivated area. Rubichon's estimates are probably very approximate. What does seem certain is that everything combined to increase further the concentration of landed property even before the eighteenth century: the small peasant farmer was more or less condemned either to extend his holding and survive, or to lose it one day and become a wage-labourer. This tendency, combined with the enclosures which eliminated common land and encouraged concentration, meant that large estates, more adaptable and profitable, were gradually extended, benefiting the landed gentry, the rich yeomen and the tenant farmers. This was the direct opposite of what happened in France, where the 'feudal' regime collapsed literally overnight on 4 August 1789, when the capitalist concentration of land was only just beginning; from now on the land was

English peasant woman on her way to market. Illustration from a manuscript of 1623-5. (British Library.)

irremediably divided among many peasant and bourgeois proprietors. Maurice Rubichon, an unconditional admirer of the English rural order, inveighed against the subdivision of France which 'was already carved up into 25 million plots before the Revolution', and now 'the figure is 115 million'.[85] Can this all be laid at the door of the *Code Napoléon*, which provided for equal inheritance? Was England preserved from fragmentation only by the survival of primogeniture among the landed gentry? Or was the establishment of capitalist farming the crucial factor?

Finally in our estimate of the role played by agriculture in the industrial revolution, we should not forget that the English countryside had from a very early date been integrated into the island's national market; as a component part of this network, English farms managed until the early nineteenth century, with a few exceptions, to feed the population of the towns and industrial conurbations; they were the essential component in a domestic market which provided the initial natural clientèle for English industry in its early days. The country's expanding agriculture was the iron industry's leading customer. Farm implements – horse-shoes, plough-shares, scythes, sickles, threshing machines, harrows, rollers – all required considerable quantities of iron; in 1780, this amounted to a demand for about 200 or 300,000 tons a year.[86] These figures cannot be accepted as they stand for the first part of the eighteenth century which is the particular focus of our inquiry, but if during that period iron imports from Sweden and Russia were rising steadily, was this not because the English domestic iron industry had insufficient capacity to meet the increasing demand largely accounted for by agriculture? And does that not suggest that agriculture was on the move before the development of industry?

The demographic revival

During the eighteenth century, the population increased in England as it increased throughout Europe and the entire world: 5,835,000 in 1700; just over 6 million in 1730; 6,665,000 in 1760. Then the movement accelerated: 8,216,000 in 1790; 12 million in 1820; almost 18 million in 1850.[87] Mortality rates fell from 33·7% to 27% in 1800 and 21% for the decade 1811-21, while the birth rate reached the record level of 37% or even higher. The statistics quoted vary somewhat from author to author, but they all tell much the same story.[88]

The massive biological increase meant more intensive cultivation of the countryside, the growth of all the towns, and the record expansion of the industrial conurbations. Historical demographers have identified three reference groups of English counties which in 1701 had comparable population figures.[89] By 1831, all three had expanded in absolute terms, but now the industrial counties represented 45% of the population as compared to a third in 1701; while the agricultural counties now contained only 26% of total population as compared to 33%. Some counties had progressed at a quite spectacular rate: the population of Northumberland and Durham had doubled, while that of Lancashire, Staffordshire and Warwickshire had tripled.[90] No doubt is therefore possible: industrialization unquestionably played a leading role in the rise of the English population. Detailed studies bear out this impression. If we take the single age-group 17 to 30, we find that in industrial Lancashire in 1800, 40% of this age group were married as compared to 19% in the agricultural areas of the county at the same time. So industrial employment also appears to have encouraged early marriage, thus accelerating demographic advance.

A soot-blackened England was coming into being, with its factory towns and workers' terraces. It was certainly no Merrie England. Like many other travellers, Alexis de Tocqueville described it in his travel journal: in July 1835[91] he stayed in Birmingham and went on to Manchester. These were enormous, still unfinished cities, thrown up quickly and badly, without any thought of planning; but they were full of life. The necklace of dense, bustling urban concentrations – Leeds, Sheffield, Birmingham, Manchester, Liverpool – were the heart and soul of the English industrial revolution. If Birmingham was still quite human, Manchester already seemed a vision of hell. Its population had increased tenfold between 1760 and 1830, rising from 17,000 to 180,000 inhabitants.[92] Because of land shortage, the factories perched on its hills had five, six or even twelve storeys. Mansions and workers' two-up-two-downs sprawled all over the town, higgledy-piggledy. There were puddles and mud everywhere: for every paved street, there were ten dirty lanes. Men, women and children herded into squalid housing – up to 15 or 16 people might be crammed into a single basement; the 50,000 Irish immigrants were part of a typically wretched sub-proletariat. The same was true of Liverpool, where Tocqueville observed 'sixty thousand Irish Catholics', adding 'the misery is almost as great as in Manchester, but it is concealed'. So in all these cities spawned by the industrial revolution, even the massive rise in the English-born population was not always enough to provide the necessary mass of workers; immigrants had to come to the rescue from Wales, Scotland and especially Ireland. And since mechanization had multiplied the number of unskilled tasks at all the key points of industrial development, calls were made on the labour of women and children, like immigrants a docile and underpaid workforce.

So the industrial revolution brought together all the manpower it required – whether for manual work or for the 'tertiary sector' where the new age was already creating jobs. All successful industry, as Ernest Labrousse[93] has pointed out, generates its own bureaucracy, and so it was in England. A further indicator of the abundance of the labour supply was the enormous number of domestic servants, probably reflecting a long-standing situation, but one which the industrial revolution did not mitigate, indeed the opposite. At the beginning of the nineteenth century, domestic servants made up over 15% of the population of London.

After 1750 then, England had no labour shortage, indeed she had so many children she hardly knew what to do. Were they a burden or on the contrary a source of energy? Consequence or cause? That these workers were useful, indeed indispensable, is obvious: they provided the necessary human dimension of the industrial revolution. Without these thousands or millions of people, nothing would have been possible. But that is not the point: we need to establish a correlation. The population explosion and the wave of industrialization were two mighty processes taking place side by side. But did one determine the other? Unfortunately both of them are very imperfectly recorded in the available documents. The population history of England has to be reconstituted from incomplete parish records. Any proposition we may make is subject to caution and liable to be overturned by future research when the enormous labour of counting and checking is tackled. Similarly, can we be really sure we know enough to trace an accurate graph of industrialization, broadly identifiable with the output curve? 'It seems reasonable to suppose', Phyllis Deane writes, 'that without the growth of output dating from the 1740s, the associated growth in population would eventually have been checked by a rise in the death rate due to declining standards of living.'[94] 1740 is certainly, on the graph in Figure 51, the

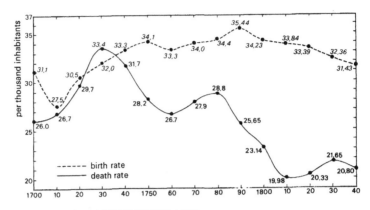

51 BIRTH AND DEATH RATES IN ENGLAND
These two curves are based on estimates we will assume to be valid, though they vary from author to author. The difference between them shows the rise in the English population after the 1730s. (From G.M. Trevelyan, *English Social History*, 1942, p. 361.)

point at which the birth rate and the mortality rate diverge: from this point on, births exceeded deaths. If true, this simple observation is proof in itself that the demographic revolution *followed* the rise of industry and was, in very large measure, created by it.

Technology: a necessary but probably not sufficient condition

If there is one factor which has lost ground as a key explanation of the industrial revolution, it is technology. Marx believed it was crucial; recent historiography has put forward some solid arguments against seeing it as a *primum mobile* or even a pump-primer, to use Paul Bairoch's expression. And yet inventions often occur before industrial capacity – but for that very reason they may often occur in a vacuum. The efficient application of technology lags, by definition, behind the general movement of the economy; it has to wait to be called on, sometimes several times, to meet a precise and persistent demand.

In textiles for instance, the two major processes are spinning and weaving. In the seventeenth century, one weaver required the services of seven or eight spinners (or rather spinsters, since they were usually women). Logically therefore it was in spinning, the operation requiring the greatest workforce, that technical innovation was needed. Nevertheless it was the loom which in 1730 saw the first labour-saving device, Kay's flying shuttle. This elementary invention – the shuttle was launched by a spring and manoeuvred by hand – which speeded up the weaving process, did not come into widespread use until after 1760 – possibly because it was precisely in the 1760s that three new inventions to speed up *spinning* appeared and were very quickly adopted: the spinning jenny in 1765 in a simple version within the means of cottage industry; Arkright's water-frame (1769); and ten years later, Crompton's 'mule', so-called because it combined the characteristics of the other two machines.[95] From now on, spinning became ten times more productive, and increased quantities of imported raw cotton began arriving from the West Indies, the East Indies and before long the southern colonies in America. All the same the rate of spinning continued to limp along behind the speed of weaving until the 1840s. Even when the steam-engine revolutionized spinning in about 1800, handloom weavers managed to keep pace, the number of weavers increased and their wages rose. The handloom was not in the end displaced until after the Napoleonic Wars and then only slowly, despite the technical improvement introduced by the Roberts power-looms in about 1825. The reason was that until about 1840 it was neither essential nor indeed advantageous (given the sharp drop in weavers' wages resulting from competition from machines and the unemployed) to replace it with the power-loom.[96]

Paul Bairoch is therefore right when he says: 'During the first decades of the industrial revolution, technology was to a much greater extent a factor governed *by* the economy than one governing the economy'. Innovations were quite clearly dependent on the state of the market: they were introduced only when they met persistent demand from consumers. In the case of the English domestic market, average annual consumption of cotton was 1,700,000 pounds in the period 1737-40; 2,100,000 in 1741-9; 2,800,000 pounds in 1751-60; and 3,000,000 pounds in 1761-70. And 'these were small quantities compared to what England was consuming twenty years later': in 1769 (before mechanization) cotton consumption per head was 300 grammes – enough to 'allow the production of one shirt per year per inhabitant'.[97] But this may in fact have been a critical threshold, since in 1804-7, when the same level was reached in France, mechanization of the cotton industry began there too.

If demand stimulated invention however, it was itself dependent on price levels. England really did have from the early eighteenth century, a popular market ready to buy up large amounts of Indian cottons precisely because they were cheap. Defoe, when poking fun at the extravagances of the fashion for printed cottons, points out that chambermaids were wearing these imported fabrics before their mistresses. This domestic market did, it is true, diminish as the craze for printed cottons sent the price up, but the real reason was the authoritarian clamp-down on imports of Indian cottons to England, except for re-export (a step incidentally which indicates how booming the market was). This being so, it may have been not so much pressure of English demand as competitive Indian prices, K.N. Chaudhuri suggests,[98] which stimulated technical inventions. The latter in any case occurred, significantly, in cotton and not in the national industry for which there was the highest demand from consumers, namely wool or even linen. The woollen industry was not mechanized until much later.

The same was true of the English metal industry: the effect of prices on innovation was perhaps as great or even greater than that of demand alone. We have already noted that coke-smelting, a technique invented by Abraham Darby, was practised in his own blast furnaces in Coalbrookdale in Shropshire as early as 1709, but that no other entrepreneur followed his example until the middle of the century. Even in 1775, 45% of the output of pig-iron was being produced by charcoal-fired furnaces.[99] Paul Bairoch attributes the belated success of the process to increasing pressure of demand, which is certainly the case.[100] But Charles Hyde has clearly explained the circumstances surrounding the late introduction of coke-smelting. Why was this method so disdained for the forty years before 1750, by the seventy-odd blast furnaces then operating in England? Why were at least eighteen furnaces built between 1720 and 1750 using the old process?[101] Simply because for one thing these enterprises were very profitable, their high selling prices being protected by heavy duties imposed on imported Swedish steel, by the absence of regional competition on account of prohibitive transport costs, and by a prosperous export trade in finished iron products.[102] Secondly, because production costs were raised clearly by the use of coke (about

The blast furnaces in Coalbrookdale, Shropshire, where Abraham Darby was the first industrialist to use coke as a fuel in England in 1709. Note however on this 1758 engraving, that there are on the banks of the Severn (bottom right) four charcoal-burning ovens. In the foreground, a large metal cylinder produced on the spot is being transported in a horse-drawn wagon. Engraving by Perry and Smith, 1758. (Armand Colin Picture Library.)

£2 per ton) and the cast-iron thus produced, being more difficult to work was not particularly tempting to the steel-masters if its price was no lower than the market price.[103]

Why then did things change after 1750, without any new technical inventions, when in a period of twenty years, twenty-seven coke-fired blast-furnaces were built and twenty-five of the old models were closed down? Why did the steel-masters from now on take far more coke-smelted pig-iron? The answer is that increased demand for ferrous metals sent the price of charcoal sharply up (and this represented about half the cost of producing pig-iron),[104] while after the 1730s, coke-smelting benefited from a drop in coal prices. So that the situation was reversed: in about 1760, the cost price of charcoal-fired smelting was about £2 per ton greater than that of iron produced by the rival method. This being so, one wonders yet again why the old procedure survived so long – still accounting for about half total ouput in 1775. Probably the cause was the phenomenal rise in demand which paradoxically protected the lame duck. Demand was so great that prices remained high, and producers using coke did not bother to drop their prices far enough to eliminate their competitors – until about 1775, after which date the price difference between the different smelting methods increased and charcoal-burning was rapidly abandoned.

So it was not the introduction of steam power or Boulton and Watt's machine which brought about the adoption of coke as fuel for blast-furnaces. The die was already cast: with or without steam, coke would have triumphed in the end.[105] That is not to deny the role played by steam in the coming expansion of British metal-working: on one hand by operating the great power-bellows, it made it possible to increase the size of furnaces considerably; secondly, by freeing the steel industry from the need to be located near running water, it opened up new regions to metal-working, in particular the Black Country and Staffordshire, a region rich in iron ores and coal but short of fast-running rivers.

At about the same time as smelting, iron-refining was also liberated from the constraints and high prices of charcoal. Whereas in 1760, coal was only used in the ironworks in the final stages, for reheating and hammering previously refined iron, the practice of 'potting' introduced coal-firing into the entire refining process in about 1780. National ouput of iron bars went up 70% almost over-night.[106] Here again, Charles Hyde dispels some myths: it was not puddling, perfected after a difficult transitional period between 1784 and 1795, which drove charcoal from the iron-works: charcoal had already been eliminated.[107] Puddling was however, the crucial step in British metallurgy, a revolution both in *quantity* and *quality* which made British iron a world-beater – whereas it had previously been both quantitatively and qualitatively inferior.

Was it perhaps the improved *quality* of metal which was responsible for the fantastic triumph of the machine, not only in the factory but in everyday life too? The various incarnations of the steam-engine, as recorded in histories of technology, make striking reading. The earliest steam-engines used wood, brick,

Iron was beginning to replace wood by the last years of the eighteenth century in England. The bridge over the Wear, at Sunderland, built in 1796. (British Library.)

heavy structures and a few metal tubes; by 1820, they were a network of metal pipes. In the early days, the boiler and the various elements subject to pressure had posed many problems. Newcomen's engine had been built with the aim of remedying the deficiencies in Savery's older model, whose joints tended to explode under the pressure of the steam. But Newcomen's sturdy machine was built with brick supports and hearth, a wooden beam, copper boiler, a tin cylinder and lead piping. Only slowly and with difficulty would these costly materials be replaced with good quality iron. Watt himself was unable to construct an airtight cylinder in the Carron works in Scotland. Eventually it was Wilkinson who solved this problem, thanks to a boring-machine of his own invention.[108]

All such problems seemed to be disappearing by the first decades of the nineteenth century, at the same time as wood was being replaced by metal in mechanical construction and a number of small metal parts of all kinds were being manufactured, making it possible 'to vary the traditional structure of machines'.[109] In 1769, John Smeaton had built the first hydraulic wheel with a cast-iron axle for the Carron ironworks. It was a failure; the porous cast-iron did not stand up to sub-zero temperatures. The wide diameter wheels which had gone into operation on London Bridge the year before, 1768, were still made of wood – but in 1817, they were replaced by iron wheels.[110]

So while it was crucial in the long-term, metallurgy was not in the forefront of development in the eighteenth century. 'The iron industry', writes David Landes, 'has sometimes received more attention than it deserves in histories of the industrial revolution.'[111] This is probably fair comment, if one is a stickler for chronology. But the industrial revolution was a continuous process which had to invent itself as it went along, one that was on tenterhooks, so to speak, for the innovation that was bound to come. The total was always being added to. And it was always the most recent advance which gave meaning to those that had gone before. Coal, coke, cast-iron, iron and steel were all important in their own right. But all of them were as it were validated by steam – and steam itself took time to find its true place with Watt's rotary steam-engine, before the railway age. Emile Levasseur calculated[112] that in the year 1840, when the first phase of the industrial revolution was over, one CV (horse-power provided by steam) was the equivalent of twenty-one men, and that by such reckoning, France had at her disposal a million slaves of a special kind – a total destined to expand at an *exponential* rate: by 1880 this figure would be 98 million, that is two and a half times the real population of France at the time – so what must the figure have been for England?

Why the cotton revolution should not be underestimated

As the curtain-raiser for the English industrial revolution, the cotton boom has long been a favourite subject with historians – but that was in the past and fashions change. Recent research has tended to diminish the role of cotton: it is these days sometimes regarded as rather minor – after all the total volume of cotton production could be measured in millions of pounds, whereas coal was measured in millions of tons. Not until 1800 did the volume of raw cotton processed in England exceed 50 million pounds, that is 23,000 tons, which as E.A. Wrigley has pointed out, is only the equivalent of 'the annual output of 150 miners in a coal mine'.[113] Moreover, since innovations in the cotton industry are part of a long line of changes particular to the older textile industries (wool, cotton, silk and linen) beginning even earlier than the sixteenth century, everything suggests that the cotton industry was an *ancien régime* phenomenon, or, as John Hicks put it, that it was 'the last chapter in the development of the old industry rather than the first in the new, as it is usually described'. Might it not be possible at a pinch to imagine success on a comparable scale in fifteenth-century Florence?[114] It was in rather the same vein that Ernest Labrousse at the Lyon conference of October 1970, described Kay's famous flying shuttle, so much admired in its own day, as 'a child's clockwork toy'.[115] The cotton revolution was accomplished without any major technical innovations. The light weight and comparatively high value of cotton enabled it to use the existing means of transport and the modest power provided by waterwheels in the Pennine valleys and elsewhere. It was only towards the end of the boom that the cotton industry moved over to steam and away from the scarcity and unreliability of the available water-power, but the steam-engine was certainly not invented for this purpose. And last but not least, the textile industry had always called for more labour than capital.[116]

Should we then accept John Hicks's label – an *ancien régime* revolution? There was all the same a crucial difference between the cotton revolution and all previous revolutions: it succeeded. Far from slumping back into stagnation, the cotton boom ushered in a period of long-term growth, which eventually turned into 'continuous growth'. And 'in the first phase of British industrialization, no other industry was of comparable importance'.[117]

The real danger these days is of playing down the cotton revolution. It is true that its antecedents go back a very long way, since cotton was being processed in Europe as early as the twelfth century. But the yarn which could be extracted from the cotton bales imported from the Levant, while fine, was not very strong. So it could not be used alone, but only as the weft to be combined with a linen warp. This hybrid fabric was called fustian (*futaine, Barchent*) – the poor relation of the textile world, coarse in appearance, but rather dear – and what was more, difficult to launder. So when in the seventeenth century traders began importing to Europe not only the raw material but also woven and printed calicoes from India, beautiful all-cotton fabrics, cheap and often patterned in attractive colours which – unlike European dyes – stood up to washing, it was a real breakthrough. Shipped in by the Indies companies, aided and abetted by fashion, these fabrics soon conquered Europe. In order to protect their textile industry (not so much fustian as woollens) England in 1700 and 1720, and France as early as 1686, forbade the sale of Indian cottons on national soil. The cottons however, kept on coming, in theory for re-export, but a roaring contraband trade meant that they found their way everywhere, gladdening the eye and satisfying a long-lasting fashion which laughed at prohibitions, police raids and confiscations.

The cotton revolution, first in England, but very soon all over Europe, began by imitating Indian industry, went on to take revenge by catching up with it, and finally outstripped it. The aim was to produce fabrics of comparable quality at cheaper prices. The only way to do so was to introduce machines – which alone could effectively compete with Indian textile workers. But success did not come immediately. That had to wait for Arkwright's water-frame (1769) and Crompton's mule (1775–8) which made it possible to produce yarn as fine and strong as the Indian product, one that could be used for weaving fabric entirely out of cotton. From now on, the market for Indian cottons would be challenged by the developing English industry – and it was a very large market indeed, covering England and the British Isles, Europe (where various continental cotton industries were however soon putting up their own competition), the coast of Africa, where black slaves were exchanged for lengths of cotton, and the huge market of colonial America, not to mention Turkey and the Levant – or India itself. Cotton was always produced primarily for export: in 1800 it represented a quarter of all British exports; by 1850 this had risen to fifty per cent.[118]

All these foreign markets, conquered one after another, as additional or substitute outlets depending on circumstances, explain the extraordinary rise in output: 40 million yards in 1785; 2025 million yards in 1850.[119] At the same time, the price of the finished product fell, from an index of 550 in 1800 to an index of 100 in 1850, whereas the price of grain and most foodstuffs fell by no more than a third over the same period. Profit margins which were originally fantastic ('not five per cent, or ten per cent, but hundreds ... and thousands per cent', as an English politician later said)[120] were drastically reduced. However, the invasion of world markets was sufficient to make up for the diminishing returns. 'Profits are still sufficient', wrote a contemporary in 1835, 'to allow of a great accumulation of capital in the manufacture.'[121]

If the takeoff did occur after 1787, cotton was certainly responsible. Eric Hobsbawm points out that its rate of expansion closely resembles that of the British economy as a whole. Other industries progressed along with cotton – and were later dragged down with it when it collapsed, something which continued into the twentieth century.[122] The impression the British cotton industry made on contemporaries was one of unprecedented vitality. In about 1820, when machines were on the point of taking over from handloom weavers as well, cotton was already the country's major user of steam-power. In about 1835, it was using at least 30,000 horse-power provided by steam and only 10,000 horse-power of hydraulic energy.[123] To measure the strength of this new intruder, one has only to consider the extraordinary development of Manchester, a thoroughly modern city, with 'its hundreds of factories, five, six or even more storeys high, each topped with an immense chimney-stack and a plume of black smoke',[124] asserting its supremacy over the neighbouring towns including the port of Liverpool, only a short while earlier the great slave-trading port, and now on the way to being the chief entry point for raw cotton, especially from the United States.[125]

The ancient and glorious woollen industry, by comparison, continued for many years to present a rather old-fashioned spectacle. An English manufacturer reminiscing in 1826 about the old days recalled how the appearance of the spinning jenny among artisan families had relegated the antiquated spinning wheels to the attic and converted the whole labour force to cotton in about 1780: the spinning 'of wool had disappeared altogether and that of linen was nearly gone; cotton, cotton, cotton, has become the almost universal material for employment'.[126] The jenny was subsequently adapted for spinning wool, but complete mechanization came twenty years later than in the cotton industry.[127] It was in Leeds (which had now replaced Norwich as the wool capital) that spinning (not of course weaving) began to be mechanized, but the wool was still a rural cottage industry in 1811.

> The [Leeds] cloth market [Louis Simond reports] consists of a large building and a large square market, built round a courtyard, proof against fire, the walls being made of brick, the floors of iron. Two thousand six hundred

Robert Owen's cotton mill at New Lanark, on the Clyde, late eighteenth, early nineteenth century. Industrially, Scotland followed closely in England's footsteps. (Document in possession of T.C. Smout.)

country manufacturers, part-farmers, part-weavers, keep stalls here twice a week, for only an hour at a time. They each have their stall along the walls of a long gallery ... the lengths of cloth are piled up behind them and they hold samples in their hands. The purchasers pass down the double line comparing samples, and since prices are agreed almost unanimously, deals are quickly made. With few words and little wasted time on either side, much business is done.[128]

It is quite clear that we are still in the pre-industrial age. Overall control was in the hands of the purchaser, that is the merchant. So wool did not follow in the steps of cotton's industrial revolution. Similarly, cutlery and ironmongery in Sheffield and Birmingham went on being produced in the many family workshops; and that is not to mention the innumerable old-fashioned trades, some of which were to survive into the twentieth century.[129]

After the cotton revolution which was for a long time the spearhead of the movement, came the iron revolution. But the England of railways and steamships, of heavy equipment which required massive capital investment but yielded relatively low profits, surely owed its existence to the huge amounts of capital which had already accumulated in the country. So even if cotton did not *directly* influence the machine revolution and the coming of the heavy metal industry, profits from cotton certainly paid the first bills. One cycle propelled the other on its way.

Victory in long-distance trade

It is hardly an exaggeration to speak of the English *commercial revolution* in the eighteenth century, of the extraordinary expansion of trade. During this century, industries producing for the home market saw their output rise from an index of 100 to 150; but those producing for export saw theirs rise from 100 to 550. It is clear that foreign trade was far out in front. This 'revolution' has of course itself to be explained, and the explanation will require nothing less than a worldwide survey. As for the links between the commercial and industrial revolutions, these are close and reciprocal: the two revolutions powerfully reinforced one another.

England's fortunes abroad lay in the constitution of a mighty trading empire giving the British economy access to the largest trading area in the world, from the Caribbean to India, China and Africa. If we divide this great empire in two – Europe on one hand and the overseas countries on the other, it may be possible to see more clearly the origins of what is after all an extraordinary career.

In the years either side of 1760 when both British and world trade were steadily expanding, it is interesting to note that England's trade with nearby Europe was declining in relative terms while overseas trade was on the increase. If we divide British trade with Europe into three columns – imports, exports, re-exports – we find that it is only in the last column, re-exports, that the share going to Europe remained a large one, more or less continuously throughout the eighteenth century (1700–1: 85%; 1750–1: 79%; 1772–3: 82%; 1797–8: 88%). This was not true of imports from Europe to Britain whose share fell steadily (65%, 55%, 45% and 43% for the same dates); while British exports to the continent fell even faster (85%, 77%, 49% and 30%).[130]

This double decline is significant: the centre of gravity so to speak of English trade was moving further away from Europe, as British trade increased with the American colonies (soon to be the United States) and with India, especially after Plassey. This bears out a rather shrewd remark by the author of *Richesse de la Hollande* (1778)[131] which may provide us with a clue to the answer. Accarias de Sérionne argues that England, held back by the high domestic prices and labour costs which made her the most expensive country in Europe, could no longer cope with competition from the French and Dutch on the markets closest to home. She was being beaten to it in the Mediterranean, in the Levant, in Italy and in Spain (in Cadiz that is, since England managed to compete quite successfully in Spanish America, operating out of the 'free ports' in Jamaica). Admittedly, in two crucial European markets, England remained ahead: in Portugal, which was one of her most ancient and solid conquests; and in Russia where she acquired indispensable supplies for the navy and for industry (timber, masts, jute, iron, pitch, tar). It is hardly forcing the overall picture however to say that England seemed to be making no further progress in Europe, indeed her trade there was dwindling; but she was triumphing in the rest of the world.

This triumph requires careful analysis. It is easy to see how by and large

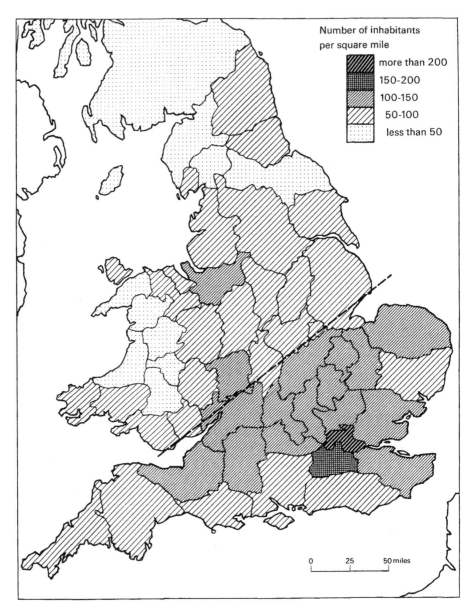

Number of inhabitants
per square mile

more than 200
150-200
100-150
50-100
less than 50

0   25   50 miles

52   THE TWO NATIONS IN 1700
Population and wealth distribution divide the country in two, either side of a line running from
Gloucester on the Severn to Boston on the banks of the Wash. (From H.C. Darby, *op. cit.*,
p. 524.)

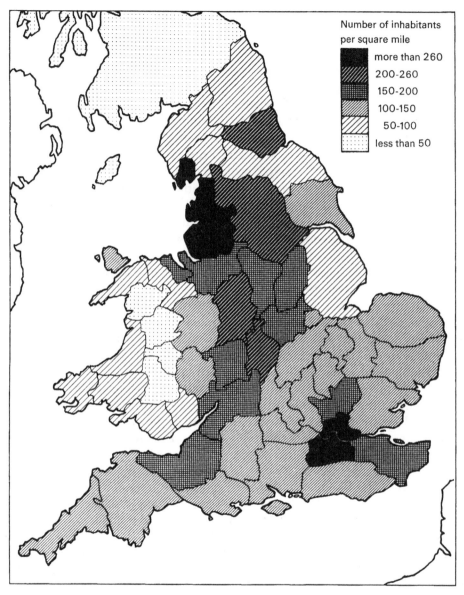

Number of inhabitants
per square mile

more than 260
200-260
150-200
100-150
50-100
less than 50

53   THE NEW POPULATION MAP IN 1800
What had previously been the poorest region of England, the north, now experienced a
population explosion, to become modern industrial England. (*Ibid.*, p. 525.)

England pushed her trade to these outer margins. In most cases, success was achieved by force: in India in 1757, in Canada in 1762 or on the coasts of Africa, England shouldered her rivals aside.[132] But it was not always or only a matter of force, since the newly-independent United States continued to increase on a massive scale the volume of goods they bought from the Old Country (though not their exports to it).[133] Similarly after 1793-5, the wars in Europe played into England's hands, obliging her to look to the rest of the world, while France and Holland were now forced out of worldwide trading. 'It is well known', writes a French observer who had lived in England throughout the Revolutionary and Napoleonic Wars, 'that no country in the four quarters of the earth has been able to trade for the last ten years (1804-13) without England's goodwill.'[134]

It is easy to see the advantages England derived from this concentration on the countries of the 'periphery', a reserve to be drawn on by the world-economy she dominated. Her high domestic prices, which were an incentive to modify the means of production (machines were used because labour costs were high) also drove her to seek supplies of raw materials (or even articles suitable for immediate re-sale in Europe) from low-cost countries. But if this was the case, a powerful reason must be the way in which English trade, with the services of the best navy in the world, had triumphed over distance. In no other country in the world, including Holland, was the division of labour so far advanced in the shipping sector as it was in England, whether in shipbuilding, shipfitting, financial backing or maritime insurance. A glance inside the London coffee-houses where the insurers foregathered – the Jerusalem, the Jamaica, Sam's and after 1774 the new Lloyd's coffee house in the Royal Exchange – would tell us more than any long treatise: insurance brokers carried orders from their customers from one insurance firm to another to find takers. Even foreigners knew the best addresses in town.[135] Lloyd's was an unrivalled centre for news and information. Insurers were better informed about a ship's position than her owners: they generally knew very well when they were on to a good thing.

But Britain, protected by her fleet, also knew very well when she was on to a good thing. There is no need here to describe for the hundredth time how during the Revolutionary and Napoleonic Wars, Britain managed to outwit the vigilance and comparative hostility of that part of the European continent which France was trying to blockade against her rival. The British always succeeded in finding a way in – at Tonningen in Denmark (until 1807), at Emden and Heligoland (until 1810); no sooner was one gateway abandoned than another opened.[136] And British trade worldwide continued imperturbably, sometimes benefiting from force of habit. The East India Company confidently carried on shipping Indian cottons home during the Napoleonic Wars: 'Thousands of bales of cotton had been lying idle in the Company's warehouses for ten years, when somebody thought of giving them to the Spanish *guerilleros* to make themselves shirts and trousers'.[137]

The commercial revolution cannot of course in itself explain the industrial revolution.[138] But no historian would deny the effect of commercial expansion on the economy which it certainly helped to reach new heights. Many historians have chosen however to minimize that effect. The problem is fundamentally the same as the bitter dispute between those who attribute capitalist growth exclusively to the virtues of *internal* evolution and those who see it as being created from outside, by the systematic exploitation of the world – a debate which has little purpose since both explanations are perfectly acceptable. Contemporary admirers of Britain were already inclining to the first explanation. Louis Simond wrote in 1812: 'The sources of England's wealth must be sought in her extensive domestic circulation [of goods], in her advanced division of labour and in the superiority of her machines.'[139] 'I suspect that people have exaggerated ... the importance of England's foreign trade'.[140] Another observer even writes: 'The vulgar notion that England owes her wealth to foreign trade is ... as false as it is firmly held, like all vulgar ideas'.[141] And he adds confidently: 'As for foreign trade, it is of no importance to any state, not even England, whatever may be said by those profound political thinkers who dreamed up the Continental system'. The 'system' was the Continental Blockade, an act of folly according to Maurice Rubichon, a Frenchman who hated France under the empire as much as he had hated it under the revolution. Was it not folly to strike at England's trade, folly to blockade the continent, folly to have sent the French fleet and the flower of the French army off to Egypt in 1798, on the inaccessible Indies route – pure folly and a waste of time for, our informant continues, what was England getting out of the Indies? About thirty ships at most, 'and half their cargo consists of the drinking water and provisions required for such a long sea-voyage'.

If such absurd ideas were in circulation at the time, was this not because many people believed, like Cantillon, that there was no such thing as a favourable or unfavourable trade balance: what a country sold could only be the equivalent of what it bought, – what Huskisson the future president of the Board of Trade called 'the Interchange of reciprocal and equivalent benefits'.[142] I need hardly say that England's trading position – with Ireland, India, the United States or anywhere else – was most emphatically *not* one of 'equivalent benefits'.

It is true that while the data available, based on customs records, gives us a fairly good idea of the rising volume of British trade, it does not allow one to calculate the British trade *balance*, as Phyllis Deane[143] has explained in a lengthy analysis impossible to summarize here. Estimates based on these records might incline one to assume only a small positive balance and possibly even a negative one. This brings us back to our previous discussion about the trade balance of Jamaica or the French West Indies. Customs records, besides their intrinsic shortcomings, refer only to goods entering or leaving English ports. They do not register movements of capital, nor the slave trade – that 'triangular' form of commerce which was outside customs control – nor freight handled by the merchant navy, nor the money sent back by planters in Jamaica, or nabobs in India, nor the profits from the country trade in the Far East.

In the port of Bristol: Broad Quay, early eighteenth century. Museum of Bristol City Art Gallery. (Photo by the museum.)

This being so, is it still possible, after recognizing the undeniable volume and extraordinary increase of foreign trade, to minimize its relative importance when total domestic trade is compared to total external trade? David Macpherson in his *Annals of Commerce* (1801)[144] was already estimating the former at two or three times the size of the latter[145] and even in the absence of reliable figures, there can be little doubt that the volume of internal trade was the greater. That by no means solves the problem, as I have already said, and I do not intend to go back over the debate about the relative importance of domestic and foreign trade. But as regards economic growth and the industrial revolution in England, the size of the domestic market by no means eclipses the significance of foreign trade. The mere fact that British industry in the eighteenth century increased its production for export by about 450% (index: 100 in 1700, 544 in 1800) and its production for the home market by only 52% (100 in 1700, 152 in 1800) is sufficiently indicative of the role of foreign markets in British production. After 1800, that role grew steadily greater: between 1800 and 1820, exports of British-made goods increased by 83%.[146] To bring about the industrial revolution, both areas of growth, internal and external, pooled their strength as multipliers. One could not have done it without the other.

Indeed I recognize the force of the argument advanced by the Indian historian Amalendu Guha,[147] who suggests that rather than compare *totals*, we compare *surpluses* – that is the surpluses England derived from India and the surplus savings in England which went into investment. According to various calculations, English investments amounted to about £6 million in 1750 (5% of G.N.P.) and to £19 million in 1820 (7%). Set alongside these figures, are the £2 million regularly derived every year from India between 1750 and 1800 so very insignificant? We do not know in detail how this money, the profits from India (in particular the wealth of the nabobs), was distributed throughout the British economy. But it was certainly neither wasted nor inactive. It went to raise the level of wealth of the island in general; and it was upon such levels of wealth that England's triumphs rested.

The spread of inland transport

However important the multiplier effect of foreign trade, I have already said too much about the national market in this book[148] to run any risk of underestimating its importance. In any case, if one accepts that, broadly speaking, domestic trade amounted to about two or three times foreign trade,[149] and that the latter (after allowing for re-exports) represented on average between 1760 and 1769 about £20 million a year in round figures,[150] then domestic trade must have represented £40 to £60 million; and if profits were 10% of the whole,[151] these must have been of the order of £4 or £6 million a year – an enormous sum. The industrial revolution was directly linked to this active circulation of goods within the economy. But why did it develop so early in England?

We have already seen that this can be explained in part by the revolutionary centralizing role of London, by the growing number of markets and the spread of the money economy which was reaching every part of the island, and by the volume of trade – to be seen in the traditional fatstock fairs, in the long-unrivalled and famous gatherings at Stourbridge fair, in the thriving market-towns which formed a circle round London, in the specialized wholesale markets inside the city itself, and the increased numbers of middlemen, redistributing incomes and profits among a growing mass of economic participants, as Defoe accurately observed. In short, much of the explanation lies in the sophistication and modernization of a network of commercial relations tending increasingly to operate under its own steam. Lastly and perhaps most of all, there was the proliferation of new means of transport, something which preceded the demands of trade, and then helped it to expand.[152]

Here too, we meet a problem already encountered earlier in this book. But it may be worthwhile looking at it afresh with reference to the remarkable circulation of goods in England. The first means of transport by which this was handled was the enormous volume of coastal shipping. The sea from this point of view as from many others, was England's first natural advantage. The coasters or 'colliers' represented three-quarters of the British navy, employing at least 100,000 sailors in 1800.[153] This being so, coasting was the school of seamanship for the crews which England turned to such good use elsewhere. Everything travelled by coaster: grain in bulk, and particularly coals from Newcastle, which sailed from Tyneside to the Thames estuary. Two score or so ports scattered around the English coasts handled this almost continuous stream of traffic, some of them ideally situated and easy of access, others used out of necessity despite their inconvenience. The Channel ports, which offered a handy refuge, were also, Defoe noted, the home or at any rate *a* home of 'smuggling and roguing'.[154]

The second advantage enjoyed by goods circulating in England was the inland network of waterways. The industrial and commercial importance of Norwich, which is a long way from the coast, can very largely be put down to the fact that the town could be directly reached from the sea, 'without lock or stop'.[155] T.S. Willan, with his customary brevity and precision,[156] has demonstrated the revolutionary importance of shipping on the rivers, which could carry sea-going vessels or at any rate their cargoes, far inland, forming as it were an extension of the marine waterway which coastal shipping had woven around the island.

England's navigable rivers, slow-flowing as a rule, were no longer used after about 1600 in the state in which nature had left them. In order to carry coal and other heavy goods in demand in the towns (particularly building materials) they were gradually improved, their navigable stretches extended, some of their meanders by-passed, and locks were built. The lock, T.S. Willan has argued, was an invention worthy to be ranked with the steam-engine.[157] The improvement of rivers was a sort of apprenticeship preparing the way for canals: the earliest canals simply prolonged or connected river routes. But vice versa, some rivers were only made navigable (or virtually 'canalized') when it became clear that they could be used to connect newly-built canals.

So canal fever was not really an attack of fever or folly, simply a speculative endeavour – one which did not pay off in fifty per cent of cases, it is sometimes argued; but one could retort that in the other fifty it did: whenever the route had been judiciously chosen, whenever coal (the crucial commodity) used the new waterway, whenever the necessary credit to launch the scheme had been well-handled by the building corporation or by the individual entrepreneur.

Canal fever began in 1755 with the Sankey canal, built to carry coal from St Helen's to Liverpool,[158] which preceded by a few years the justly celebrated and totally successful Duke of Bridgewater's canal, linking the Worsley coal mines to Manchester.[159] When the Duke of Bridgewater undertook on his own these works 'which required a greater circulation of paper money than is to be found in the feeble establishment pompously known as the Bank of France, he had not of course like the latter seen his paper money discredited; nor was he obliged like the latter to have in his cellars cash to the value of a quarter of his notes in circulation; and this was just as well – for he often did not have so much as a crown to pay the postillion who drove him along the works'.[160]

On this occasion, the entrepreneur played his cards well. He already owned a mine, which made it easier to borrow money: everyone knows that people only lend to the rich. But his plans were well worked out. By delivering the coal from his mines directly to Manchester, he succeeded in selling it for half the old price and was able to make an annual profit of 20% on his outlay and expenditure. Canals were only a folly when built by those without a clear plan in mind, for if the cost of transport by sea is taken as the unit of reference, canal transport cost only three times as much. (Carting was nine times as expensive and pack animals twenty-seven times).

Meanwhile on land, the turnpikes (the first of which was begun in 1654) had made it possible to build up a very respectable network of main roads. Financed, like the canals, by individual entrepreneurs (the state was interested only in strategic roads heading towards Scotland or Ireland) the turnpikes replaced old roads which may not have been as terrible as they are sometimes described, but which were unsuitable for wheeled traffic and often impassable in winter.

But even the new roads with their hard surfaces[161] (produced by simple techniques which had made little advance even on Roman methods) and the craze for canals did not solve all problems, for instance those of transporting coal from the pithead to the dockside. In the last years of the eighteenth century, iron rails made their first appearance – putting the railway before the engine, as Clapham put it.[162] Baron Dupin[163] translated the English 'rail road' as *route-ornière*, misleadingly since *ornière* means a groove and suggests that the rail was hollow in the middle to take the solid wheel of a carriage. But a rail is of course a raised bar and the very earliest rails were in fact made of wood. They carried wagons which also had wooden wheels: these were being used as early as the seventeenth century in the quarries at Bath, in the Cornish tin-mines and for moving coal round Newcastle.[164] On these rails, usually completed by an external sill which prevented the wheel from slipping off, a horse could pull a load three times heavier than on an ordinary road. The really dramatic change was the replacement of the wooden rail by the iron rail in 1767 or so. From 1800 efforts were being made to develop a steam-engine which could pull loads: the first

The Duke of Bridgewater (1736–1803), in front of his canal. Engraving, 1767. (Armand Colin Picture Library.)

locomotive, Stephenson's Rocket, appeared in 1814.

There were already railways (without locomotives) '76 leagues long' around Newcastle in 1816,[165] and they were even longer in the county of Glamorgan in Wales, which includes the ports of Cardiff and Swansea and the mines at Merthyr Tydfil. A Scottish system had also been developed around Glasgow and Edinburgh and it was there that 'the greatest number of schemes of this kind [have been put to] capitalists in recent years'.[166] One of these rail roads went right into the city of Glasgow, observed Baron Dupin who thought that it might be possible to 'lay rails like this down one side of the very sloping streets in the main French towns, in several streets on the Montagne-Sainte-Geneviève in Paris for instance'.[167] In 1833, a book describing 'a voyage from Manchester to Liverpool by railway and steam engine' by M. Cuchetet caused a sensation in France. It gave details of these 'iron roads',[168] of the station in Water Street,[169] of the various engines used, 'among which that of Mr Robert Stephenson, known as

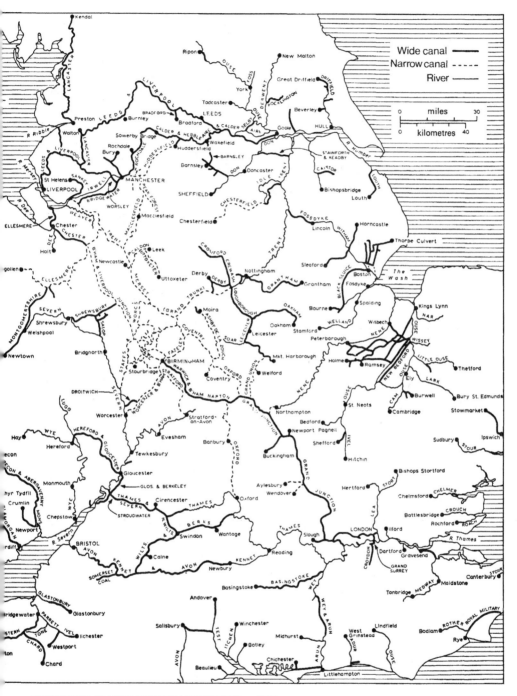

54 PRINCIPAL NAVIGABLE WATERWAYS c. 1830
From H. J. Dyos and D.H. Aldcroft, *op. cit.* T.S. Willan's map, for the period 1660–1700, in
Figure 38.

the "Samson", is the most advanced at present'[170] – engines 'which are no bigger than the average water-barrel carried by a water-carrier'.[171]

From the wooden rail to the steam-train, railways were an important part of the development of the 'carrying trade' in Britain. One does not have to be an expert to be convinced that this increased speed of transport sustained England's growth as a whole. Even in the twentieth century,[172] there is a correlation between growth and ease of transport facilities. The speed of communications also means that instructions and news travel faster and is vital to the business world. Would Thomas Williams have been able to establish and maintain his copper monopoly and all his other business interests, from Cornwall to Shetland in the 1790s, if his business letters from London to Lancashire and Wales had not been able to travel as fast as the modern post?[173]

But when it comes to transport, we must not only think of England's increasingly dense inland network of rivers, canals, roads and railways. Long-distance transport should not be forgotten – these things were all connected. In 1800, a Frenchman observed that when there was a severe shortage of grain at home, 'England shipped in 600,000 quintals of rice from India at 12 francs a quintal in transport costs, whereas it would be impossible to find a carrier in a little town in Brittany who would take a quintal of grain to some other town in Lorraine for less than 40 or 50 francs; yet the distance is no more than 150 leagues'.[174]

> Here in London, we have been able to see over the past twenty years [1797 to 1817 probably] that as soon as England enters into conflict with Italy, and can no longer obtain there as in the past the silk she needs for her factories, the [East India] Company plants mulberry trees in India and annually provides thousands of bales of silk; that as soon as England enters into conflict with Spain, and can no longer obtain there as in the past the indigo she needs for her factories, the Company has this plant too grown in India, and annually provides thousands of chests of indigo; that as soon as England enters into conflict with Russia and can no longer obtain the hemp she needs for her navy, the Company plants it in India to meet the demand; England is threatened with hostilities with America and may be unable to obtain cotton, so the Company provides the amount required by the spinners and weavers; England [is] in conflict with her [own] colonies . . . the Company provides the sugar and coffee Europe needs.

These remarks are no doubt open to question. But the interesting thing about them is that they were made by the very same observer who counselled against the 'vulgar notion'[175] that England's wealth was derived from foreign trade and who assured us that she could have been self-sufficient. So she might have been, but it would have been on a very different footing, and would have meant leaving the conquest of the world to some other country.

The West India Dock in London, early nineteenth century. Sugar, rum and coffee being unloaded. (Photo Batsford.)

The mills of history grind exceedingly slow

Everything I have said so far has pointed towards a number of conclusions. In the first place, that in this instance (the industrial revolution) as in every instance that history seeks to study in depth, it is not the short-term, the history of events that matters most. Everything achieved by this revolution took a long time: coke-smelting, the mechanization of weaving, the true agricultural revolution, a steam-engine that worked, railways that ran. The industrial revolution was a long time being born, and before it could develop and begin to move, there had to be a good deal of destruction, adaptation and 'restructuring'. If we are to believe Charles Wilson and Eric Hobsbawm,[176] the industrial revolution was already there in embryo in England by the Restoration (1660), yet nothing emerged very quickly. Throughout the apparently absurdly backward seventeenth century however, the age that seemed to drag its feet, the *ancien régime* was steadily being eroded and overthrown: the traditional structures of agriculture and landed property were being impaired or destroyed; the guilds were losing their grip, even in London after the Great Fire of 1666; the Navigation Act was renewed; and the last constructive measures of a mercantilist policy of protection were being enacted. Everything was really on the move, so that the kingdom, wrote Defoe in 1724, 'changes its face from day to day'; every day something new appeared to engage the attention of travellers.[177] England was ceasing to be an under-developed country in the present-day sense of the word: she was raising her levels of output and her standard of living, perfecting the tools of her economic activity. Above all, she possessed an economy whose different sectors were in harmony, each being far enough developed not to present the risk of creating a dangerous bottleneck at the first serious crisis. England was therefore poised for advance, whatever the direction chosen or the occasion that might arise.

All the same, can we really be satisfied with this image of a smoothly coordinated and evenly developing combination of sectors, capable between them of providing all the interconnected elements of the industrial revolution and meeting demands from other sectors? It conveys a misleading vision of the industrial revolution as a consciously pursued objective, as if Britain's society and economy had conspired to make possible the new Machine Age. At a pinch, this picture of a revolutionary, yet somehow pre-determined experience might be applied to the industrial revolutions being pursued at the present time, with previous models available to act as markers along the road. But this was certainly not how the English revolution developed. It was not moving towards any goal, rather it encountered one, as it was propelled along by that multitude of different currents which not only carried forward the industrial revolution but also spilled over into areas far beyond it.

Beyond the industrial revolution

It is evident from the very vocabulary we use that the industrial revolution, massive phenomenon though it was, was not the only or even the major overall occurrence in a period heavy with developments. *Industrialism*, the adoption by a whole society of an industrial mode of life, is clearly something broader than the 'revolution' itself. And it is even more evident that *industrialization*, the transition from a predominantly agricultural society to one in which manufacture dominates – a far-reaching movement in itself – takes us beyond the radius of the preceding analysis. The industrial revolution proper was an accelerating factor so to speak in this process. As for *modernization*, this is something bigger again than even industrialization: 'Industrial development is not the whole story of the modern economy'.[178] And the ground covered by the term *growth* is even wider – extending to the whole of history.

That said, is it possible to use the data and realities of growth in order to stand back and view the industrial revolution from outside, in the context of a wider movement?

Types of growth

To start us on the way, we may consider the reflection of D.C. North and R.P. Thomas that 'the industrial revolution was not the source of modern growth'.[179] Growth was certainly something separate from the industrial revolution, even if the latter was undoubtedly borne on the back of the former. I would be inclined to agree with John Hicks that 'the industrial revolution of the last two hundred years was perhaps no more than a vast secular boom'.[180] When he refers to a 'boom' does this not simply mean growth – growth which was not confined to the period of the industrial revolution, and which in fact preceded it. The word growth itself, which has only become fashionable recently – since the 1940s[181] – denotes in today's language 'a complex process of *long-term* development'.[182] But do we really have a precise measure of this concept? Economists do not on the whole talk about growth in periods earlier than the nineteenth century. And they are in any case far from agreed in explaining how it works. Some believe that all growth is balanced, others that all growth is unbalanced or uneven. *Balanced growth* (as described by Nurske, Young, Hartwell) affects all sectors at the same time, in a fairly steady forward movement, based on demand, and drawing considerably on the national market which is the principal motive force behind development. The *unbalanced or uneven growth* school (Innis, A.O. Hirshman, Schumpeter, Rostow) views growth as beginning in one privileged sector which transmits the impetus to others. Growth therefore consists of the process of catching up with the leader, and in this perspective it is supply, that is the voluntarist side of economics (as A. Fanfani would say), which comes to prominence; in this kind of development, it is the effect of outside markets rather than the expansion of the domestic market that matters, even if the latter is on the point of becoming a national market.

Having made this distinction, R.M. Hartwell[183] has demonstrated to his own satisfaction that the industrial revolution was the result of balanced growth. His arguments are excellent. But he is thereby extending to the late eighteenth century forms of growth which economists as a rule confine to the nineteenth. He might just as well, without too greatly distorting concrete reality (in so far as it is known) have adapted the second theory – that of unbalanced growth – to the process of the industrial revolution. It is the latter theory which many historians have in fact – not always fully consciously perhaps – preferred in the past; and they might still choose it today on reflection. In the first place, it is a dramatic and *événementiel* explanation, convincing and easy to grasp at first sight. After all there really *was* a cotton boom, and this was unquestionably the first industry to go in for mass production. So could it not be said that cotton started the ball rolling?

But why should the two theories be regarded as mutually exclusive? Why cannot they be valid simultaneously or in succession, in the normal dialectic which contrasts and brings together long-term and short-term movements? Is the distinction between them not more theoretical than practical? There are plenty of examples to show that progress in a single sector can launch a burst of growth, as we have already seen in this chapter, and others could no doubt be cited from the present-day world. But we have also seen that such growth is likely to collapse sooner or later, to run into difficulties, unless it is able to rely on a wider, multi-sectoral response. So rather than discuss the merits of *balanced* and *unbalanced* growth, would it not be better to speak of *continuous* and *discontinuous* growth? This is a very real distinction since it corresponds to that profound, indeed structural break, which took place, in the West at least, in the nineteenth century. Simon Kuznets is quite right, to my mind, to distinguish between 'traditional' growth and 'modern' growth.[184]

Modern growth is that continuous or sustained growth of which François Perroux[185] was able to say long ago that it was independent of rising or falling prices, a remark which surprised, disturbed and even worried historians used to studying 'traditional' centuries very different from the nineteenth. François Perroux and Paul Bairoch, who took up this point, are of course quite right. In the United Kingdom as a whole, total national income and per capita income progressed without faltering through a long period of falling prices (1810–50), a long price rise (1850–80), and another fall (1880–90) – at annual rates of 2.8% and 1.7% for the first period; 2.3% and 1.4% for the second and 1.8 and 1.2% for the third.[186] This was that wonder of wonders, continuous growth. It never came to a total halt, even during times of crisis.

Before this transformation, traditional growth had hiccupped along in a succession of stop-go movements, sometimes even backward jumps, for centuries on end. Several very long phases can be distinguished: 1100–1350; 1350–1450; 1450–1520; 1520–1720; 1720–1817.[187] These phases present contradictory features: population rose during the first, collapsed during the second, climbed again during the third, stagnated during the fourth; and shot up during the last. Every time the population increased, both output and national income grew, as if to prove the truth of the belief that population equals wealth. But on every occasion per capita income declined or even fell sharply, whereas it improved during phases of economic stagnation – as the long-term graph[188] established by E.H. Phelps Brown and Sheila Hopkins has shown. There was thus a clear *divergence* between national income and per capita income: a rise in the national product was always achieved on the backs of those who did the work: this was the law of the *ancien régime*. And I would suggest, contrary to what has been said and repeated elsewhere, that the early phases of the industrial revolution in Britain were sustained by an *ancien régime* pattern of growth. There was no economic miracle, no continuous growth before 1815, or possibly even 1850; some people would argue that it did not occur until after 1870.

How can growth be explained?

Whatever form growth takes, it raises the level of the economy, as the incoming tide floats the boats in a harbour; it engenders an infinite number of inter-related balances and imbalances; it enables slumps to be avoided, it creates employment and conjures up profits. It is the movement that enables the world to regain its secular rhythm after every slowdown or contraction. But this movement which seems to explain everything else is itself difficult to explain. Growth *per se* is a mysterious thing[189] – even for today's economists with their sheafs of statistics. One can only advance hypotheses – without much confidence since as we have seen, at least two possible explanations have been suggested, namely balanced and unbalanced growth: but we are not obliged to choose between them.

In this situation, the distinction made by Simon Kuznets between 'what makes economic growth possible' and 'the way it actually *happens*', could be a crucial one.[190] Is not 'growth potential' precisely that 'balanced' development which is only acquired slowly, through the continuous interaction of the different factors and agents of production, by a transformation of the structural relations between land, labour, capital, the market, the state and social institutions? Growth of this kind is inevitably a matter of *the long-term (la longue durée)*. It enables us to trace back the origins of the industrial revolution to the thirteenth, seventeenth or eighteenth century if we choose to. The 'way growth actually happens' on the other hand cannot but be a question of more immediate circumstances (*la conjoncture*), the product of a comparatively recent time-span, of particular conditions, of technical discoveries, of some national or international opportunity, or even of pure chance. If for instance, India had not been the world's leading producer (both model and competitor) of woven cotton, the industrial revolution would probably have happened just the same in Britain, but would it have started in cotton?

If one accepts this yoking together of the long and the short-term analysis, one can without too much difficulty combine the explanation of the two forms of growth – the one of necessity balanced, the other of necessity unbalanced and advancing by fits and starts, lurching 'from crisis to crisis', replacing one growth industry with another, one market with another, one energy source with another, one means of pressure with another, depending on the circumstances of the moment.

For sustained growth to occur, long-term factors – the forces which accumulate progress over time – must already have produced 'whatever it is that makes economic growth possible', and every time an obstacle is encountered, there must be some new source of dynamism waiting in the wings to take over from the one that is running (or has run) out of steam. Sustained growth is like a relay race with no final whistle. If growth could not be maintained from the thirteenth to the fourteenth century, it was because the mills which had launched it could provide only a limited impetus and there was no other source of energy to take over from them; but a more powerful reason possibly was that the agriculture of the time could not keep pace with population increase and found itself faced with falling yields. Until the industrial revolution, every burst of growth came up against what I called in the first volume of this book, 'the limits of the possible', a ceiling imposed by agricultural output, by the available means of transport, sources of power or market demand. Modern growth begins when that ceiling or limit recedes indefinitely into the distance – which is not to say of course that some kind of ceiling may not be reached in the future.

Growth and the division of labour

Every advance made by growth concerns the *division of labour*. The latter is a derivative phenomenon, trailing along behind growth which drags it in its wake so to speak. But the increasing complexity of the division of labour can eventually be taken as a reliable indicator of the progress made towards growth, or even as a means of measuring it.

Contrary to what Marx believed and wrote in good faith, Adam Smith did not invent the idea of the division of labour. He merely conferred the status of a general theory on an ancient idea already adumbrated by Plato, Aristotle and Xenophon, and mentioned long before his own time by William Petty (1623–87), Ernst Ludwig Carl (1687-1743), Adam Ferguson (1723-1816) and Cesare Beccaria (1735–93). But from the time of Adam Smith, economists regarded the idea as something akin to Newton's law of gravity. Jean-Baptiste Say was one of the first to rebel against the vogue and thereafter the concept of the division of labour rather went out of fashion. Durkheim wrote of it that 'it is merely a derivative phenomenon ... [which] takes place on the surface of social life, and this is particularly true of the economic division of labour, which is but skin deep'.[191] Is this really so? I have often imagined the division of tasks as something like the *intendance* – the supply corps which follows the army and organizes occupied territory. Was the improved organization of exchange – and by the same token the enlargement of its scope – such a small thing? The extension of the services or tertiary sector – a major phenomenon of our own times – forms part of the division of labour and lies at the heart of socio-economic theories of today. The same is true of the destructuring and restructuring of social features which accompany growth, for growth does not merely increase the division of labour, it reshuffles the cards, eliminating old functions and proposing new ones, in a process which reshapes both economy and society. The industrial revolution represented a new and completely disorienting division of labour, preserving and refining the mechanisms at work but bringing disastrous consequences in social and human terms.

The division of labour: the end of the road for the putting-out system

The most frequent form taken by industry in town and country was the putting-out system,[192] a pattern of working which had become general throughout Europe and had enabled mercantile capitalism from a quite early stage to take advantage of the surplus of cheap labour in the countryside. The rural artisan worked at home, helped by his family, while still keeping a field and a few animals. Raw materials – wool, flax, cotton – were provided by the merchant in town who ran the operation, received the finished or semi-finished product and paid the bill. The putting-out system thus combined town and country, craft and farming, industrial and family labour, and at the top, mercantile and industrial capitalism. To the artisan, it meant a life that was balanced if not exactly peaceful; to the entrepreneur, it meant the possibility of keeping fixed capital costs down and more particularly of coping with the only too frequent gaps in demand: when sales fell off, he simply reduced his orders and employed fewer people – perhaps suspending operations entirely. In an economy where it was demand, not supply, which restricted industrial output, out-working provided industry with the necessary elasticity. It could be halted or re-started at a word of command.[193]

Even the manufactories, which were the earliest concentrations of labour, the first attempt at *economies of scale*, often retained this pattern which provided room for manoeuvre: they usually relied on a large number of outworkers. And in any case, manufactories represented only a small fraction of output,[194] until the factory with its machines perfected the all-conquering solution of mass-production; and that took time.

The disruption brought by the new system was indeed slow to emerge. Even in the vanguard industry of cotton, the family workshop survived for a long time, since handloom weaving co-existed with mechanized spinning for a good half-century. As late as 1817, one witness described it as exactly the same as in the old days, 'with the sole exception of the flying shuttle invented and introduced by John Kay in about 1750'.[195] The power-loom, driven by steam, was not operational until the 1820s or so. The long period when rapid spinning in modern factories was out of step with traditional handloom weaving did of course radically upset the former division of labour. Whereas previously the spinning wheels had hardly been able to keep up with the demands of the weaver, the position was reversed as spinning increasingly became mechanized. Handloom weaving was forced to call on more and more workers, who had to work at breakneck speed, but could earn high wages. Rural workers began to abandon their small-holdings and joined the ranks of the full-time weavers which were visibly swollen too by the recruitment of large contingents of women and children. In 1813–14, out of 213,000 handloom weavers, 130,000 – more than half – were under the age of fourteen.

It is of course true that in a society where every man living by the sweat of

While there were from a very early date modern machines in the cotton mills round Edinburgh and Glasgow, the manufacture of woollen cloth in the Highlands of Scotland remained very archaic. Even in 1772, the women in this engraving are fulling the cloth with their feet. On the left, two women appear to be grinding corn at a primitive quern. (National Library of Scotland.)

his brow was always on the borderline between hunger and starvation, it had always been normal for children to work alongside their parents in the fields, in the family workshop or shop. So true indeed that in the early days, new firms and factories hired not individuals but whole families who offered themselves as a team, to mines or cotton mills. In Robert Peel's factory in Bury in 1801-2, out of 136 workers, 95 belonged to 26 families.[196] So the family workshop moved straight into the factory, with all the advantages that this method offered in the way of discipline and efficiency. Small teams (made up of one adult plus one or two children) were not only possible but positively advantageous. Technical progress sooner or later put an end to the practice however. Thus in the textile industry after 1824, the new automatic mule perfected by Richard Roberts required, if it was to work at full stretch,[197] that the man or woman watching the machine had as many as nine young (or very young) assistants, whereas the old mules only required one or two. Thus the family structure was broken up inside the factory, producing a completely different context and atmosphere for child labour.

Shortly before this, another far more disastrous process of disruption had begun with the coming of the power-loom. This time it was the handloom weavers who were doomed to disappear. The power-loom, 'with which a child can produce as much as two or three men',[198] was truly a social catastrophe, on top of so many others. Thousands of weavers were thrown on to the streets. Wages collapsed so drastically that the starvation rates at which labour could be bought kept some wretched handloom weavers in work longer than would rationally have been expected.

At the same time, the new division of labour, as it urbanized working-class society, was tearing apart the world of the poor, as they chased after work which vanished in front of them; it eventually took them to unfamiliar places, far from the countryside they knew and in the end diminished their way of life. Living in towns, deprived of the traditional resources of kitchen garden, cow, and farm-yard fowls, working in great factories under the stern gaze of the overseers, being forced to obey, losing all freedom of movement, accepting fixed working-hours – all these were immediate effects hard to bear. It meant changing a whole way of life and view of the world, to the point of alienation from one's own existence. It meant changing diet – eating poor food and less of it. Neil J. Smelser has given us a sociological and historical account of the life of the uprooted workers in the new all-conquering cotton industry.[199] It was many years before working-class society succeeded in creating protection in the shape of new attitudes and organizations – friendly societies, cooperative banks and so on.[200] Trade unions would only come later. And it is not much use asking the rich what they thought of the new town-dwellers. They saw them as 'mindless, vicious, quarrelsome and rebellious' and to make matters worse, 'as a rule poor'.[201] What the workers themselves thought of factory labour was expressed rather differently – with their feet. In 1838, only 23% of the textile workforce were adult males; the great mass were women and children, who put up less resistance.[202] Never before had social discontent in England been so severe as in the years 1815–45 which saw the rise in turn of Luddite machine-breakers, of political radicals, who would have liked to break down the structures of society, of trade unionism and of Utopian socialism.[203]

The industrialists

The division of labour did not only affect the base but also – perhaps even more quickly – the top levels of industrial firms. Hitherto, in Britain as on the continent, the rule had been the indivisibility of the chief commercial functions – a businessman could be a jack of all trades: merchant, banker, insurer, ship-owner, industrialist. When the English 'country banks' appeared for instance, their proprietors were corn-merchants, brewers, or wholesalers with many in-

A weaving workshop in eighteenth-century England, by Hogarth. In the foreground the owner is looking through the books; behind him, women are working at looms. (Photo British Museum.)

terests, who had been motivated to set up banks by their own needs and those of their neighbours.[204] These men with a finger in every pie were found wherever one turned: they were directors of the East India Company (naturally) or the Bank of England where they influenced decisions and exerted patronage, they had seats in the House of Commons, gradually climbed the ladder of honours, and were soon governing the country which was already subordinate to their interests and passions.

But by the late eighteenth and early nineteenth century, a new type was emerging, the 'industrialist', a man of action who would before long, even before the formation of Peel's second ministry (1841), be making an appearance on the political stage, in the House of Commons itself. In the course of acquiring their independence, these men had broken one by one the ties between pre-industry and mercantile capitalism. With them there appeared a new form of capitalism, one that went from strength to strength, firmly based on industrial production. The new 'entrepreneurs' were above all organizers. 'Relatively few', remarks Peter Mathias, 'were the pioneers of major innovations or inventions in their own right.'[205] The talents they claimed to possess, the tasks they set themselves, were those of being conversant with new techniques, able to handle their foremen and workers and lastly having an expert knowledge of the market so as to be able to direct output themselves, changing course whenever necessary. They tended to do without the merchant as middleman, preferring themselves to supervise the purchase and transport of the raw materials they needed, to see that it was of the correct quality and arrived regularly. Since they were producing for a mass market, they wanted to be able to assess for themselves the state of the market and to adapt production accordingly. The Fieldens, mill-owners in Todmorden, had their own agents in the United States in the early nineteenth century, who bought supplies of cotton for the factory.[206] 'The great London porter brewers bought little malt in the open market at Mark Lane or Bear Quay [but] ... employed factors' in the barley-growing regions of East Anglia – who were kept on a very tight rein if the following letter from a London brewer to his factor is anything to go by: 'I have sent you by coach a sample of the last pale malt you sent in. It is so infamously bad ... that I will not receive another sack of it into my brewhouse. Should I have occasion ever to write such another letter, I shall entirely alter my plan of buying'.[207]

Such behaviour was a sign of the completely new dimensions of industry, including brewing which a Frenchman in 1812 described as 'truly one of the curiosities of the city of London':

> The brewery of Barclay & Co is one of the most impressive. The whole enterprise is powered by a 'fire-pump' of thirty horse-power and although there are employed there nearly 200 men and a large number of horses, they are almost all used for outside tasks. There is nobody to be seen inside this prodigious factory and everything in it operates by a hidden hand. Great rakes move up and down and stir the boilers 12 feet high and 20 feet in diameter, which contain the hops and stand over the fire. Elevators carry 2500 bushels of draff[208] a day to the top of the building from where it is distributed in various pipes to the places where it is to be used; the barrels are transported without being touched; the pumping machine itself which accomplishes all this is so precisely constructed, there is so little friction or shock within it, that without exaggerating, it makes hardly any more sound than a watch ticking, and one can hear a pin drop anywhere in the building. The vats into which the liquid is poured when it has received the final preparations, are of gigantic dimensions: the largest holds 3000 barrels of 36 gallons each, which at 8 barrels to the ton is equal to the cargo of a 375-ton ship; and there are forty or fifty of these containers, the smallest of which holds 800 barrels, that is 100 tons ... The smallest vat, when full of beer is worth £3000 sterling and calculating on this basis the contents of the others, the cellar alone contains a capital of £300,000 sterling. The barrels in which the beer is carried to consumers, themselves cost £80,000 sterling and the

entire establishment probably requires a capital of no less than half a million pounds sterling; the building is fire-proof, the floors being made of metal and the walls of brick; 250,000 barrels of beer a year come out of it, enough to load an entire fleet of 150 ships each carrying 200 tons cargo.[209]

These colossal breweries had moreover organized the distribution of their output, not only in London itself, where they supplied beer directly to half the ale-houses in town, but also in Dublin, where they had agents.[210] This is an important point: industrial enterprise was moving towards total independence. Peter Mathias cites the example of the building entrepreneur Thomas Cubitt, who emerged as a man of fortune in about 1817, having become rich during the Napoleonic Wars. His success owed nothing to technical innovation, and everything to new management techniques: he got rid of the sub-contractors who had traditionally handled the building trade; he acquired a permanent workforce and organized his own credit arrangements.[211]

This recently-found independence was the sign of a new age. The division of labour between industry and other kinds of business was nearing completion. Historians tell us that this is the beginning of industrial capitalism, and so it is. But they also tell us that this is when 'true' capitalism begins; I find that a much more questionable proposition. Is there such a thing as 'true' capitalism?

British economy and society by sector

The composition of every society undergoing long-term growth is inevitably affected by the division of labour. This was everywhere at work in England. The division of political power between Parliament and Crown in 1660, at the Restoration, and in particular with the Bill of Rights of 1688, marks the beginning of a division with far-reaching consequences. Another example would be the way a cultural sector (from education to the theatre, newspapers, publishing houses and learned societies) was gradually emerging as an increasingly independent world. The world of commerce was also being split apart, a process I have rather too briefly described. And lastly a modification of the occupational structure was taking place, along the lines of the classic scheme first defined by Fischer in 1930 and by Colin Clark in 1940, namely that the *primary* sector (agriculture) although still dominant, was shrinking as first the *secondary* (industrial) and then the *tertiary* (services) sector expanded. R.M. Hartwell's exceptional contribution to the Lyon Colloquium of 1970[212] provides a good opportunity to consider for a moment a problem which is not often discussed.

It is true that the distinction between the three sectors is far from crystal clear, and there are grounds for uncertainty on the exact borderline between even the first and second sectors (agriculture and industry sometimes overlap); as for the third, which is an amalgam of everything, questions could certainly be asked about its composition or its identification. It is usually taken to include all the 'services' – commerce, transport, banking, administration – but is it right to include domestic servants in this category? Should the hordes of domestic servants (in about 1850, this was the second largest occupational group in England after agriculture, with over a million people)[213] be placed in a sector theoretically marked by superior productivity? This does not seem right. But with this reservation, let us accept the Fischer-Clark proposition that a growing tertiary sector is invariably a sign of a developing society. In the United States today, the services sector accounts for half the population – a record percentage indicating that American society is the most advanced in the world.

R.M. Hartwell argues that historians and economists have seriously overlooked the importance of the tertiary sector in English growth of the eighteenth and nineteenth centuries. The development of a *services revolution* he suggests, could be seen as the counterpart of the agricultural revolution in relation to the industrial revolution.

The place of services in the economy certainly expanded: it cannot be denied that transport developed, that commerce gave rise to many new functions; that the number of shops was always increasing and that they were tending to specialize; that businesses were expanding steadily if not on the whole particularly fast; that they were developing their own bureaucracies; that new categories of occupations were coming into being or taking on new functions: factors, accountants, inspectors, actuaries, commissioners. Banks had very small staffs it is true, but there were large numbers of them. The state, with its thousands of administrative responsibilities was acquiring its own bureaucracy, beginning to swell into an oversize body. There were more top-heavy state bureaucracies on the continent admittedly, but the British state was by no means a slim organization, despite delegating many of its functions. We shall not count the army, the navy or domestic service in the tertiary sector. But we should unquestionably make room in it for the growing numbers of liberal professions – doctors, lawyers, etc. The latter had begun their way up in the days of Gregory King and were being turned out in droves by the Westminster law schools.[214] By the end of the eighteenth century all the professions were expanding steadily and tending to change their structures and traditional forms of organization.

Did the tertiary revolution in eighteenth-century England have any effect on industrial takeoff? It is hard to reply, particularly since as Colin Clark himself explained, division into sectors has always been present in some form, and is still going on as a long-term feature of the economy. There is certainly no evidence that the expansion of the tertiary sector launched growth.[215] But it was unquestionably a sign that growth was taking place.

The division of labour and the geography of Britain

Let us now turn to the devastating effect that the division of labour had on the economic geography of Britain. This was something very different from the elimination of provincial autarkies in France during the economic expansion of the eighteenth century.[216] In England, the process was not one of development so much as upheaval – things were practically turned upside down. The interaction between the different regions of England – projected on to the physical landscape of the island where it has left visible signs – is the most powerful and telling document one could imagine on the growth of the British economy and the industrial revolution it brought with it. It is surprising that this question has not inspired any full-length study, although there is at least one remarkable essay on historical geography[217] and a very rich literature on the history of the regions.[218]

The question has been clearly perceived however, by E.L. Jones in his paper at the 1965 Munich conference,[219] by David Ogg[220] in 1934, by G.M. Trevelyan[221] in 1942: between them they have said the important thing, which is that the economic geography of England had for centuries been articulated either side of a line from Gloucester on the Severn, to Boston, the little town on the Wash which used to export wool to Florence and the Hanseatic ports.[222] Leaving Wales on one side, this line bisected England into two roughly equal parts of contrasting character. South-east England, especially the Thames valley and surrounding areas, had the lowest rainfall in the island, and the most eventful history. Here was to be found 'every type of urban development which had grown up over the centuries: ecclesiastical seats, regional markets, university cities, staging posts, entrepôt towns, [former] manufacturing centres'.[223] All the accumulated advantages of history were combined here – the capital city, a rich commercial life, a countryside domesticated and modernized to meet the needs of the capital; last but not least, between London and Norwich to the north, and between London and Bristol to the west, lay the prime zones of English pre-industry. North-west England by contrast, was an area of high rainfall; on its ancient uplands the main activity was sheep grazing. Compared to the south it was a sort of periphery, a backward area, as indeed the figures indicate: in the seventeenth century, the population ratio between north and south (excluding London) was 1:4; for wealth (calculated from taxes) the figures were 5:14.[224]

This ancient imbalance was completely overturned by the industrial revolution. The previously privileged south saw its traditional industries decline. It did not succeed, for all its capitalist wealth and commercial strength, in attracting and keeping the new industry. It was on the contrary that other England, north of the dividing line, which was 'in the space of a few generations'[225] transformed into a rich and astonishingly modern country.

The road from London to Scotland via Northampton and Manchester today runs through the Pennine coalfield with its series of basins where once men and machines crowded together and where there sprang up almost overnight the most dynamic and the most 'satanic' of industrial conurbations. The evidence is still visible there today: every coal basin had its own speciality, its types of industry, its own history and its own great city – Birmingham, Manchester, Leeds, Sheffield – which grew up simultaneously, shifting the industrial balance of England to the north. Here industrialization and urbanization proceeded at breakneck speed; the various Black Countries of England were machines devouring and disorienting the population who flocked to them. Geography is not of course the only explanation for these mighty constructions, but it helps us to see more clearly the harsh determinism exerted by coal, the constraints of communications, the role of manpower resources and, too, the heavy weight of the past. Perhaps the brutal new features of eighteenth- and nineteenth-century England essentially needed some kind of social vacuum as their site.

North-west England was not, it should be said, a desert in the way that journalists describe the west of France for instance as 'the French desert'. But it was undoubtedly in economic terms a *periphery*, like Scotland, compared to the London area. This time however, the periphery, including Scotland, joined up with the core, made up for lost time and reached the same level. In terms of our core-periphery theories, it is an exception of glaring dimensions – as T.C. Smout has pointed out in his work on Scotland.[226] There is no shortage of explanations: the advanced core region (southern England) was within easy access of the periphery (and in any case the term 'periphery', if undoubtedly applicable to Scotland, is perhaps only partly applicable to north-west England). More significantly, Scotland and the 'other' England caught up with the south by means of very rapid industrialization. And it is well attested that industrialization prospers when it is introduced to low-income areas, where the very poverty of the workforce gives it a competitive advantage – as can be seen today by looking at South Korea, Hong Kong and Singapore, and in the past by comparing northern Europe with Italy.

Finance and capitalism

The history of capital reaches well beyond the first industrial revolution – preceding it, encompassing it and continuing after it. During this period of exceptional economic growth which encouraged progress everywhere, capital, like everything else, was transformed and expanded as industrial capitalism asserted itself, soon becoming all-important. But was this the new form in which capitalism was finally to make its mark as it were in world history, to begin its own 'true' career? Was it only in this form that it reached perfection and became its true self, with modern mass production and the huge weight of fixed capital that this required? Was everything that had come before merely preparing the way, a series of embryonic forms of capitalism, curiosities fit only for the historical museum? This is often the impression more or less directly conveyed by standard historical analysis. While it may not be a totally misleading impression, neither is it entirely correct.

In my view, capitalism is a venture that goes back a very long way: by the time of the industrial revolution it already had a considerable wealth of experience behind it and not only in the commercial sphere. So in England in the early years of the nineteenth century, capital was present in all its classic forms which

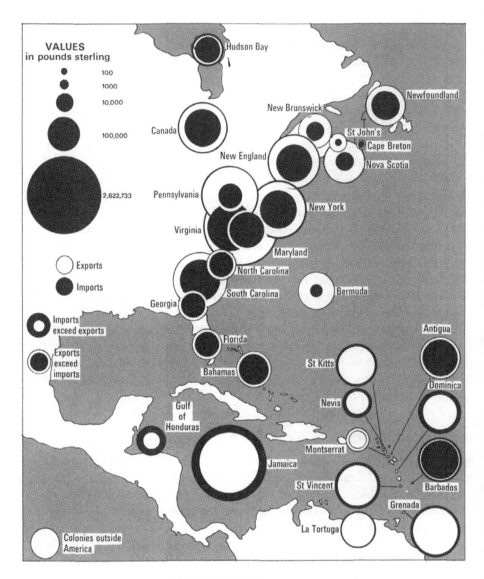

VALUES
in pounds sterling

- 100
- 1000
- 10,000
- 100,000

2,622,733

○ Exports

● Imports

◉ Imports
exceed exports

◉ Exports
exceed
imports

Hudson Bay

Newfoundland

New Brunswick

St John's

Cape Breton

Canada

New England

Nova Scotia

Pennsylvania

New York

Virginia

Maryland

North Carolina

Bermuda

South Carolina

Georgia

Florida

Antigua

St Kitts

Dominica

Bahamas

Nevis

Gulf
of
Honduras

Montserrat

Barbados

Jamaica

St Vincent

Grenada

La Tortuga

Colonies outside
America

55 GREAT BRITAIN'S TRADE WITH WITH THE REST OF THE WORLD IN 1792
From statistics in French archives (A.E. M. et D. Angleterre 10 f° 130). White stands for exports
(E), black for imports (I). The inside of the circle is black or white depending on whether exports
exceeded imports or vice versa. Circles that look empty signify approximate equality between
imports and exports. This was the case in Turkey (I = £290,559; E = £273,715); Italy (£1,009,000
and £936,263); and Ireland (£2,622,733 and £2,370,866). There was an imbalance in Britain's
favour with the United States; Portugal (£977,820 and £754,612); and France after the Eden
treaty (£717,034 and £1,221,666). Some general totals: Europe £11,170,860 and £12,813,435;
America: £5,603,947 and £8,159,502; Asia £2,671,547 and £2,627,887; Africa £82,917 and

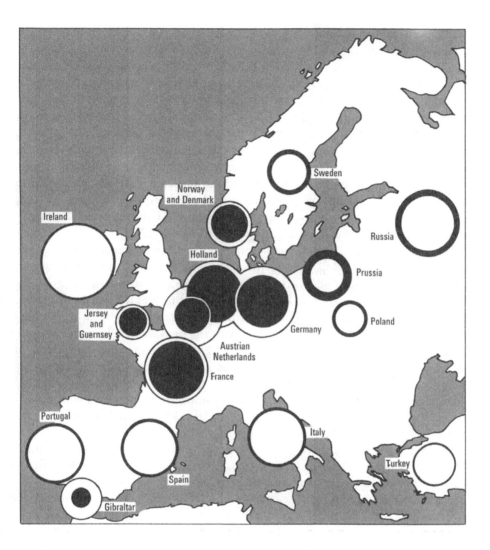

£1,367,539. Total imports were £19,529,273 to £24,878,362 exports, that is a positive balance of over £5 million. Exports of 'English-manufactured' goods were worth £18,509,796, re-exports of goods manufactured abroad £6,568,565. British trade was carried by 15,463 ships entering her ports and 15,010 leaving, a total of 30,470 ships, 3620 of which were foreign. The average tonnage of English ships was 122 tons, their average crew 7 men. For Franco-British trade there were 3160 return voyages, 430 by foreign ships. For trade with Asia there were 28 departures and 36 returns, all in English ships, average tonnage 786 tons, average crew 93.

(This record does not count the substantial English coastal shipping, mostly of coal.)

were moreover all very much alive: agricultural capital, which in itself constituted half of England's wealth even in 1830; industrial capital, which had been
growing very slowly until its sudden expansion; and a very ancient commercial
capital, smaller in *relative* terms but ready to expand worldwide, creating the
colonialism for which a name and justification would soon have to be found;
finally (if we can lump together the worlds of banking and finance) there was
financial capital which did not wait for the triumph of the City of London to
come into being. For Hilferding,[227] it was the twentieth century, with its profusion of huge corporations and the immense concentration of money in every
form which brought about the advent and the supremacy of finance capitalism
in a sort of unholy trinity in which industrial capitalism was God the Father,
commercial capitalism – a secondary phenomenon – God the Son, and finance
capitalism the Holy Ghost, penetrating everything else.[228]

Rather than take up this perhaps rather questionable image, let us draw the
conclusion that Hilferding rejects the notion of a purely industrial form of
capitalism, that he sees the world of capital as a range of possibilities, within
which the financial variety – a very recent arrival as he sees it – has tended to win
out over the others, penetrating and dominating them from within. It is a view
with which I am very willing to concur, with the proviso that I see the plurality
of capitalism as something going back a long way. Finance capitalism was no
newborn child of the 1900s; I would even argue that in the past – in say Genoa
or Amsterdam – following a wave of growth in commercial capitalism and the
accumulation of capital on a scale beyond the normal channels for investment,[229]
finance capitalism was already in a position to take over and dominate, for a
while at least, all the activities of the business world.

In the English case, it is clear that the range of types of capitalism, including
the rise of 'finance capitalism', already existed well before 1900. Much earlier, in
the wave of revolutions which marked England's tempestuous growth, a financial revolution had even run alongside the country's industrialization; it may not
have launched the latter, but it certainly accompanied it and made it possible. It
is often said that the English banks did not finance industrialization. But recent
studies have shown that both long and short-term credit was available for
industrial enterprise in the eighteenth and even the nineteenth century.[230]

The Bank of England, founded in 1694, was the centre of an entire banking
system. Around it and based on it were the private London banks: 73 of them in
1807, about a hundred during the 1820s.[231] In the provinces, the 'country banks'
which had certainly appeared by the early eighteenth century and which multiplied in the wake of the South Sea Bubble only to collapse with it afterwards,
numbered only a dozen in 1750, but 120 in 1784, 290 in about 1797, 370 in 1800
and at least 650 in about 1810.[232] One author even puts the number at about 900
in the same period, probably counting the branches which several of them
opened. It is true that this spontaneous generation was the triumph of Lilliput
(banks could not have more than six partners)[233] and that their numbers were

created not so much to meet the needs of speculation (which was however by no means a privilege of Londoners), as to meet particular local needs and circumstances. A country bank[234] was often simply an extra counter opened in an already well-established firm where the handling of bills, discounting and credit were no more than good neighbourliness, often carried on quite informally. These improvised bankers came from all kinds of backgrounds. The Fosters of Cambridge were millers and cornmerchants; in Liverpool most of the banks were branches of commercial houses; the Lloyds of Birmingham were originally ironmasters; the Smiths of Nottingham were hosiers; the Gurneys of Norwich were yarn merchants and worsted manufacturers; most Cornish bankers were mine-owners; elsewhere they might be malt or hop merchants, brewers, drapers, mercers or turnpike treasurers.[235]

In short, eighteenth-century banks were the product of local circumstances, rather like the first new industrial undertakings. Provincial England needed credit, it needed facilities for the circulation of bills of exchange, it needed cash, and the private banks fulfilled all these functions since they even had the right to issue bank notes. Indeed this was a major source of profit for them since at least at first, until people had sufficient confidence in them to deposit cash with them, they could only extend their credit by printing money.[236] In theory these banks had gold reserves sufficient to cover their issues, but if there was a crisis accompanied by public panic as in 1745, they were obliged to send in haste to London banks for cash to avoid bankruptcies. These could not always be avoided, during the crises of 1793 and 1816 in particular. And such failures are evidence in themselves that the local banks made large-scale loans, not only in the short but in the long-term.[237]

In general however the system was solid enough, since it was in practice, though not officially, underwritten by the Bank of England, which acted as the 'lender of last resort'.[238] Its own cash reserves were usually adequate to cover unexpected repayments by private banks, in London or the provinces, in times of difficulty. After 1797, when the bank notes of the Bank of England were no longer convertible into gold, they became for local banks the currency into which they undertook in the last resort to change their own notes. A clear sign of general stability was that the private banks became deposit banks, thereby increasing their ability to make loans to farmers or landowners as well as to industrialists, pit-owners or canal builders.[239] The latter took full advantage of the opportunity – the Duke of Bridgewater's loans are a perfect example.

After 1826, when joint stock banks were authorized by law, these made up the new generation of more solidly based banks with greater capital resources than the earlier generation. Were they any more prudent? Not at all since they had to compete with the existing banks for customers, therefore to take more risks. Their numbers grew visibly: there were 70 of them in 1836 but between 1 January and 26 November of that year, no fewer than 42 joint stock banks 'have been set up and are entering into competition with those which already exist'.[240]

The Coal Exchange in London. Engraving by Rowlandson. (Photo Roger-Viollet.)

Soon there would be over a hundred, and with their many branches they would number as many as the country banks which now began to look rather old-fashioned establishments.

London however was for a long time closed to the joint stock banks, but in the end they forced their way in and in 1854 were admitted to the Clearing House of the London banks, that is they could take a full part in the circulation of money and credit of which London was the unique, sophisticated and initiatory centre. The Clearing House, which had been created in 1773 for compensatory payments between banks, was described by the admiring Frenchman Maurice Rubichon in 1811:

> The mechanism for circulation [he writes] is organized in such a way that one could say that in England there is neither money nor paper. Forty London cashiers handle between them almost all the payments and transactions of the kingdom. Meeting every evening, they exchange in the most natural way

the paper they hold respectively so that a thousand-louis [sic] note is often enough to settle the circulation of several million.[241]

Very impressive no doubt – but are these not exactly the terms used by observers in the sixteenth and seventeenth century to describe the mechanisms of the traditional fairs of Lyon or Besançon-Piacenza? The only difference – but an important one – was that clearing meetings were held daily in London, whereas in the great fairs of the past it was four times a year.

On the other hand, banks fulfilled a function that fairs could not. 'In this country', wrote a perspicacious Frenchman, 'no individual, whether in trade or not, keeps his money at home; he keeps it deposited with a banker or rather cashier, on whom he can draw, who keeps his accounts and settles his expenses depending on the state of his credit'.[242] Money accumulated in banks did not lie idle, but became available for risk, since neither banker nor cashier let it moulder in their coffers. As Ricardo put it, the distinctive function of the banker began when he used other people's money.[243] Then there was the money which circulated under pressure, between the Bank of England and the British government, or between the bank as lender of last resort and the other banks and commercial or even industrial firms. And the popular savings banks collected the money saved by the poor – a large amount as a French correspondent writes, for 'the poor man's fortune [in the mass] in England is greater than the rich man's fortune in more than one kingdom'.[244]

To complete the picture, one should mention the establishment in London of a third generation of pseudo-banks – the bill-brokers who founded what were known as discount houses. It should also be pointed out that the private banks in the City of London, which acted as agents and correspondents for regional banks, were able to redistribute credit and to transfer surplus capital from regions like south-east England to the active north-west, a procedure easily grasped, as capital was invested in the best interests of lenders, borrowers and middlemen.

A full account would also examine the Bank of England. The first thing to be said about it is that it was not only a government bank and thereby both blessed with privileges and encumbered with responsibilities; it was also a private bank with its own shareholders and as such a very sound investment: the 'shares ... [originally] created at one hundred pounds sterling stood at £136 in 1803 and are worth £355 today' (6 February 1817).[245] Throughout the eighteenth century they provided fuel for speculation on the Stock Exchanges in both London and Amsterdam. Secondly, the use of Bank of England notes was steadily spreading, reaching the country as a whole and not only the region round the capital to which they had originally been confined. In Lancashire, in Manchester and Liverpool, workers refused to be paid in notes issued by private banks which were often undervalued by shopkeepers.[246] London plus Lancashire was already a large catchment area. But after 1797, the Bank of England bank note became a surrogate form of gold coinage throughout the entire country.

One ought also to look inside the Stock Exchange where new listings were flooding in. In 1825, there were 114 new quotations, 20 in railways, 22 for loans and banks, 17 for foreign mines (especially in Latin America) plus 11 gas-lighting companies. These 114 new quotations alone represented investments of £100 million[247] at least on paper, since funds were not all paid in immediately.

The haemorrhage of English capital towards foreign investment had already begun. It was a movement which had reached fantastic levels by the end of the nineteenth century but was already well under way by 1815,[248] with variable results admittedly, and indeed in 1826 there was a wholesale crisis. Speculation in finance and the Stock Exchange and the export of capital nevertheless continued via the extremely lively money market. By about the 1860s, while industrial output was still growing fast (it had almost doubled in ten years and was to continue expanding at high rates until at least 1880)[249] and when investment *at home* was probably as high as it had ever been in British history,[250] financial investment abroad, which had been rising rapidly since mid-century, was already in some years reaching the same level as the *total* investment on British soil.[251] Moreover the *percentage* accounted for by trade and transport in national income increased steadily, rising from 17.4% in 1801 to 15.9% in 1821, 22% in 1871 and 27.5% in 1907.[252]

How then can one think of 'industrial' capitalism as the only 'true' capitalism, triumphing over commercial capitalism ('false' capitalism?) and finally, reluctantly, making way for ultra-modern finance capitalism? Financial, industrial and commercial capitalism (since capitalism never stopped being connected with trade) coexisted throughout the nineteenth century, as they had before the nineteenth century and would do after it.

What did change constantly over time were the rates and the timing of profits: these could vary from sector to sector, country to country and it was in the light of such variations that the respective volumes of capital investment themselves changed. Between 1830 and 1870 or so, the period of most intense industrialization in Britain, the capital/revenue quotient seems to have reached its highest known level.[253] But is this explained simply by the virtues of industrial capitalism in itself – or by the fact that British industry was able to expand during these years to match the enormous world markets which Britain unquestionably dominated? This seems to be indicated by the contrast with Parisian capitalism which during the same period took the course which it regarded as most profitable and opportune *for itself* and the one from which it could best challenge Britain, and fell back on finance. Paris became quite widely accepted as a centre for movements of capital within Europe.

> Over the last twenty years [wrote the Chevalier Séguier from Paris in September 1818] Paris has become the principal centre for banking operations in Europe, whereas London is not really a banking city. The result is that an English capitalist who wants to effect some banking operation, say a transfer of funds from one country to another, is obliged to turn to one of the European banking

centres and since Paris is the nearest, it is there that most English transactions are handled today.[254]

His remarks might not stand up to scrutiny, but there is no doubt that Paris was carving out a place for itself alongside and in the shadow of London, that it was becoming reasonably competitive, and if Bagehot is right in his history of the Stock Exchange, the pendulum swung against Paris only after 1870. It was after the Franco-Prussian War, he writes, that the English became bankers to the rest of Europe.[255]

How important was the short-term economic climate?

Does this question – the last in the chapter and one which cannot be answered categorically – take us away from our original purpose which was to go beyond the historical context of the industrial revolution? Yes to some extent, because the time-span I have in mind here is the comparatively short-term (nothing longer than a Kondratieff). So it does divert us from the long-term and brings us to vantage points nearer the reality under observation: we shall be looking at certain details in close-up.

The economic fluctuations of varying length which seem to succeed one another like waves rolling in from the sea, are a rule in world history, a rule which has reached down the ages to us and will carry on operating. Like a repeated rhythm – Charles Morazé uses the term 'dynamic structures' – these movements are as if pre-ordained. Focusing on this kind of movement takes us inevitably to the heart of the problems we have been looking at, but by particular paths, namely those of the history of prices, the interpretation of which has been one of the major problems of historiography over the last forty or fifty years. In this field, British historians are by no means overshadowed, indeed they were the first and some of the best collectors of price series. But they do not look at the short-term climate (*la conjuncture*) in the same way as other (notably French) historians.

To oversimplify a complex issue, I would say that British historians do not regard the *conjuncture* as an exogeneous force – as the French school does, its point of view having been more or less explicitly formulated by Ernest Labrousse, Pierre Villar, René Baehrel and Jean Meuvret. For these writers, and for me, the *conjuncture* determines the processes which accompany it, it exerts an influence on human existence. For our British colleagues, the *conjuncture* of a given country is determined by national events or processes. For example, French historians see the stagnation and fall of prices between 1778 and 1791 as being explained by the international *intercycle* (short-term cycle) identified by Labrousse; British historians see them as the result of the war with the American colonies (1776–83) and its consequences. I am myself too aware of the mutual benefits of both perspectives not to accept that both views may be valid, and that the explanation ought to take both into account. But depending whether one or the other is preferred, responsibilities, or perhaps I should say efficient causes, might change position and nature.

T.S. Ashton[256] and those who agree with him[257] are clearly right when they list the series of factors which may influence short-term change. Top of the list comes war. No one will disagree with that. More precisely, fluctuations arose from swings between war and peace (the Seven Years' War, 1756-63; the American War of Independence, 1775-83; the French Revolutionary and Napoleonic Wars, 1793-1802, 1803-15). Then there are the fluctuations in the rural economy (which remained Britain's major economic sector, it must be remembered, until about the 1830s): the harvest might be good, average or poor and bad years (1710, 1725, 1773, 1767, 1792-3, 1795-6, 1799-1800) always marked the start of the so-called *ancien régime* crises[258] which affected the whole of economic life. Even in the nineteenth century, the increasingly frequent and massive calls made on foreign wheat had repercussions on the British economy, if only because payment had to be made quickly (and in cash say the correspondents) to ensure the rapid arrival of sacks of grain or barrels of flour.

Another influence on fluctuations in the English economy was the trade cycle, the set of upward and downward swings which had their effect on the general situation. And there was also the money supply, gold and silver coinage on the one hand and notes of every provenance on the other. The London Stock Exchange (which was always 'sensitive', and to which fear was a more frequent visitor than optimism)[259] was a curious seismograph which not only registered all the movements around it but also had the diabolical power of itself triggering off earthquakes: as it did in 1825-6, 1837 and 1847. Every ten years or so, as had already been the case towards the end of the eighteenth century, the summits of economic life would be shaken by a credit crisis, while at the same time traditional *ancien régime* type crises were still possible.[260]

Such are the conclusions of our British colleagues. As for French historians, rightly or wrongly they see the *conjuncture* as a reality in its own right, although it is far from easy to *explain* in its own right. We agree with Léon Dupriez and Wilhelm Abel that prices form some sort of totality. Dupriez has even spoken of a *prices structure*. Prices, according to this view, are related to each other and if they go up and down together it is because their particular variations are combined. Above all, this is not a 'vibration' confined to one economy, however important that country may be. Britain did not create her own price levels, nor the fluctuations in her trade, nor even her own money supply; the other economies in the world – the whole world – all contributed and all economies moved almost in unison. This is what we as historians found most striking when we first began work in this field: for some indication of the surprising results, see René Baehrel's very revealing and persuasive work.

The climate which raised, halted or lowered prices in England was not a climate obeying a time-scale peculiar to England, but one governed by 'world time' (cf. chapter 1). It may very well be the case that this 'world time' was in part dictated by Britain, or even that London was its essential epicentre - but the rest of the world helped to shape and determine a movement which was by no means the private property of the British Isles. The consequences are obvious. The 'sounding-board' for prices was the entire world-economy of which Britain was the core. So the economic movement affecting Britain was in part of external origin, and events outside Britain, notably in nearby Europe, may have something to do with British history. Europe and Britain were contained within the same economic climate - which does not mean to say that their experience was identical. When describing a conjunctural *crisis* in the economy, I have on the contrary stressed that it does not and cannot have the same impact on the strong and the weak (for instance on Italy and Holland in the seventeenth century); consequently that it is the occasion of a redistribution of functions and of international economic relations, usually ending up by making the strong stronger and the weak weaker. This is why I do not agree with the argument used by Peter Mathias[261] to deny the role played, between 1873 and 1896, by the downward curve of a Kondratieff cycle and its responsibility for the 'Great Depression' which affected England during these years. While growth rates in both Germany and America also fell during the same period, he argues, it is clear that the situation was very different in Germany, the United States and Britain, and that the British Isles fell back in *relative* terms, losing their share in the world economy. That is perfectly true: what would become evident to the world in 1929 was casting its shadow before. But the fact remains that growth slowed down *simultaneously* in Germany, the United States, Britain and indeed in France. And it is the way the *graphs* all dip together, whatever the actual price level in each country, which is the surprising but undeniable thing about this crisis.

What was obvious in the nineteenth century and is even more obvious in the world today, namely an economic trend affecting huge areas in a similar way and at very much the same time, can already be detected in the eighteenth century or even earlier. So it is very tempting to compare what was happening in Britain between the 1780s and 1812-17, with what was going on in France, which we can study thanks to Ernest Labrousse's exhaustive study. But we should not assume too much too soon: the French picture will not be directly reflected across the Channel. We have a number of different graphs to consider and they do not all speak the same language. If we could compare price, wage and output trends from country to country according to the same criteria, it would be much easier to spot coincidences and divergences, and the problem of similarity or difference would be quickly resolved. This is not the case. But if we compare the British and French graphs for prices of goods produced and consumed, we can see straight away that the French graph behaves much more dramatically than the British. Perhaps this is only to be expected: the water may boil less fiercely at the centre of the world than elsewhere. It is not very easy, on the British price curve taken from Deane and Cole, to spot an intercycle between 1780 and 1792; rather

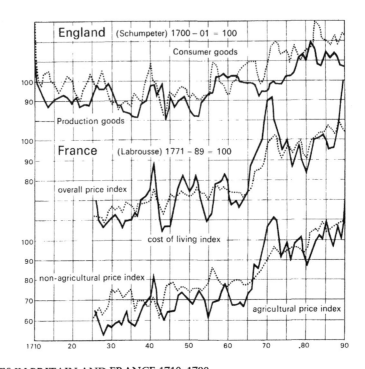

56 PRICES IN BRITAIN AND FRANCE 1710-1790
The Labrousse intercycle shows up clearly on the French graphs, but does it appear in the British figures? (After G. Imbert, *Des Mouvements de longue durée Kondratieff*, 1959, p. 207.)

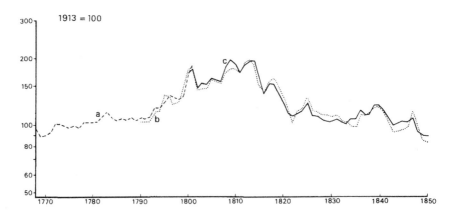

57 LONG-TERM TRENDS IN BRITISH PRICES
In the smoothed-out graph showing long-term change, the 'stability' referred to by Leon Dupriez can easily be detected between 1772 and 1793. The nearest thing to the French intercycle is the plateau of the 1780s. The Kondratieff cycle begins, as in France, in about 1791, reaches its peak in 1810-12 (in France in about 1817) and falls to its lowest point in 1850-1. The three different lines (continuous, dashes and dots) represent different series of calculations. (After P. Deane and W.A. Cole, *British Economic Growth 1688-1959*, 1962.)

prices mark a sort of plateau, a period of 'stability' as Léon Dupriez would call it, arguing that this period of stagnation began in 1773. On the other hand, the graphs quite emphatically concur about the Kondratieff cycle which follows: it begins in 1791, peaks in 1812 and reaches its lowest point in 1851.

We may conclude that the British industrial revolution experienced two movements, roughly between 1781 and 1815, a first and second wind so to speak, the first a rather difficult period, the second easier. In very broad terms, this was also the rhythm experienced by France and the rest of the continent. Louis XVI's France, racked with problems and about to open the door to violent political upheaval, had something in common with George III's England, which was also going through a bad patch. In England there would be no political explosion at the end of the road, but the road itself would be a painful one. For about ten years there was a pause in the upward movement which had hitherto blessed the British economy. It would not be true to say that everything began to go wrong, but it was certainly not going as right as in the past. England, like France, was paying the price for the fantastic efforts and money expended on the American war. And the crisis which followed complicated things greatly, redistributing functions and underlining differences between sectors. Trade expanded in spectacular fashion in both France and England, but in both countries the trade balance was upset, running into deficit. Vigorous attempts at recovery were undertaken, but with only limited success. Could not the signature of the Eden Treaty in 1786, a truce between two hostile and mutually distrustful powers, be regarded as an effort to run for cover?

As a rule the result of an abnormally long depression acts as a severe test of business concerns, in which those which adapt and stand up to attack will survive, while those too weak to survive go to the wall. It was England's good fortune to have entered these rough waters just as the 'second generation' of inventions was coming into being: the spinning jenny (1768); the water-powered frame (1769); the powered drill (1775); the rotary steam-engine (1776–81); iron puddling (1784); the first usable threshing machine (1786); the perfected form of the lathe (1794) – cumulatively a huge technical investment paving the way for recovery.

In 1791, the skies cleared: prices rose, business picked up, there was a greater division of labour, resulting in greater productivity. English agriculture benefited from this until Waterloo, and middle-sized farms survived thanks to high food prices. It was indeed the generally favourable situation which made it possible to indulge in the insane expenditure on the Revolutionary and Napoleonic Wars (£1,000 million was spent by England alone).[262] But since this age was not the private property of Britain, the continent also saw the creation of modern industry, though on a smaller scale.

The improving situation however sent prices up faster than wages in Britain. Since the population was also expanding, the result was a drop in living standards as per capita income fell, in current prices, between 1770 and 1820.[263] In 1688, it had been £9.1; in 1770, it was £19.1; in 1798, £15.4; in 1812, £14.2; in 1822, £17.5. Even clearer evidence is provided by the graphs calculated by E.H. Phelps Brown and Sheila Hopkins, showing the wages of English stone-masons between the thirteenth and nineteenth centuries, reproduced with explanations in Figure 58. This is quite a conclusive graph, since it shows over a period of centuries the regular correlation between price rises and the fall in real wages: rising prices seem to produce an increase in output and a rise in population – interrelated phenomena, causally linked – but wages invariably fall; under the conditions of the *ancien régime*, progress was always at the expense of the living standards of the workers. And this rule, which is indeed the unmistakable sign of the *ancien régime*, can still be seen at work, according to the Brown-Hopkins figures, between 1760 and 1810-20, with wages hitting their lowest levels in about the 1800s, just as the graph for the economic situation in general is moving towards its highest point.[264] When the wage situation improved after 1820, as prices fell, it was simply that the old rules were asserting themselves. The real miracle, the real change did not happen until the beginning of the next Kondratieff cycle, after about 1850 (another key date both in Britain and on the continent). This time when prices moved up, wages kept pace; continuous growth had at last appeared.

This brings me to the heart of a debate which too many historians have perhaps cannily avoided; it concerns the price that Britain paid for becoming 'the first industrial nation'. I am inclined to agree with the earliest historians who studied this question, that there was indeed a deterioration in the well-being of the British masses, a decline in real wages, for farm labourers as well as for workers in factories or transport. I tend to think (and I must proceed with caution here, since I am no expert on this period) that the first phase of industrialization between 1760 and 1815 was even more painful than the period which followed Waterloo, although unrest among both workers and peasants was more widespread and more endemic after the British victory that it had been before. But is not unrest itself evidence that things were, if not good, at least improving or reaching sufficient levels to support it? It is however true and this was the *extra* price of industrial growth compared with the other forms of growth which had preceded it) that between 1817 and 1850 the rise in real wages and per capita income registered on the Brown-Hopkins graph was in part cancelled out for the labouring masses by the dramatic impact of over-rapid urbanization – which combined the catastrophic effects of wretched housing, unhealthy and even contaminated food (for lack of sufficient means of transport), with the social upheaval which tore individuals away from their family roots and the resources of the village community. But between 1780 and 1815, with the collapse of real wages (beginning it should be noted in 1760,[265] that is with the sharp rise in output and population which characterized the latter half of the eighteenth century and not only with the outbreak of the American War of Independence) the situation was even more dramatic.

'Two generations were sacrificed to the creation of an industrial base.' This conclusion by present-day historians[266] based on the witness of contemporaries, is certainly borne out if we view England in the period through the eyes of the French commander and *mestre-de-camp* Pillet.[267] Wounded and taken prisoner at Cintra in Portugal in 1807, he lived for many years in England until his release, and if he had no great love for the country (what prisoner ever loves his jailers?) he was a perceptive observer, writing without bitterness and apparently with a natural inclination to impartiality. His memories of England were of very hard times: 'I have seen all her factories without work', he writes, 'her people troubled with famine and crushed by taxation, her paper money discredited'.[268] In 1811, 'the manufacturers being unable to pay their workmen gave them for wages the products of their own manufacture; and in order to buy bread, these unfortunate creatures had to sell them on the spot at two-thirds of their real value'.[269] Another witness, Louis Simond, who was also a lucid observer and an admirer of England, noted at the same date[270] that 'the worker cannot buy with his regular pay the bread, meat and clothes necessary for his upkeep and that of his family'. As for farm labourers, 'their wages lag ... painfully behind the general rate for everything'. In Glasgow in 1812, he observed[271] that 'the wages of the cotton workers ... are no more than a quarter what they were nineteen years ago, although everything has doubled in price in the meantime'. We may query the exact figures he gives, but not the general impoverishment he was condemning.

But Commander Pillet saw further still, it seems to me, in the sense that as a military man he was aware of England's extraordinary military effort. In order to provide men for the army, the English government was recruiting soldiers 'in a much more frightening proportion that any of the appeals made to our population'.[272] The upkeep of the armies was a colossal burden: there were over 200,000 men under the colours (and English soldiers' pay was four times that of the French)[273] and the enormous fleet had to be maintained too. Hence perhaps the inflexible harshness with which soldiers and sailors were treated, as members of the most wretched classes of society, 'the scum of the earth'.[274] Of a younger son who went to the bad and whose family bought him a commission in the army, it was said, 'the rascal is fit to be hanged and good only to become a redcoat'.[275] This was England's true sub-proletariat, supplied with men by the poverty of the actual proletariat, worker, peasant or vagrant. What should we blame? Perhaps not industrialization, nor capitalism which was now storming the commanding heights of wealth, nor even the war itself nor the general economic climate in which everything was bathed – but all of these at once.

Many historians do not wish to face up to this disturbing fact. They simply refuse to admit it. One will argue that there is no precise or satisfactory method of measuring living standards. Another will say that the situation of the working class was worse or at any rate no better, before the first examples of mechanization. A third says he does not believe that prices ever fell between 1790 and 1830. But what prices are we talking about – nominal or real prices? And do the graphs not plainly tell us that prices first rose then fell? And what about wages?

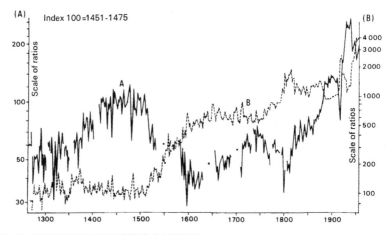

(A) Index 100=1451-1475 (B)

58   THE 'HOUSEWIFE'S SHOPPING BASKET'
This graph, like those calculated by Abel and Fourastie-Grandamy (cf. vol. I, p. 134), shows how historians of the economy have tried to extract from a price-wage relation something like per capita income. The English stonemason was paid a certain wage and consumed a certain number of essential products. A group of such essential products, sometimes described as 'the housewife's shopping basket', has been used as an indicator. The dotted line shows changes in the price of the shopping basket, the continuous line the relation between wages and the contemporary price of the shopping basket (the period 1451–75 was chosen as an index = 100). Comparison of the graphs shows that any period when prices were stable or dropping (1380–1510; 1630–1750) saw an improvement in consumption and well-being. When prices rise there is a fall in living standards; between 1510 and 1630 and again between 1750 and 1820, in the early days of the industrial revolution. After that, wages and prices rise in unison. (After E.H. Phelps-Brown and Sheila Hopkins, in *Essays in Economic History*, ed. E. Carus-Wilson, II, pp. 183 and 186.)

It seems abundantly clear that the English people paid very dearly for their victories, even for the advance in agriculture which enriched only a certain class of farmers, and much more heavily for the machines, the technical triumphs, the commanding lead in trade, the pre-eminence of London, the fortunes of the industrialists and the shareholders in the Bank of England – the price for all these and not merely for the military victories of its armies and navy and the Battle of Waterloo was a high one. It is only fair to add that later, after 1850, the British people as a whole, whatever the inequalities of society, shared in Britain's triumphs on the world stage. It is the destiny of a people which finds itself at the centre of a world-economy to be *in relative terms* the richest and least badly-off. Dutch men and women in the seventeenth century or the 'Americans' of today, whatever their position in society, enjoyed or continue to enjoy the privilege which was possessed by the British in the nineteenth century.

Material progress and living standards

Seen through the lens of the *conjuncture*, the British industrial revolution of the eighteenth and nineteenth centuries appears in rather a new light. This is one more vantage-point from which to view the complicated landscape of growth. The industrial revolution was a collection of problems hard to disentangle, borne along on a wider stream. Its very size forces us to ask questions about the broader history of the world, about the real transformations and motives behind growth, about the beginnings of continuous growth (1850 seems a more appropriate date than 1830-2 which is often suggested as marking the end of the first stage of the industrial revolution). It also urges us to reflect on long-term European growth of which the industrial revolution marks the most spectacular phase, between a past which was long uncertain and a present to which uncertainty seems to be returning.

If we measure growth by the two variables G.N.P. and per capita income (or as I would prefer to say G.N.P. and the real wages of the Brown-Hopkins stonemason), we might follow Wilhelm Abel[276] in observing that these two variables increased side by side in the twelfth and thirteenth centuries – providing an early model of 'sustained growth'. After 1350 and until 1450, G.N.P., the volume of output and the mass of the population declined, but the well-being of survivors increased, they were relieved of the tasks imposed upon them by progress, and benefited from the lull. During the much-vaunted sixteenth century (specialists in the sixteenth century are rather 'nationalist' about their century) and until 1625-50, both population and output rose once more, Europe became more densely settled, but general well-being steadily decreased. Progress always took its toll. After 1650 the 'seventeenth-century crisis', which historians have conscientiously painted in very black colours, lasted until 1720, 1730 or 1750. And the same phenomenon occurred as in the period after 1350: a measure of individual well-being went hand in hand with economic stagnation. René Baehrel is right.[277] Then the process began again in the eighteenth century: a rise in 'prosperity' and a drop in real wages.

From the middle of the nineteenth century, which broke the rhythm of growth established during the *ancien régime*, the world apparently embarked upon a new age: the secular trend was characterized by a simultaneous rise in population, prices, G.N.P., and wages, interrupted by only short cyclical depressions as if 'sustained growth' was here to stay.

But only 120 years have passed between 1850 and 1970. Have the long crises of the secular trend gone for ever with the coming of Modern Times? It is difficult to answer because the truth is that the secret of these secular movements, the key even to their simple correlations is still unknown to us; consequently we lack a substantial element in historical explanation. As a result many historians, and not the least among them, find it easy to be ironic about these historical cycles which can be observed and noted but not explained. Do they really exist?

Is it really possible to believe that human history obeys all-commanding rhythms which ordinary logic cannot explain? I am inclined to answer yes, even though the phenomenon is as puzzling as the climatic cycles, whose existence we are forced to admit, since the evidence stares us in the face, although the experts can still only suggest hypotheses about their origin. I do believe in these tidal movements which seem to govern the physical and economic history of the world, even if the favourable or unfavourable indicators which trigger them off, and which are the product of so many relationships, remain a mystery. I believe in them so firmly that since the beginning of our present difficulties, in 1972–4, I have often asked myself: is this the downward slope of a Kondratieff cycle? Or are we indeed embarking upon a much longer slide, a reversal of the secular trend? If so, are not the day-to-day remedies proposed to meet the crisis completely illusory? For the reversal of the secular trend is a structural crisis which could only be resolved by thorough-going structural demolition and reconstruction.

Only a few years ago, when I outlined these arguments in a lecture, my prognosis of a long-term crisis made my audiences smile. To make forecasts like this in the name of history, and in the name of a long sequence of secular cycles in the past which we can only identify without being able to explain them, is of course a very risky business. But today's economists, armed with all the data about the present experience, also seem to be reduced to hypotheses. Are they not just as incapable as the rest of us of predicting the *length* or even of explaining the nature of the crisis into which we are plunging a little further every day?

By Way of Conclusion:
Past and Present

WHAT I HAVE DONE in this book – and it was not so very difficult though it did raise a number of problems – was to introduce the word *capitalism* with its various meanings and ambiguities, into the broad arena of early modern world history. Was I right to welcome it in? To use it as an *essential* model, applicable to several centuries? A model is like a ship: built on land, launched on water. Will it float? Can it sail? If it is seaworthy, perhaps its analytic cargo will be valid too.

Capitalism, as I have understood it, has proved throughout this book to be a good barometer. Taking it as a guide has meant being able to tackle in a direct and useful way the basic problems and realities: the long-term (*la longue durée*); divisions of economic life; world-economies; secular trends and other fluctuations; the complex and complicating tangles of social hierarchies, not to say the class struggle; the ever-present yet varying role played by dominant minorities; even the series of industrial revolutions. What better subject then for these final pages than this explosive topic, the central focus of all the problems and debates raised in the book? But is it really worth recapitulating here, even briefly, all the evidence, arguments and examples the reader has already met in what has gone before and which we should be able to take as read? I am of the view that the classic conclusion, in which a book's central arguments are rehearsed imperturbably for one last time, as if closing the door on everything that has been said, is inappropriate in a work of history, which can never claim to be complete, to have told the truth once and for all.

At the end of such a lengthy undertaking, I feel rather the need to throw open the doors and windows, to give the house a good airing, even to go outside it. Having constructed as I went along my conceptual framework which ought to be applicable to more than the pre-industrial modern period (otherwise it can hardly claim to belong to history in the deepest sense) I should rather like to launch it on the waters and in the setting of another period. And while we are at it, why not take the present day as that period? Why not, that is, take the realities we have ourselves seen and felt? This would take us out of the magic world of retrospective history and into the living landscape which needs no reconstruction, but lies before us in all its richness and confusion.

There is nothing illogical about this: is it not the secret aim and underlying motive of history to seek to explain the present?[1] And today, now that it is in touch with the various social sciences, is history not also becoming a science of a kind, imperfect and approximate as they are, but ready to ask questions as much as to answer them, to be a measure of the present as well as of the past? That at any rate is what encourages me to embark on a venture I consider not only possible and useful but even pleasurable. Let us disregard, without excessive heart-searching, the risks inherent in a comparison which will take little notice of that bogey of the historian, anachronism. As we emerge from our long journey through the past, the present may be a refreshing way of getting our bearings – and even perhaps a test of truth.

It goes without saying that I make no claim to explain the present in the light of history. I would simply like to see how the explanations and expository schemas I have used stand up to the rough waters of today. Is the model I have built on the frame of pre-nineteenth-century capitalism still seaworthy? Can it withstand the violent buffetings it will clearly receive in the twentieth century? I do not believe that the present contradicts the past; on the contrary, it helps to illuminate it and vice versa. There is no shortage of analogies. But such continuity as there is can only apply to the West, to the so-called 'free world', which no longer encompasses the entire globe as it did before 1917. With the dramatic experiments carried out by the socialist countries, capitalism has vanished from large areas of the planet. So today's world is one which contains both continuity and discontinuity, and this contradiction will always remain on the horizon of the problems I shall be considering in the following order: capitalism as a long-term structure; capitalism as part of the social complex; whether capitalism is in a fit condition to survive or not (though if it were to disappear, would all the inequality in our societies vanish overnight? I rather doubt it); and finally capitalism as distinct from the market economy, which is for me the essential message of this long quest.

Capitalism and the long-term (la longue durée)

Throughout this book, I have argued that capitalism has been *potentially* visible since the dawn of history, and that it has developed and perpetuated itself down the ages. On this point I give my vote to Theodor Mommsen,[2] to Michael Rostowtzeff[3] and to Henri Pirenne.[4] Far in advance, there were signs announcing the coming of capitalism: the rise of the towns and of trade, the emergence of a labour market, the increasing density of society, the spread of the use of money, the rise in output, the expansion of long-distance trade or to put it another way the international market. When, in the first century AD, India seized or at any rate penetrated the islands of the East Indies; when Rome held an area even greater than the Mediterranean in her power; when China invented paper money in the ninth century; when the West reconquered the Mediterranean between the eleventh and thirteenth century; when a world market began to take shape in the sixteenth century, the 'biography of capital' was starting to be written in one form or another. Many historians, more cautious than I, refuse to go back any further than the sixteenth or even eighteenth century, identifying capitalism more or less with the cataclysmic explosion of the industrial revolution. But even in this 'short-term' perspective, we are talking about three or five centuries, and therefore about a long-lived structure – which is not the same thing as an absolutely unchanging reality. The long-term is made up of a succession of repeated movements, with variations and revivals, periods of decline, adaptation or stagnation – what sociologists would describe as *structuration, destructuration* and *restructuration*. Sometimes too there are major breaks with the past – and the industrial revolution was certainly one such. But I would maintain, rightly or wrongly, that throughout even this formidable transformation, capitalism remained essentially true to itself. Is it not in the nature of capitalism, a sort of rule of the game, that it thrives on change, drawing strength from it, being ready at any moment to expand or contract itself to the dimensions of the all-enveloping context which, as we have seen, limits in every period the possibilities of the human economy everywhere in the world?

It would however be a mistake to imagine capitalism as something that developed in a series of stages or leaps – from mercantile capitalism to industrial capitalism to finance capitalism, with some kind of regular progression from one phase to the next, with 'true' capitalism appearing only at the late stage when it took over production, and the only permissible term for the early period being mercantile capitalism or even 'pre-capitalism'. In fact as we have seen, the great 'merchants' of the past never specialized: they went in indiscriminately, simultaneously or successively, for trade, banking, finance, speculation on the Stock Exchange, 'industrial' production, whether under the putting-out system or more rarely in manufactories. The whole panoply of forms of capitalism – commercial, industrial, banking – was already deployed in thirteenth-century Florence, in seventeenth-century Amsterdam, in London before the eighteenth century. It is undoubtedly the case that in the early nineteenth century, the coming of machines made industrial production a high-profit sector and capitalism went over to it on a massive scale. But it was by no means confined to this sector. When the first fantastic profits of the cotton boom in Britain fell, in the face of competition, to 2 or 3%, the accumulated capital was diverted to other industries, steel and railways for instance; to an even greater extent though, there was a return to finance capitalism, to banking, to more speculation than ever on the Stock Exchange, to major international trade, to the profits derived from exploitation of the colonies, to government loans etc. And here again, there was little or no specialization: the Wendel family in France were steelmasters, bankers, mill-owners in the Vosges and suppliers of military equipment for the Algiers expedition in 1830.[5]

Secondly, despite everything that has been written about the liberal competitive capitalism of the nineteenth and twentieth centuries, monopoly is by no means a thing of the past. It has simply taken on new forms, a whole range of them, from trusts and holding companies to the famous American multinational firms which in the 1960s tripled the number of their subsidiaries abroad. In 1973, 187 of them, with subsidiary companies in at least five foreign countries, accounted for 'not only three-quarters of US investment abroad, but also for half the total of US exports and one third of total sales of manufactured goods on the US market'. Accused of taking jobs away from workers in their own country by setting up subsidiaries abroad, of contributing to the trade deficit and of playing a disastrous role in the international money markets, including speculation against the dollar, they were the object of inquiries by the American Senate for several years – but seem to be none the worse for it today. The multinationals too have a finger in every pie – in industry of course (since they invest in low-wage countries); in finance inevitably, given the size of their short-term disposable funds ('more than twice the reserves of the central banks and the international monetary institutions', so that a 2% shift in their liquidities would be enough to provoke an acute monetary crisis anywhere in the world, according to a US Senate committee); but they also have commercial interests: it was advanced in defence of the multinationals in 1971 that they were responsible for a majority of American exports (62%) whereas they actually produced only 34% of them.[6]

In short, the chief privilege of capitalism, today as in the past, remains the ability to *choose* – a privilege resulting at once from its dominant social position, from the weight of its capital resources, its borrowing capacity, its communications network, and, no less, from the links which create between the members of a powerful minority – however divided it may be by competition – a series of unwritten rules and personal contacts. Its sphere of action has undoubtedly widened, since all sectors of the economy are now open to it and in particular it has very largely penetrated that of production. But it is also true that just as in the past capitalism did not control the whole of the market economy, so today there are still quite considerable areas of activity with which it does not concern itself, leaving them to a market economy still operating under its own steam, to small business and to the determination of producers and workers in modest enterprises. Capitalism has its own preserves: top-level real estate and Stock Exchange speculation, banking, large-scale industrial production which by virtue of its size, and the strength of its organization, has considerable freedom in price-fixing and in international trade. Sometimes, but only in special circumstances, capitalism concerns itself with agricultural production or even transport – for instance those shipping companies which sail under flags of convenience in order to escape tax and which have made it possible to amass fantastic fortunes. And since it does have the freedom to choose, capitalism can always change horses in mid-stream – the secret of its vitality.

Its capacity to adapt, its versatility and consistent strength do not of course shield capitalism from every risk. In major crises, numbers of capitalists go under, but there are always others who survive or take their place. Creative responses are indeed often made outside capitalist circles, since innovation has more than once come from below. But such solutions almost automatically find their way to the owners of capital and the end result is a revitalized capitalism often even stronger than before, more energetic and efficient than the old. The vicomte d'Avenel was surprised and on the whole pleased to note that with the passage of time wealth changes hands many times, so that on a single estate for instance several different 'races' of owners may succeed one another.[7] He was right, but such takeovers do not in the end eliminate either private wealth or private property. The same is true of capitalism: it may change all the time but it carries on inheriting the succession. What Henry Hope, a leading Amsterdam businessman once said of trade in 1784 after the fourth Anglo-Dutch War, could also be said of capitalism: 'It is often ill but it never dies'.[8]

Capitalism and the social context

The worst error of all is to suppose that capitalism is simply an 'economic system', whereas in fact it lives off the social order, standing almost on a footing with the state, whether as adversary or accomplice: it is and always has been a massive force, filling the horizon. Capitalism also benefits from all the support that culture provides for the solidity of the social edifice, for culture – though unequally distributed and shot through with contradictory currents – does in the end contribute the best of itself to propping up the existing order. And lastly capitalism can count on the dominant classes who, when they defend it, are defending themselves.

Of the various social hierarchies – the hierarchies of wealth, of state power or of culture, that oppose yet support each other – which is the most important? The answer as we have already seen, is that it may depend on the time, the place and who is speaking.

A businessman might reply that at present politics is the most important, that the power of the state is such that neither banking nor industrial capital stand a chance compared to it. And there are certainly serious commentators who have written of the all-powerful state, crushing everything in its path, stifling initiative in the private sector, sapping the beneficial freedom of the 'innovator'. The state, they say, is a mastodon that must be driven back into its cave. But it is of course possible to read the opposite – that capital and economic power are entrenched everywhere, crushing the freedom of the individual. We should not let ourselves be deceived: the truth is of course that both state and capital – a certain kind of capital at any rate, the monopolies and big corporations – coexist very comfortably, today as in the past; capital does not seem to be doing so badly. It has, as it always did, burdened the state with the least remunerative and most expensive tasks: providing the infrastructure of roads and communications, the army, the massive costs of education and research. Capital also lets the state take charge of public health and bear most of the cost of social security. Above all, it shamelessly benefits from all the exemptions, incentives, and generous subsidies granted by the state – which acts as a machine collecting the flow of incoming money and redistributing it, spending more than it receives and therefore obliged to borrow. Capital is never very far away from this providential source of bounty. 'Contrary to the myth of the private sector as the source of initiative whose dynamism is stifled by government action, late [or as some people would say mature] capitalism has found, in the range of activities peculiar to the state, the means of ensuring the survival of the entire system' – the capitalist system needless to say. This reflection comes from a review by the Italian economist Federico Caffe[9] of two books generally in agreement with this position, by C. Offe[10] on contemporary Germany, and James O'Connor[11] on the United States in 1977. Lastly, it is thanks to its friendly relations, indeed symbiosis, with the state – the dispenser of fiscal incentives (to stimulate the great god investment), of lucrative contracts, of measures which make it easier to reach foreign markets – that 'monopoly capitalism', which J. O'Connor contrasts with the 'competitive sector', prospers. Consequently, O'Connor argues, 'the growth of the state sector [including the welfare state] is indispensable for the expansion of private industry and in particular the monopolist industries'. Although 'economic power and political power are formally separate, there is a close network of informal relations between them.'[12] I will not quarrel with that – but collusion between the state and capital is nothing new. It dates back to the beginning of the modern period and is so regular that every time a state falters – whether the state of Castile in 1557 or the French monarchy in 1558 – capitalism visibly misses a beat too.

The relations between capitalism and culture are even more ambiguous because they contain a contradiction: culture is both support and challenge, guard dog and rebel. It is true that a challenge will often wear itself out after its most violent explosions. The protests in Luther's Germany against the monopolies of big firms like the Fuggers and Welsers, in the end came to nothing. Almost invariably, culture becomes a mainstay of the existing order and capitalism derives not a little of its security from it.

We are still being told today that capitalism is if not the best, at any rate the least bad regime, that it is more efficient than socialism while at the same time leaving individual property intact, that it favours individual initiative (shades of Schumpeter's innovator). The arguments in its favour are sprayed like artillery fire over a broad range, sometimes apparently very far from the target. Thus since money for instance is clearly a structure which furthers injustice, every thesis in favour of social inequality is another argument for capitalism. Keynes in 1920[13] pronounced himself unconditionally in favour of 'inequality in the distribution of wealth' which was in his view the best way of swelling the accumulated capital indispensable to the vigour of economic life. Sixty years later, *Le Monde* in August 1979 was telling us that 'inequalities of every kind are a natural phenomenon so what is the point of denying them?'[14]

In a debate like this, any and every authority can be invoked, from Fustel de

Coulanges or Georges Dumezil to Konrad Lorenz[15] or a certain recent critic of Michelet, inveighing against the liberal camp. It is argued that human nature is unchangeable, therefore that society is unchangeable too; that it has always been unjust, unequal, subject to hierarchy. History is thus dragged in to testify. Even the old myth of the 'hidden hand' of the market, adjusting supply and demand better than any human intervention, will not lie down and die. Its message is that by pursuing his own interest, the individual will serve the interest of all – so let battle commence and may the best man win! America has become intoxicated with the myth of the self-made man, who builds up his fortune from scratch, an honour and an example to the nation. There are certainly plenty of rags-to-riches stories in America and elsewhere, but not only is honesty not always their most conspicuous feature, they are less common than is often supposed. Sigmund Diamond[16] has brought relish to the task of discovering how many of the so-called self-made men in the United States actually concealed the headstart they had received from a family fortune built up over several generations, just like the 'bourgeois' fortunes in Europe after the fifteenth century.

What has disappeared however is the euphoria and complacency of early nineteenth-century capitalism; and the new defensive language is in fact a response to the vehemence of socialist attacks, rather as in the sixteenth century the Counter-Reformation was a response to the Reformation. There has been a predictable sequence of blast and counterblast. And since no element in society exists in isolation, the deepening crisis in our present-day economies and societies is indicative of a profound cultural crisis too, as we know from our experience of 1968. Herbert Marcuse[17] who, without wishing to, became the guru of this revolution, was quite justified in saying (23 March 1979) that 'it is stupid to describe 1968 as a defeat'. 1968 shook the foundations of society, broke habits and taboos, even destroyed apathy: the fabric of family and society was sufficiently torn for new life styles to be created at every level of society. It is in this sense that it really was a cultural revolution. After 1968, capitalism, at the heart of much-decried western society, was in a less secure position than before, under attack not only from socialists and orthodox Marxists but from new groups opposed to power in every form, whose rallying-cries include 'Down with the state!'

But time passes; ten or fifteen years are nothing in the slow-moving history of society, but a long interval in the lifetime of an individual. Those active in 1968 have been reabsorbed into a long-suffering society whose patience gives it prodigious powers of resistance and recuperation. Inertia is the feature it lacks the least. So the cultural revolution may not have been a failure – but one would have to think very hard before pronouncing it an outright success. In any case have there ever been any outright successes in cultural matters? The Renaissance and the Reformation were both outstanding and long-lived cultural revolutions, coming one after the other. It was already an explosive enterprise to have reintroduced Greece and Rome to Christian civilization; to tear apart the seamless robe of the Church was even more earth-shaking. Yet in the end the dust settled, everything was absorbed into the existing order and the wounds healed. The Renaissance ended with Machiavelli's *Prince* and the Counter-Reformation. The Reformation loosed upon the world a new dominant Europe, supremely capitalist; in Germany it produced a crew of petty princelings – not a happy result. And did Luther not betray the rebel cause in the Peasant War of 1525?

Can capitalism survive?

Boris Porchnev[18] some years ago gently reproached me and other 'bourgeois' (i.e. western) historians, for talking at length about the origins and early stages of capitalism without ever considering its end. I have at least some excuse – since I have confined my studies to the early modern period it is not my fault if at the end of the nineteenth century, capitalism was still going strong. And while western capitalism is undoubtedly going through a period of uncertainty and crisis, I do not believe that it is on the point of collapse. It no longer, admittedly, excites the admiration which Marx himself could not help feeling for it; nor is it viewed, as it once was by Max Weber or Werner Sombart, as the culminating stage of a long development. But that does not mean that any system which might replace it in some relatively smooth evolution might not turn out to be strikingly similar.

I may be quite wrong, but I do not have the impression that capitalism is likely to collapse of its own accord, in some form of 'endogenous' deterioration; for any collapse to take place, there would have to be some external impact of great violence; and a credible alternative would have to be available. The colossal weight of a whole society and the powers of resistance of an alert ruling minority are not likely to be easily overthrown by ideological speeches and programmes or by momentary electoral success. Wherever socialism has triumphed in the world, it has been as the result of some external pressure and in circumstances of extreme violence – whether the Russian revolution of 1917, the setting up of socialist states in East Europe after the Second World War, the victory of the Chinese revolution in 1949, the triumph of the Cuban guerillas in 1959, or the liberation of Vietnam in 1975. And all these movements were founded on absolute confidence in the socialist future which may be less forthcoming today.

No one will deny that the present crisis, dating from the early 1970s, is a threat to capitalism. It is far more serious than that of 1929 and even large firms will probably be swallowed up in it. But capitalism as a system has every chance of surviving. *Economically* speaking (I do not say *ideologically*) it might even emerge strengthened from the trial.

We have after all seen what role was usually played by crises in pre-industrial Europe: they tended to eliminate the small firm (small that is in capitalist terms), the fragile undertaking created in times of economic euphoria, or the old-fashioned business – that is to say they reduced competition rather than increasing it and usually ended with the bulk of economic activities concentrated in a few hands. In this respect, nothing has changed. At national and international level, there has indeed been a 'new deal' but it has benefited the strongest, and I am inclined to agree with Herbert Marcuse[19] who argued in a recent debate with Jean Elleinstein that 'crises are essential to the development of capitalism; inflation and unemployment etc. [nowadays] encourage the centralization and concentration of capitalism. This is the beginning of a new phase of development but it is by no means the final crisis of capitalism'. Centralization and concentration are indeed the silent demolition and construction workers of our social and economic architecture. Back in 1968, Giovanni Agnelli, the chairman of Fiat, was predicting that 'in twenty years there may be no more than six or seven makes of car in the world'. And today nine companies between them account for 80% of world car production. Secular crises (and as I have said, the present crisis looks suspiciously like one) exact a penalty for the increasing discrepancy between the structures of supply, demand, profit, employment, etc. Breakdowns begin to occur and in the inevitable readjustments, some activities are reduced or even eliminated altogether. But new avenues of profit open up at the same time for the benefit of the survivors.

Major crises also provoke a new deal of a sort in international relations. Here too the weak tend to get weaker and the strong stronger, although world hegemony may change hands and geographical location. The world has profoundly changed, in many ways, in the last few decades. The American economy has shifted towards the south and west (a contributory factor to the decline of New York) – to such an extent that Jacques Attali[20] has even spoken of a shift of the world's centre of gravity from the Atlantic to the Pacific, with a new economic axis running between the United States and Japan. And there has also been a split in the Third World, with the new wealth of the oil-producing countries and the accentuated poverty and distress of the other less developed countries. But these years have also seen the industrialization (effected largely from outside by western nations and in particular by the multinational companies) of the backward countries which were until recently confined to the role of exporters of raw materials. In short, capitalism has had to rethink its policies in those large areas of the world which the western world-economy had for so long dominated – exploitable areas with low living standards, like Latin America, Africa now in theory liberated, or India. It is possible that India has now crossed a critical threshold: having been long accustomed to famine (in 1943, 3 or 4 million people died in Bengal) India has now made such progress in agriculture that with the aid of two or three good harvests she found herself for the first time, in 1978, heavily in surplus – and therefore obliged to think about exporting grain because of the quite unexpected problems of storage, difficult to solve at short notice. This does not however mean that the stage has yet been reached when the mass of Indian villagers will be the buyers of manufactured objects 'made in India'. Poverty remains widespread and the population is still increasing at the rate of

13 million a year.[21] So I think it can be assumed that even faced with a new Third World, capitalism will, for some time to come, be able to reorganize its means of domination or devise new ones, using yet again the formidable strength of acquired position and the weight of the past.

'Tradition and previous generations', Marx wrote, 'weigh like a nightmare on the minds of the living' - and not only on the minds, on the very existence of the living too, one might add. Jean-Paul Sartre may have dreamed of a society from which inequality would have disappeared, where one man would not exploit another. But no society in the world has yet given up tradition and the use of privilege. If this is ever to be achieved, all the social hierarchies will have to be overthrown, not merely those of money or state power, not only social privilege but the uneven weight of the past and of culture. The experience of the socialist countries proves that the disappearance of a single hierarchy - the economic hierarchy - raises scores of new problems and is not enough on its own to establish equality, liberty or even plenty. A clear-sighted revolution, if such a thing is even possible - and if it were, would the paralysing weight of circumstances allow it to remain so for long? - would find it very difficult to demolish what should be demolished, while retaining what should be retained: freedom for ordinary people, cultural independence, a market economy with no loaded dice, and a little fraternity. It is a very tall order - especially since whenever capitalism is challenged, it is invariably during a period of economic difficulty, whereas far-reaching structural reform, which would inevitably be difficult and traumatic, requires a context of abundance or even superabundance. And the present population explosion is likely to do little or nothing to encourage the more equitable distribution of surpluses.

A conclusion to end conclusions: capitalism and the market economy

It is in the end at the political level that the distinction - to my mind beyond doubt - between capitalism in its various guises and 'the market economy' takes on its full significance.

The rise of capitalism in the nineteenth century has been described, even by Marx, even by Lenin, as eminently, indeed healthily competitive. Were such observers influenced by illusions, inherited assumptions, ancient errors of judgment? In the eighteenth century, compared to the unearned privileges of a 'leisured' aristocracy, the privileges of merchants may perhaps have looked like a fair reward for labour; in the nineteenth century, after the age of the big companies with their state monopolies (the Indies companies for instance) the mere freedom of trading may have seemed the equivalent of true competition. And industrial production (which was however only one sector of capitalism) was still quite frequently handled by small firms which did indeed compete on the market and continue to do so today. Hence the classic image of the entrepreneur serving the public interest, which persisted throughout the nineteenth century, while the virtues of laissez-faire and free trade were everywhere cele-brated.

The extraordinary thing is that such images should still be with us today in the language spoken by politicians and journalists, in works of popularization and in the teaching of economics, when doubt long ago entered the minds of the specialists, certainly before 1929. Keynes was already writing about imperfect competition. Today's economists go even further and distinguish between market prices and monopoly prices, that is they see a two-tier structure, a monopolist sector and a 'competitive sector'. This two-stage model is to be found in J. O'Connor's writing as well as in Galbraith's.[22] Is it therefore wrong to describe as the 'market economy' what some people would call the 'competitive sector'? At the top come the big monopolies, while underneath them competition is confined to small or medium-sized concerns.

The distinction is by no means universal in everyday discussion, but the habit is gradually growing of using 'capitalism' to refer to big business only. Increasingly capitalism is being used as a *superlative*. In France for instance, which are the concerns held up to public abuse? The 'trusts', the multinational corporations – that is, public hostility is accurately and rightly directed at the top. The little shop where I buy my daily paper could hardly be called a capitalist enterprise, though if it belongs to a chain of shops, the chain could be said to be part of capitalism. Nor could one describe as capitalist the little firms or independent manufacturing enterprises sometimes known in France as 'the 49s' because they want to keep the total of their employees under the magic number of 50, to avoid the fiscal or union regulations affecting larger concerns. These small businesses are legion. But they are visible in large numbers in the bitter conflicts which now and then put both them and the problem which presently concerns us in the limelight.

Over the twenty years or so before the crisis of the 1970s, New York – at that time the leading industrial city in the world – saw the decline one after another of the little firms, sometimes employing less than thirty people, which made up its commercial and industrial substance – the huge clothing sector, hundreds of small printers, many food industries and small builders – all contributing to a truly 'competitive' world whose little units were both in competition with, yet dependent upon each other. The disorganization of New York was the result of the squeezing out of these thousands of businesses which in the past made it a city where consumers could find in town anything they wanted, produced, stored and sold on the spot. It was the big firms, with their big production units out of town, which ousted the little men. The bread which an old-fashioned bakery used to make for New York schools is now brought in from New Jersey.[23]

Here then is a good example, in the most advanced country in the world, of what a competitive economy could be – an obsolete economy to be sure, employing small numbers and managed on a personal basis. It has now gone for ever, leaving a gap in the heart of New York which will never be filled. But there are still examples of this old-fashioned activity to be seen today. Prato, the big textile centre near Florence, is the best example I can think of, a real hive of thriving small family businesses, with a workforce ready to turn its hand to anything, quick to follow changes in fashion or the markets, with old-world practices sometimes reminiscent of the putting-out system. The big Italian textile firms are all suffering from the crisis at the moment, but there is still full employment in Prato.

But it is not my intention to list examples, simply to point out that there is a sort of lower layer in the economy – it may be small or large, and we may call it what we like, but it exists and is made up of independent units. So we should not be too quick to assume that capitalism embraces the whole of western society, that it accounts for every stitch in the social fabric. Neither the little workshops of Prato nor the small printers of New York can be regarded as examples of true capitalism – that would be completely wrong, both socially and in terms of economic organization.

Finally, it should be said that the competitive sector does not account for everything large-scale capitalism leaves aside or abandons. Today, just as in the eighteenth century, there is quite a sizeable lower floor, a sort of bargain basement, below the other two storeys; some economists estimate it at about 30 to 40% of economic activity in the *industrialized* countries. This surprisingly large figure, for which estimates have only recently appeared, is made up of all the activities outside the market and state controls – fraud, barter of goods and services, moonlighting, housework – that domestic economy which St Thomas Aquinas regarded as the *economia pura* and which still of course exists today. It is still possible then to use the three-tier model whose relevance to the past has already been discussed. It can still be applied to the present. And our statistics which do not find room anywhere for the 'basement' of the economy, give us only an incomplete picture.

This is enough to make one think again before assuming that our societies are organized from top to bottom in a 'capitalist system'. On the contrary, putting it briefly, there is a dialectic still very much alive between capitalism on the one hand, and its antithesis, the 'non-capitalism' of the lower level on the other. It is sometimes said that big business tolerates small firms, although if it really tried it could sweep them aside. How generous! In much the same way, Stendhal thought that in Renaissance Italy, a cruel world if ever there was one, the big cities let the small towns survive out of the goodness of their hearts. I have argued (and I think I am right) that the big cities would not have been able to survive without the smaller ones at their service. As for the big companies of today, Galbraith argues that they only respect small businesses because the latter, being on such a small scale, have much higher unit production costs, which makes it possible for market prices to be fixed at levels providing handsome profits for the larger firms – as if the big companies, if they were left alone in the field, could not perfectly well fix prices and profits at any level they liked! The truth is that they need the smaller firms, first and foremost to carry out the humble tasks indispensable to any society, but which capitalism does not care to handle. Secondly, like the eighteenth-century manufactories which frequently drew on family workshops in the surrounding districts, the big firms farm out certain tasks to sub-contractors, who deliver finished or semi-finished goods. There are small workshops in Savoy today turning out metal parts for faraway factories. Then too there is a need for retailers and middlemen. All these chains of sub-contractors may be directly dependent on capitalism but they are in themselves merely another branch of small business.

Indeed it seems that if the conflict between capitalism and the layer beneath were a strictly economic one – which it is not – both sides would have an interest in peaceful coexistence – the conclusion reached by a recent conference of economists.[24] But government policies may intervene. Since the last war, several European countries have consciously adopted policies designed to eliminate small business on the New York pattern: they are seen as a hangover from the past and a sign of economic backwardness. The state itself creates monopolies – to take just one example, *Électricité de France* (the nationalized French electricity company) is today being accused of being a state within the state, holding up the development of alternative forms of energy. And it is the biggest private firms which receive state aid and subsidy, whereas banks are supposed to restrict credit to small firms – which amounts to condemning them to vegetate or vanish.

There could be no more dangerous policy. This is to repeat in another form the fundamental error committed by the socialist countries. Read what Lenin wrote: 'Small-scale commercial production is, every moment of every day, giving birth *spontaneously* to capitalism and the bourgeoisie ... Wherever there is small business and freedom of trade, capitalism appears'.[25] He is even supposed to have said: 'capitalism begins in the village market-place'. His conclusion was that in order to get rid of capitalism, its very roots that is, individual production and the freedom of trade had to be dug out. Are Lenin's remarks not in fact a homage to the enormous creative powers of the market, of the lower storey of exchange, of the self-employed artisan or even of individual resourcefulness – creative powers which provide the economy not only with a rich foundation but with something to fall back on in times of crisis, war, or serious economic collapse requiring structural change? The lowest level, not being paralysed by the size of its plant or organization, is the one readiest to adapt; it is the seedbed of inspiration, improvisation and even innovation, although its most brilliant discoveries sooner or later fall into the hands of the holders of capital. It was not the capitalists who brought about the first cotton revolution; all the new ideas came from enterprising small businesses. Are things so very different today? One of the leading representatives of French capital said to me the other day: 'It is never the inventors who make a fortune'; they have to hand over to someone else. But they have the ideas in the first place! A recent report from M.I.T. points out that over the last fifteen years more than half the jobs created in the United

States have been in small firms employing less then 50 workers.

Finally, if we are prepared to make an unequivocal distinction between the market economy and capitalism, might this offer us a way of avoiding that 'all or nothing' which politicians are constantly putting to us, as if it were impossible to retain the market economy without giving the monopolies a free hand, or impossible to get rid of monopolies without nationalizing everything in sight? The programme proposed by the 'Prague spring' – socialism at the top, but freedom and 'spontaneity' at the base – was put forward as a double solution to a double and unsatisfactory reality. But what kind of socialism will be able to maintain the freedom and mobility of the individual enterprise? As long as the solutions put forward amount to replacing the monopoly of capital with the monopoly of the state, compounding the faults of the former with those of the latter, it is hardly surprising that the classic left-wing solutions do not arouse great electoral enthusiasm. If people set about looking for them, seriously and honestly, economic solutions could be found which would extend the area of the market and would put at its disposal the economic advantages so far kept to itself by one dominant group in society. But the problem does not essentially lie there; it is social in nature. Just as a country at the centre of a world-economy can hardly be expected to give up its privileges at international level, how can one hope that the dominant groups who combine capital and state power, and who are assured of international support, will agree to play the game and hand over to someone else?

30 October 1979.

Notes

Translator's note: Wherever possible, when a French edition of an English-language source is quoted in the text, the original has been traced and the page reference in the notes amended. This has not always been possible. References to works originally published in French have been left unaltered, except where there is a recent and easily available English translation.

Abbreviations used in notes:

A.d.S.	Archivio di Stato.
A.E.	Affaires Etrangères (Foreign Affairs), Paris.
A.N.	Archives Nationales, Paris.
B.M.	British Museum (now British Library), London.
B.N.	Bibliothèque Nationale, Paris.
C.S.A.	Central State Archives, Moscow.
P.R.O.	Public Record Office, London.

NOTES TO FOREWORD

1. The expression 'world time', which was used for the French title of this volume, (Le Temps du Monde) is borrowed from Wolfram EBERHARD, Conquerors and Rulers. Social Forces in Medieval China, 2nd edn., 1965, pp. 13 ff., quoted by Immanuel WALLERSTEIN, The Modern World System, 1974, p. 6.

2. Ashin DAS GUPTA, 'Trade and Politics in 18th Century India', in Islam and the Trade of Asia, ed. D. S. RICHARDS, 1970, p. 183.

3. René BOUVIER, Quevedo 'homme du diable, homme de Dieu', 1929, p. 83.

4. Jean IMBERT, Histoire économique des origines à 1789, 1965; Hans HAUSHERR, Wirtschaftsgeschichte der Neuzeit, 1954; Hubert RICHARDOT and Bernard SCHNAPPER, Histoire des faits économiques jusqu'à la fin du XVIIIᵉ siècle, 1963; John HICKS, A Theory of Economic History, 1969.

5. Allgemeine Wirtschaftsgeschichte des Mittelalters und der Neuzeit, 2 vols., 1958.

6. Friedrich NOVALIS, quoted in L'Encyclopédie, 1966, p. 43.

7. René CLEMENS, Prolégomènes d'une théorie de la structure économique, 1952, esp. p. 92.

8. Witold KULA, in conversation, many years ago. Cf. On the Typology of Economic Systems. The Social Sciences. Problems and Orientation, 1968, pp. 109-27.

9. José GENTIL DA SILVA, exact reference mislaid and untraceable by the author himself when consulted.

10. W. W. ROSTOW, Politics and the Stages of Growth, 1971.

11. Article by K. S. KAROL in Le Monde, 23 July 1970.

12. Quoted by Cyril S. BELSHAW, Traditional Exchange and Modern Markets, 1965. p. 5.

13. Joseph SCHUMPETER, History of Economic Analysis, 2nd edn., 1955, I, p. 6.

14. Jean POIRIER, 'Le commerce des hommes', in Cahiers de l'Institut de

science économique appliquée, n° 95, November 1959, p. 5.

15. Marc GUILLAUME, *Le Capital et son double*, 1975, p. 11.

16. Jean-Baptiste SAY, *Cours complet d'économie politique pratique*, I, 1828, p. 7.

17. Fernand BRAUDEL, 'Histoire et sciences sociales: la longue durée', in *Annales E.S.C.*, 1958, pp. 725-53.

18. J. SCHUMPETER, *op. cit.*, ch. 2 passim. (According to Mrs Elizabeth BOODY-SCHUMPETER, a fourth method would have been through sociology.)

NOTES TO CHAPTER I

1. See above, Volume II, chapter 5, on the use of the term 'set'.

2. SIMONE DE SISMONDI, *Nouveaux Principes d'économie politique*, ed. Jean WEILLER, 1971, p. 19.

3. *Ibid.*, p. 105, n. 1.

4. I first found this word used in the special sense employed here in Fritz RÖRIG's book, *Mittelalterliche Weltwirtschaft, Blüte und Ende einer Weltwirtschaftsperiode*, 1933. Hektor AMMANN, in *Wirtschaft und Lebensraum der Mittelalterlichen Kleinstadt*, n.d., p. 4, rightly qualifies this as 'eine Art Weltwirtschaft', 'a sort of world economy'.

5. Léon-H. DUPRIEZ, 'Principes et problèmes d'interprétation', p. 3, in *Diffusion du progrès et convergence des prix. Etudes internationales*, 1966. The ideas expressed in this chapter have much in common with those of I. WALLERSTEIN, *op. cit.*, although I do not always agree with him.

6. Fernand BRAUDEL, *La Mediterranée, ...*, 1st French edn., 1949, pp. 325, 328 ff.

7. Fernand BRAUDEL, *The Mediterranean and the Mediterranean World in the Age of Philip II*, English trans., 2 vols., 1972-3, I, p. 387 (hereafter referred to as *Medit*; all page references are to the English edition of 1972-3, published by Collins, which is a translation of the second French edition of 1966).

8. A. M. JONES, 'Asian Trade in Antiquity', in *Islam and the Trade of Asia, op. cit.*, p. 5.

9. I have used the expressions 'rules' or 'tendencies', following the example of Georges GURVITCH (*règles tendancielles*) to avoid using the stronger 'laws'.

10. Paul SWEEZY, *Modern Capitalism*, 1974, p. 143.

11. Immanuel Wallerstein's expression.

12. Georg TECTANDER VON DER JABEL, *Iter persicum ou description d'un voyage en Perse entrepris en 1602 ...*, 1877, pp. 9, 22-4.

13. Pedro CUBERO SEBASTIÁN, *Breve Relación de la peregrinación que ha hecho de la mayor parte del mundo*, 1680, p. 175.

14. Louis-Alexandre FROTIER DE LA MESSELIÈRE, *Voyage à Saint-Pétersbourg ou Nouveaux Mémoires sur la Russie*, 1803, p. 254.

15. *Medit*., I, p. 282.

16. Philippe de COMMYNES, *Mémoires*, III, 1965 edn., p. 110.

17. René DESCARTES, *Oeuvres*, I, *Correspondance*, 1969, p. 204.

18. Charles de BROSSES, *Lettres familières écrites d'Italie en 1739 et 1740*, 1858, p. 219.

19. Jacques de VILLAMONT, *Les Voyages ...*, 1607, p. 203.

20. *Ibid.*, p. 209.

21. Meaning of course 'free-thinking'.

22. Brian PULLAN, *Rich and Poor in Renaissance Venice*, 1971, p. 3.

23. *Voyage d'Angleterre, de Hollande et de Flandres*, 1728, Victoria and Albert Museum, 86, NN 2, f° 177. The 'Brownists' referred to are the members of the Protestant sect inspired by the teachings of Robert Browne in the 1580s.

24. *Ibid.*, f°s 178-9.

25. Hugo SOLY, 'The "Betrayal" of the Sixteenth Century Bourgeoisie: a Myth? Some considerations of the Behaviour Pattern of the Merchants of Antwerp in the Sixteenth Century', in *Acta historiae neerlandicae*, 1975, pp. 31-49.

26. Louis COULON, *L'Ulysse françois ou le voyage de France, de Flandre et de Savoie*, 1643, pp. 52-3 and 62-3.

27. Alonso MORGADO, *Historia de Sevilla*, 1587, f° 56.

28. Who was also king of Portugal until 1640.

29. Evaldo CABRAL DE MELLO, *Olinda restaurada. Guerra e Açucar no Nordeste 1630-1654*, 1975, p. 72.

30. *Ibid.*

31. Charles CARRIÈRE, Marcel COURDURIÉ, *L'Espace commercial marseillais aux XVIIe et XVIIIe siècles*, typescript, p. 27.

32. A.N., Marine, B7 463, 11 (1697).

33. Patrick CHORLEY, *Oil, Silk and Enlightenment. Economic Problems in XVIIIth century Naples*, 1965. See also Salvatore CIRIACONO, *Olio ed Ebrei nella Repubblica veneta del Settecento*, 1975, p. 20.

34. See above, Volume II, chapter 4.

35. *Medit.*, I, pp. 125 ff.

36. *Ibid.*, p. 391 and note 177. The reference *is* to oil, not 'wine' as the English edition reads mistakenly. *Mea culpa.* (S.R.)

37. Ernst WAGEMANN, *Economía mundial*, 1952, II, p. 95.

38. Johann Heinrich Von THÜNEN, *Der isolierte Staat in Beziehung auf Landwirtschaft und Nationalökonomie*, 1876, I, p. 1.

39. E. CONDILLAC, *Le Commerce et le gouvernement*, 1776, 1966 edn., pp. 248 ff. for instance describes the economy of an imaginary island.

40. *Siedlungsgeographische Untersuchungen in Niederandalusien*, 1935.

41. See above, Volume II, pp. 36-42.

42. In *The Wealth of Nations*, quoted by Pierre DOCKÈS, *L'Espace dans la pensée économique*, 1969, pp. 408-9.

43. See below, this chapter.

44. H. PIRENNE, *Histoire de Belgique*, III, 1907, p. 259.

45. A. EMMANUEL, *L'Echange inégal*, 1969, p. 43.

46. In a paper given at the Prato conference, April 1978.

47. *Ibid.*

48. Johann BECKMANN, *Beiträge zur Œkonomie* ..., 1781. III, p. 427. In about 1705, there were 84 trading firms, of which 12 were Spanish, 26 Genoese, 11 French, 10 English, 7 from Hamburg, 18 Dutch or Flemish; François DORNIC, *op. cit.*, p. 85, citing Raimundo de LANTERY, *Memorias*, Part II, pp. 6-7.

49. Jean GEORGELIN, *Venise au Siècle des Lumières*, 1978, p. 671.

50. Tibor WITTMAN, 'Los metales preciosos de América y la estructura agraria de Hungria a los fines del siglo XVI', in *Acta historica*, XXIV, 1967, p. 27.

51. Jacques SAVARY, *Dictionnaire universel de commerce* ..., 1759-1765, V, col. 669.

52. Jacques DOURNES, *Pötao, une théorie du pouvoir chez les Indochinois Jörai*, 1977, p. 89.

53. Abbé PRÉVOST, *Histoire générale des voyages*, VI, p. 101.

54. J. PAQUET, 'La misère dans un village de l'Oisans en 1809', in *Cahiers d'histoire*, 1966, 3, pp. 249-56.

55. Germaine LEVI-PINARD, *La Vie quotidienne à Vallorcine au XVIIIe siècle*, 2nd edn., 1976.

56. 'Cervières, une communauté rurale des Alpes briançonnaises du XVIIIe siècle à nos jours', in *Bulletin du Centre d'histoire économique et sociale de la région lyonnaise*, 1976, n° 3, pp. 21 ff.

57. Quoted by Isaac de PINTO, *Traité de la circulation et du crédit*, 1771, pp. 23-4.

58. H. C. DARBY, *An Historical Geography of England before A.D. 1800*, 1951, p. 444.

59. E. NARNI-MANCINELLI, Matteo PAONE, Roberto PASCA, 'Inegualanzia regionale e uso del territorio: analisi di un' area depressa della Campania interna', in *Rassegna economica*, 1977.

60. Christiane KLAPISCH-ZUBER, *Les Maîtres du marbre. Carrare 1300-1600*, 1969, pp. 69-76.

61. Moscow, C.S.A., 705/409, f° 12, 1785.

62. *Le Monde*, 27 June 1978.

63 and 64. See above, Volume II, chapter 5, p. 459.

65. T.S. WILLAN, *Studies in Elizabethan Foreign Trade*, 1959, p. v.

66. Pierre BRUNEL, *L'Etat et le Souverain*, 1977, p. 12.

67. The *Dogado* was the name given to the complex of lagoons, islets and estuaries on the north coast of the Adriatic which constituted the approach to Venice. (*Enc. Ital.*, XIII, p. 89).

68. Elena FASANO, *Lo Stato mediceo di Cosimo I*, 1973.
69. Georges LIVET, *L'Équilibre européen de la fin du XVᵉ à la fin du XVIIIᵉ siècle*, 1976.
70. Claude MANCERON, *Les Vingt Ans du roi*, 1972, p. 121.
71. Ragnar NURSKE, *Problems of Capital Formation in Underdeveloped Countries*, 1953, p. 4.
72. P. CHAUNU, *Séville et l'Atlantique*, VIII, 1, 1959, p. 1114.
73. A. EMMANUEL, *op. cit.*, p. 32.
74. David RICARDO, *Principles of Political Economy and Taxation*, Everyman edn., 1955, p. 81.
75. G. TOMASI DI LAMPEDUSA, in *Il Gattopardo (The Leopard)*, Milan, 1958.
76. Maurice LEVY-LEBOYER, François CROUZET and P. CHAUNU.
77. Until the creation on 24 March 1776 of the *Caisse d'Escompte*.
78. See below, chapter 2.
79. *Op. cit.*, p. 10.
80. I. WALLERSTEIN, *The Modern World System*, part II, chapter 2 (read in typescript).
81. J. GEORGELIN, *Venise au siècle des Lumières*, *op. cit.*, p. 760.
82. *Ibid.*, p. 14 and *passim*.
83. *Medit.*, II, p. 696.
84. Jacques GERNET, *Le Monde chinois*, 1972, p. 429.
85. See below, chapter 5.
86. Quoted by H.R.C. WRIGHT, Proceedings of Leningrad congress, 1970, V, p. 100.
87. W. KIENAST, *Die Anfänge des europäischen Staatensystems im späteren Mittelalter*, 1936.
88. *Geschichte der Kriegskunst . . .*, 1907.
89. I am quoting from memory. The incident is recounted in the papers of Diego Suárez, which used to be in the archives of the Government-General building in Algiers.
90. E. CABRAL DE MELLO, *Olinda restaurada . . .*, *op. cit.*, *passim*.
91. *Ibid.*, p. 246.
92. I have exchanged some correspondence on this subject with Professor CRUZ COSTA of the University of São Paulo.
93. On the introduction of the bayonet, see J.U. NEF, *War and Human Progress*, 1954, pp. 251-4.
94. Quoted by J.U. NEF *War and Human Progress*, p. 156.
95. Pasquale VILLANI, 'La società italiana nei secoli XVI e XVII', in *Ricerche storiche ed economiche in memoria di C. Barbagallo*, 1970, I, p. 255.
96. Philippe Auguste d'ARCQ, *La Noblesse militaire*, 1766, pp. 75-6; my italics.
97. B.G. ZANOBI, in Sergio ANSELMI, *Economia e Società; le Marche tra XV e XX secolo*, 1978, p. 102.
98. Cf. I. WALLERSTEIN, *op. cit.*, p. 87.
99. Federico BRITO FIGUEROA, *Historia económica y social de Venezuela*, I, 1966, *passim*.
100. Sir George STAUNTON, *An authentic account of an Embassy . . . to the Emperor of China . . . from the papers of . . . the Earl of MacCartney*, 1797, page reference to French edn. untraceable in original.
101. Louis-Narcisse BAUDRY DES LOZIÈRES, *Voyage à la Louisiane et sur le continent de l'Amérique septentrionale fait dans les années 1794-1798*, 1802, p. 10.
102. Peter LASLETT, *The World We Have Lost*, 1979 edn., p. 30 ff.
103. *Medit.*, I, p. 468.
104. See above, Volume II, p. 147.
105. *Ibid.*
106. A.d.s. Venice, Senato Zecca, 42, 20 July 1639.
107. Abbé Jean-Bernard LE BLANC, *Lettres d'un François*, 1745, II, p. 42.
108. *Ibid.*, p. 43.
109. *Ibid.*, p. 1.
100. *Ibid.*, III, p. 68.
111. Jacques ACCARIAS DE SERIONNE, *La Richesse de l'Angleterre*, 1771, p. 61.
112. These questions were discussed at the 1978 Prato conference, with contributions from T.C. SMOUT (on Scotland), H. KELLENBENZ and P. BAIROCH.
113. A. DAS GUPTA, *art. cit.*, in *Islam and the Trade of Asia*, ed. D.S. RICHARDS, 1970, p. 206.
114. *Précis de sociologie d'après V. Pareto*, 2nd edn., 1971, p. 172.
115. G. IMBERT, *Des Mouvements de longue durée Kondratieff*, 1959.
116. *Théorie économique du système féodal: pour un modèle de l'économie polonaise*, 1970, p. 48.

117. Cf. the recent discussion of the Kondratieff cycle: W. W. ROSTOW, 'Kondratieff, Schumpeter and Kuznets: Trend Periods Revisited', in *The Journal of Economic History*, 1975, pp. 719-53.
118. W. BRULEZ, 'Séville et l'Atlantique: quelques reflexions critiques', in *Revue belge de philologie et d'histoire*, 1964, n° 2, p. 592.
119. P. CHAUNU, *Séville et l'Atlantique*, VIII, 1, 1959, p. 30.
120. Dietrich EBERLING and Franz IRSIGLER, *Getreideumsatz, Getreide und Brotpreise in Köhn, 1368-1797*, 1976.
121. F. BRAUDEL and F. SPOONER, 'Prices in Europe from 1450 to 1750', in *The Cambridge Economic History of Europe*, IV, 1967, p. 468.
122. P. CHAUNU, *op. cit.*, p. 45.
123. *Gazette de France*, p. 489.
124. Pierre CHAUNU, *Les Philippines et le Pacifique des Ibériques*, 1960, p. 243, n. 1.
125. L. DERMIGNY, *La Chine et l'Occident. Le commerce à Canton au XVIIIᵉ siècle, 1719-1833*, I, 1964, p. 101, n. 1.
126. 'En Inde aux XVIᵉ et XVIIᵉ siècles: trésors américains, monnaie d'argent et prix dans l'Empire mogol', in *Annales E.S.C.*, 1969, pp. 835-59.
127. Quoted by Pierre VILAR, Stockholm Congress, 1960, p. 39.
128. Rondo Cameron, 'Economic History, Pure and Applied' in *Journal of Economic History*, March 1976, pp. 3-27.
129. *Il Problema del trend secolare nelle fluttuazioni dei prezzi*, 1935.
130. G. IMBERT, *op. cit.*
131. *Ibid.*
132. 'Les implications de l'emballement mondial des prix depuis 1972', in *Recherches économiques de Louvain*, September 1977.
133. In *Annales E.S.C.*, 1961, p. 115.
134. P. LEON, in Stockholm Congress, 1960, p. 167.
135. *La Crise de l'économie française à la fin de l'Ancien Régime et au début de la Révolution*, 1944, pp. viii-ix.
136. *Théorie économique du système féodal...*, *op. cit.*, p. 84.
137. 'Gazettes hollandaises et trésors américains' in *Anuario de historia económica y social*, 1969, p. 333.
138. P. VILAR, *L'Industrialisation en Europe au XIXᵉ siècle*, Colloque de Lyon, 1970, p. 331.
139. Joan Robinson, *Economic Heresies*, 1971, p. 18.
140. P. BEYSSADE, *La Philosophie première de Descartes*, typescript, p. 111.
141. Earl J. HAMILTON, 'American Treasure and the Rise of Capitalism' in *Economica*, November 1929, pp. 355-6.
142. E.H. Phelps BROWN, S.V. HOPKINS, 'Seven Centuries of Building Wages', in *Economica*, August 1955, pp. 195-206.
143. Charles SEIGNOBOS, *Histoire sincère de la nation française*, 1933.

NOTES TO CHAPTER 2

1. The foregoing remarks are based on Paul ADAM's typescript, *L'Origine des grandes cités maritimes indépendantes et la nature du premier capitalisme commercial*, p. 13.
2. Paul GROUSSET, preface to Régine PERNOUD, *Les Villes marchandes aux XIVᵉ et XVᵉ siècles*, 1948, p. 18.
3. *Studi di storia economica*, 1955, I, p. 630.
4. 'Income tax' was the term used for the tax levied by Pitt the Younger in 1799.
5. Henri PIRENNE, *La Civilisation occidentale au Moyen Age du XIᵉ au milieu du XVᵉ siècle*, in *Histoire générale*, ed., G. GLOTZ, VIII, 1933, pp. 99-100.
6. *Cours complet d'économie politique pratique*, *op. cit.*, I, p. 234.
7. *Traité de la circulation et du crédit*, *op. cit.*, p. 9.
8. Renée DOEHAERD, *Le Haut Moyen Age occidental, économies et sociétés*, 1971, p. 289.
9. P. ADAM, *op. cit.*, p. 11.
10. An expression used by Henri Pirenne during a lecture given in Algiers in 1931.
11. 'The Closing of the European Frontier', in *Speculum*, 1958, p. 476.
12. Wilhelm ABEL, *Agrarkrisen und Agrarkonjunktur*, 1966, p. 19.

13. Johannès BÜHLER, *Vida y cultura en la edad media*, 1946, p. 204.
14. B.H. SLICHER VAN BATH, *The Agrarian History of Western Europe, A.D. 500–1850*, 1966, p. 24.
15. Yves RENOUARD, *Les Villes d'Italie de la fin du Xe au début du XIVe siècle*, 1969, I, p. 15.
16. Karl BOSL, *Die Grundlagen der modernen Gesellschaft in Mittelalter*, 1972, II, p. 290.
17. He has often said this in my hearing. Cf. Armando SAPORI, 'Caratteri ed espansione dell'economia comunale italiana', in *Congresso storico internazionale per l'VIII° centenario della prima Lega Lombarda*, Bergamo, 1967, pp. 125–36.
18. 'What accelerated technological progress in the Western Middle Ages?', in *Scientific Change*, ed. CROMBIE, 1963, p. 277.
19. 'Les bases monétaires d'une suprématie économique: l'or musulman du VIIe au XIe siècle', in *Annales E.S.C.*, 1947, p. 158.
20. *L'Économie rurale et la vie des campagnes dans l'Occident médiéval*, 1962, I, p. 255.
21. *La Nascità dell'Europa, sec. X–XIV*, 1966, pp. 121 ff.
22. 'La civiltà economica nelle sue esplicazioni dalla Versilia alla Maremma secoli X–XVII', in *Atti del 60° Congresso Internazionale della 'Dante Alighieri'*, p. 21.
23. *Wirtschaftsgeschichte Deutschlands von 16. bis 18. Jahrhundert*, 1951, I, p. 327.
24. *Mittelalterliche Weltwirtschaft . . .*, 1933, p. 22.
25. Similar remarks on the influence of Frankfurt-am-Main can be found in Hans MAUERSBERG, *Wirtschafts- und Sozialgeschichte zentraleuropäischer Städte in neuerer Zeit*, 1960, pp. 238–9.
26. H. PIRENNE in *Histoire générale*, ed. G. GLOTZ, VIII, *op. cit.*, p. 144.
27. *Ibid.*, p. 11.
28. *Ibid.*, p. 90. Henri LAURENT, *Un Grand Commerce d'exportation. La draperie des Pays-Bas en France et dans les pays méditerranéens, XIIe–XVe siècles*, 1935, pp. 37–9.
29. H. PIRENNE, *op. cit.*, p. 128.
30. They did so eventually on 30 January 1598, by order of Queen Elizabeth; the text is given in Philippe DOLLINGER, *La Hanse (XIIe–XVIIe siècles)*, 1964, pp. 485–6.
31. Tibor WITTMAN, *Les Gueux dans les 'bonnes villes' de Flandre (1577–1584)*, 1969, p. 23; Hippolyte FIERENS-GEVAERT, *Psychologie d'une ville, essai sur Bruges*, 1901, p. 105; E. LUKCA, *Die Grosse Zeit der Niederlande*, 1937, p. 37.
32. Datini Archives, Prato, 26 April 1399.
33. H. PIRENNE, *op. cit.*, p. 127.
34. J.A. VAN HOUTTE, 'Bruges et Anvers, marchés "nationaux" ou "internationaux" du XIVe au XVIe siècle', in *Revue du Nord*, 1952, pp. 89–108.
35. *Brügges Entwicklung zum mittelalterlichen Weltmarkt*, 1908, p. 253.
36. *Op. cit.*, p. 16.
37. On the whole of this paragraph see P. DOLLINGER, *op. cit.*
38. H. PIRENNE, *op. cit.*, pp. 26–7.
39. P. DOLLINGER, *op. cit.*, p. 42.
40. Witold HENSEL, Aleksander GIEYSZTOR, *Les Recherches archéologiques en Pologne*, 1958, pp. 54 ff.
41. P. DOLLINGER, *op. cit.*, p. 21.
42. Renée DOEHAERD, 'A propos du mot "Hanse"', in *Revue du Nord*, January 1951, p. 19.
43. P. DOLLINGER, *op. cit.*, p. 10.
44. *Medit.*, I, p. 140.
45. P. DOLLINGER, *op. cit.*, p. 177.
46. *Ibid.*, p. 54.
47. See above, Volume II, p. 359.
48. P. DOLLINGER, *op. cit.*, p. 39.
49. *Ibid.*, p. 148.
50. *Ibid.*, p. 39.
51. *Ibid.*, p. 59.
52. *Ibid.*, p. 86.
53. Henry SAMSONOWICZ, 'Les liens culturels entre les bourgeois du littoral baltique dans le bas Moyen Age', in *Studia maritima*, I, pp. 10–11.
54. *Ibid.*, p. 12.
55. *Ibid.*
56. *Ibid.*
57. P. DOLLINGER, *op. cit.*, p. 266.
58. *Ibid.*, p. 55.
59. *Ibid.*, p. 130.

60. *Ibid.*, p. 95.
61. *Ibid.*, pp. 100-101.
62. Marian MALOWIST, *Croissance et regression en Europe, XIVᵉ-XVIIᵉ siècles*, 1972, pp. 93, 98.
63. P. DOLLINGER, *op. cit.*, p. 360.
64. M. MALOWIST, *op. cit.*, p. 133.
65. *Ibid.*, p. 105.
66. Eli F. HECKSCHER, *Mercantilism*, Eng. trans., 1955, I, p. 329.
67. *Histoire des prix et des salaires dans l'Orient médiéval*, 1969, p. 237.
68. Robert-Henri BAUTIER, 'La marine d'Amalfi dans le trafic méditerranéen du XIVᵉ siècle, à propos du transport du sel de Sardaigne' in *Bulletin philologique et historique du Comité des Travaux historiques et scientifiques*, 1959, p. 183.
69. M. del TREPPO, A. LEONE, *Amalfi medioevale*, 1977. This book challenges the traditional history of Amalfi which concentrates exclusively on trade.
70. M. LOMBARD, *art. cit.*, in *Annales E.S.C.*, 1947, pp. 154 ff.
71. Armando CITARELLA, 'Patterns in Medieval Trade: The Commerce of Amalfi before the Crusades', in *Journal of Economic History*, December 1968, p. 533 and n. 6.
72. R.-H. BAUTIER, *art. cit.*, p. 184.
73. R.S. LOPEZ, *op. cit.*, p. 94.
74. Y. RENOUARD, *op. cit.*, p. 25, n. 1.
75. Elena C. SKRZINSKAJA, 'Storia della Tana' in *Studi veneziani*, X, 1968, p. 7. *'In mari constituta, caret totaliter vineis atque campis'*.
76. M. CANARD, 'La Guerre sainte dans le monde islamique', *Actes du IIᵉ Congrès des sociétés savantes d'Afrique du Nord*, Tlemcen, 1936, in II, pp. 605-23.
77. The chrysobull of Alexius Comnenus in May 1082 exempted the Venetians from all payment (H. PIRENNE, *op. cit.*, p. 23).
78. Giuseppe TASSINI, *Curiosità veneziane*, 1887, p. 424.
79. Gino LUZZATTO, *Studi di storia economica veneziana*, 1954, p. 98.
80. Benjamin DAVID, 'The Jewish Mercantile Settlement of the 12th and 13th century in Venice: Reality or Conjecture?', in *A.J.S. Review*, 1977, pp. 201-25.
81. Wolfgang von STROMER, 'Bernardus Tauronicus und die Geschäftsbeziehungen zwischen der deutschen Ostalpen und Venedig vor Grundung des Fondaco dei Tedeschi', in *Grazer Forschungen zur Wirtschafts- und Sozialgeschichte*, III.
82. G. LUZZATO, *op. cit.*, p. 10.
83. *Ibid.*, pp. 37-8.
84. Giorgio GRACCO, *Società e stato nel medioevo veneziano (secoli XII-XIV)*, 1967.
85. Heinrich KRETSCHMAYR, *Geschichte von Venedig*, 1964, I, p. 257.
86. W. HEYD, *Histoire du commerce du Levant au Moyen Age*, 1936, p. 173.
87. Not as terrible as all that, according to Donald E. QUELLER Gerald W. DORY, 'Some Arguments in Defense of the Venetians on the Fourth Crusade', in *The American Historical Review*, n° 4, October 1976, pp. 717-37.
88. R.S. LOPEZ, *op. cit.*, pp. 154 ff.
89. Jacques MAS-LATRIE, *Histoire de l'Ile de Chypre sous le règne des princes de la maison de Lusignan*, 1861, I, p. 511.
90. On this point, see above, Volume II, p. 200.
91. Richard HENNIG, *Terrae incognitae*, 1950-1956, III, p. 109 ff.
92. A view rejected by F. BORLANDI , 'Alle origini del libro di Marco Polo', in *Studi in onore di Amintore Fanfani*, 1962, I, p. 135.
93. Elizabeth CHAPIN, *Les Villes de foires de Champagne des origines au début du XIVᵉ siècle*, 1937, p. 107, n. 9.
94. Henri PIRENNE, *op. cit.*, I, p. 295.
95. H. LAURENT, *op. cit.*, I, p. 39.
96. Robert-Henri BAUTIER, 'Les foires de Champagne', in *Recueil Jean Bodin*, V, 1953, p. 12.
97. H. PIRENNE, *op. cit.*, p. 89.
98. Félix BOURQUELOT, *Étude sur les foires de Champagne*, 1865, I, p. 80.
99. Hektor AMMANN, 'Die Anfänge des Activhandels und der Tucheinfuhr aus Nordwesteuropa nach dem Mittelmeergebiet', in *Studi in onore di Armando Sapori*, p. 275.
100. The derivation of this name is unknown – it *may* have been the name of the street in Florence where the *Arte de Calimala* had its warehouses (*Dizionario enciclopedico italiano*).
101. *Medit.*, I, p. 317.

102. *Ibid.*
103. H. LAURENT, *op. cit.*, p. 80.
104. Henri PIGEONNEAU, *Histoire du commerce de la France*, I, 1885, pp. 222–3.
105. *Ibid.*
106. Mario CHIAUDANO, 'I Rothschild del Duecento: la Gran Tavola di Orlando Bonsignori' in *Bulletino senese di storia patria*, VI, 1935.
107. R.-H. BAUTIER, *op. cit.*, p. 47.
108. F. BOURQUELOT, *op. cit.*, I, p. 66.
109. H. LAURENT, *op. cit.*, p. 38.
110. *Ibid.*, pp. 117–18.
111. R.-H. BAUTIER, *op. cit.*, pp. 45–6.
112. Vital CHOMEL, Jean EBERSOLT, *Cinq Siècles de circulation internationale vue de Jougne*, 1951, p. 42.
113. See below, section on Venice.
114. Wolfgang von STROMER, 'Banken und Geldmarkt: die Funktion der Wechselstuben in Oberdeutschland und den Rheinlanden', paper given to the *Settimana di Prato*, 18 April 1972, 4th week, F. Datini.
115. Augusto GUZZO, Introduction to the *Secondo Colloquio sull'età dell' Umanesimo e del Rinascimento in Francia*, 1970.
116. Giuseppe TOFFANIN, *Il Secolo senza Roma*, Bologna, 1943.
117. Guy FOURQUIN, *Les Campagnes de la région parisienne à la fin du Moyen Age*, 1964, pp. 161–2.
118. But NB the attempt by Philippe IV de Valois to renew the privileges of the Champagne fairs in 1344–9. Cf. M. de LAURIÈRE, *Ordonnances des rois de France*, 1729, II, pp. 200, 234, 305.
119. *Banca e moneta dalle Crociate alla Rivoluzione francese*, 1949, p. 62.
120. *Ibid.*
121. Raymond de ROOVER, 'Le rôle des Italiens dans la formation de la banque moderne' in *Revue de la banque*, 1952, p. 12.
122. See above, Volume II, p. 124.
123. Carlo CIPOLLA, *Money, Prices and Civilization*, 1956, pp. 33–4.
124. H. KRETSCHMAYR, *op. cit.*, II, p. 234.
125. *Ibid.*, pp. 234–6.
126. *Ibid.*, p. 239.
127. *The Foundations of Capitalism*, 1959, pp. 29 ff.
128. Hannelore GRONEUER, 'Die Seeversicherung in Genua am Ausgang des 14. Jahrhunderts' in *Beiträge zur Wirtschafts- und Sozialgeschichte des Mittelalters*, 1976, pp. 218–60.
129. H. KRETSCHMAYR, *op. cit.*, II, p. 300.
130. Christian BEC, *Les Marchands écrivains à Florence 1375–1434*, 1968, p. 312.
131. *Medit.*, I, p. 339.
132. *Ibid.*
133. *Bilanci generali*, 1912 (ed. Reale commissione per la pubblicazione dei documenti finanziari delle Repubblica di Venezia, 2nd series).
134. See below, chapter 4.
135. *Bilanci generali*, 2nd series, I, 1, Venice, 1912.
136. *Ibid.*, Documenti n° 81, pp. 94–7. Text printed in H. KRETSCHMAYR, *op. cit.*, II, pp. 617–19.
137. *Medit.*, I, p. 498.
138. It is *normally* agreed that the ratio between the annual coinage issued by the mint and the amount of money in circulation was 1 to 20.
139. Pierre-Antoine, Comte DARU, *Histoire de la République de Venise*, 1819, IV, p. 78.
140. Oliver C. COX, *The Foundations of Capitalism*, 1959, p. 69 and n. 18 (following MOLMENTI).
141. See below, this chapter.
142. A.d.S. Venice, Notario del Collegio, 9, f° 26 v°, n° 81, 12 August 1445.
143. *Ibid.*, 14, f° 38 v°, 8 July 1491; Senato Terra, 12, f° 41, 7 February 1494.
144. *Medit.*, II, pp. 894–5.
145. Ad.S. Venice, Senato Terra, 4, f° 107 v°.
146. P. MOLMENTI, *La Storia di Venezia nella vita privata* . . ., 1880, I, pp. 124, 131–2.
147. Piero PIERI, 'Milizie e capitani di ventura in Italia del Medio Evo', in *Atti della Reale Accademia Peloritana*, XL, 1937–8, p. 12.
148. H. KRETSCHMAYR, *op. cit.*, II, p. 386.
149. Girolamo PRIULI, *Diarii*, ed. A. Segre, 1921, I, p. 19.
150. Federico CHABOD, 'Venezia nella politica italiana ed europea del Cinquecento', in *La Civiltà veneziana del Rinascimento*, 1958, p. 29. On the arrival of the ambassadors from Spain and from 'king' Maximilian, Archivio Gonzaga, series E, Venezia 1435, Venice, 2 January 1495.

151. H. HAUSHERR, *op. cit.*, p. 28.
152. *Bilanci*, I, pp. 38-9. Not in 1318, as William McNEILL writes in *Venice, the Hinge of Europe 1081-1797*, 1974, p. 66, but before 1228, cf. *Bilanci . . .*, I, pp. 38-9, on the site of the *Fondaco dei Tedeschi*: '*qui tenant fonticum Venetie ubi Teutonici hospitantur*'.
153. J. SCHNEIDER, 'Les villes allemandes au Moyen Age. Les institutions économiques', in *Recueil de la Société Jean Bodin*, VII, *La Ville, institutions économiques et sociales*, 1955, part 2, p. 423.
154. Antonio H. DE OLIVEIRA MARQUES, 'Notas para a historia de Feitoria portuguesa da Flandes no seculo XV', in *Studi in onore di Amintore Fanfani*, 1962, II, pp. 370-476, esp. p. 446. Anselmo BRAACAMP FREIRE, 'A Feitoria da Flandes', in *Archivio historico portuguez*, VI, 1908-1910, p. 322 ff.
155. *Medit.*, I, p. 471.
156. G. LUZZATTO, *op. cit.*, p. 149.
157. *Medit.*, I, p. 302.
158. Alberto TENENTI, Corrado VIVANTI, 'Le film d'un grand système de navigation: les galères marchandes vénitiennes, XIVᵉ-XVIᵉ siècles', in *Annales E.S.C.*, 1961, p. 85.
159. *Op. cit.*, pp. 62 ff.
160. Federigo MELIS, *La Moneta*, typescript, p. 8.
161. Federigo MELIS, 'Origenes de la Banca Moderna', in *Moneda y Credito*, March 1971, pp. 10-11.
162. Federigo MELIS, *Storia della ragioneria, contributo alla conoscenza e interpretazione delle fonti più significative della storia economica*, 1950, pp. 481 ff.
163. Federico MELIS, *Sulle fonti della storia economica*, 1963, p. 152.
164. See above, Volume II, pp. 289 ff.
165. R. HENNIG, *op. cit.*, III, pp. 119 ff and IV, p. 126.
166. G. TASSINI, *op. cit.*, p. 55.
167. E. LATTES, *La Libertà delle banche a Venezia*, 1869, chapter 2.
168. Gino LUZZATTO, *Storia economica di Venezia, dal XIᵉ al XVIᵉ s.*, 1961, p. 101.
169. G LUZZATTO, *op. cit.*, p. 212.
170. G. LUZZATTO, *op. cit.*, p. 78.
171. G. LUZZATTO, *Studi . . .*, *op. cit.*, pp. 135-6.
172. *Ibid.*, p. 130.
173. Reinhold C. MUELLER, 'Les prêteurs juifs à Venise', in *Annales E.S.C.*, 1975, p. 1277.
174. G. LUZZATTO, *Studi . . .*, *op. cit.*, p. 104.
175. *Ibid.*, p. 104.
176. *Ibid.*, p. 106, n. 67.
177. 'Le rôle du capital dans la vie locale et la commerce extérieur de Venise entre 1050 et 1150', in *Revue belge de philologie et d'histoire*, XIII, 1934, pp. 657-96.
178. 'Aux origines du capitalisme vénitien', review of the preceding article in *Annales E.S.C.*, 1935, p. 96.
179. R. MOROZZO DELLA ROCCA, A. LOMBARDO, *I Documenti del commercio veneziano nei secoli XI-XIII*, 1940, quoted by G. LUZZATTO, *Studi . . .*, p. 91, n. 9.
180. G. LUZZATTO, *Storia economica . . .*, *op. cit.*, p. 82.
181. *Ibid.*, pp. 79-80.
182. Raymond de ROOVER, 'Le marché monétaire au Moyen Age et au début des temps modernes', in *Revue historique*, July-Sept., 1970, pp. 7 ff.
183. *Medit.*, I, p. 378.
184. *Ibid.*
185. F. MELIS, *La Moneta*, *op. cit.*, p. 8.
186. Frederic C. LANE, *Venice, a maritime republic*, 1973, p. 166.
187. *Ibid.*, p. 104.
188. *Industry and Economic Decline in 17th Century Venice*, 1976, pp. 24 ff.
189. A.d.S. Venice, Senato Terra, 4, fᵒ 71, 18 April 1458.
190. Domenico SELLA, 'Les mouvements longs de l'industrie lainière à Venise aux XVIᵉ et XVIIᵉ siècles', in *Annales E.S.C.*, Jan.-March 1957, p. 41.
191. Brian PULLAN, *Rich and Poor in Renaissance Venice*, 1971, pp. 33 ff; Ruggiero MASCHIO, 'Investimenti edilizi delle scuole grandi a Venezia (XVI-XVII sec.); paper given to Prato conference in April 1977.
192. A.d.S. Venice, Senato Mar, II, fᵒ 126, 21 February 1446.
193. D. SELLA, *art. cit.*, pp. 40-1.
194. Ömer Lutfi BARKAN, 'Essai sur les données

statistiques des régistres de recensement dans l'Empire ottoman aux XVᵉ et XVIᵉ siècles', in *Journal of economic and social history of the Orient*, August 1957, pp. 27 and 34.

195. A Senate decision of 18 February 1453 declares unequivocally the need '*ob reverentiam Dei, bonum christianorum honorem, nostri dominii et pro commodo et utilitate mercatorum et civium nostrorum*', to go to the aid of Constantinople, a city of which it could be said that 'it is considered to be a part of our State and should not fall into the hands of infidels', '*civitas Constantinopolis que dici et reputari potest esse nostri dominii, non deveniat ad manos infidelium*', A.d.S., Venice, Senato Mar, 4, 170.

196. A.d.S. Venice, Senato Secreta, 20, fᵒ 3, 15 January 1454.

197. H. KRETSCHMAYR, *op. cit.*, II, pp. 371 ff.

198. Damião PEREZ, *Historia de Portugal*, 1926-1933, 8 vols.

199. Ralph DAVIS, *The Rise of the Atlantic Economies*, 2nd ed., 1975, p. 1.

200. See in particular the works of Vitorino MAGALHAẼS-GODINHO.

201. R. DAVIS, *op. cit.*, p. 4.

202. Gonzalo de REPARAZ , *La Epoca de los grandes descubrimientos españoles y portugueses*, 1931.

203. Prospero PERAGALLO, *Cenni intorno alla colonia italiana in Portogallo nei secoli XIVᵉ, XVᵉ, XVIᵉ*, 2nd edn., 1907.

204. Virginia RAU, 'A family of Italian merchants in Portugal in the XVth century: the Lomellini', in *Studi in onore di A. Sapori, op. cit.*, pp. 717-726.

205. Robert RICARD, 'Contribution à l'étude du commerce génois au Maroc durant la période portugaise, 1415-1550' in *Annales de l'Inst. d'Etudes orientales*, III, 1937.

206. Duarte PACHECO PEREIRA, *Esmeraldo de situ orbis . . .*, 1892, quoted by R. DAVIS, *op. cit.*, p. 8.

207. *Op. cit.*, p. 11.

208. V. MAGALHAẼS-GODINHO, 'Le repli vénitien et égyptien et la route du Cap, 1496-1533'. in *Éventail de l'histoire vivante*, 1953, II, p. 293.

209. Richard EHRENBERG, *Das Zeitalter der Fugger*, 1922, 2 vols.

210. Hermann VAN DER WEE, *The Growth of the Antwerp Market and the European Economy (14th-16th Centuries)*, 1963, II, p. 127.

211. Henri PIRENNE, *Histoire de Belgique*, 1973, II, p. 58.

212. G.D. RAMSAY, *The City of London*, 1975, p. 12.

213. Émile COORNAERT, 'Anvers a-t-elle eu une flotte marchande?', in *Le Navire et l'économie maritime*, ed. Michel MOLLAT, 1960, pp. 72 ff.

214. *Ibid.*, pp. 71 and 79.

215. G.D. RAMSAY, *op. cit.*, p. 13.

216. H. PIRENNE, *op. cit.*, II, p. 57.

217. G.D. RAMSAY, *op. cit.*, p. 18.

218. Lodovico GUICCIARDINI, *Description de tous les Pays-Bas*, 1568, p. 122.

219. H. VAN DER WEE, *op. cit.*, II, p. 203.

220. E. COORNAERT, 'La genèse du système capitaliste: grand capitalisme et économie traditionelle à Anvers au XVIᵉ siècle', in *Annales d'histoire économique et sociale*, 1936, p. 129.

221. O.C. COX, *op. cit.*, p. 266.

222. Hermann VAN DER WEE, *op. cit.*, 3 vols.

223. *Ibid.*, II, p. 128.

224. *Ibid.*, II, p. 120.

225. J. VAN HOUTTE, *op. cit.*, p. 82.

226. Renée DOEHAERD, *Etudes anversoises*, 1963, I, pp. 37 ff, 62-3.

227. Anselmo BRAACAMP FREIRE, *art. cit.*, pp. 322 ff.

228. H. VAN DER WEE, *op. cit.*, I, Appendix 44/1.

229. *Ibid.*, II, p. 125.

230. *Ibid.*, II, pp. 130-1.

231. *Ibid.*, II, p. 131.

232. *Ibid.*, II, p. 129.

233. *Ibid.*

234. Anselmo BRAACAMP FREIRE, *art. cit.*, p. 407.

235. V. MAGALHAẼS-GODINHO, *L'Economie de l'Empire portugais aux XVᵉ et XVIᵉ siècles*, 1969, p. 471.

236. John U. NEF, 'Silver production in central Europe, 1450-1618', in *The Journal of Political Economy*, 1941, p. 586.

237. *Medit.*, I, p. 545.

238. Richard GASCON, *Grand Commerce et vie urbaine au XVIᵉ siècle, Lyon et ses marchands*, 1971, p. 88.

239. H. VAN DER WEE, *op. cit.*, II, p. 156.

240. Earl J. HAMILTON, 'Monetary inflation in Castile, 1598-1660', in *Economic History*, 6, January 1931, p. 180.

241. 1529, the Paix des Dames; 1535, the occupation of Milan by Charles V.

242. Fernand BRAUDEL, 'Les emprunts de Charles Quint sur la place d'Anvers', in Colloques Internationaux du C.N.R.S., *Charles Quint et son temps*, Paris, 1958, p. 196.

243. H. VAN DER WEE, *op. cit.*, II, p. 178, n. 191.

244. Pierre CHAUNU, *Séville et l'Atlantique*, VI, pp. 114-5.

245. See below, chapter 3.

246. J. VAN HOUTTE, *op. cit.*, p. 91.

247. *Medit.*, I, p. 480.

248. H. VAN DER WEE, *op. cit.*, II, p. 179.

249. Hugo SOLY, *Urbanisme en Kapitalisme te Antwerpen in de 15. de Eeuw*, summary in French, p. 457 ff.

250. T. WITTMAN, *op. cit.*, p. 30.

251. P. DOLLINGER, *op. cit.*, pp. 417-18; cf. the illustration on p. 106.

252. H. VAN DER WEE, *op. cit.*, II, pp. 228-9.

253. *Ibid.*, p. 238.

254. *Ibid.*, II, p. 186.

255. Charles VERLINDEN, Jan CRAEYBECKX, E. SCHOLLIERS, 'Mouvements des prix et des salaires en Belgique au XVIᵉ siècle', in *Annales E.S.C.*, 1955, pp. 184-5.

256. John LOTHROP MOTLEY, *La Revolution des Pays Bas au XVIᵉ siècle*, II, p. 196.

257. *Ibid.*, III, p. 14.

258. *Ibid.*, III, ch. 1.

259. *Medit.*, I, p. 482 and n. 122. For an up-to-date discussion of the question, see William D. PHILLIPS and Carla R. PHILLIPS, 'Spanish wool and Dutch rebels: the Middleburg incident of 1574', in *American Historical Review*, April 1977, pp. 312-30.

260. H. VAN DER WEE, 'Anvers et les innovations de la technique financière aux XVIᵉ et XVIIᵉ siècles', in *Annales E.S.C.*, 1967, p. 1073, and *The Growth of the Antwerp Market . . .*, II.

261. H. VAN DER WEE, in *art. cit. Annales E.S.C.*, 1967, p. 1071.

262. *Ibid*, p. 1073, n. 5.

263. *Ibid.*, p. 1076.

264. Raymond de ROOVER, *L'Evolution de la lettre de change, XVIᵉ-XVIIIᵉ siècles*, 1953, p. 119.

265. *Les Gueux dans les 'bonnes villes' de Flandre, 1577-1584*, Budapest, 1969.

266. B.N., Ms. Fr. 14666, f° 11 v°. Report of 1692.

267. Giovanni BOTERO, *Relationi universali*, 1599, p. 68.

268. *Ibid.*

269. Comtesse de BOIGNE, *Mémoires*, 1971, I, p. 305.

270. Jacques HEERS, *Gênes au XVᵉ siècle*, 1961, p. 532.

271. Jérôme de LA LANDE, *Voyage d'un Français en Italie*, 1769, VIII, pp. 492-3.

272. The unpublished *Voyage* by the Comte d'ESPINCHAL, 1789, Clermont-Ferrand Library.

273. *Ibid.*

274. *Ibid.*

275. Vito VITALE, *Breviario della storia di Genova*, 1955, I, p. 148.

276. *Ibid.*, p. 163.

277. *Medit.*, I, p. 390.

278. V. VITALE, *op. cit.*, I, p. 346.

279. *Ibid.*, p. 349.

280. *Ibid.*, p. 421.

281. Hannelore GRONEUER, *art. cit.*, pp. 218-260.

282. *Ibid.*

283. A.N., K 1355, 21 May 1684.

284. A.N., A.E., B¹ 529, 12 April, 1710.

285. B.N., Ms. Fr., 16073, f° 371.

286. Giuseppe FELLONI, *Gli Investimenti finanziari genovesi in Europa tra il Seicento e la Restaurazione*, 1971, p. 345.

287. Fernand BRAUDEL, 'Endet das "Jahrhundert der Genuesen" im Jahre 1627?', in Festschrift for Wilhelm Abel, p. 455.

288. Roberto S. LOPEZ, *Studi sull'economia genovese nel Medio Evo*, 1936, pp. 142 ff.

289. Roberto S. LOPEZ, frequently referred to this in conversation, and in one of his unpublished lectures.

290. *Medit.*, I, pp. 342-3.

291. As Camelo TRASSELLI has often argued in his lectures.

292. Cf. the text and references in V. VITALE, *op. cit.* (see note 275 above).

293. R.S. LOPEZ, *Genova marinara del Duecento: Benedetto Zaccaria, ammiraglio e mercante*, 1933, p. 154.

294. Carmelo TRASSELLI, 'Genovesi in Sicilia' in *Atti della Società ligure di storia patria*, IX (LXXXIII), fasc. II, p. 158.
295. *Ibid.*, pp. 155–78.
296. *Ibid.*, and *viva voce*.
297. *Ibid.*
298. Carmelo TRASSELLI, 'Sumario duma historia do açucar siciliano', in *Do Tempo e da Historia*, II, 1968, pp. 65–9.
299. See above, Volume II, pp. 420–1.
300. Gerónimo UZTARIZ, *Théorie et pratique du commerce et de la marine*, 1753, p. 52.
301. Renée DOEHAERD, *Les Relations commerciales entre Gênes, la Belgique et l'outremont*, 1941, I, p. 89.
302. R. RICARD, *art. cit.* (see note 205).
303. Ramon CARANDE, 'Sevilla fortaleza y mercado', in *Anuario de historia del derecho español*, II, 1925, pp. 33, 55 ff.
304. Virgina RAU, 'A family of Italian merchants in Portugal in the XVth century: the Lomellini', in *Studi in onore di Armando Sapori*, pp. 717–726.
305. André-E. SAYOUS, 'Le rôle des Génois lors des premiers mouvements réguliers d'affaires entre l'Espagne et le Nouveau Monde', in *C.r. de l'Académie des Inscriptions et Belles-Lettres*, 1930.
306. Felipe RUIZ MARTÍN, *Lettres marchandes* . . ., p. xxix.
307. *Ibid.*
308. *Medit.*, I, p. 339.
309. F. BRAUDEL, 'Les emprunts de Charles Quint sur la place d'Anvers', *art. cit.*, p. 192.
310. R. CARANDE, *art. cit.*
311. Henri LAPEYRE, *Simón Ruiz et les asientos de Philippe II*, 1953, pp. 14 ff.
312. *Medit.*, I, 343–4.
313. Felipe RUIZ MARTÍN, *Lettres marchandes* . . . ., p. xxxviii.
314. Giorgio DORIA, 'Un quadriennio critico: 1575–1578. Contrasti e nuovi orientamenti nella società genovese nel quadro della crisi finanziaria espagnola', in *Mélanges Franco Borlandi*, 1977, p. 382.
315. Giorgio DORIA, paper given at Madrid Conference, 1977.
316. *The International Economy and Monetary Movements in France*, 1972, pp. 23 ff.
317. Felipe RUIZ MARTÍN, *Lettres marchandes* . . . , p. xliv.
318. *Ibid.*, p. xxxii.
319. *Ibid.*, pp. xxx–xxxi.
320. *Medit.*, I, p. 503.
321. This ordinance created the *escudo*, or gold crown which replaced the *excellente* of Granada. Cf. *Medit.*, I, p. 472 and note 66.
322. Henri PIRENNE, *Histoire de Belgique*, IV, 1927, p. 78.
323. *Medit.*, I, pp. 504 ff.
324. *Ibid.*, I, pp. 510–11. F. RUIZ MARTÍN. *El Siglo de los Genoveses*, unpublished.
325. Fernand BRAUDEL, 'La vita economica di Venezia nel secolo XVI', in *La Civiltà veneziana del Rinascimento*, p. 101.
326. *Ibid.*
327. *Medit.*, I, p. 322 and n. 232, and p. 503, n. 275.
328. See above, chapter 1, n. 48.
329. F. BRAUDEL, *art. cit.*, 'Endet das "Jahrhundert" . . .', pp. 455–68.
330. A.E. FEAVEARYEAR, *The Pound Sterling*, 1931, pp. 90–1.
331. A.E., M et D, Hollande, 122, f° 248 (report from Aitzema, 1647).
332. José GENTIL DA SILVA, *Banque et crédit en Italie au XVII^c siècle*, 1969, I, p. 171.
333. F. BRAUDEL, *art. cit.*, 'Endet das "Jahrhundert" . . .', p. 461.
334. Michel MORINEAU, 'Gazettes hollandaises et trésors américains', in *Anuario de Historia economica y social*, 1969, pp. 289–361.
335. J. DE LA LANDE, *Voyage en Italie*, op. cit., IX, p. 362.
336. *Ibid.*, IX, p. 367.
337. *Gli Investimenti finanziari genovesi in Europa tra il Seicento e la Restaurazione*, 1971.
338. *Ibid.*, p. 472.
339. *Ibid.*, p. 168, note 30.
340. *Ibid.*, p. 249.
341. *Ibid.*, pp. 392, 429, 453.
342. B.N., Ms Fr. 14671, f° 17, 6 March 1743.
343. G. FELLONI, *op. cit.*, p. 477.
344. Since Genoa allowed Protestant merchants to settle in the city, so presumably could handle their competition.
345. Carmelo TRASSELLI.
346. José GENTIL DA SILVA, *op. cit.*, pp. 55–6.

NOTES TO CHAPTER 3

1. Throughout this chapter, the term Holland is frequently used, following the rather unsatisfactory usage of the present day, to refer to the whole of the United Provinces.

2. Violet BARBOUR, *Capitalism in Amsterdam in the Seventeenth Century*, 1963, p. 13.

3. See above, Chapter 2.

4. Richard TILDEN RAPP, 'The Unmaking of the Mediterranean Trade . . .' in *Journal of Economic History*, September 1975.

5. G. de USTARIZ, *op. cit.*, p. 97. The area of the United Provinces, it might be useful to recall, was of the order of 34,000 km².

6. *Oeuvres complètes*, I, p. 455. Turgot had translated into French the work of the English economist Josiah Tucker, (1712–1799) *A Brief Essay on the advantages and disadvantages which respectively attend France and Great Britain with regard to trade.*

7. A.N., K 1349, 132, f° 20.

8. *The Complete English Tradesman . . .*, 1745, II, p. 260. Defoe tells us that he has this on good authority but does not say whose.

9. A.N., Marine, B⁷, 463, f° 30.

10. G. de USTARIZ, *op. cit.*, p. 98.

11. Jean-Baptiste d'ARGENS, *Lettres juives*, 1738, III, p. 192.

12. Jacques ACCARIAS DE SERIONNE, *Les Interêts des nations de l'Europe développés relativement au commerce*, 1766, I, p. 44.

13. Jean-Nicolas de PARIVAL, *Les Délices de la Hollande*, 1662, p. 10.

14. A.E., M. et D. 72, Hollande, November 1755.

17. L. GUICCIARDINI, *op. cit.*, p. 288.

16. GAUDARD DE CHAVANNES, *Voyage de Genève à Londres*, 1760, unpaged.

17. *Viaje fuera de España*, 1947, p. 1852.

18. C. R. BOXER, *The Dutch Seaborne Empire*, 1969, p. 7.

19. J.-N. de PARIVAL, *op. cit.*, p. 76.

20. *Ibid.*, p. 56.

21. *Ibid.*, p. 82.

22. *Ibid.*, p. 13.

23. *Ibid.*, p. 26.

24. *Ibid.*, p. 12.

25. 'The Role of the Rural Sector in the Development of the Dutch Economy, 1500–1700', *Journal of Economic History*, March 1971, p. 267.

26. Jean-Claude FLACHAT, *Observations sur le commerce et sur les arts d'une partie de l'Europe, de l'Asie, de l'Afrique et des Indes orientales*, 1766, II, p. 351.

27. Charles WILSON, *England's Apprenticeship 1603–1763*, 1965, 3rd ed. 1967, p. 71; Immanuel WALLERSTEIN, *The Modern World System*, II, ch. 11.

28. Barry SUPPLE, *Commercial Crisis and Change in England 1600–1642*, 1959, p. 34.

29. Jean-Claude BOYER, 'Le capitalisme hollandais et l'organisation de l'espace dans les Provinces-Unies', *Colloque franco-hollandaise*, typescript, esp. p. 4.

30. J.-N. de PARIVAL, *op. cit.*, p. 83.

31. Jan de VRIES, 'An Inquiry into the Behavior of wages in the Dutch Republic and the Southern Netherlands, 1500–1800', typescript, p. 13.

32. Pieter de LA COURT, *Mémoires de Jean de Witt*, 1709, pp. 43–4. (English trans., attrib. to John de Witt, *The True Interest and Political Maxims of the Republic of Holland and West Friesland*, 1702.)

33. *Op. cit.*, p. 216.

34. Abbé SCAGLIA, in Hubert G.R. READE, *Sidelights on the Thirty Years' War*, London, 1924, III, p. 34, quoted by John U. NEF, *War and Human Progress*, 1950, p. 14.

35. Ivo SCHÖFFER, 'Did Holland's Golden Age co-incide with a Period of Crisis?', *in: Acta historiae neerlandica*, 1966, p. 92.

36. *Journal de Verdun*, November 1751, p. 391.

37. A.N., K 879, 123 and 123 *bis*, n° 18, f° 39.

38. J.L. PRICE, *The Dutch Republic during the 17th Century*, 1974, pp. 58 ff.

39. P. de LA COURT, *op. cit.*, p. 28.

40. J.-N. de PARIVAL, *op. cit.*, p. 104.

41. Johann BECKMANN, *Beiträge zur Œkonomie . . . 1779–1784*, II, p. 549.

42. *Op. cit.*, p. 37.

43. A.N., A.E., B¹ 619, 6 March 1670.
44. J. SAVARY, *op. cit.*, I, p. 84.
45. J.-B. d'ARGENS, *op. cit.*, III, p. 194.
46. *Le Guide d'Amsterdam*, 1701, pp. 2 and 81.
47. *Ibid.*, pp. 82–3.
48. *Gazette d'Amsterdam*, 1669, 14, 21, 28 February and 18 June.
49. *Le Guide d'Amsterdam*, *op. cit.*, p. 1.
50. J. ACCARIAS DE SÉRIONNE, *op. cit.*, I, p. 173.
51. J.L. PRICE, *op. cit.*, p. 33.
52. J.-N. de PARIVAL, *op. cit.*, p. 41.
53. W. TEMPLE, *Observations upon the Provinces of the United Netherlands*, 1720, p. 59 (Cambridge edn., 1932, p. 126).
54. *Le Guide d'Amsterdam*, 1701, pp. 1–2.
55. G.V. MENTINK and A.M. VAN DER WOUDE, *De demografische outwikkeling te Rotterdam en Cool in de 17ᵉ en 18ᵉ eeuw*, 1965.
56. J.-N. de PARIVAL, *op. cit.*, p. 33.
57. Friedrich LÜTGE, *Geschichte der deutschen Agrarverfassung vom frühen Mittelalter bis zum 19. Jahrhundert*, 1967, p. 285. IVO SCHÖFFER, in: *Handbuch der europäischen Geschichte*, ed. Theodor SCHIEDER, IV, 1968, p. 638. (*Hannekemaier* means 'day-labourer' in Dutch, and *peopen* and *moffen* were pejorative colloquial terms used to describe Germans.)
58. A.N., Marine, B⁷, 463, fᵒ 39, (1697).
59. More significant than the Jews from Germany, the Sephardic Jews were mostly Portuguese and had their own cemetery at Ouwerkerque (*Le Guide d'Amsterdam*, 1701, p. 38; see also the bibliography in Violet BARBOUR, *op. cit.*, p. 25, n. 42); on Portuguese Jews, see E.M. KOEN's article 'Notarial records relating to the Portuguese Jews in Amsterdam up to 1639', in *Studia Rosenthaliana*, January 1973, pp. 116–27.
60. *Die Juden und das Wirtschaftsleben*, 1911, p. 18; *Medit.* (English translation), I, pp. 629 ff and II, 816.
61. *Medit.*, I, pp. 629 ff.
62. Ernst SCHULIN, *Handelsstaat England*, 1969, p. 195.
63. See above vol. II, pp. 157–9.
64. Léon VAN DER ESSEN, *Alexandre Farnèse, prince de Parme, gouverneur général des Pays-Bas, 1545-1592*, IV, 1935, p. 123.
65. C.R. BOXER, *op. cit.*, p. 19, note 5.
66. *Voyage en Hollande*, in: *Œuvres complètes*, 1969, XI, p. 336, quoted by C. MANCERON, *op cit.*, p. 468.
67. J.-N. de PARIVAL, *op. cit.*, p. 36.
68. J. ALCALA ZAMORA Y QUEIPO DE LLANO, *España, Flandes y el Mar del Norte (1618-1639). La última ofensiva europea de los Austrias madrileños*, 1975, p. 58.
69. W. TEMPLE, *op. cit.*, p. 26.
70. J.-N. de PARIVAL, *op. cit.*, p. 19.
71. A.-N., K 1349, 132, fᵒ 162 vᵒ ff. (1699).
72. A.N., M 662, dos. 5, fᵒ 15 vᵒ.
73. A.N., K 1349, 132, fᵒ 168.
74. Jacques ACCARIAS DE SÉRIONNE, *La Richesse de la Hollande*, 1778, I, p. 68.
75. A.E., C.P. Hollande, 94, fᵒ 59.
76. J. ACCARIAS DE SÉRIONNE, *op. cit.*, I, p. 69.
77. Which went in the end to the big merchants, A.N., M 662, dossier 5, fᵒ 13 vᵒ.
78. A.N. K 1349, 132, fᵒ 174 and vᵒ.
79. For some reason (an unintended omission?) there is no mention of oil.
80. A.N., A.E., B¹, 624.
81. J. ACCARIAS DE SÉRIONNE, *op. cit.*, I, p. 255.
82. *Ibid.*, II, p. 54.
83. C. WILSON, *Anglo-Dutch Commerce and Finance in the Eighteenth Century*, 1941, p. 3.
84. P. de LA COURT, *op. cit.*, p. 28.
85. Quoted by C. WILSON, *Profit and Power. A Study of England and the Dutch Wars*, 1957, p. 3.
86. I. de PINTO, *op. cit.*, p. 263.
87. Jacques ACCARIAS DE SÉRIONNE, *La Richesse de l'Angleterre*, 1771, notably pp. 42 et 44.
88. J.-B. d'ARGENS, *op. cit.*, III, p. 193.
89. A.N., A.E., B¹, 619, Pomponne's correspondence, the Hague, 16 May 1669. The 20,000 ships Colbert speaks of are pure exaggeration. In 1636, the Dutch fleet consisted of 2300 to 2500 vessels, plus the 2000 herring-busses. Cf. J.L. PRICE, *op. cit.*, p. 43. My estimate (600,000 tons) corresponds to W. VOGEL's 'Zur Grösse der Europäischen

Handelsflotten', in *Forschungen und Versuche zur Geschichte des Mittelalters und der Neuzeit*, 1915, p. 319.

90. W. TEMPLE, *op. cit.*, p. 47, (Cambridge edn., 1932, p. 97).

91. J.-B. TAVERNIER, *Les Six Voyages* ..., 1676, II, p. 266.

92. A.N., Marine, B⁷, 463, f° 45, 1697.

93. A.N., M 785, dos. 4, f°ˢ 68-9.

94. *Ibid.*

95. With the hull opened at the after end to accommodate the masts.

96. *Le Guide de l'Amsterdam*, 1701, p. 81.

97. Maltese Archives, 65-26.

98. L. DERMIGNY, *Le Commerce à Canton* ..., *op. cit.*, p. 161, note 4.

99. A.N., G⁷, 1695, f° 52, 15 February 1710.

100. On this expedition, cf. Isaac DUMONT DE BOSTAQUET, *Mémoires*, 1968.

101. A.N., K 1349, n° 132, f° 130.

102. Moscow C.S.A., 50/6, 537, 1, 12/23 January 1787.

103. 'Dutch Capitalism and the European World economy', in: *Colloque franco-hollandais*, 1976, typescript, p. 1.

104. 'Les interdépendances économiques dans le champ d'action européen des Hollandais (xvi⁰-xviii⁰ siècles)', in: *Colloque franco-hollandais*, 1976, typescript, p. 76.

105. Francisco de SOUSA COUTINHO, *Correspondencia diplomatica... durante a sua embaixada en Holanda*, 1920-1926, II, 227, 2 January 1648: '*que como he de tantas cabeças e de tantos juizos differentes, poucas vezes se acordão todos inda pera aquillo que milhor lhes està*'.

106. A.R.J. TURGOT, *op. cit.*, I, p. 373.

107. That is exercising control from above (in theory at least).

108. A.N., K 1349, f° 11.

109. W. TEMPLE, cited by C. BOXER, *The Dutch Seaborne Empire*, *op. cit.*, p. 13.

110. A.N., K 1349, f° 35 v°. Holland alone provided over 58% of the tax contribution of the United Provinces.

111. I. SCHÖFFER, in: *Handbuch* ..., *op. cit.*, p. 654.

112. C. PROISY D'EPPES, *Dictionnaire des girouettes ou nos contemporains d'après eux-mêmes*, 1815.

113. 'The Low Countries', in: *The New Cambridge Modern History*, IV, 1970, p. 365.

114. K.H.D. HALEY, *The Dutch in the 17th Century*, 1972, p. 83.

115. A.N., K 1349, f° 7 and 7 v°.

116. B.M. VLEKKE, *Evolution of the Dutch Nation*, 1945, pp. 162-6, quoted by C.R. BOXER, *op. cit.*, p. 11, note 4.

117. J.-N. de PARIVAL.

118. A word derived from *calfat*, *calfateur* = caulker, 'Someone of no consequence'.

119. J.-N. de PARIVAL, *op. cit.*, p. 190.

120. *Le Guide d'Amsterdam*, *op. cit.*, p. 21.

121. *Op. cit.*, p. 39, quoted in C.R. BOXER, *op. cit.*, p. 37.

122. I. de PINTO, *op. cit.*, pp. 334-5.

123. J.L. PRICE, *op. cit.*, p. 220.

124. *Ibid.*, p. 224, quoted in French: '*Le françois qui est pour les intelligents ... le flament qui n'est que pour les ignorants*'.

125. A.N., K 849.

126. Marcel MARION, *Dictionnaire des institutions de la France aux XVII⁰ et XVIII⁰ siècles*, 1923, p. 521.

127. On the early cultivation of potatoes in the Low Countries, see Chr. VANDENBROEKE, 'Cultivation and Consumption of the Potato in the 17th and 18th Century', in: *Acta historiae neerlandica*, V, 1971, pp. 15-40.

128. A.N., K 849, n° 18, f° 20.

129. I. de PINTO, *op. cit.*, p. 152.

130. J.-N. de PARIVAL, *op. cit.*, p. 41.

131. A.N., K 1349, 132, f° 215.

132. A.N., K 849, f°ˢ 17-18.

133. *Ibid.*

134. *Ibid.*

135. I. de PINTO, *op. cit.*, p. 147.

136. *Journal du commerce*, January 1759.

137. Warsaw, Central Archives, Radziwill Collection, 18 August 1744.

138. I. de PINTO, *op. cit.*, p. 94.

139. The term used, *faire paroli*, comes from gaming, 'to outbid or raise the stakes'.

140. J. de VRIES, 'An Inquiry into the Behavior of Wages ...', *art. cit.*, p. 13.

141. Jules MICHELET, *Histoire de France*, XIV, 1877, p. 2.

142. A.E., C.P. Hollande, 35, f° 267 v°, 15 May 1646.

143. The *Vereenigde Oost-Indische Compagnie*, the Dutch East India Company.

144. A.N., K 1349, 50 v°.
145. *Ibid.*
146. *Op. cit.*, p. 53.
147. A.E., C.P. Hollande, 46, f° 309.
148. The 17 directors of the V.O.C.
149. C.R. BOXER, *op. cit.*, p. 46, quoted by G. PAPAGNO, *art. cit.*, pp. 88-9; see below, note 271.
150. A.N., M 785, dos. 4, f°s 16-17.
151. J.G. VAN DILLEN, 'Isaac Le Maire et le commerce des Indes orientales', in: *Revue d'histoire moderne*, 1935, pp. 121-37.
152. A.N., A.E., B¹, 619, 18 June 1665.
153. J. DU MONT, *Corps universel diplomatique du droit des gens, contenant un recueil des traitez* ..., 1726, IV, p. 274.
154. José Gentil DA SILVA, 'Trafics du Nord, marchés du "Mezzogiorno", finances génoises: recherches et documents sur la conjoncture à la fin du XVIᵉ siècle', in: *Revue du Nord*, avril-juin 1959, p. 146.
155. I. WALLERSTEIN, *The Modern World System, op. cit.*, I, p. 211; P. JEANNIN, *art. cit.*, p. 10.
156. *Moeder* in the sense of original, basic.
157. Cited by I. WALLERSTEIN, *op. cit.*, pp. 198-9.
158. *Medit.*, I, p. 140; V. VAZQUEZ DE PRADA, *Lettres marchandes d'Anvers*, 1960, I, p. 48.
159. J.G. DA SILVA, *Banque et crédit en Italie* ..., I, p. 593, note 183.
160. *Ibid.*
161. Germaine TILLION, *Les Ennemis complémentaires*, 1960.
162. A. GRENFELD PRICE, *The Western Invasions of the Pacific and its Continents*, 1963, p. 29.
163. Simancas, E°-569, f° 84 (nd.); Virginia RAU, 'Rumos e vicissítudes do comércio do sal portuguès nos seculos XIV à XVIII', in: *Revista da Faculdade de Letras* (Lisboa), 1963, n° 7, pp. 5-27.
164. Felipe RUIZ MARTÍN, unpublished study.
165. *Medit.*, I, p. 590.
166. *Medit.*, I, p. 63.
167. *Medit.*, I, p. 638; Jean-Pierre BERTHE, 'Les Flamands à Séville au XVIᵉ siècle', in: *Fremde Kaufleute auf der iberischen Halbinsel*, ed. H. KELLENBENZ, 1970, p. 243.

168. Jacob VAN KLAVEREN, *Europäische Wirtschaftsgeschichte Spaniens im 16. und 17. Jahrhundert*, 1960; *Medit.*, I, pp. 636 ff.
169. J. VAN KLAVEREN, *op. cit.*, pp. 116-17.
170. A.N., K 1349, no 133. Memorandum about the government of the Provinces of the Netherlands, f°s 3 and 4. H. PIRENNE, *op. cit.*, 1973, III, p. 60.
171. 'Gazettes hollandaises et trésors américains', in: *Anuario de Historia económica y social*, 1969, pp. 289-361.
172. Earl J. HAMILTON, *art. cit.*, in: *Economic History*, 1931, pp. 182 sq.
173. *Medit.*, I, p. 510.
174. *Medit.*, I, pp. 640-2.
175. *Navigatio ac itinerarium Johannis Hugonis Linscotani in Orientalem sive Lusitanorum Indiam* ..., 1599.
176. Abbé PRÉVOST, *op. cit.*, VIII, p. 75.
177. *Ibid.*
178. See the useful summary which opens W.H. MORELAND'S classic study, *From Akbar to Aurangzeb*, 1922, pp. 1-44.
179. Simancas, Estado Flandes 619, 1601.
180. Abbé PRÉVOST, *op. cit.*, VIII, pp. 75-6.
181. A.N., K 1349, quoted by BOXER, *op. cit.*, p. 23.
182. W.H. MORELAND, *op. cit.*, p. 19, note 1.
183. A.N., K 1349, f° 36.
184. R. DAVIS, *op. cit.*, p. 185.
185. A.d.S. Genoa, Spagna, 15.
186. C.S.P. East Indies, p. 205, Cottington to Salisbury, 18 February 1610.
187. L. DERMIGNY, *op. cit.*, I, p. 107.
188. *Ibid.*, I, p. 106.
189. David MACPHERSON, *Annals of Commerce*, 1805, II, p. 233.
190. L. DERMIGNY, *op. cit.*, I, p. 105, note 1.
191. A.N., Marine, B⁷, 463, f° 145; J. SAVARY, *op. cit.*, V, col. 1196.
192. A.N., K 1349, f° 44.
193. C.G.F. SIMKIN, *The Traditional Trade of Asia*, 1968, p. 188.
194. W.H. MORELAND, *op. cit.*, p. 63.
195. C.G.F. SIMKIN, *op. cit.*, p. 225.
196. C.R. BOXER, *op. cit.*, p. 143.
197. *Ibid.*, p. 196.
198. W.H. MORELAND, *op. cit.*, p. 32.
199. *Ibid.*, p. 38.
200. C.G.F. SIMKIN, *op. cit.*, pp. 199 ff; A.N., K 1349.

201. Constantin RENNEVILLE, *Voyage de S. van Rechteren ...*, 1703, II, p. 256.
202. D. MACPHERSON, *op. cit.*, II, p. 466.
203. Hermann KELLENBENZ, 'Ferdinand Cron', in: *Lebensbilder aus dem Bayerischen Schwaben*, 9, pp. 194-210.
204. Duarte GÓMES SOLIS, *Mémoires inédits de ...* (1621) ed. Bourdon, 1955, p. 1; J. CUVELIER, L. JADIN, *L'Ancien Congo d'après les archives romaines, 1518-1640*, 1954, p. 499, 10 April 1632.
205. A.N., K 1349, 132, f° 34.
206. Cf. *The Famous Voyage of Sir Francis Drake*, in J. HARRIS. *Navigantium atque Itinerantium Bibliotheca*, vol. I, 1764.
207. *Medit.*, I, pp. 302 et 305.
208. The capture of Amboyna was followed by the massacre of the English, who were arrested for conspiracy and executed after a sham trial, W.H. MORELAND, *op. cit.*, p. 23.
209. Abbé RAYNAL, *Histoire philosophique et politique des établissements et du commerce des Européens dans les deux Indes*, 1775, III, p. 21.
210. C. RENNEVILLE, *op. cit.*, V, p. 119.
211. Kristof GLAMANN, *Dutch Asiatic Trade, 1620-1740*, 1958, p. 68.
212. *Ibid.*, p. 168.
213. W.H. MORELAND, *op. cit.*, p. 64.
214. K. GLAMANN, *op. cit.*, p. 58.
215. A. LIOUBLINSKAIA, *Lettres et mémoires adressés au chancelier P. Séguier, 1633-1649*, 1966. Letter of Champigny, Aix, October 1647, pp. 321-2.
216. F. de SOUSA COUTINHO, *op. cit.*, II, p. 313. Letter to marquis of Niza, 17 February 1648.
217. K. GLAMANN, *op. cit.*, p. 120.
218. *Ibid.*, p. 131.
219. A.N., Marine, B⁷, 463, f° 253, report of 1687.
220. *Ibid.*
221. K. GLAMANN, *op. cit.*, pp. 91-2.
222. A.N., Marine, B⁷, 463, f⁰ˢ 177-8.
223. *Ibid.*, f⁰ˢ 161, ff.
224. *Ibid.*
225. L. DERMIGNY, *op. cit.*, I, p. 281.
226. A.N., Marine, B⁷, 463, f⁰ˢ 158-60.
227. *Ibid.*
228. François PYRARD DE LAVAL, *Seconde Partie du voyage ... depuis l'arrivée à Goa jusques à son retour en France*, 1615, II, p. 353.
229. Abbé PRÉVOST, *op. cit.*, VIII, pp. 126-9.
230. Or by throwing 'the superfluous pepper into the sea' (Ernst Ludwig CARL, *Traité de la richesse des princes et de leurs États et des moyens simples et naturels pour y parvenir*, 1722-1723, p. 236).
231. C. RENNEVILLE, *op. cit.*, V, p. 124.
232. A.N., Marine, B⁷, 463, 251-2.
233. C.G.F. SIMKIN, *op. cit.*, p. 197.
234. W.H. MORELAND, *op. cit.*, p. 77.
235. C.G.F. SIMKIN, *op. cit.*, p. 197.
236. K. GLAMANN, *op. cit.*, pp. 19 et 207.
237. *Ibid.*, p. 166.
238. *Ibid.*, p. 265.
239. *Ibid.*, 231.
240. L. DERMIGNY, *op. cit.*, III, p. 1164.
241. *Op. cit.*, p. 265.
242. A.N., G⁷, 1697, f° 117, 21 August 1712.
243. G. de UZTÁRIZ, *op. cit.*, p. 103.
244. K. GLAMANN., *op. cit.*, p. 6; J. SAVARY, *op. cit.*, V, col. 1606 ff.
245. C.G.F. SIMKIN, *op. cit.*, p. 192.
246. A.E., Mémoires, Hollande, 72, 243.
274. K. GLAMANN, *op. cit.*, p. 60.
248. Abbé PRÉVOST, *op. cit.*, IX, p. 55.
249. A.N., Marine, B⁷, 463, f° 205.
250. Warships had much bigger crews: the 11 ships which left Texel with Matelief in 1605 carried a total of 1357 crewmen, or an average of 123 men per ship. So the estimate might be anywhere between 8000 (50 per ship) and 16,000 men (100 per ship). C. RENNEVILLE, *op. cit.*, III, p. 205.
251. A.N., Marine, B⁷, 463, f° 205.
252. J.-P. RICARD, *op. cit.*, p. 376.
253. *Essai politique sur le commerce*, 1735, p. 51.
254. Moscow, C.S.A., 50/6, incomplete reference.
255. By a team led by Ivo SCHÖFFER.
256. C.G.F. SIMKIN, *op. cit.*, p. 182.
257. J. SAVARY, *op. cit.*, V, col. 1610-1612.
258. A.N., A.E., B⁷, 619, The Hague, 25 June 1670.
259. J. SAVARY, *op. cit.*, I, col. 25 and V, col. 1612.
260. K. GLAMANN, *op. cit.*, pp. 244 ff.
261. *Ibid.*, pp. 252 ff.
262. *Ibid.*, p. 248.
263. Moscow, C.S.A., 50/6, 539, 57,

Amsterdam, 25 July–5 August 1788.

264. *Op. cit.*, p. 249.

265. *Ibid.*, p. 265.

266. *Ibid.*, pp. 229–31.

267. *Op. cit.*, I, p. 465.

268. C. BOXER, *The Dutch Seaborne Empire*, *op. cit.*, p. 52; *Les Six Voyages ...*, 1681, II, p. 420.

269. W.H. MORELAND, *op. cit.*, p. 315.

270. A.N., Marine, B⁷, 463, f⁰ˢ 245 and 257–8.

271. Giuseppe PAPAGNO, 'Struttura e istituzioni nell' espansione coloniale: Portogallo e Olanda', in: *Dall' Età preindustriale all'età del capitalismo*, ed. G.L. BASINI, 1977, p. 89.

272. Francesco CARLETTI, *Ragionamenti del mio viaggio in torno al mondo*, 1958, pp. 213 ff.

273. K. GLAMANN, *op. cit.*, pp. 33 ff.

274. *Ibid.*, p. 34. Cornelis Bicker, in 1622, was a *bewindhebber* in the West Indies Company, while his brother Jacob was in the East India Company.

275. *Ibid.*, pp. 35–6.

276. W.H. MORELAND, *op. cit.*, p. 61.

277. *Grande Enciclopedia portuguesa brasileira*, III, article 'Baïa'.

278. R. HENNIG, *op. cit.*, p. 8; Victor von KLARWILL, *The Fugger News Letters*, 1924–1926, I, p. 248.

279. In the sense of a charter granted.

280. A.N., K 1349, 132, f⁰ 107 v⁰.

281. A.d.S. Florence, Correspondence with Genoa, V, 32.

282. J. ACCARIAS DE SÉRIONNE, *Richesse de la Hollande*, *op. cit.*, pp. 137–8.

283. J. CUVELIER, L. JADIN, *op. cit.*, pp. 501–2.

284. K. GLAMANN, *op. cit.*, p. 155.

285. Cf. above, chapter 1.

286. British Museum, Sloane, 1572, f⁰ 65.

287. A.N., K. 1349, 132, f⁰ 117 v⁰.

288. J. DU MONT, *op. cit.*, VI, p. 215.

289. *Sertão* = (lit.) undergrowth, the bush.

290. *Journal du voyage de deux jeunes Hollandais*, *op. cit.*, p. 377.

291. A.N., Marine, B⁷, 463, f⁰ˢ 216–17.

292. B.N., Ms. Portugais, 26, f⁰ 216 and 216 v⁰, Lisbon, 8 October 1668.

293. P. de LA COURT, *op. cit.*, p. 52.

294. J. DU MONT, *op. cit.*, I, p. 15.

295. Simancas, Estado Flandes, 2043.

296. A.N., K 1349, 132, f⁰ 34 v⁰.

297. Maltese archives, 6505, early eighteenth century.

298. A.N., K 1349, 132, f⁰ 135.

299. L. GUICCIARDINI, *op. cit.*, p. 108.

300. C. WILSON, *Anglo-Dutch commerce ...*, *op. cit.*, p. 20.

301. 1748, I, pp. 339–40.

302. *Ibid.*

303. A.N., B¹, 619, Pomponne's correspondence, 1669. Konrad Van Beuningen was the ambassador of the United Provinces to the king of France.

304. *Ibid.*, D'Estrades, the Hague, 5 February, 1665.

305. D. DEFOE, *A Plan of the English Commerce*, 1728, p. 192.

306. LE POTTIER DE LA HESTROY, A.N., G⁶, 1687 (1703), f⁰ 67.

307. A.N., B¹, 619, 27 June 1669.

308. *Ibid.*, 30 October 1670.

309. J.-F. MELON, *op. cit.*, Eng. transl. *A Political Essay upon Commerce*, by D. Bindon, 1739, p. 334.

310. *Ibid.*, p. 334.

311. *Ibid.*, p. 335.

312. That is it required a constant supply of liquid currency.

313. Moscow, C.S.A., 50/6, 490, 17 April 1773.

314. J. ACCARIAS DE SÉRIONNE, *Les Intérêts des nations ...*, *op. cit.*, II, p. 200.

315. J. SAVARY, *op. cit.*, I, col. 331 ff.; J. ACCARIAS DE SÉRIONNE, *op. cit.*, I, p. 278.

316. J. ACCARIAS DE SÉRIONNE, *op. cit.*, II, p. 250.

317. *Ibid.*, II, p. 321.

318. *Ibid.*, I, p. 226.

319. *Ibid.*

320. A.N., A.E., B¹, 165. 13 February 1783.

321. J. ACCARIAS DE SÉRIONNE, *op. cit.*, I, p. 278.

322. *Ibid.*

323. *Ibid.*

324. C.P. KINDLEBERGER, *Manias, Bubbles, Panics and Crashes and the Lender of Last Resort*, ch. 2.

325. J. SAVARY, *op. cit.*, I, col. 8.

326. The terms *transport* and *transfer* were both used.

327. J. ACCARIAS DE SÉRIONNE, *op. cit.*, II, pp. 314–15.

328. 'Traites et retraites' – the former meant a withdrawal, the latter a payment.

withdrawal, the latter a payment.

329. Giulio MANDICH, *Le Pacte de Ricorsa et le marché étranger des changes*, 1953.

330. C. WILSON, *Anglo-Dutch Commerce ...*, *op. cit.*, p. 167.

331. J. ACCARIAS DE SÉRIONNE, *op. cit.*, I, p. 226.

332. *Ibid.*, II, p. 210.

333. *Ibid.*, I, p. 397.

334. The English gold coins, value one pound sterling, which were first minted in 1489 by Henry VII.

335. A.d.S. Naples, Affari Esteri, 804.

336. The exchange rate at which it became more advantageous to send gold abroad than to pay by banker's draft. (R. BARRAINE, *Nouveau dictionnaire de droit et de sciences économiques*, 1974, p. 234).

337. A.N., Marine, B⁷, 438, Amsterdam, 13, 26 December 1774.

338. In *L'Express*, 28 January 1974.

339. J. ACCARIAS DE SÉRIONNE, *op. cit.*, II, p. 201.

340. A.N. Marine B⁷ 438, f⁰ 6, Amsterdam 17 March 1774, letter from Maillet du Clairon.

341. F. RUIZ MARTÍN, *Lettres marchandes ...*, p. xxix.

342. *Medit.*, II, p. 700.

343. Eric J. HOBSBAWM, *The Age of Revolution*, pp. 44–5.

344. C. WILSON, *Anglo-Dutch Commerce ...*, *op. cit.*, pp. 88–9.

345. 'Obligations' was sometimes the term used.

346. A.E., C.P. Hollande, 513, f⁰ 360, the Hague, 9 March 1764.

347. Moscow, C.S.A., 480, 50/6.

348. Moscow, C.S.A., 12/23, mars 1784, 50/6, 522, f⁰ 21 v⁰. NB the expression *prime* or bonus. A French document (A.E., C.P., Hollande, 577 f⁰ 358, 12 December 1788) refers simply to the *bénéfice* (profit). The profit on a Russian loan of 3 million florins was 120,000 fl., that is 4%.

349. See above chapter 2.

350. Moscow, C.S.A., 480, 50/6, f⁰ 13, Amsterdam, 2–13 April 1770.

351. *Ibid.*, f⁰ 6, Amsterdam, 29 March–9 April 1770.

352. Moscow, C.S.A., 472, 50/6, f⁰ 3 v⁰-4, Amsterdam, 18–29 March 1763, and 25 March–5 April 1763.

353. Moscow, C.S.A., 539, 50/6, 62, v⁰, 26 August 1788.

354. A.E., C.P., 578, f⁰ 326, 2 June 1789.

355. *Ibid.*, 579, f⁰ 3, 3 July 1789.

356. *Ibid.*, f⁰ˢ 100 v⁰ ff., 18 août 1789.

357. Sweden, 448 000 km², Norrland, 261 500, southern Sweden, 186 500.

358. Maurice ZIMMERMAN, *États scandinaves, régions polaires boréales*, in: P. VIDAL DE LA BLACHE, L. GALLOIS, *Géographie universelle*, III, 1933, p. 143.

359. G.K. Bücher's well-known distinctions between the household economy, the urban economy and the territorial economy.

360. See above, chapter 1.

361. P. DOLLINGER, *La Hanse ...*, *op. cit.*, p. 52.

362. Claude NORDMANN, *Grandeur et liberté de la Suède (1660–1792)*, 1971, p. 93.

363. *Ibid.*, p. 17.

364. Counting the land surface only, no more than 3 inhabitants per km².

365. *Op. cit.*, p. 17.

366. A distinction is usually made between Sweden's 'greatness' before 1721 and her 'freedom' in the eighteenth century.

367. *Ibid.*, p. 94.

368. *Ibid.*, p. 45.

369. P. DOLLINGER, *op. cit.*, pp. 527–8.

370. V. BARBOUR, *op. cit.*, p. 102.

371. C. NORDMANN, *op. cit.*, p. 50.

372. *Ibid.*, p. 453.

373. Eli F. HECKSCHER and E.F. SÖDERLUND, *The Rise of Industry*, 1953, pp. 4–5.

374. C. NORDMANN, *op. cit.*, p. 243.

375. J. SAVARY, *op. cit.*, V, col. 1673.

376. Sometimes described as 'masked' ships.

377. C. NORDMANN, *op. cit.*, pp. 63–4.

378. L. DERMIGNY, *op. cit.*, I, pp. 173, *sq.*

379. 'The Economic Relations between Peasants, Merchants and the State in North Eastern Europe, in the 17th and 18th Centuries', paper at Bellagio conference, 1976.

380. See above, Vol. II, pp. 225 ff.

381. The *Bücher von Bauernschulden* which could be used as evidence in court.

382. Pierre JEANNIN, *L'Europe du Nord-Ouest et du Nord aux XVIIᵉ et XVIIIᵉ siècles*, 1969, p. 93.

383. The *hemman* was the hereditary property of the Swedish peasant. The

spelling *heman* is sometimes found, e.g.
in A.N., K 1349.

384. C. NORDMANN, *op. cit.*, p. 15.

385. Maria BOGUCKA, 'Le marché monétaire de Gdansk et les problèmes du crédit public au cours de la première moitié du XVIIᵉ siècle', Prato conference, typescript, 1972, p. 5.

386. *Op. cit.*, V, col. 579-80.

387. M. BOGUCKA, art. cit., p. 3.

388. Walter ACHILLES, 'Getreidepreise und Getreidehandelsbeziehungen europäischer Räume im 16. und 17. Jahrhundert', in: *Zeitschrift für Agrargeschichte und Agrarsoziologie*, April 1959, p. 46.

389. Marian MALOWIST, *Croissance et régression en Europe*, 1972, p. 172.

390. Sven-Erik ASTRÖM, paper at Bellagio conference, 1976 (quoted note 379 above).

391. As demonstrated by Witold KULA, *Théorie économique du système féodal*, 1970, pp. 93 ff.

392. J. SAVARY, *op. cit.*, V, col. 578.

393. LE POTTIER DE LA HESTROY, *doc. cit.*, fᵒ. 17.

394. Père MATHIAS DE SAINT-JEAN (alias Jean ÉON), *Le Commerce honorable...*,1646, pp. 89-90.

395. P. BOISSONNADE, P. CHARLIAT, *Colbert et la Compagnie de commerce du Nord (1661-1689)*, 1930, pp. 31 ff.

396. LE POTTIER DE LA HESTROY, *doc. cit.*, fᵒ. 18.

397. A.N., A.E., B¹, 619, the Hague, 5 Sept. 1669.

398. A.N. G⁷, 1695, 52.

399. A.N., M 662, nᵒ 5, fᵒ 1 vᵒ.

400. *Ibid.*, fᵒ 98.

401. *Ibid.*, fᵒ 59 vᵒ.

402. *Ibid.*, fᵒ 115.

403. C. NORDMANN, *op. cit.*, pp. 54-5.

404. LE POTTIER DE LA HESTROY, *doc. cit.*, fᵒ. 25.

405. Père MATHIAS DE SAINT-JEAN (alias Jean ÉON), *op. cit.*, pp. 30 ff., pp. 87 ff.

406. See Chapter 2.

407. *Anglo Dutch Commerce...*, *op. cit.*, pp. 6-7.

408. *Ibid.*

409. *Ibid.*, p. 10 et note 5.

410. *A Plan of the English commerce*, 1728, p. 163.

411. C. WILSON, *op. cit.*, pp. 7-10.

412. E. SCHULIN, *op. cit.*, p. 230. 'All our merchants must turn Dutch factors'

413. C. WILSON, *op. cit.*, pp. 16-17.

414. *Ibid.*, p. 11.

415. C. WILSON, *England's Apprenticeship...*, *op. cit.*, p. 322.

416. *La République hollandaise des Provinces-Unies*, 1968, p. 33.

417. *Op. cit.*, pp. 223 ff.

418. Constantin RENNEVILLE, *Voiage de Paul van Caerden aux Indes orientales*, 1703, II, p. 133.

419. A company which pre-dated the creation of the V.O.C.

420. C. RENNEVILLE, *op. cit.*, pp. 170-3.

421. Jean MEYER, *Les Européens et les autres*, 1975, p. 253.

422. Art. cit., August 1763.

423. C.H.E. de WIT, quoted by J.L. PRICE, *op. cit.*, p. 220 and note 9.

424. A.N., Marine, B⁷, 435, fᵒ 2.

425. *Gazette de France.* 24 April 1772.

426. *Ibid.*

427. A.N., Marine, B⁷, 434, fᵒ 30; 435, fᵒˢ 1 ff. 'The failure of the house of Clifford and Son has been followed by two or three others of less importance but which have further increased fears and caused a complete loss in confidence.'

428. Moscow, C.S.A., 50/6, 506, fᵒ 49.

429. A contrast remarked upon by C. CARRIÈRE, M. COURDURIÉ, *op. cit.*, I, p. 85: 'The agricultural cycle does not exactly fit in with the activity of the great international port' (Marseille in this instance).

430. *Anglo-Dutch Commerce...*, *op. cit.*, p. 176.

431. J. ACCARIAS DE SÉRIONNE, *Les Intérêts de l'Europe...*, *op. cit.*, II, p. 205.

432. M.G. BUIST, *At Spes non fracta. Hope and Co, 1770-1815*, 1974, pp. 12-13.

433. M. TORCIA, *Sbozzo del commercio di Amsterdam*, 1782, p. 9.

434. A.E., C.P. Hollande, 513, fᵒ 64 vᵒ.

435. C. WILSON, *op. cit.*, p. 168.

436. M. TORCIA, *op. cit.*, p. 9.

437. A.d.S Venise, Inghilterra 119, fᵒ 92, 92 vᵒ.

438. C. WILSON, *op. cit.*, pp. 167-168.

439. *Gazette de France*, 584, Hamburg, 22 Aug. 1763.

440. *Ibid.*, 624, Copenhagen, 3 September 1763.
441. Moscow, C.S.A., 50/6, 472, f° 50, 12 Aug 1763.
442. *Ibid.*
443. *Ibid.*, f° 51 v°.
444. *Ibid.*
445. 'Disconte' is used for 'escompte' in the original.
446. Moscow, C.S.A., 50/6, 472, f° 44.
447. A.N., A.E., C.P. Hollande, 513, f° 64 v°.
448. *Surchéance = Surséance = sursis*, reprieve.
449. A.d.S. Naples, Affari Esteri 800, the Hague, 2 August 1763.
450. *Ibid.* A report from Berlin had been received.
451. *Gazette de France*, 544, 4 August 1763.
452. A.d.S. Naples, Affari Esteri 800.
453. *Gazette de France*, 296, the Hague, 22 April 1763.
454. M. TORCIA, *op. cit.*, p. 9.
455. Moscow, C.S.A. 50/6, 490, 1/2.
456. *Ibid.*
457. *Ibid.*
458. *Ibid.*
459. *Anglo-Dutch Commerce...*, pp. 169 ff.
460. A.N. Marine, B⁷, 435, Amsterdam, 7, 5 April 1773.
461. A.N., Marine, B⁷, 438, Amsterdam, 7, 28 March 1774.
462. A.N., Marine, B⁷, 435, Amsterdam, 3, 4 February 1773.
463. Thursday 24 October 1929. Cf. J.K. GALBRAITH, *The Great Crash*, 1929, 1955.
464. Intercycle, the ten to twelve year cycle.
465. C.E. LABROUSSE, *La Crise de l'économie française...*, *op. cit.*, p. XXII.
466. Robert BESNIER, *Histoire des faits économiques jusqu'au XVIIIᵉ siècle*, 1962-1963, p. 249.
467. Moscow, C.S.A., 50/6, 539, f° 47.
468. C.P. THURNBERG, *Voyage en Afrique et en Asie, principalement au Japon, pendant les années 1770-1779*, 1794, p. 30.
469. A.E. C.P. Hollande, 543, Amsterdam, 28 December 1780.
470. Expression from the book by Pieter GEYL, *La Révolution batave (1783-1798)*, 1971.
471. I. SCHÖFFER, *op. cit.*, pp. 656 and 657.
472. Moscow, C.S.A., 50/6, 531, f° 51.
473. *Ibid.*, 534, f° 126 v°.
474. *Ibid.*, 530, f° 62.
475. *Ibid.*, 531, f° 92-3, Amsterdam, 18/29 December 1786.
476. *Ibid.*, 50/6, 531, f° 66.
477. *Ibid.*
478. M.G. BUIST, *op. cit.*, p. 431.
479. That is the stadtholder.
480. A.E. C.P. Hollande, 565, f° 76-83.
481. P. GEYL, *op. cit.*, p. 90.
482. A.E. C.P. Hollande, 575, f° 70.
483. P. GEYL, *op. cit.*, pp. 94, ff.
484. *Ibid.*, p. 95.
485. A.E. C.P. Hollande, 575, f° 253 ff., the Hague, 14 December 1787; cf. also A.E., C.P. Hollande, 578, f° 274, the Hague, 15 May 1789.
486. *Ibid.*
487. A.E., C.P. Hollande, 576, f° 46, 3 April 1788.
488. A.E., C.P. Hollande, 575, f° 154 v°, 25 October 1787.
489. Moscow, C.S.A., 50/6, 533, f° 60.

NOTES TO CHAPTER 4

1. Jean ROMEUF, 1958; Alain COTTA, 1968; H. TEZENAS DU MONTCEL, 1972, and even BOUVIER-AJAM et al., 1975. The term 'domestic market' is perhaps more usual, at least in certain contexts, in English, but for the sake of clarity 'national market' is used throughout for *marché national*. (Tr.)
2. Cf Pierre VILAR, 'Pour une meilleure compréhension entre économistes et historiens. "Histoire quantitative" ou économétrie rétrospective?', in *Revue historique*, 1965, pp. 293-311.
3. Jean MARCZEWSKI, *Introduction à l'histoire quantitative*, 1965; R.W. FOGEL, in particular *The Economics of Slavery*, 1968; among his many articles, 'Historiography and retrospective econometrics' in *History and Theory*, 1970, pp. 245-64; 'The New Economic

History, I, Its findings and methods, in *Economic History Review*, 1966, pp. 642–56.

4. See above, vol. II.

5. Cf. Pierre CHAUNU's article 'La pesée globale en histoire', in *Cahiers Wilfredo Pareto*, 1968.

6. François PERROUX, 'Prises de vue sur la croissance de l'économie française 1780–1950' in *Income and Wealth*, V, 1955, p. 51.

7. W. SOMBART, *Der moderne Kapitalismus*, 1928, II, pp. 188–9, suggests that the primitive local market and the international market both appear earlier than intermediary markets, including the national market.

8. See above, chapter 1.

9. Louis CHEVALIER, *Démographie générale*, 1951, esp. p. 139.

10. 'Études sur l'ancienne communauté rurale en Bourgogne. II. La Structure du manse' in *Annales de Bourgogne*, XV, 1943, p. 184.

11. These minuscule units may be very old indeed. Frédéric HAYETTE thinks that the villages of Europe grew up within the framework of settlement patterns of the Roman era and only began to emerge from these in the eighth and ninth centuries. 'The Origins of European Villages', in *The Journal of Economic History*, March 1977, pp. 182–206 and the comments of J. A. RAFTIS, pp. 207–9.

12. Guy FOURQUIN, in Pierre LEON, *Histoire économique et sociale du monde*, 1977, I, p. 179; the area of a *commune* in France could be smaller than 10 km² in rich regions but might be as much as 45 km² in poor regions.

13. LEVI-PINARD, *La Vie quotidienne à Vallorcine*, op. cit., p. 25.

14. Michael WEISSER, 'L'économie des villages ruraux situés aux alentours de Tolède', typescript, 1971, p. 1.

15. *Crises agraires en Europe (XIIᵉ-XXᵉ siècle)*, 1973, p. 15.

16. Cf. Pierre CHEVALIER, *La Monnaie en Lorraine sous le règne de Léopold (1698–1729)*, 1955, p. 126, n. 3 (1711).

17. Lucien GALLOIS, *Paris et ses environs*, n.d. (1914), p. 25.

18. Letter from R. BRUNET, 25 November 1977: 'There seems to be a typical size of 1000 km² which cannot, I think, be a matter of chance'.

19. According to R. BRUNET, these are, in ascending order, Beauvaisis: 800 km² (questionable); the Woëvre: 800 km²; pays d'Auge: 1200 to 1400 km²; Valois: 1000 km²; Othe: 1000 km².

20. Guy CABOURDIN, *Terre et hommes en Lorraine du milieu du XVIe siècle à la guerre de Trente Ans, Toulois et comté de Vaudémont*, 1975, I, p. 18.

21. Jean NICOLAS, *La Savoie au XVIIIe siècle*, 1978, p. 138. Tarentaise: 1693 km², Maurienne: 1917 km²; Chablais: 863 km²; Genevois: 1827 km².

22. Before 1815, from information provided to me by Paul Guichonnet.

23. Marco ANSALDO, *Peste, fame, guerra, cronache di vita valdostana del sec. XVII*, 1976.

24. Emile APPOLIS, *Le Diocèse civil de Lodève*, 1951, pp. v and vi, 1 and 1 n. 2.

25. G. CABOURDIN, op. cit.

26. Marzio ROMANI, lecture at Paris, 8 December 1977.

27. Lucien FEBVRE in *Annales E.S.C.*, 1947, p. 205.

28. Armand BRETTE, *Atlas des bailliages ou juridictions assimilées, ayant formé unité électorale en 1789*, n.d., p. viii: 'Out of over 400 *bailliages* which formed electoral constituencies in 1789, probably not one did not have some parishes which were divided in half, uncertain or disputed by neighbouring *bailliages*'.

29. In this long paragraph, the terms province, region, natural region and consequently the terms provincial market and regional market are interchangeable. On these problems see André PIATIER, *Existe-t-il des régions en France?*, 1966; *Les Zones d'attraction de la région Picardie*, 1967; *Les Zones d'attraction de la région Auvergne*, 1968.

30. 'Tableau de la France' in *Histoire de France*, II, 1876, p. 79.

31. 'Ritratti di cose di Francia' in *Opere complete*, 1960, pp. 90–1.

32. J. DHONDT, 'Les solidarités médiévales. Une société en transition: la Flandre en 1127–1128' in *Annales E.S.C.*, 1957, p. 529.

33. P. CHEVALIER, *op. cit.*, p. 35.
34. 1712–1770. Maria Theresa appointed him administrator of the Austrian Netherlands from 1753 till his death.
35. A.d.S. Naples, Affari Esteri 801, the Hague, 2 September 1768. On the facilities granted by the government in Brussels for importing wool to Ostend, cf. *ibid.*, 27 May 1768.
36. *The Opposition to Louis XIV*, 1965, p. 217.
37. P. CHAUNU, in: F. BRAUDEL and E. LABROUSSE. *Histoire économique et sociale de la France*, I, vol. I, p. 28.
38. Joseph CALMETTE, *L'Élaboration du monde moderne*, 1949, pp. 226–7.
39. Ernest GOSSART, *L'Établissement du régime espagnol dans les Pays-Bas et l'insurrection*, 1905, p. 122.
40. Eli F. HECKSCHER, *Mercantilism*, 1955, I, pp. 45 ff.
41. Thorold ROGERS, *History of agriculture and prices in England*, 1886, quoted by HECKSCHER, *op. cit*, I, p. 48
42. *ibid.*
43. Abbé COYER, *Nouvelles Observations sur l'Angleterre par un voyageur*, 1749, pp. 32–3.
44. A.N., Marine, B⁷, 434, *c.* 1776.
45. A. PONZ, *op cit*, I, p. 1750.
46. Marcel REINHARD, 'Le voyage de Pétion à Londres (24 novembre–11 décembre 1791)', in: *Revue d'histoire diplomatique*, 1970, pp. 35–6.
47. Otto STOLZ, 'Zur Entwicklungsgeschichte des Zollwesens innerhalb des alten deutschen Reiches', in: *Vierteljahrschrift für Sozial-und Wirtschaftsgeschichte*, 1954, 46, I, pp. 1–41.
48. *Bilanci . . .*, *op. cit.*, I, p. CI, 20 December 1794.
49. Ricardo KREBS, *Handbuch der europäischen Geschichte*, ed. Theodor SCHIEDER, 1968, vol. 4. p. 561.
50. E. HECKSCHER, *op. cit.*, I, p. 108.
51. Charles CARRIÈRE, *Négociants marseillais au XVIIIᵉ siècle*, 1973, pp. 705 and 710–12. About 1767.
52. A.N., H 2940; L.-A. BOITEUX, *La Fortune de mer*, 1968, p. 31, after Philippe MANTELLIER, *Histoire de la communauté des marchands fréquentant la rivière de Loire*, 1867.
53. J. SAVARY, *op cit.*, I, col. 22–3.
54. A.d.S. Genoa, Lettere Consoli 1/26, 28 (London, 11/12 December 1673).
55. A.N., F 12, 65, f° 41 (1 March 1719).
56. A.N., H 2939 (printed document).
57. *Ibid.*
58. P. DOCKÈS, *op. cit.*, p. 182.
59. R. BESNIER, *op. cit.*, p. 99.
60. Moscow, C.S.A., 93/6, 439, f° 168. Paris, 20 November–1 December 1786.
61. *Gazette de France*, 3 January 1763 (London 24 December 1762).
62. I. de PINTO, *op cit.*, p. 2.
63. Traian STOIANOVICH, unpublished typescript.
64. Michel MORINEAU, 'Produit brut et finances publiques: analyse factorielle et analyse sectorielle de leurs relations', unpublished paper, Prato conference, 1976.
65. 'Zur Entwicklung des Sozial Produckts in Deutschland im 16. Jahrhundert', in: *Jahrbuch für Nationalökonomie und Statistik*, 1961, pp. 448–89.
66. Art. cit., p. 18.
67. 'L'unite économique des Balkans et la Méditerranée à l'époque moderne', in: *Studia historiae oeconomicae*, Poznan, 1967, 2, p. 35.
68. *La Catalogne dans l'Espagne moderne . . .*, 1962, III, p. 143.
69. B.N., Ms. fr. 21773, f° 31.
70. *Die Entstehung der Volkswirtschaft*, 1911, p. 141.
71. I am using the term anachronistically to refer forward to the future Banks of England, France, etc.
72. C.P. KINDLEBERGER, *Manias, Bubbles, Panics and Crashes and the Lender of Last Resort*.
73. Irfan HABIB, 'Potentialities of capitalist development in the economy of Mughal India', *Journal of Economic History*, 1969, p. 41 and note 30.
I. HABIB, 'Usury in Medieval India', in *Comparative Studies in Society and History*, VI, July 1964.
74. 'Commercial Expansion and the Industrial Revolution', in: *The Journal of European Economic History*, IV, 3, 1975, pp. 613–54.

75. *Cádiz y el Atlántico, 1717-1778*, 1976.
76. P. Dockès, *op. cit.*, p. 157.
77. Emmanuel Le Roy Ladurie, 'The chief defects of Gregory King', in *The Territory of The Historian*, trans. B and S. Reynolds, 1979, pp. 173-91.
78. Pierre de Boisguilbert, *Détail de la France*, 1699, ed. I.N.E.D., 1966, II, p. 584.
79. *Op. cit.*, pp. 153 ff.
80. François Perroux, quoted by Jean Lhomme, in: *Georges Gurvitch, Traité de sociologie*, 3rd ed., 1967, I, p. 352, note 2.
81. Date of the publication of the pioneering study by Arthur Lyon Bowley and Josiah C. Stamp, *National Income*.
82. 'Europe's Gross National Product, 1800-1875', in: *The Journal of European Economic History*, 1976, p. 273.
83. *Comptabilité nationale*, 1965, pp. 3, 6, 28, 30. Cf. F. Fourquet. *Histoire des services collectifs de la comptabilité nationale*, 1976, p. v.
84. The term seems to have been used for the first time by William Petty in *Political Arithmetick*, 1671-1677.
85. Letter from Louis Jeanjean, 9 January 1973.
86. See above Vol. II.
87. Simon Kuznets, *Economic Growth of Nations, Total Output and Production Structure*, 1971, pp. 66 ff.
88. Jacques Attali, Marc Guillaume, *L'Anti-économique*, 1974, p. 32.
89. As pointed out by F. Perroux, quoted by C. Vimont, in: Jean Romeuf, *Dictionnaire des sciences économiques*, 1958, II, p. 984.
90. *Ibid.*, p. 982.
91. *Dictionnaire économique et financier*, 1975, p. 1014.
92. In: Jean Romeuf, *op cit.*, p. 985.
93. 'Estimations du revenu national dans les sociétés occidentales pré-industrielles et au XIXᵉ siècle', in: *Revue économique*, March 1977.
94. *Ibid.*
95. *Ibid.*, p. 193.
96. A.d.S. Venice, Senato Mar, 23, f° 36, 36 v°, 29 September 1534.
97. That is the population of Venice plus the Dogado.

98. Based on the annual wage-bill for woollen-workers (20,000 people, 5000 workers, 740,000 ducats) assuming the population of Venice to have been 200,000.
99. P. Mantellier, *op. cit.*, p. 388. For Frank Spooner's calculations, cf Figure 31 below.
100. Vauban, *Projet d'une dixme royale*, 1707, pp. 91-3.
101. Charles Dutot, *Réflexions politiques sur les finances et le commerce*, 1738.
102. *Ibid.*, I, pp. 366 ff.
103. J.D. Gould, *Economic Growth in History*, 1972, p. 4.
104. *Ibid.*, p. 5.
105. See the first version of Vol I of this book (*Capitalism and Material Life 1400-1800*, trans. M. Kochan, Fontana edn., (1974) p. 129.)
106. H. Van der Wee, 'Productivité, progrès technique et croissance économique du XIIᵉ au XVIIIᵉ siècle', unpublished paper, Prato conference, 1971.
107. On 'Gross Product and Public Finance, 18th and 19th centuries'.
108. 2nd ed. 1952.
109. J. de Vries, *The Dutch Rural Economy in the Golden Age, op. cit.*, p. 95.
110. Cf. P. Bairoch, 'Population urbaine et taille des villes en Europe de 1600 à 1700', in: *Revue d'histoire économique et sociale*, 1976, n° 3, p. 21.
111. M. Reinhardt, 'La population des villes, sa mesure sous la Révolution et l'Empire'. in: *Population*, 1954, p. 287.
112. *Op. cit.*, I, 1952, pp. 61 ff.
113. In 1700, 81% of the world's active population was in the primary sector (agriculture, forestry, fishing etc.) In 1970 the figure was 54.5% cf. Paul Bairoch, 'Structure de la population active mondiale de 1700 à 1970', in: *Annales E.S.C.*, 1971, p. 965.
114. Pieter de La Court, *Mémoires de Jean de Witt*, 1709, pp. 30-1.
115. Gregory King, *An Estimate of the Comparative Strength of Great Britain and France ...*, 1696.
116. François Quesnay, *Tableau oeconomique*, 1758.
117. K. Glamann, informative letter of 12 October 1976. Cf Figure 29.

118. *François Quesnay et la physiocratie*, 1958, I, pp. 154 ff.
119. 'Zur Entwicklung des Sozialprodukts ...,' art. cit., p. 489.
120. Jean MARCZEWSKI, 'Le produit physique de l'économie française de 1789 à 1913', in: *Histoire quantitative de l'économie française, Cahiers de l'I.S.E.A.*, n° 163, July 1965, p. XIV.
121. *Ibid.*
122. *Ibid.*
123. *Medit.*, I, (Eng. trans) pp. 420 ff.
124. Robert E. GALLMAN and E.S. HOWLE, 'The Structure of U.S. Wealth in the Nineteenth Century', Conference of Southern Economic Association; Raymond W. GOLDSMITH, 'The Growth of Reproducible Wealth of the United States of America from 1805 to 1950' in: *Income and Wealth of the United States: Trends and Structure*, II, 1952.
125. *Op. cit.*, p. 66.
126. 'La fortune privée de Pennsylvanie, New Jersey, Delaware (1774)', in: *Annales E.S.C.*, 1969, p. 245.
127. Hubert BROCHIER, Pierre TABATONI, *Économie financière*, 2nd ed., 1963, p. 131.
128. J.H. MARIÉJOL, in: Ernest LAVISSE, *Histoire de France*, 1911, VI, Part I, p. 37.
129. P.G.M. DICKSON, 'Fiscal Need and National Wealth in 18th Century Austria', paper given at Prato conference, 1976.
130. *Op cit.*, see above note 115.
131. VAUBAN, *op cit.*, p. 153.
132. 'Taxation in Britain and France 1715–1810', paper given at Prato, 1976, published in: *The Journal of European Economic History*, 1976, pp. 608-9.
133. Museo Correr, Donà delle Rose Collection, 27.
134. A.N., K 1352.
135. See above, note 98.
136. Lucien FEBVRE, 'Un chapitre d'histoire politique et diplomatique: la réunion de Metz à la France' in: *Revue d'histoire moderne*, 1928, p. 111.
137. Jacques BLOCH-MORHANGE, *Manifeste pour 12 millions de contribuables*, 1977, p. 69; and a suggestive article by two economic journalists, David WARSH and Lawrence MINARD, 'Inflation is now too serious a matter to leave to economists' in: *Forbes*, 15 November 1976, p. 123.
138. In Britain, Nicholas KALDOR, Dudley JACKSON, H.A. TURNER, Frank WILKINSON; in the United States, John HOTSON; in France, J. BLOCH-MORHANGE and cf. the article by David WARSH and Lawrence MINARD.
139. J. ROBINSON, *The Accumulation of Capital*, 1956, p. 19.
140. *An Economic History of Sweden*, 1954, pp. 61, 69, 70, 116.
141. 'Le revenu national en Pologne au XVIᵉ siècle', in: *Annales E.S.C.*, 1971, n° 1, pp. 105-13.
142. 'L'urbanisation de la France au XIXᵉ siècle', in: Conference of French economic historians, 1977.
143. E.A. WRIGLEY, 'The Supply of Raw Materials in the Industrial Revolution', in: *The Economic History Review*, 1962, p. 110.
144. *The International Economy and Monetary Movements in France 1493–1725*, 1972, p. 306.
145. *Op cit.*, II, p. 587.
146. *Staat und Staatsgedanke*, 1935, p. 62.
147. *Le Bourgeois*, 1911, p. 106.
148. Jean BOUVIER, forthcoming article in *Annales, E.S.C.*
149. P. ADAM, *op. cit.*,
150. René GANDILHON, *Politique économique de Louis XI*, 1941, p. 322.
151. In: F. BRAUDEL and E. LABROUSSE, *Histoire économique et sociale de la France*, II, 1970, pp. 166-7.
152. The document is in the personal possession of Paul Guichonnet. There is a photocopy at the Maison des Sciences de l'Homme, Paris.
153. B.N., Ms. fr. 21773, fᵒˢ 133 ff.
154. Régine ROBIN, *La Société française en 1789: Semur-en-Auxois*, 1970, pp. 101-9.
155. B.N., Ms. fr. 21773, fᵒˢ 133 ff.
156. *Ibid.*
157. *Histoire économique de la France*, 1939, p. 232.
158. R. GASCON, in: F. BRAUDEL and E. LABROUSSE, *op. cit.*, I, p. 256.
159. Cardinal François MATHIEU, *L'Ancien Régime en Lorraine et en Barrois*, 1907, p. XIII.

160. René BAEHREL, *Une Croissance: la Basse-Provence rurale (fin du XVIe siècle-1789)*, 1961, *passim*, notably pp. 77 ff.

161. J. ACCARIAS DE SÉRIONNE, *Les Intérêts des nations de l'Europe ...*, *op. cit.*, I, p. 224.

162. J. HUGUETAN, *Voyage d'Italie curieux et nouveau*, 1681, p. 5.

163. A.N., 129, A.P., 1.

164. A.N., 125, A.P., 16 (1687).

165. B.N., Ms. fr. 21773, f°s 73 to 75 v°.

166. Arthur YOUNG, *Travels in France*, 1892 ed., p. 16.

167. A. PONZ, *op. cit.*, p. 1701.

168. E. LABROUSSE, in: F. BRAUDEL and E. LABROUSSE, *op. cit.*, II, p. 173.

169. A.N., G⁷ 1674, f⁰ 68, Paris, 17 December 1709; A.N., G⁷, 1646, f⁰ 412, Orleans, 26 August 1789.

170. *Ibid.*, f°s 371, 382; 1647, f⁰ 68, Orleans, 1, 22 April, 17 December 1709.

171. Moscow, C.S.A., 93/6, 394, f⁰ 24 and 24 v⁰, 30 September 1783.

172. H. RICHARDOT, *op. cit.*, p. 184, quoted by P. DOCKÈS, *op. cit.*, p. 20.

173. In: F. BRAUDEL and E. LABROUSSE, *op. cit.*, I, p. 22.

174. *Ibid.*, I, p. 39.

175. P. DOCKÈS, *op cit.*, p. 156.

176. *Ibid.*, p. 308.

177. *Ibid.*, pp. 23 and 353.

178. Quoted by Marcel ROUFF, *Les Mines de charbon en France au XVIIIe siécle*, 1922, p. 83, note 1.

179. 9 April 1709, quoted by Claude-Frédéric LÉVY, *Capitalistes et pouvoir au siècle des Lumières*, 1969, p. 325.

180. Quoted by P. DOCKÈS, *op. cit.*, p. 298.

181. Raymond COLLIER, *La Vie en Haute-Provence de 1600-1850*, 1973, p. 36.

182. R. GASCON, in: F. BRAUDEL, E. LABROUSSE, *op. cit.*, I, vol. I, p. 328.

183. José Gentil DA SILVA, *Banque et crédit en Italie ...*, *op. cit.*, p. 514.

184. *Ibid.*, pp. 94, 285, 480, 490.

185. M. MORINEAU, 'Lyon l'italienne, Lyon la magnifique', in: *Annales E.S.C.*. 1974, p. 1540; F. BAYARD, 'Les Bonvisi, marchands banquiers à Lyon', in: *Annales E.S.C.*, 1971.

186. A.N., G⁷, 1704, 111.

187. R. GASCON, in: F. BRAUDEL, E. LABROUSSE, *op. cit.*, I, p. 288.

188. Frank C. SPOONER, *op. cit*, cf. note 144 above.

189. Denis RICHET, *Une Société commerciale Paris-Lyon dans la deuxième moitié du XVIe siècle*, 1965, lecture given to Paris and Ile-de-France History Society.

190. *Histoire de Marseille*, III, pp. 236-7.

191. D. RICHET, *op. cit.*, p. 19.

192. *Œuvres*, ed. G. SCHELLE, 1913, I, p. 437.

193. P. DOCKÈS, *op. cit.*, p. 247.

194. Jules DELABORDE, *Gaspard de Coligny, amiral de France*, 1892, III, p. 57.

195. *Mémoires de Jean Maillefer, marchand bourgeois de Reims*, 1890, p. 52.

196. E. BRACHENHOFFER, *Voyage en France 1643-1644*, 1925, pp. 110, 113.

197. Lewis ROBERTS, *The Merchants Mapp of Commerce*, 1639, quoted by E. SCHULIN, *op. cit.*, p. 108.

198. B.N., Ms. fr. 21773, f°s 31 ff.

199. *Ibid.*

200. *Ibid.*

201. André RÉMOND, 'Trois bilans de l'économie française au temps des théories physiocratiques', in: *Revue d'histoire économique et sociale*, 1957, pp. 450-1.

202. Mostly in A.N., G⁷.

203. C.-F. LÉVY, *op. cit.*, p. 332.

204. Jacques SAINT-GERMAIN, *Samuel Bernard, le banquier des rois*, 1960, p. 202.

205. C.-F. LÉVY, *op. cit.*, p. 338.

206. Mathieu VARILLE, *Les Foires de Lyon avant la Révolution*, 1920, p. 44.

207. A.N., KK, 1114, f°s 176-7. Memorandum by M. d'Herbigny, *intendant* of Lyon, with observations by M. de la Michodière, *intendant* in Lyon in 1762.

208. M. VARILLE, *op. cit.*, p. 45.

209. A.N., G⁷, 359-60.

210. P. de BOISLISLE, *Correspondance des contrôleurs généraux ...*, 1874-1897, II, p. 445.

211. A.N., G⁷, 363, 25 July 1709.

212. *Ibid.* 15 July.

213. *Ibid.* 2 August 1709.

214. M. VARILLE, *op. cit.*, p. 44.

215. Guy ANTONIETTI, *Une Maison de banque à Paris au XVIIIe siècle, Greffulhe, Montz et Cie, 1789-1793*, 1963, p. 66.

216. A.D. Loire-Atlantique, C 694, document pointed out to me by Claude-Frédéric LÉVY

217. Edgar FAURE, *La Banqueroute de Law*, 1977, p. 55.

218. *Op. cit.*, map n° 1.

219. Henri HAUSER, 'La question des prix et des monnaies en Bourgogne', in: *Annales de Bourgogne*, 1932, p. 18.

220. *The Elizabethans and America*, quoted by I. WALLERSTEIN, *The Modern World System, op. cit.*, p. 266, note 191.

221. Fritz HARTUNG, Roland MOUSNIER, 'Quelques problèmes concernant la Monarchie absolue', in: *International conference of historical sciences* Rome, 1955, vol. IV, p. 45.

222. In: F. BRAUDEL, E. LABROUSSE, *Histoire économique et sociale de la France*, II, p. 525.

223. R. BESNIER, *op cit.*, p. 35.

224. *Beauvais et le Beauvaisis de 1600 à 1730. Contribution à l'histoire sociale de la France du XVII⁰ siècle*, 1960, pp. 499 ff.

225. Jean DELUMEAU, 'Le commerce extérieur de la France', in: *XVII⁰ siècle*, 1966, pp. 81-105; by the same author, *L'Alun de Rome*, 1962, pp. 251-4.

226. Emmanuel LE ROY LADURIE, preface to A. d'ANGEVILLE, *Essai sur la statistique de la population française*, 1969, p. xx.

227. Michel MORINEAU, 'Trois contributions au Colloque de Göttingen', in: *Vom Ancien Régime zur französischen Revolution*, ed. Albert CREMER, 1978, p. 405, note 61.

228. *Ibid.*, pp. 404-5.

229. J.C. TOUTAIN, paper given at Edinburgh International Economic History Conference, 1978, typescript.

230. Between 1702 and 1713, French privateers captured 4543 prizes from the enemy, E. LABROUSSE in F. BRAUDEL, E. LABROUSSE. *op. cit.*, II, p. 191.

231. Quoted by Charles FROSTIN, 'Les Pontchartrain et la pénétration commerciale française en Amérique espagnole (1690–1715), in: *Revue historique*, 1971, p. 310.

232. Michel AUGÉ-LARIBÉ, *La Révolution agricole*, 1955, p. 69.

233. Abbé Ferdinando GALIANI, *Dialogues sur le commerce des bleds*, 1949, p. 548.

234. A.N., F¹², 724.

235. M. MORINEAU, 'Produit brut et finances publiques ...', art. cit.

236. Edward Fox, *History in a Geographic Perspective, The Other France*, 1971.

237. B.N. Ms. fr. 21773.

238. *Ibid.*, fᵒˢ 127 vᵒ-131.

239. A.N., G⁷, 1685, 67.

240. E. Fox, *op. cit.*, p. 63.

241. *Les Négociants bordelais, l'Europe et les îles au XVIII⁰ siècle*, 1974, pp. 381 ff.

242. B.N., Ms. fr. 21773, fᵒ 148.

243. A.N., G⁷, 1692, fᵒ 146.

244. Louis TRENHARD, *Histoire des Pays-Bas français*, 1972, p. 330.

245. Art, cit., p. 437.

246. Jean MEYER, *L'Armement nantais de la seconde moitié du XVIII⁰ siècle*, 1969, p. 62.

247. A.N., G⁷, 1686, fᵒˢ 59 and 60.

248. *Gazette d'Amsterdam*, 1672.

249. A.N., Colonies, F 2A, 16 et F 2A, 15 (4 March 1698).

250. A.N., 94 AQ 1 (8 January 1748).

251. A.N., G⁷, 1698, 224 (19 February 1714).

252. *Ibid.*, 223 (7 February 1714).

253. According to Victor HUGO, *En voyage: Alpes et Pyrénées*, 1890.

254. A *généralité* was an administrative division of which an *intendant* was in charge.

255. François de DAINVILLE, 'Un dénombrement inédit au XVIII⁰ siècle: l'enquête du contrôleur général Orry, 1745', in: *Population*, 1952, pp. 49 ff.

256. Art. cit., pp. 443 and 446.

257. E. LABROUSSE, in: F. BRAUDEL, E. LABROUSSE, *op. cit.*, II, p. 362.

258. Marcel MARION, *Les Impôts directs sous l'Anrien Régime principalement au XVIII⁰ siècle*, 1974, pp. 87-112; it was a tax created in 1749, based on the *dixième*; 'it was never much more than a tax on the income from land and fell far below an actual twentieth', M. MARION, *Dictionnaire des Institutions*, p. 556.

259. Jean-Claude PERROT, *L'Age d'or de la statistique régionale française, an IV-1804*, 1977.

260. A.N., F¹², 721 (11 June 1783).

261. *Toulouse et la région Midi-Pyrénées au siècle des Lumières, vers 1670-1789*, 1974, p. 836 and general conclusion.

262. On this problem cf. Anne-Marie COCULA, 'Pour une définition de l'espace aquitain au XVIII⁰ siècle', in: *Aires et structures du commerce français*, ed.

Pierre LÉON, 1975, pp. 301–9.

263. Philippe de VRIES, 'L'animosité anglo-hollandaise au XVIIe siècle', in: *Annales E.S.C.*, 1950, p. 42.

264. *Letters and Papers, Foreign and Domestic of the Reign of Henry VIII*, ed. BREWER, III/II, 1867, p. 1248, quoted in E. HECKSCHER, *op. cit.*

265. Abbé J.-B. LE BLANC, *op. cit.*, I, p. 137.

266. *Travels in France*, *op. cit*, p. 5.

267. A.L. ROWSE, 'Tudor Expansion: the Transition from Medieval to Modern History', in: *William and Mary Quarterly*, 1957, p. 312.

268. SULLY, *Mémoires*, III, p. 322.

269. Abbé J.-B. LE BLANC, *op, cit.*, III, p. 273.

270. Jean-Gabriel THOMAS, *Inflation et nouvel ordre monétaire*, 1977, p. 58.

271. J. SAVARY, *op. cit.*, III, col. 632.

272. J.-G. THOMAS, *op. cit.*, pp. 60–1.

273. J.D. GOULD used the term as the title for his book on the subject, *The Great Debasement*, 1970.

274. A penny-weight (dwt.) was one twentieth of an ounce. The silver content of 11 ounces 2 dwt to 12 ounces works out at $222/240 = 37/40$.

275. J.D. GOULD, *op. cit.*, table on page 89.

276. Raymond de ROOVER, *Gresham on Foreign Exchange*, 1949, p. 67.

277. *Ibid.*, p. 68.

278. *Ibid.*, pp. 198 ff. and 270 ff.

279. A.E. FEAVEARYEAR, *The Pound Sterling. A History of English Money*, 1963, pp. 82–3.

280. J. Keith HORSEFIELD, *British Monetary Experiments 1650–1710*, 1960, pp. 47–60.

281. Created by Charles II in 1663.

282. A.E., C.P. Angleterre, 173, f° 41.

283. *Ibid.*, f° 132, 8 October 1696.

284. J.K. HORSEFIELD, *op. cit.*, p. 50.

285. Jacques E. MERTENS, *La Naissance et le développement de l'étalon-or, 1696–1922*, 1944, p. 91.

286. J.-G. THOMAS, *op cit.*, pp. 68–9.

287. J.K. HORSEFIELD, *op. cit.*, p. 85.

288. *Op. cit.* p. 80. 'In France all funds are known indiscriminately as "paper" ... This expression is deplorable'.

289. Louis SIMOND, *Voyage d'un Français en Angleterre pendant les années 1810 et 1811*, 1816, II, pp. 228 ff.

290. Maurice RUBICHON. *De l'Angleterre*,

1815–1819, p. 357. 'After 1808, guineas completely vanished from circulation', L. SIMOND, *op. cit.*, I, p. 319 and II, p. 232.

291. L. SIMOND, *op. cit.*, pp. 227–8.

292. Arnold TOYNBEE, in the French edition, *L'Histoire*, 1951, p. 263. (Quotation untraceable in English.)

293. Bartolomé BENNASSAR, *L'Angleterre au XVIIe siècle (1603–1714)*, n.d., p. 21.

294. See above, vol. II., Ch. 1.

295. T.S. WILLAN, *The Inland Trade*, 1976.

296. Daniel DEFOE, *The Complete English Tradesman*, 5th ed. 1745, I, pp. 340–1.

297. *Ibid.*

298. *Ibid.*, I, p. 342.

299. T.S. WILLAN, *River Navigation in England, 1600–1750*, 1964, p. 133.

300. Quoted by Ray Bert WESTERFIELD, *Middlemen in English Business particularly between 1660 and 1760*, 1915, p. 193.

301. T.S. ASHTON, *An Economic History of England: the 18th century*, 1972, pp. 66–7.

302. René-Martin PILLET, *L'Angleterre vue à Londres et dans ses provinces pendant un séjour de dix années*, 1815, p. 23.

303. J.K. HORSEFIELD, *op. cit.*, p. 15.

304. Eric J. HOBSBAWM, *Industry and Empire*, 1968, p. 11, and Sydney POLLARD, David W. CROSSLEY, *The Wealth of Britain, 1085–1966*, 1968, pp. 165–6.

305. J. ACCARIAS DE SÉRIONNE, *Les Intérêts de l'Europe ...*, *op. cit.*, I, p. 46.

306. E. HOBSBAWM, *op, cit.*, p. 253.

307. S.G.E. LYTHE et J. BUTT, *An Economic History of Scotland, 1100–1939*, 1975, pp. 70 ff.

308. T.C. SMOUT, *A History of the Scottish People*, 1969, p. 242.

309. *Ibid.*, pp. 165 ff.

310. T.C. SMOUT, Paper at Prato Conference, 1978.

311. J. ACCARIAS DE SÉRIONNE, *La Richesse de l'Angleterre*, *op. cit.*, p. 52.

312. T.C. SMOUT, *op. cit.*, p. 226.

313. Charles BAERT-DUHOLANT, *Tableau de la Grande-Bretagne, de l'Irlande et des possessions angloises dans les quatre parties du monde*, Paris, an VIII, I, p. 202.

312. The Pale was a 'palisade which moved forward and back depending on the

fortunes of war'. P. VIDAL DE LA BLACHE, *Etats et nations de l'Europe*, 4th edn., n.d., p. 307.

315. For instance J.H. PLUMB in a chapter of his book, *England in the Eighteenth Century*, 1973, pp. 178 ff. under the unexpected title 'The Irish Empire'.

316. Christopher HILL, *Reformation to Industrial Revolution, A social and economic history of Great Britain*, 1967, p. 131.

317. J.H. PLUMB, *op. cit.*, p. 179.

318. *Épocas do Portugal económico*, 1929. The cycles refer to the successive cycles of commodity production in Brazil: the dyewood cycle, the sugar cycle, the gold cycle, etc.

319. C. BAERT-DUHOLANT, *op. cit.*, I, pp. 320-55.

320. I. de PINTO, *op. cit.*, p. 272.

321. A.N., A.E., B¹, 762, f° 253. My italics.

322. *Ibid.*

323. Moscow, C.S.A., 35/6, 312, f° 162, 9 December 1779, 2 February 1780.

324. A.E., C.P. Angleterre, 533, f° 73, 14 March 1780.

325. J.H. PLUMB, *op. cit.*, p. 164.

326. *États et nations de l'Europe*, *op. cit.*, p. 301.

327. Pablo PEBRER, *Histoire financière et statistique générale de l'Empire britannique*, 1834, II, p. 12.

328. Jonathan SWIFT, *History of the Four Last Years of the Queen*, written in 1713 and published posthumously in 1758, quoted by P.G.M. DICKSON, *art. cit*, pp. 17-18.

329. D. DEFOE, *op. cit.*, II, p. 234.

330. A.N., 257 AP 10.

331. *Journal du Commerce*, 1759, pp. 105-106; quoted by I. de PINTO, *op. cit.*, p. 122.

332. Quoted by P.G.M. DICKSON, art cit., p. 23.

333. A.N., 257 AP 10.

334. L.C.A. DUFRESNE DE SAINT-LÉON, *Études sur le crédit public*, 1824, p. 128.

335. J.-B. SAY, *op. cit.*, VI, 1829, p. 187.

336. I. de PINTO, *op. cit.*, pp. 41-2.

337. P.G.M. DICKSON, *op. cit.*, p. 16.

338. *Ibid.*

339. Moscow, C.S.A., n.d., 35/6, 3190, f° 114.

340. Cracow Archives, Czartoryski collection 808, f° 253.

341. Moscow, C.S.A., 3301, f° 11 v°, Simolin, 5-16 April 1782.

342. Museo Correr, P.D., C 903/14.

343. Orville T. MURPHY, 'Du Pont de Nemours and the Anglo-French Commercial Treaty of 1786', in: *The Economic History Review*, 1966, p. 574.

344. D. GUÉRIN, *La Lutte des classes sous la Première République, bourgeois et 'bras nus' 1793-1797*, 1946, p. 51.

345. A.N., A.E., B¹, 762, f° 151, 26 June 1787.

346. A.E., M. et D, Angleterre, 10.

347. A.N., A.E., B¹, 762.

348. J. SAVARY, *op. cit.*, V, col. 744.

349. M. RUBICHON, *op. cit.*, II, p. 354.

350. A.N., A.E., B¹, 762, f° 161.

351. *Ibid.*, f° 162.

352. *Ibid.*, f° 255.

353. A.E., M. and D. Angleterre, 10, f°s 96 et 106.

354. *Ibid.*

355. VORONTSOV Archives Moscow, 1876, IX, p. 44, London, 4/15 November 1785.

356. J. VAN KLAVEREN, 'Die historische Erscheinung der Korruption', II, in: *Viertel-jahrschrift für Sozial und Wirtschaftsgeschichte*, 1958, p. 455.

357. A.N., A.E., B¹, 762, f° 255, 18 December 1789.

358. R. BESNIER, *op. cit.*, p. 38.

359. P. MATHIAS and P. O'BRIEN, art. cit., pp. 601-50.

360. T.J. MARKOVITCH, *Histoire des industries françaises: les industries lainières de Colbert à la Révolution*, 1976.

361. A.N., G⁷, 1692, f° 34.

362. Albert CREMER, 'Die Steuersystem in Frankreich und England am Vorabend der französische Revolution', in: *Von Ancien-Régime zur französischen Revolution*, 1978, pp. 43-65.

363. *Op. cit.*, I, pp. 31 and 275.

NOTES TO CHAPTER 5

1. Throughout this chapter I have been guided by two books, Michel DEVEZE, *L'Europe et le monde à la fin du XVIIIᵉ siècle*, 1970; Giorgio BORSA, *La Nascità del*

mondo moderno in Asia orientale, 1977.

2. This is not the ideal expression since it includes in 'non-Europe' the eastern part of the continent. But can one say 'non-West'? Charles VERLINDEN, in *L'Avènement des temps modernes*, ed. Jean-Claude MARGOLIN, 1977, p. 676, writes of 'L'Europe vraiment européenne', 'truly European Europe'.

3. Giuliano GUOZZI, *Adamo e il Nuovo Mondo. La nascità dell'antropologia come ideologia coloniale: dalle genealogie bibliche alle teorie razziali*, 1977.

4. Edmundo O'GORMAN, *The Invention of America*, 1961; François PERROUX uses the same expression in *L'Europe sans rivage*, 1954, p. 12: 'Europe, which – in many senses of the word – invented the world ...'.

5. Francisco LÓPEZ DE GÓMARA, *Historia general de las Indias, Primera Parte*, 1852, p.156.

6. Friedrich LÜTGE, *Deutsche Sozial- und Wirtschaftsgeschichte*, 1966, p. 288; H. BECHTEL, *op. cit.*, II, p. 49.

7. *Les Fonctions psychologiques et les œuvres*, 1948.

8. C. MANCERON, *op. cit.*, p. 524.

9. B.N., Ms. fr. 5581, f⁰ 23, 2 December 1717.

10. P. CHAUNU, *Séville et l'Atlantique...*, *op. cit.*, VIII, p. 48.

11. Alonso de ERCILLA, *La Araucana* (published in 1569), 1910, ch. XXVII, p. 449.

12. Alvaro JARA, *Tierras nuevas, expansión territorial y ocupación del suelo en América (s. XVI-XIX)*, 1969; Pierre MONBEIG, *Pionniers et planteurs de São Paulo*, 1952.

13. François CHEVALIER, *La Formation des grands domaines au Mexique. Terre et société aux XVIᵉ-XVIIᵉ siècles*, 1952, p. 4.

14. Frédéric MAURO, *Le Brésil du XVᵉ à la fin du XVIIIᵉ siècle*, 1977, p. 145.

15. Roland MOUSNIER, in: Maurice CROUZET, *Histoire générale des civilisations*, V, 1953, p. 316.

16. D. PEDRO DE ALMEIDA, *Diario*, p. 207, quoted by Oruno LARA, *De l'Atlantique à l'aire caraïbe; nègres cimarrons et révoltes*

d'esclaves, XVIᵉ-XVIIᵉ siècles, n.d., II, p. 349.

17. The *quilombo*, a Brazilian word meaning the place of refuge for runaway slaves.

18. Frédéric MAURO, paper given at Prato, 1978.

19. D. A. BRADING, *Miners and merchants in Bourbon Mexico 1763-1810*, Cambridge, 1971, p. 233.

20. 'Introduction à l'histoire de Guadalajara et de sa région', C.N.R.S. Conference, *Le Rôle des villes dans la formation des régions en Amérique latine*, pp. 3 ff.

21. *Les Mécanismes de la vie économique dans une société coloniale; le Chili (1680-1830)*, 1973, pp. 262 ff.

22. Pedro CALMÓN, *Historia social do Brasil*, 1937, p. 191. The exodus took place in 1871.

23. Georg FRIEDERICI, *El Caracter del Descubrimiento y de la Conquista de América*, 1973, p. 113.

24. D. A. BRADING, *op. cit.*, p. 5

25. *Capitalism and Slavery*, 4th ed., 1975.

26. *Ibid.*, p. 30.

27. Karl MARX, *Capital, I*, quoted by Pierre VILAR, Problems of the formation of capitalism', in: *Past and Present*, 1956, p. 34.

28. Marcel BATAILLON, *Etudes sur Bartolomé dé Las Casas*, 1965, p. 298.

29. M. DEVÈZE, *op. cit.*, p. 358.

30. M. DEVÈZE, *Antilles, Guyanes, la mer des Caraïbes de 1492 à 1789*, 1977, p. 173.

31. Nicolás SÁNCHEZ ALBORNOZ, *La Población de América latina*, 2nd ed., 1977, pp. 62 ff.

32. J. L. PHELAN, *The Millennial Kingdom of the Franciscans in the New World*, 1956, p. 47.

33. Juan A. and Judith E. VILLAMARIN, *Indian Labor in Mainland Colonial Spanish America*, 1975, p. 17.

34. Jean-Pierre BERTHE, 'Aspects de l'esclavage des Indiens en Nouvelle-Espagne pendant la première moitié du XVIᵉ siècle' in; *Journal de la société des américanistes*, LIV-2, p. 204, note 48.

35. Alvaro JARA, paper given at Prato, 1978.

36. Father AJOFRIN, 1763, quoted by D. A.BRADING, *op. cit.*, p. 276.

37. Anibal B. ARCONDO, 'Los precios en una

economia en transición. Cordóba durante el siglo XVIII' in: *Revista de economia y estadística*, 1971, pp. 7-32.

38. According to Daniel DEFOE, *Moll Flanders*, Abbey Classics, edn., quoted by E. WILLIAMS, *op. cit.*, p. 18.

39. M. DEVÈZE, *Antilles, Guyanes . . ., op. cit.*, p. 185.

40. Édouard FOURNIER, *Variétés historiques et littéraires*, 1855-1863, VII, p. 42, note 3.

41. R. MOUSNIER, *op. cit.*, p. 320.

42. Giorgio SPINI, *Storia dell' età moderna*, 1960, p. 827.

43. E. WILLIAMS, *op. cit.*, p. 19.

44. D. W. BROGAN, introduction to E. WILLIAMS, *op. cit.*, p. viii.

45. In 1860, with the coming of the railways, Cuba developed monster-sized sugar plantations of 11,000 acres, whereas in Jamaica, the largest were barely as much as 2000, E. WILLIAMS, *op. cit.*, pp. 151-2.

46. E. WILLIAMS, *op. cit.*, p. 26.

47. Adam SMITH, *The Wealth of Nations*, 1961 edn, ed. E. CANNAN, II, p. 99.

48. 'Sociedad colonial y sublevaciones populares; el Cuzco, 1780', typescript, p. 8.

49. Émile-G. LÉONARD, *Histoire générale du protestantisme*, III, 1964, pp. 6, 692 ff.; 'L'Église presbytérienne du Brésil et ses expériences ecclésiastiques', in: *Études évangéliques*, 1949.

50. J. LYNCH, *The Spanish American Revolutions, 1803-1826*, 1973, p. 128, quoted by Nicole BOUSQUET, *La Dissolution de l'Empire espagnol au XIXe siècle*, unpub. thesis, 1974, p. 106.

51. François COREAL, *Voyages aux Indes occidentales*, 1736, I, p. 244.

52. P. CHAUNU, *Séville et l'Atlantique . . ., op. cit.*, t. VIII₁, p. 597.

53. C. FREIRE FONSECA, *Economia natural y colonizacão do Brasil (1534-1843)*, 1974, unpublished thesis.

54. Cf. first edn. of Vol I, *Capitalism and Material Life, op. cit.*, p. 60.

55. J. ACCARIAS DE SÉRIONNE. *Les Intérêts des nations de l'Europe . . .*, I, 1766, p. 56.

56. F. COREAL, *op. cit.*, I, pp. 220-1.

57. F. MAURO, *Le Brésil . . .*, p. 138.

58. J. ACCARIAS DE SÉRIONNE, *op. cit.*, I, p. 85. *Bravos* in this context meant 'savages'.

59. Marcel GIRAUD. *Histoire de la Louisiane française*, 1953, I, pp. 196-7.

60. Quoted by J. M. PRICE, in Virginia B. PLATT and David C. SKAGGS, *Of Mother Country and Plantations*, 1972, p. 7.

61. Charles M. ANDREWS, *The Colonial Period of American History. The Settlements*, I, 1970, pp. 518-19.

62. Enrique FLORESCANO, *Precios del maiz y crisis agricolas en Mexico (1708-1810)*, 1969, p. 314.

63. Russell WOOD, in *Journal of Economic History*, March 1977, p 62, note 7.

64. D. A. BRADING, *op. cit.*, p. 347.

65. German ARCINIEGAS, *Este Pueblo de America*, 1945, p. 49, compares this crisis to a sort of Middle Ages.

66. F. COREAL, *op. cit.*, I, pp. 353-4. Popayan is a province of Colombia, south-east of Bogota.

67. N. BOUSQUET, *op. cit.*, p. 42. Socorro, a town in Colombia in Santander province.

68. François CHEVALIER, 'Signification sociale de la fondation de Puebla de Los Angeles', in; *Revista de historia de América*, 1947, n° 23, p. 127.

69. Reginaldo de LIZARRAGA, 'Descripción del Perú, Tucuman, Río de la Plata y Chile' in: *Historiadores de Indias*, 1909, II, p. 465.

70. D. A. BRADING, *op. cit.*, p. 17.

71. A. N., Marine, B⁷, 461, f° 39. William Pitt the Elder (1708-1778) received the title of Earl of Chatham in 1766.

72. M. DEVÈZE, *L'Europe et le monde . . ., op. cit.*, p. 331, after M. L. HANSEN, *The Atlantic Migration (1607-1860)*, and H. COWAN, *British Emigration to North America*, 1961.

73. *Ibid.*

74. A.N., A.E., B III, 441. 'Palatines' meant natives of the Palatinate.

75. *Ibid.*

76. I.e. the shipowner's account.

77. *Livres*, paid to the shipowner.

78. A.N., Colonies, C 11 4 11, f°ˢ 205 ff.

79. A.N. Colonies, C 11 4 11.

80. R. MOUSNIER, *op. cit.*, p. 320.

81. A.N., A.E., B. III, 441, 1782.

82. A.N., A.E., C.C.C. Philadelphia, 7, f° 358, New York, 27 October 1810.

83. Fawn BRODIE, *Thomas Jefferson; an*

Intimate History, 1976.

84. A.N., A.E., B III, 441, 1781.

85. *Ibid.*

86. J. F. JAMESON, *The American Revolution considered as a Social Movement*, 1925, pp. 46 ff.

87. *Ibid.*, p. 48.

88. *Ibid.*, p. 31.

89. P. J. GROSLEY, *Londres*, 1770, p. 232.

90. J. F. JAMESON, *op. cit.*, p. 31.

91. Michel FABRE, *Les Noirs américains*, 2nd ed., 1970.

92. A.N., Marine, B⁷, 467, 17 February 1789.

93. Adam. SMITH, *op. cit.*, 1961 edn., vol. 2, p. 97.

94. Bernard BAILYN, *The New England Merchants in the 17th Century*, 1955, pp 16 ff.

95. A.N., Marine, B⁷, 458.

96. A.N., A.E., B III, 441.

97. P. J. GROSLEY, *op. cit.*, p. 232.

98. J. ACCARIAS DE SÉRIONNE, *Les Intérêts des nations . . .*, I, pp. 211-13.

99. E. WILLIAMS, *op. cit.*, p. 147, quoting J. W. FORTESCUE, *A History of the British Army*, 1899-1930, IV, part I, p. 325.

100. R. MOUSNIER, *op. cit.*, p. 327.

101. A.d.S.Naples, Affari Esteri, 801, the Hague, 21 October 1768.

102. J. ACCARIAS DE SÉRIONNE, *Les Intérêts des nations . . .*, *op. cit.*, I, p. 73, note a.

103. J. ACCARIAS DE SÉRIONNE, *La Richesse de l'Angleterre*, *op. cit.*, p. 96.

104. A.E., C.P. United States, 53, fᵒˢ 90 ff. Georgetown, founded in 1786 is now a suburb of Washington.

105. The date usually quoted is that of the victory of Sucre at Ayacucho on 9 December 1824. I prefer the date of 1825, that is when London first became excited about investment in South America.

106. Earl Diniz MacCARTHY MOREIRA, 'Espanha e Brasil: problemas de relacionamento (1822-1834)' in: *Estudos ibero-americanos*, July 1977, pp. 7-93.

107. Jacob VAN KLAVEREN, *Europäische Wirtschaftsgeschichte Spaniens . . .*, *op. cit.*, 1960, p. 177.

108. LE POTTIER DE LA HESTROY, *doc. cit.*, fᵒ 34.

109. Ernst Ludwig CARL, *op. cit.*, II, p. 467.

110. A.E., C.P. (Angleterre), 120, fᵒ 237.

111. Quoted by Lewis HANKE, 'The Portuguese in Spanish America', in: *Revista de historia de América*, 1962, p. 27.

112. British Museum, Add. 28370, fᵒˢ 103-104, El duque de Medina Sidonia to Matheo Vázquez, San Lucar, 17 September 1583.

113. *Ibid.*, fᵒ 105.

114. A.N., Marine, B⁷, 232, fᵒ 325, quoted by E. W. DAHLGREN, *Relations commerciales et maritimes entre la France et les côtes de l'océan Pacifique*, 1909, p. 37.

115. Some historians have even spoken of a quota of only 4 per cent at the end of the seventeenth century, which I find hard to believe. A. GARCIA-BAQUERO GONZALEZ, *op. cit.*, I, p. 82.

117. F. COREAL, *op. cit.*, I, p. 308.

118. CARRIÈRE, *Négociants marseillais . . .*, *op. cit.*, I, p. 101.

119. A.E., M. et D. (Amérique) 6, fᵒˢ 287-91.

120. A.N., F¹², 644, fᵒ 66, March 1722.

121. A.N., A.E., B¹, 625, the Hague, 19 February 1699.

122. N. BOUSQUET, *op. cit.*, p. 24; Simon COLLIER, *Ideas and Politics of Chilean Independence, 1808-1833*, 1963, p. 11.

123. Alice CANABRAVA, *O Comércio português no Rio da Prata (1580-1640)*, 1944; Marie HELMER, 'Comércio e contrabando entre Bahia e Potosi no século XVI', in: *Revista de historia*, 1953, pp. 195-212.

124. H. E. S. FISHER, *The Portugal Trade*. 1971, p. 47.

125. J. ACCARIAS DE SÉRIONNE, *Les Intérêts des nations . . .*, *op. cit.*, I, p. 86.

126. Quoted by J. VAN KLAVEREN, 'Die historische Erscheinung der Korruption, in ihrem Zusammenhang mit der Staats- und Gesellschaftsstruktur betrachtet', I, in: *Vierteljahrschrift für Sozial- und Wirtschaftsgeschichte*, December 1957, pp. 305-6, note 26.

127. Gonzalo de REPARAZ, 'Los caminos del contrebando', in: *El Comercio*, Lima, 18 February 1968.

128. A.N., K 1349, fᵒ 124 and 124 vᵒ.

129. A.N., G⁷, 1692, memorandum from Granville-Locquet, fᵒ 206 vᵒ.

130. N. BOUSQUET. *op. cit.*, p. 17, after Pierre CHAUNU, 'Interpretación de la

Independencia de América Latina' in: *Perú Problema*, n° 7, 1972, p. 132; J. VICENS VIVES, *An Economic History of Spain*, 1969, p. 406.

131. Claudio SANCHEZ ALBORNOZ agrees that he did write this, but neither of us has been able to find the exact reference.

132. A.E., M. et D. (America) 6, f° 289.

133. The *asiento*, the monopoly of providing black slaves for the Spanish colonies in America, was practised from the sixteenth century. At the beginning of the War of the Spanish Succession (1701) it went to France. In 1713, it took the form of an international treaty when Philip V granted it to England: the agreement signed with the South Sea Company arranged for the annual shipment of 48,000 slaves over a period of 30 years and permitted the Company to send two ships of 500 tons, the *navios de permiso* to the colonial fairs. Although article 16 of the treaty of Aix-la-Chapelle renewed it in 1748 for another 4 years, the English company in fact gave it up in 1750.

134. M. DEVÈZE. *L'Europe et le monde . . .*, pp. 425-6.

135. Decree of 18 May 1756, A. GARCIA-BAQUERO GONZALEZ, *op. cit.*, I, p. 84.

136. N. BOUSQUET, *op. cit.*, p. 8.

137. Ships which in theory sailed individually but whose cargoes had been registered (*registradas*) on departure.

138. A. de Indias, E 146, quoted by G. DESDEVISES DU DEZERT, *L'Espagne de l'Ancien Régime*, III, 1904, p. 147.

139. *Ibid.*, p. 148. The fourteenth port, opened in 1788, was San Sebastian.

140. Moscow, C.S.A., 50/6, 500, 3, Amsterdam, 12/23 January 1778.

141. Oscar CORNBLIT, 'Society and Mass Rebellions in Eighteenth Century Peru and Bolivia', in: *St Antony's Papers*, 1970, pp. 9-44.

142. The chambers of commerce, which arranged and controlled foreign trade and enjoyed considerable privileges.

143. Cf. J. R. FISHER. *Government and Society in Colonial Peru*. 1970, esp. pp. 124 ff.

144. D. A. BRADING, *op. cit.*, pp. 226, 232.

145. Ibid., p. 18; A. E., C. C., Mexico, 1, f°s 2-15.

146. 'Obstacles to Economic Growth in 19th Century Mexico', in *American Historical Review*, February 1978, pp. 80 ff.

147. *Ibid.*, p. 82.

148. A. HANSON JONES, art. cit.

149. J. VICENS VIVES, *Historia social y económica de España y America, op. cit.*, IV, p. 463.

150. According to the calculations, also rather doubtful, of Holden FURBER in *John Company at work*, 1948, p. 309. These calculations do not include contraband.

151. A.E., C.P., (United States) 59, f° 246 v°.

152. Jurgen SCHNEIDER, 'Le commerce français avec l'Amérique latine pendant l'âge de l'indépendance (première moitié du XIXᵉ siècle)' in: *Revista de historia de América*, 1977, pp. 63-87.

153. Nico PERRONE, 'Il manifesto dell'imperialismo americano nelle borse di Londra e Parigi' in *Belphagor*, 1977, pp. 321 ff. There was a flight of capital to Europe; 'most of it was sent to France', a situation referred to in November 1828, A.E., M. et D., (America) 40, 501, f°s 4 ff.

154. A.N., A.E., B. III, 452.

155. 'Feudalismo y capitalismo in América latina', in: *Boletín de estudios latino-americanos y del Caribe*, December 1974, pp. 21-41.

156. For what follows, see A.N., Marine, B⁷, 461, Memorandum on the situation of the United States concerning domestic industry and foreign trade, dated February 1789.

157. *op. cit.*, p. 49.

158. Quoted by B. H. SLICHER VAN BATH, art. cit., p. 25.

159. See above, Vol.II.

160. E. FLORESCANO, *op. cit.*, p. 433.

161. C. GIBSON, *The Aztecs under Spanish Rule*, 1964, p. 34.

162. M. BATAILLON, *op. cit.*, p. xxxi.

163. *Ibid.*, p. xxx.

164. *Der Charakter der Entdeckung und Eroberung Amerikas durch die Europäer*, 1925, I, pp. 453-4.

165. E. WILLIAMS, *op. cit.*, pp. 30 ff and 126.

166. 'Lo zucchero e l'Atlantico', in: *Miscellanea di Studi sardi e del commercio atlantico*, III (1974), pp. 248-77.

167. M. DEVÈZE, *L'Europe et le monde . . .*, pp. 263 ff.

168. Robert CHALLES, *Voyage aux Indes d'une escadre française (1690-1691)*, 1933, pp. 85-7.

169. The Contra Costa was the term for the Indian Ocean coast of Southern Africa.

170. W. G. RANDLES, *L'Empire du Monomotapa du XVe au XVIIIe siècle*, 1975, p. 7.

171. Roland OLIVER and G. MATTHEW, *History of East Africa*, 1966, p. 155.

172. Auguste TOUSSAINT, *L'Océan Indien au XVIIIe siècle*, 1974, p. 64.

173. Moscow C.S.A., 18 October 1774, complete reference mislaid.

174. K. G. DAVIES, *The Royal African Company*, 1957, pp. 5 and 6.

175. N. SÁNCHEZ ALBORNOZ, *op. cit.*, p. 66.

176. W. G. L. RANDLES, *L'Ancien Royaume du Congo des origines à la fin du XIXe siècle*, 1968; J. CUVELIER and L. JADIN, *op. cit.*; G. BALANDIER, *La Vie quotidienne au royaume de Kongo du XVIe siècle*, 1965.

177. J. SAVARY, *op. cit.*, see the article 'manille', III, col. 714.

178. J. CUVELIER and L. JADIN, *op. cit.*, p. 114.

179. Pierre POIVRE, *Voyages d'un philosophe, ou Observations sur les mœurs et les arts des peuples de l'Afrique, de l'Asie et de l'Amérique*, 1768, p. 22.

180. *La Cosmographie universelle . . .*, 1575, f° 67.

181. Philip CURTIN, *Economic Change in Precolonial Africa. Senegambia in the Era of the Slave Trade*, 1975, pp. 235, 237-47.

182. Cf. first edn. of Vol I, *Capitalism and Material Life*, p. 23.

183. B. BAILYN, *op. cit.*, p. 16.

184. Père Jean-Baptiste LABAT, *Nouvelle Relation de l'Afrique occidentale*, 1728, IV, p. 326, a propos of Gambia.

185. P. CURTIN, *op. cit.*, p. xxii.

186. *Ibid.*, p. 4.

187. W. G. L. RANDLES, *L'Ancien Royaume du Congo . . .*, *op. cit.*, p. 69.

188. *Ibid.*, p. 87.

189. O. LARA, *op. cit.*, II, pp. 291-2.

190. J. BERAUD-VILLARS, *L'Empire de Gao. Un État soudanais aux XVe et XVIe siècles*, 1942, p. 144.

191. W. G. L. RANDLES, *L'Ancien Royaume du Congo . . .*, *op. cit.*, p. 132.

192. *Ibid.*

193. *Ibid.*, p. 135.

194. W. G. L. RANDLES, *L'Empire du Monomotapa . . .*, *op. cit.*, p. 18.

195. W. G. L. RANDLES, *L'Ancien Royaume du Congo . . .*, *op. cit.*, p. 216.

196. *Konkwistadorzy Portugalscy*, 1976.

197. Paul MILIOUKOV, Charles SEIGNOBOS, Louis EISENMANN, *Histoire de Russie*, I, 1932, p. 158, note 1; *Medit.*, p. 191.

198. J.-B. LABAT, *op. cit.*, V, p. 10.

199. A term meaning 'adventurers'.

200. W. G. RANDLES, *L'Ancien Royaume du Congo . . .*, *op. cit.*, pp. 217 ff.; C. VERLINDEN, in J. C. MARGOLIN, *op. cit.*, p. 689. The word *pombeiro* may come from *pumbo*, the busy market in what is now Stanley Pool.

201. Gaston MARTIN, *Nantes au XVIIIe siècle. L'ère des négriers (1714-1774)*, 1931, pp. 46 ff.

202. P. CURTIN, *op. cit.*

203. *Ibid.*, pp. 334 ff.

204. Y. BERNARD, J.-C. COLLI, D. LEWANDOWSKI, *Dictionnaire . . .*, *op. cit.*, p. 1104.

205. M. DEVÈZE, *L'Europe et le monde . . .*, *op. cit.*, p. 310, and references to C. W. NEWBURY, Reginald COUPLAND, C. LLOYD, D. CURTIN, H. BRUNSCHWIG.

206. A.E., C.C.C. London, 12, f°s 230 ff., Letter from Séguier, 12 May 1817.

207. *Considérations... sur l'abolition générale de la Traite des Nègres adressées aux Négociateurs qui doivent assister au Congrès de Vienne, par un Portugais*, September 1814, pp. 17-18. (B.N., Paris, LK 9, 668.)

208. This paragraph owes much to Jacqueline KAUFMANN-ROCHARD's book, *Origines d'une bourgeoisie russe, XVIe-XVIIe siècles*, 1969.

209. C. VERLINDEN, *op. cit.*, see note 2 above, pp. 676 ff.

210. I. WALLERSTEIN, *op. cit.*, p. 320.

211. Walther KIRCHNER, 'Über den russischen Aussenhandel zu Beginn der Neuzeit', in: *Vierteljahrschrift für Sozial- und Wirtschaftsgeschichte*, 1955.

212. B. H. SUMMER, *Survey of Russian*

History, 1947, p. 260, quoted by R. M. MATTON, in: *Russian Imperialism from Ivan the Great to the Revolution*, ed. Taras HUNCZAK, 1970, p. 106.

213. George VERNADSKY, *The Tsardom of Moscow, 1547-1682*, V, 1969, p. 166.

214. Artur ATTMAN, *The Russian and Polish Markets in International Trade 1500-1650*, 1973, pp. 135 ff.

215. *Ibid.*, pp. 138-40.

216. The *rijksdaaler* or *rigsdaler* or *rixdollar*, the official thaler of the Netherlands, minted since the Estates-General of 1579.

217. M. V. FECHNER's book (in Russian) on Russian trade with the East, 1952; Leon Poliakoff kindly provided me with a resumé of the whole book and translations of key passages.

218. A. GERSCHENKRON, *Europe in the Russian mirror*, 1970, p. 54.

219. Marian MALOWIST, 'The economic and social Development of the Baltic Countries, xvth-xviith century', in : *Economic History Review*, December 1959, pp. 177-189.

220. A.N., K 1352, f⁰ 73, c. 1720.

221. *Ibid.*

222. Samuel H. BARON, 'The Fate of the Gosti in the reign of Peter the Great', in: *Cahiers du monde russe et soviétique*, October-December 1973, pp. 488-512.

223. J. KAUFMANN-ROCHARD, *op. cit.*, p. 88.

224. *Ibid.*, pp. 87 and 227.

225. *Ibid.*, pp. 227-8.

226. J. KULISCHER, *Wirtschaftsgeschichte Russlands*, I, p. 447.

227. Or *riad*: a gallery of shops.

228. 1 pood = 16.38 kg.

229. J. KULISCHER, *op. cit.*, I pp. 447 ff.

230. On the following, see Jerome BLUM, *Lord and Peasant in Russia from the 9th to the 19th century*, pp. 106 ff.

231. Michael CONFINO, *Systemes agraires et progrès agricole. L'assolement triennal en Russie aux XVIIIᵉ-XIXᵉ siècles*, 1970, p. 99.

232. Frédéric Le PLAY, *L'Ouvrier Européen*, 1877-9, quoted in J. BLUM, *op. cit.*, pp. 316-17.

233. Vorontsov Archives, *op. cit.*, xxii, p. 327.

234. J. BLUM, *op. cit.*, p. 283. Roger PORTAL, 'Manufactures et classes sociales en Russie au XVIIIᵉ siècle', in *Revue historique*, April-June 1949, p. 169.

235. Peter Simon PALLAS, *Voyages ... dans plusieurs provinces de l'Empire de Russie et dans l'Asie septentrionale*, Paris, 1794, I, p. 14, note 1.

236. J. BLUM, *op. cit.*, pp. 302-3.

237. *Ibid.*, pp. 293-4.

238. *Ibid.*, pp. 300-1.

239. *Ibid.*, p. 288.

240. *Ibid.*, p. 290.

241. *Ibid.*, p. 473.

242. J. KAUFMANN-ROCHARD, *op. cit.*, p. 191.

243. Louis Alexandre FROTIER DE LA MESSELIÈRE, *Voyage à Saint-Pétersbourg ou Nouveaux Mémoires sur la Russie, op cit.*, p. 116.

244. Auguste JOURDIER, *Des forces productives, destructives et improductives de la Russie*, 1860, p. 118.

245. J. P. KILBURGER, *Kurzer Unterricht von dem russischen Handel*, quoted by J. KULISCHER, *op. cit.*, p. XII, pp. 248 and 329.

246. J. KAUFMANN-ROCHARD, *op. cit.*, p. 46.

247. Adam OLEARIUS, *Voyage en Moscovie, Tartarie et Perse*, 1659, p. 108, quoted by J. KAUFMANN-ROCHARD, *op. cit.*, p. 46.

248. J. KULISCHER, *op. cit.*, p. 338.

249. J. BLUM, *op. cit.*, p. 286.

250. J. KAUFMANN-ROCHARD, *op. cit.*, pp. 39 ff.

251. Vorontsov Archives, *op. cit.*, XXI, p. 333.

252. J. KAUFMANN-ROCHARD, *op. cit.*, p. 65.

253. François BARRÊME, *Le Grand Banquier*, 1685, p. 216.

254. A.N., Marine, B⁷, 457, 1780.

255. A.E., M. et D. (Russia), 7, f⁰ 298, c. 1770.

256. A.E., M. et D. (Russia), 2, f⁰ 176, 1773.

257. P. Philippe AVRIL, *Voyage en divers États d'Europe et d'Asie, entrepris pour découvrir un nouveau chemin à la Chine ...*, 1692, p. 103.

258. Eugenio ALBERI, *Relazioni degli ambasciatori veneti durante il secolo XVI*, 1839-1863, III, 2, Giac. Soranzo, p. 199.

259. A.d.S. Venice, Inghilterra, London, 18-19 June 1703.

260. J. SAVARY, *op. cit.*, V, col. 658 ff.

261. Boris NOLDE, *La Formation de l'Empire russe*, 2 vol., 1952-1953.

262. François-Xavier COQUIN, *La Sibérie, peuplement et immigration paysanne au XIXᵉ siècle*, 1969, pp. 9-10.
263. *Ibid.*
264. p. CAMENA D'ALMEIDA, in: *Géographie universelle*, V, 1932, p. 258.
265. Details from F.-X. COQUIN, *op. cit.*, p. 109.
266. A.E., M. et D. (Russia), 2, fᵒˢ 187 vᵒ-188.
267. F.-X. COQUIN, *op. cit.*, p. 11.
268. *Ibid.*, p. 12.
269. A.E., M et D. (Russia), 7, fᵒˢ 246-9. 'Observations pour l'abbé Raynal'.
270. P. CAMENA D'ALMEIDA, *op. cit.*, p. 217.
271. J. G. GMELIN, *Voyage en Sibérie ...*, 1767, II, p. 50.
272. *Ibid.*, II. 123.
273. J. KAUFMANN-ROCHARD, *op. cit.*, p. 200.
274. *Gazette de France*, 4 April 1772, p. 359.
275. W. LEXIS, 'Beiträge zur Statistik der Edelmetalle nebst einigen Bemerkungen über die Wertrelation', in: *Jahrbuch für Nationalökonomie und Statistik*, XXXIV, 1908, p. 364.
276. C. M. FOUST, 'Russian Expansion to the East through the 18th Century', in: *Journal of Economic History*, 1961, p. 472.
277. Maurice-Auguste de BENYOWSKY, *Voyages et mémoires ...*, 1791, p. 63.
278. P. S. PALLAS, *Voyage à travers plusieurs provinces de l'Empire russe*, 1771-1776, III, p. 490.
279. *Ibid.*, p. 487.
280. M.-A. de BENYOWSKY, *op. cit.*, p. 48.
281. A.E., M et D. (Russia), 2, fᵒ 188.
282. James R. GIBSON, *Feeding the Russian Fur Trade: provisionment of the Okhotsk seaboard and the Kamtchatka peninsula, 1689-1856*, 1970.
283. Ernst HOFFMANN, *Reise nach den Goldwäschen Ostsiberiens*, 1847, 1969 ed., pp. 79 ff.
284. In 1728, 1732, 1741, 1746, 1755.—A.E., M. et D. (Russia), 2, fᵒˢ 183-5.
285. *Ibid.*
286. J. SAVARY. *op. cit.*, V, col. 659 ff.
287. C. M. FOUST. art. cit., p. 477.
288. J. G. GMELIN, *op. cit.*, I, p. 49.
289. C. M. FOUST, art. cit., p. 477; A.N., A.E., M. et D. (Russia), 2, fᵒ 182.
290. Vorontsov Archives, *op. cit.*, IX, pp. 32-3.
291. Gino LUZZATTO, *Storia economica dell'età moderna e contemporanea*, II, 1952, p. 16.
292. A.N., A.E., B¹, 485.
293. A.d.S. Naples, Affari Esteri, 800; *Gazette de Cologne*, 23 September 1763. Russian currency could be exchanged in London apparently from 1762.
294. Moscow, C.S.A., Vorontsov Collection, 1261, 4-446.
295. Vorontsov Archives, *op. cit.*, XXI, p. 137.
296. *Ibid.*, p. 315.
297. *Ibid.*, X, p. 201.
298. J. BLUMD, *op. cit.*, p. 293.
299. R. PORTAL, art. cit., pp. 6 ff.
300. J. BLUM, *op. cit.*, p. 294.
301. A.N. Marine, B⁷, 457.
302. A.N., K 1352.
303. Vorontsov Archives, *op. cit.*, VIII, p. 363.
304. Fernand GRENARD, *Grandeur et décadence de l'Asie*, 1939, p. 72.
305. A.E., M. et D. (Turkey), 36, fᵒ 16.
306. G. TONGAS, *Les Relations de la France avec l'Empire ottoman, durant la première moitié du XVIIᵉ siècle*, 1942, p. 141.
307. Giovanni BOTERO, *Relationi universali*, 1599, II, pp. 117-18.
308. C. BOXER, 'The Portuguese in the East, 1500-1800', in: *Portugal and Brazil, an Introduction*, ed. H. V. LIVERMORE, 1953, p. 221.
309. A.d.S. Venice, Relazioni, B 31.
310. François SAVARY DE BRÈVES, *Relation des voyages de ...*, 1628, p. 242.
311. Maestre MANRIQUE, *Itinerario de las misiones que hizo el Padre F. Sebastian Manrique ...*, 1649, p. 460.
312. Abbé PRÉVOST, *op. cit.*, IX, 1751, p. 88 (Voyage of A. de Rhodes, 1648).
313. Edward BROWN, *A Brief Account of Some Travels ...*, 1673, pp. 39-40.
314. T. STOIANOVITCH, typescript, paper to *Conférence de la Commission d'histoire économique de l'Association du Sud-Est européen*, Moscow/Kiev, 1969.
315. W. PLATZHOFF, *Geschichte des europäischen Staatensystems, 1559-1660*, 1928, p. 31.
316. Herbert JANSKY, in: *Handbuch der europäischen Geschichte*, ed. T.

SCHIEDER, *op. cit.*, IV, p. 753.

317. *Ibid.*, p. 761.

318. Jorjo TADIC, 'Le commerce en Dalmatie et à Raguse et la décadence économique de Venise au XVIIᵉ siècle', in: *Aspetti e cause della decadenza economica veneziana nel secolo XVII*, 1961, pp. 235-274.

319. Robert MANTRAN, 'L'Empire ottoman et le commerce asiatique au XVIᵉ et au XVIIᵉ siècle', in: *Islam and the Trade of Asia*, ed. D.S. RICHARDS, *op. cit.*, p. 169. Baghdad was occupied in 1534, Basra in 1535 and again in 1546.

320. Moscow, C.S.A., 276-1-365, fᵒˢ 171-5.

321. A.E., M. et D. (Turkey) 11, fᵒˢ 131-51.

322. *Brouillarts* registers in which transactions were recorded from day-to-day.

323. Pierre BELON, *Les Observations de plusieurs singularitez et choses mémorables trouvées en Grèce, Asie, Judée, Égypte, Arabie et autres pays estranges*, 1553, fᵒ 181 vᵒ.

324. Abbé PRÉVOST, *op. cit.*, IX, p. 88.

325. *Gazette d'Amsterdam*, 13 December 1672. Kaminiec, today Kamenec Podolsk in the Ukraine, was in succession Turkish, Tartar, Polish until 1793, then Russian.

326. Paul-Ange de GARDANE, *Journal d'un voyage dans la Turquie d'Asie et la Perse, fait en 1807 et 1808*, 1809, p. 13.

327. Marciana Library, Scritture, Oro e argento, VII, MCCXXVIII, 55.

328. The gold ducat minted by the kings of Hungary, often imitated abroad.

329. Ugo TUCCI, 'Les émissions monétaires de Venise et les mouvements internationaux de l'or', in: *Revue historique*, July 1978, p. 97, note 23.

330. *Ibid.*, p. 109, note 65.

331. F. REBUFFAT, M. COURDURIE, *Marseille et le négoce marseillais international (1785-1790)*, 1966, pp. 126 ff.

332. C. SONNINI, *Traité sur le commerce de la mer Noire*, n.d.

333. A.N., A.E., B¹, 436, quoted by T. STOIANOVITCH, typescript, p. 35.

334. In his Paris lectures in 1955.

335. *Medit.*, II, p. 721.

336. *Ibid.*, I, p. 286.

337. Henri MAUNDRELL, *op. cit.*, 4th ed. 1800, p. 14.

338. In a local publication unfortunately mislaid.

339. A.d.S., Naples, Affari Esteri, 800, the Hague, 21 August 1761.

340. Moscow C.S.A., 4113, 158, fᵒ 4, Venice, 4/15 December 1787.

341. A.E., M. et D. (Turkey) 15, fᵒˢ 154-9.

342. *Observations sur l'état actuel de l'Empire ottoman* (written in French and never published in English), ed. Andrew S. EHRENKREUTZ, 1965, pp. 49-50.

343. *Ibid.*, p. 53.

344. *Ibid.*, p. 54.

345. By the treaty of Kučuk Kajnardzi.

346. By the treaty of Constaninople (January 1784) recognizing the cession of Crimea to Russia.

347. See above, Vol. I.

348. K. N. CHAUDHURI, *The Trading World of Asia and the English East India Company, 1660-1760*, 1978, p. 17.

349. A.E., M. et D. (Turkey), 11, fᵒˢ 131-51, 1750.

350. H. FURBER, *op. cit.*, p. 166.

351. A.E., M. et D. (Turkey), 11, fᵒ 162.

352. *Ibid.*, fᵒ 151, 1750.

353. H. FURBER, *op. cit.*, p. 66.

354. A.E., M. et D. (Turkey), 11, fᵒˢ 70 and 70 vᵒ.

355. *Ibid.*, fᵒ 162.

356. Moscow, C.S.A., 35/6, 371, fᵒ 32.

357. *Ibid.*, 93/6, 438, fᵒ 81.

358. Luigi CELLI, Introduction to *Due Trattati inediti di Silvestro Gozzolini da Osimo, Economista e Finanziere del sec. XVI*, 1892, p. 8.

359. Moscow, C.S.A., October 1787, incomplete reference.

360. M.-A. de BENYOWSKY, *Voyages et mémoires . . .*, *op. cit.*, I, p. 51.

361. 'Agenda for Ottoman History', in: *Review*, I, 1977, p. 53.

362. Moscow, C.S.A., March 1785, complete reference mislaid.

363. *Handbuch der europaïscher Geschichte*, ed. T. SCHIEDER, *op. cit.*, p. 771.

364. A.d.S. Naples, Affari Esteri, 805.

365. Michel MORINEAU, paper at Prato conference, 1977, typescript, p. 7.

366. J. ROUSSET, *Les Intérêts présens des puissances de l'Europe*, 1731, I, p. 161.

367. Ange GOUDAR, *Les Intérêts de la France mal entendus . . .*, 1756, I, p. 5.

368. For this paragraph I have drawn particularly on Giorgio BORSA, *La Nascita del mondo moderno in Asia orientale*, 1977, and Michel DEVÈZE, *L'Europe et le monde, op. cit.*

369. Maurice LOMBARD, *L'Islam dans sa première grandeur*, 1971, p. 22.

370. Cf. first edn. of Vol. I, pp. 306-7.

371. The Arab name (Zendj = 'black men') for the southern coast of Somalia as far as Mozambique.

372. *Indonesian Trade and Society*, 1955.

373. The Tamil population lives in southern India and Sri Lanka (formerly Ceylon).

374. Archibald R. LEWIS, 'Les marchands dans l'océan Indien', in: *Revue d'histoire économique et sociale*, 1976, p. 448.

375. *Ibid.*, p. 455.

376. *Ibid.*, pp. 455-6.

377. Donald F. LACH, *Asia in the Making of Europe*, 1970, I, p. 19.

378. Franco VENTURI, *L'Europe des Lumières, recherches sur le XVIIIᵉ siècle*, 1971, pp. 138-9.

379. C.G.F. SIMKIN, *op. cit.*, p. 182.

380. Giorgio BORSA, *op. cit.*, p. 31.

381. A.N., Colonies, C², 254, fᵒ 15 vᵒ.

382. L. DERMIGNY, *La Chine et l'Occident ...*, *op. cit.*, II, p. 696.

383. See above, chapter 3.

384. L. SIMOND, *Voyage d'un Français en Angleterre ...*, *op. cit.*, II, p. 280.

385. Victor JACQUEMENT, *Voyage dans l'Inde ...*, 1841-1844, p. 17.

386. M. DEVÈZE, *op. cit.*, p. 223.

387. British Museum, Sloane 1005.

388. R. CHALLIS, *Voyage aux Indes ...*, *op. cit.*, p. 436.

389. A.N., Colonies, C², 105, fᵒ 233.

390. François Martin, (1640-1706) governor general of the French *Compagnie des Indes* from 1701.

391. A. N., Colonies, C² 105, fᵒˢ 256 vᵒ and 257.

392. Maestre MANRIQUE, *op. cit.*, p. 398.

393. K. N. CHAUDHURI, *op. cit.*, pp. 447-8.

394. A.N., A.E., B III, 459.

395. A.N., Colonies, C², 75, fᵒ 165.

396. Probably bonds, the short-term Company loans. Saha PANCHANAM, 'Einige Probleme der kapitalistischen Entwicklung Indiens im 19. Jahrhundert', in *Jahrbuch fur Wirtschaftsgeschichte*, 1970, I, pp. 155-61.

397. V. I. PAVLOV, *Historical Premises for India's Transition to Capitalism*, 2nd ed., 1978, pp. 326-32.

398. K. N. CHAUDHURI, *op. cit.*, p. 455.

399. *Ibid.*, p. 456.

400. Abbé PRÉVOST, *op. cit.*, I, pp. 35, 48, 49.

401. Carlo M. Cipolla, *Guns and Sails in the early phase of European Expansion*, 1965, p. 138.

402. *Ibid.*

403. *Ibid.*

404. T. T. CHANG, *Sino-Portuguese Trade from 1514 to 1644*, 1934, p. 120, quoted by C. M. Cipolla, *op. cit.*, p. 138.

405. *The Embassy of Sir Thomas Roe to the Court of the Great Moghol*, 1899, II, p. 344, quoted by G. BORSA, *op. cit.*, p. 25.

406. C. M. CIPOLLA, *op. cit.*, p. 139, note 17.

407. K. N. CHAUDHURI, *op. cit.*, pp. 457 et 461.

408. I. Bruce WATSON, 'The Establishment of English Commerce in North-Western India in the Early Seventeenth Century', in: *Indian Economic and Social History*, XIII, n° 3, pp. 384-5.

409. K. N. CHAUDHURI, *op. cit.*, p. 461.

410. A.N., A.E., B III, 459, Memorandum from Bolts, 19 messidor an V.

411. According to which merchants and artisans agreed to deliver goods.

412. I.B. WATSON, art. cit., pp. 385-9.

413. A.N., A.E., B III, 459.

414. A.N., Colonies, C², 105, fᵒˢ 218 vᵒ-220.

415. A.N., Colonies, C¹¹, 10, 31 December 1750. See Pierre Poivre's quarrel with the commander of *Le Mascarin* in Canton in June 1750.

416. C. BOXER, *The Portuguese Seaborne Empire, 1415-1825*, 1969, p. 57, quoted by I. WALLERSTEIN, *op. cit.*, p. 332.

417. V. I. PAVLOV, *op. cit.*, p. 243.

418. E.g. Norman JACOBS, *Modern Capitalism and Eastern Asia*, 1958.

419. B. R. GROVER, 'An Integrated Pattern of Commercial Life in the Rural Society of North India during the 17th-18th centuries', in: *India Historical Records Commission*, XXXVII, 1966, pp. 121.

420. L. C. JAIN, *Indigenous Banking in India*, 1929, p. 5.

421. For a discussion of the meaning of this

word, see Irfan HABIB, *The Agarian System of Mughal India*, 1963, pp. 140 ff.

422. Irfan HABIB, 'Potentialities of Capitalistic Development in the Economy of Mughal India', in *Journal of Economic History*, 1969, pp. 32-78, esp. p. 39.

423. Satish CHANDRA, 'Some Institutional Factors in Providing Capital Inputs for the Improvement and Expansion of Cultivation in Medieval India', in: *Indian Historical Review*, 1976, p. 85.

424. *Ibid.*, p. 89.

425. B. R. GROVER, art. cit., p. 130.

426. S. CHANDRA, art. cit., p. 84.

427. I. HABIB, 'Potentialities', art. cit., *Journal of Economic History*, 1969, p. 38.

428. *Ibid.*, p. 46.

429. *Ibid.*, p 35.

430. *Ibid.*, p. 35, note 8.

431. Abbé PRÉVOST, *op. cit.*, XI, pp. 661-2.

432. *Ibid.*, pp. 651-2.

433. *Ibid.*, p. 652.

434. The Bengal maund 34.5 kg, the Surat maund 12.7 kg (K. N. CHAUDHURI, *op. cit.*, p. 472).

435. B. R. GROVER, art. cit., pp. 129-30.

436. I. HABIB, 'Potentialities ...' art. cit., p. 38. W. H. MORELAND, *op. cit.*, pp. 99-100, 103-4.

437. I. HABIB, 'Usury in Medieval India', art. cit., p. 394.

438. B. R. GROVER, art. cit., p. 138.

439. The Indian state of which Bombay is the capital.

440. I. HABIB, 'Potentialities ...,' art. cit., pp. 64-5.

441. *Ibid.*, p. 62.

442. SONNERAT, *Voyage aux Indes Orientales et à la Chine*, 1782, I, pp. 103 et 104.

443. *Jahangir's India: the Remonstrantie of Francisco Pelsaert*, 1925, p. 60, quoted in I. HABIB, 'Potentialities', art. cit., p. 62.

444. I. HABIB, 'Potentialities ..., art. cit., p. 63.

445. *Ibid.*, p. 63.

446. Abbé PRÉVOST, *op. cit.*, X, p. 1.

447. *Ibid.*, X, p. 93.

448. *Ibid.*, X, p. 237.

449. H. FURBER, *op. cit.*, p. 10.

450. I. HABIB, 'Potentialities ...', art. cit., p. 69.

451. A.N., Marine, B⁷, 443, f⁰ 254.

452. V. I. PAVLOV, *op. cit.*, p. 329.

453. H. FURBER, *op. cit.*, p. 187.

454. A.N., Colonies, C², 105, f⁰ 291, v⁰.

455. H. FURBER, *op. cit.*, pp. 189-90.

456. V. I. PAVLOV, *op. cit.*, p. 233.

457. K. N. CHAUDHURI, *op. cit.*, p. 260.

458. *Ibid.*, p. 258.

459. Abbé PRÉVOST, *op. cit.*, X, p. 65.

460. I.e. without signing a contract of compulsory delivery with the artisans.

461. A.N., A.E., B III, 459, April 1814. 'Mémoire sur le commerce de l'Inde, que fesoit l'ancienne compagnie des Indes ...', f⁰ˢ 1-32, *passim*. (To translate this list of gallicized names for Indian fabrics, K.N. CHAUDHURI's list of fabrics (*op. cit.*, Appendix 4, pp. 501-5) has been consulted.–Trans).

462. *Ibid.*, f⁰ 12.

463. Satish CHANDRA, 'Some Aspects of the Growth of a Money Economy in India during the Seventeenth Century', in: *The Indian Economic and Social History Review*, 1966, p. 326, and B. R. GROVER, art. cit., p. 132.

464. B.R. GROVER, art. cit., pp. 128, 129, 131.

465. *Ibid.*, p. 132.

466. The site of the French factory of Pondicherry, which suffered from shortages of food supplies as well as of goods.

467. A.N., Colonies, C², 75, f⁰ 69.

468. Percival SPEAR, *The Nabobs*, 1963, pp. xiv ff.

469. A.N., C², 286, f⁰ 280.

470. I. HABIB, 'Potentialities ...,' art. cit., p. 41.

471. *Ibid.*, p. 55.

472. Abbé PRÉVOST, *op. cit.*, X, p. 232.

473. Roland MOUSNIER, in: Maurice CROUZET, *Histoire générale des civilisations*, IV, 1954, p. 491.

474. Abbé PRÉVOST, *op. cit.*, X, p. 235.

475. *Trousses*, folded cloaks which were slung behind the saddle.

476. A.N., Colonies, C², 56, f⁰ˢ 17 v⁰ ff., 1724. Cloth imports in this period were worth 50,000 *écus* a year.

477. Abbé PRÉVOST, *op. cit.*, X, p. 245.

478. I. HABIB, 'Potentialities ..., art. cit., pp. 59 ff.

479. *Ibid.*, pp. 59.

480. Abbé PRÉVOST, *op. cit.*, X, p. 146.

481. François BERNIER, *Voyages* ...
    *contenant la description des États du
    Grand Mogol* ..., 1699, I, p. 94.
482. Abbé PRÉVOST, *op. cit.*, X, p. 235.
483. *Ibid.*, X, p. 95.
484. P. SPEAR, *op. cit.*, p. xiii.
485. M. N. PEARSON, 'Shivaji and the Decline
    of the Mughal Empire', in : *Journal of
    Asian Studies*, 1970, p. 370.
486. A. K. MAJUMDAR, 'L'India nel Medioevo
    e al principio dell'età moderna' in:
    Propyläen Weltsgeschichte, ... (Italian
    translation), VI, 1968, p. 191.
487. *Ibid.*, p. 189.
488. A Hindu sect devoted to Vishnu, founded
    in the early sixteenth century. The
    Sikhs founded the kingdom of Lahore.
489. H. FURBER, *op. cit.*, p. 303.
490. A. K. MAJUMDAR, *op. cit.*, p. 195.
491. *Medit* ..., I, p. 371.
492. H. FURBER, *op. cit.*, p. 25.
493. Giuseppe PAPAGNO, 'Monopolio e libertà
    di commercio nell'Africa orientale
    portoghese alla luce di alcuni documenti
    settecenteschi', in: *Rivista storica
    italiana*, 1974, II, p. 273.
494. A.N., A.E., B III, 459, Memorandium
    from Louis Monneron, 1 Prairial An IV.
495. A.N., 8 AQ 349.
496. T. RAYCHAUDHURI, *Readings in Indian
    Economy*, 1964, p. 17, quoted by V. I.
    PAVLOV, *op. cit.*, p. 87.
497. V. I. PAVLOV, *op. cit.*, pp. 86–8.
498. *Ibid.*, pp. 239 ff.
499. *Ibid.*, pp. 324–35.
500. *Ibid.*, pp. 99 ff.
501. K. N. CHAUDHURI, *op. cit.*, p. 273.
502. V. I. PAVLOV, *op. cit.*, p. 215.
503. *Ibid.*, p. 216.
504. *Ibid.*, p. 217. This was no doubt why, if
    the English did import steel to India in
    the eighteenth century, in particular for
    shipbuilding, it was always Swedish,
    never British steel.
505. Armando CORTESÃO, in: *The Suma
    Oriental* by Tome PIRES, 1944, II, pp.
    278–9; V. MAGALHÃES GODINHO, *op. cit.*,
    p. 783.

506. M. A. P. MEILINK-ROELOFSZ, *Asian Trade
    and European Influence*, 1962, pp. 13 ff.
507. O. W. WOLTERS, *Early Indonesian
    Commerce*, 1967, pp. 45 ff.
508. Abbé PRÉVOST, *op. cit.*, VIII, p. 316.
509. *Ibid.*, VIII, p. 312.
510. *Ibid.*, IX, 74 (1622).
511. *Ibid.*, XI, p. 632.
512. SONNERAT, *op. cit.*, II, p. 100.
513. On these questions see G. COEDES's
    classic study 'Les Etats hindouisés
    d'Indochine et d'Indonésie', 1948, in
    Histoire du monde, ed. M. E.
    CAVAIGNAC, vol. VII.
514. M. A. P. MEILINK-ROELOFSZ, in: *Islam
    and the Trade of Asia*, ed. D. S.
    RICHARDS, *op. cit.*, pp. 137 ff.
515. Luis Filipe F. R. THOMAZ, 'Maluco e
    Malaca', in: *A Viagem de Fernão de
    Magalhães e a questão das Molucas*, ed. A.
    TEIXERA, 1975, pp. 33 ff.
516. *Ibid.*, p. 33.
517. Quoted in PAVLOV, *op. cit.*, p. 221.
518. *Ibid.*
519. Abbé PRÉVOST, *op. cit.*, I, p. 116.
520. *Ibid.*, I, p. 115.
521. M. A. Hedwig FITZLER, 'Der Anteil der
    Deutschen an der Kolonialpolitik
    Philipps II von Spanien in Asien' in:
    *Vierteljahrschrift für Sozial-und
    Wirtschaftsgeschichte*, 1935, p. 251.
522. L. F. F. R. THOMAZ, art. cit., p. 36.
523. Abbé PRÉVOST, *op. cit.*, I, p. 336 (1592).
524. *Ibid.*, VI, pp. 62–3.
525. *Ibid.*, VIII, pp. 480 ff.
526. *Op cit.*, pp. 160 ff.
527. A.N., Colonies, C^{11}, f° 10 v°.
528. *Op. cit.*, p. 174.
529. *Voyage en Inde du comte de Modave,
    1773-1776*, ed. J. DELOCHE, 1971,
    p. 77.
530. *Ibid.*
531. 'I. Wallerstein et l'Extrême-Orient,
    plaidoyer pour un xviᵉ siècle négligé',
    Leyden Conference, October 1978,
    typescript.
532. 'Littoral et intérieur de l'Inde', Leyden
    Conference, October 1978, typescript.

NOTES TO CHAPTER 6

1. Cf. LITTRÉ, *Révolution:* 'Return of a star to
   the point it started from'.

2. Hannah ARENDT, *On Revolution*, 1963.
3. Jürgen KUCZYNSKI, 'Friedrich Engels und

die Monopole', in: *Jahrbuch für Wirtschaftsgeschichte*, 1970, 3, pp. 37–40.

4. Adolphe BLANQUI, *Histoire de l'économie politique en Europe depuis les Anciens jusqu'à nos jours*, 1837, II, p. 209. 'Hardly had it sprung from the brains of those two men of genius, Watt and Arkwright, than the Industrial Revolution took possession of England'; cf. R.M. HARTWELL, *The Industrial Revolution and economic growth*, 1971, p. 111; Peter MATHIAS, *The First Industrial Nation. An Economic History of Britain 1700–1914*, 1969, p. 3.

5. Maurice DOBB, *Études sur le développement du capitalisme*, 1969, p. 274, note 3; A. BESANÇON, in: *Quarterly Journal of Economics*, XXXVI, 1921, p. 343.

6. W.W. ROSTOW, *The Stages of Economic Growth*, 1960.

7. Simon KUZNETS, *Economic Growth of Nations*, 1971.

8. Simon KUZNETS, 'Capital formation in Modern Economic Growth', Third International Economic History Conference, Munich, 1965, I, p. 20, note 1.

9. Phyllis DEANE, *The First Industrial Revolution*, 1965, p. 117.

10. 'Encore la révolution anglaise du XVIIIᵉ siècle', in: *Bulletin de la Société d'histoire moderne*, 1961, p. 6.

11. In the preface to the French translation of T.S. ASHTON, *The Industrial Revolution*, 1955.

12. J. HICKS, *A Theory of Economic History*, *op. cit.*, pp. 151–4.

13. J.-B. SAY, *Cours complet d'économie politique*, *op. cit.*, II, p. 170.

14. T.S. ASHTON, 'The Treatment of Capitalism by Historians', in: *Capitalism and the Historians*, ed. F.A. HAYEK, 1954, p. 60.

15. P. Deane, *op. cit.*, pp. 116, 117 and note 1, after W.W. ROSTOW, *The Economics of Take off into Sustained Growth*, 1963.

16. Ignacy SACHS, *Pour une économie politique du développement*, 1977, p. 9.

17. *Ibid.*

18. This quotation from the Chilean economist Oswaldo SUNKEL, is taken from I. SACHS, *op. cit.*, p. 34.

19. Ignancy SACHS, *La Découverte du Tiers Monde*, 1971, pp. 18-30.

20. *Ibid.*

21. A.N., F¹², 1512 C, bundle 5.

22. Lynn WHITE, *Medieval Technology and Social Change*, 1962, p. 80; M. ROSTOVTZEFF, *The Social and Economic History of the Hellenistic World*, 1967, I, p. 365.

23. Stephen Finney MASON, *A History of the Sciences*, 1953, p. 48.

24. A. VIERENDEL, *Esquisse d'une histoire de la technique*, 1921, I, p. 38.

25. Edward Fox, *History in a Geographical Perspective, The Other France*, 1971, *op. cit.*

26. *La Révolution industrielle du Moyen Age*, 1975.

27. *La Crise du féodalisme*, 1976.

28. 'An Industrial Revolution of the thirteenth Century', in: *Economic History Review*, 1941.

29. The expression had earlier been used of Germany, either by G.F. von SCHMOLLER or by F. PHILIPPI.

30. Eleonora M. CARUS WILSON, 'The Woollen Industry' in: *The Cambridge Economic History*, II, 1952, p. 409.

31. *Little Red Book of Bristol*, ed. F.B. BICKLEY, 1900, 58, II, 7.

32. Frederic C. LANE, 'Units of Economic Growth historically considered', in: *Kyklos*, XV, 1962, pp. 95–104.

33. W. ABEL, *Agrarkrisen und Agrarkonjunktur*, *op. cit.*, p. 51.

34. C.M. CIPOLLA, 'The Professions, The Long View', in: *The Journal of European Economic History*, Spring 1973, p. 41.

35. G. BOIS, *op. cit.*, p. 246.

36. Roger BACON, quoted by L. WHITE, *Medieval Technology ...*, *op. cit.*, p. 134.

37. Jacob Cornelius VAN LEUR, *Indonesian Trade and Society*, 1955, p. 20.

38. See above, Vol. II.

39. Herman KELLENBENZ, *Deutsche Wirtschaftsgeschichte*, I, 1977, p. 167.

40. Gemma MIANI, 'L'économie lombarde aux XIVᵉ et XVᵉ siècles', in: *Annales E.S.C.*, June 1964, p. 571.

41. Renato ZANGHERI, 'Agricoltura e sviluppo del capitalismo', In: *Studi storici*, 1968, p. 539.

42. Eric J. HOBSBAWM, 'Il secolo XVII nello sviluppo del capitalismo', in: *Studi storici*, 1959-1960, p. 665.

43. Carlo PONI 'All' origine del Sistema di fabbrica ...', in: *Rivista storica italiana*, 1976, pp. 444. ff.

44. L. WHITE, *op. cit.*, p. 129.

45. *Ibid.*, p. 28.

46. Gino BARBIERI, *Le Origini del capitalismo lombardo*, 1961; G. MIANI, art. cit.

47. John U. NEF, 'The Progress of Technology and the Growth of Large-Scale Industry in Great Britain, 1540-1640', in: *Economic History Review*, October 1934, p. 23.

48. S. POLLARD and D.W. CROSSLEY, *The Wealth of Britain ...*, *op. cit.*, 1968.

49. John CLEVELAND, *Poems*, 1650, p. 10.

50. John U. NEF, art. cit., pp. 3-24.

51. S. POLLARD and D.W. CROSSLEY, *op. cit*, p. 85.

52. *Ibid.*, p. 130.

53. *Ibid.*, pp. 84 and 95.

54. Charles HYDE, *Technological Change and the British Iron Industry, 1700-1820*, 1977.

55. See the section on technology, later in this chapter.

56. C. HYDE, *op. cit.*, pp. 42 ff., 144.

57. S. POLLARD et D. W. CROSSLEY, *op. cit.*, pp. 105 and 136-7.

58. *Ibid.*

59. *Ibid.*, pp. 142-3.

60. John U. NEF, *The Conquest of the Material World*, 1964, pp. 141-3.

61. 'The Origins of the Industrial Revolution', in: *Past and Present*, April 1960, pp. 71-81.

62. *L'Industrialisation en Europe au XIXe siècle*, ed. Pierre LÉON, François CROUZET, Richard GASCON, Lyon, 7-10 October 1970, 1972.

63. Pierre VILAR, 'La Catalogne industrielle. Réflexions sur un démarrage et sur un destin', in: *L'Industrialisation en Europe au XIXe siècle, op. cit.*, p. 421.

64. Jacques BERTIN, *ibid.*, p. 477.

65. M.W. FLINN, *The Origins of the Industrial Revolution*, 1965, p. 96

66. H.J. HABAKKUK, 'Historical Experience of Economic Development', in: E.A.G. ROBINSON ed., *Problems of Economic Development*, 1955, p. 123.

67. Paul BAIROCH, *Révolution industrielle et sous-dévelopment*, 1974, p. 73.

68. E.L. JONES, 'Le origini agricole dell'industria', in: *Studi storici*, IX, 1968, p. 567. (This article is similar to but not identical with the same writer's 'Agricultural origins of industry', in *Past and Present*, 40, 1968, pp. 58 ff.)

69. Jethro TULL, *The Horse Hoeing Husbandry*, 1733.

70. Jonathan David CHAMBERS and Gordon Edmund MINGAY, *The Agricultural Revolution 1750-1880*, 1966, pp. 2-3.

71. *Ibid.*

72. *Ibid.*

73. *Ibid.*

74. P. BAIROCH, *op. cit.*, tables pp. 222 et 226; P. MATHIAS, *The First Industrial Nation*, *op. cit.*, table, p. 474.

75. Charles-Alexandre de BAERT-DUHOLANT, *Tableau de la Grande-Bretagne ...*, *op. cit.*, IV, pp. 242-3.

76. E.L. JONES, art. cit., pp. 568 ff. (Cf. art. cir , *Past and Present* 1968, pp. 62 ff.)

77. E.A. WRIGLEY, in: *Past and Present*, 1967, quoted by E.L. JONES, art. cit., p. 569.

78. E.L. JONES, art. cit., p. 570, or *Past and Present* article p. 63

79. *Ibid.*, pp. 572-4.

80. J.D. CHAMBERS and G.E. MINGAY, *op. cit.*, p. 18.

81. *Ibid.*, pp. 199-201.

82. M. RUBICHON, *op. cit.*, II, p. 13.

83. Abbé J.-B. LE BLANC, *Lettres d'un Français*, *op. cit.*, II, pp. 64 and 66-7.

84. M. RUBICHON, *op. cit.*, II, pp. 12-13.

85. *Ibid.*, II, p. 122.

86. P. BAIROCH, *op. cit.*, p. 87.

87. *Ibid.*, p. 215.

88. R. REINHARD, A. ARMENGAUD, J. DUPAQUIER, *Histoire générale de la population mondiale*, 1968, pp. 202 ff.

89. Roland MARX, *La Révolution industrielle en Grande-Bretagne des origines à 1850*, 1970, pp. 57-8.

90. *Ibid.*

91. Alexis de TOQUEVILLE, *Voyages en Angleterre*, 1958, pp. 59 and 78.

92. E. HOBSBAWM, *Industry and Empire*, *op. cit.*, p. 40.

93. In: *L'Industrialisation en Europe au*

XIXe siècle, op. cit., p. 590.

94. P. DEANE, *op. cit.*, p. 34.
95. E. HOBSBAWM, *op. cit.*, p. 42.
96. *A History of Technology*, ed. C. SINGER, E. J. HOLMYARD, A. R. HALL, T. L. WILLIAMS, 1958, IV, pp. 301-3.
97. P. BAIROCH, *op. cit.*, p. 20.
98. *The Trading World of Asia and The English East India Company 1660-1760*, *op. cit.*, pp. 273 ff.
99. Only 10% by 1791, Ch. HYDE, *Technological Change . . .*, *op. cit.*, p. 66.
100. P. BAIROCH, *op. cit.*, p. 249.
101. C. HYDE, *op. cit.*, p. 219.
102. *Ibid.*, pp. 47-51.
103. *Ibid.*, pp. 37-40.
104. *Ibid.*, pp. 57 and 79.
105. *Ibid.*, p. 71.
106. *Ibid.*, p. 93.
107. *Ibid.*, pp. 83-94.
108. Francis K. KLINGENDER, *Art and the Industrial Revolution*, 1968, pp. 9-10.
109. *Histoire générale des techniques*, ed. M. DAUMAS, 1962, III, p. 59.
110. *Ibid.*, p. 13.
111. David S. LANDES, *The Unbound Prometheus*, p. 88.
112. Emile LEVASSEUR, *La Population française*, 1889-1892, III, p. 74.
113. E. A. WRIGLEY, 'The Supply of Raw Material in the Industrial Revolution', in: *The Economic History Review*, art. cit., p. 13.
114. J. HICKS, *op. cit.*, 2nd ed., 1973, p. 147.
115. E. LABROUSSE, in: *L'Industrialisation de l'Europe au XIXe siècle, op. cit.*, p. 590.
116. P. DEANE, *op. cit.*, pp. 90-1.
117. E. HOBSBAWM, *Industry and Empire, op. cit.*, p. 51.
118. P. MATHIAS, *op. cit.*, p. 250.
119. E. HOBSBAWM, *The Age of Revolution*, 1973 edn., p. 54 and note.
120. *Ibid.*, p. 52.
121. *Ibid.*, p. 57.
122. *Ibid.*, p. 54.
123. J. H. CLAPHAM, *An Economic History of Modern Britain*, 1926, pp. 441-2.
124. Quoted by E. HOBSBAWM, *Industry and Empire, op. cit.*, p. 40.
125. L. SIMOND, *op. cit.*, I, p. 330. The first bale of American cotton arrived in about 1791.
126. Quoted by P. DEANE, *op. cit.*, p. 87.

127. After 1820 for cotton, after 1850 for wool; S. POLLARD and D. W. CROSSLEY *op. cit.*, p. 197.
128. L. SIMOND, *op. cit.*, II, pp. 102-3.
129. P. MATHIAS, *op. cit.*, p. 270.
130. P. DEANE, *op. cit.*, p. 56.
131. J. ACCARIAS DE SÉRIONNE, *La Richesse de la Hollande, op. cit.*
132. François CROUZET, *L'Economie britannique et le blocus continental 1806-1813*, 1958, I, p. 157.
133. P. DEANE, *op. cit.*, p. 56.
134. M. RUBICHON, *op. cit.*, II, p. 312.
135. Thomas S. ASHTON, *An Economic History of England. The 18th Century*, 1955, pp. 132 ff.
136. F. CROUZET, *op. cit.*, pp. 294 ff.
137. M. RUBICHON, *op. cit.*, II, p. 382, I have replaced the word 'guerrillas' in the original by 'guerilleros'.
138. W. W. ROSTOW, *op. cit.*, p. 560.
139. L. SIMOND, *op. cit.*, II, p. 284.
140. *Ibid.*, p. 282.
141. M. RUBICHON, *op. cit.*, I, p. 575.
142. *On Depreciation*, p. 69.
143. P. DEANE, *op. cit.*, pp. 58 ff.
144. D. MACPHERSON, *op. cit.*, III, p. 340.
145. T. S. ASHTON, *op. cit.*, p. 63.
146. P. MATHIAS, *op. cit.*, p. 466.
147. AMALENDU GUHA, review of P. MATHIAS, *The First Industrial Nation, op. cit.*, in: *The Indian Economic and Social History Review*, vol. 7, September 1970, pp. 428-30.
148. See above, chapter 4.
149. As D. MACPHERSON says, cf. note 144.
150. P. DEANE, W. A. COLE, *British Economic Growth, 1688-1959*, 1962, p. 48.
151. Which was a quite normal percentage, cf. M. RUBICHON, *op. cit.*, I, p. 574.
152. T. S. WILLAN, *The Inland Trade. op. cit.*, ch. 1.
153. R.-M. PILLET, *L'Angleterre vue à Londres et dans ses provinces, op. cit.*; 'Colliers' are of course ships carrying coal.
154. *Historical Geography of England before 1800*, 1951, ed. H. C. DARBY, p. 522.
155. D. DEFOE, *Tour . . .*, I, p. 63, quoted by H. C. DARBY, *op. cit.*, p. 498.
156. T. S. WILLAN, *River Navigation in England . . ., op. cit.*
157. *Ibid.*, p. 94.
158. C. DUPIN, *op. cit.*, p. 163, note.

159. *Ibid.*, p. 171.
160. M. RUBICHON, *op. cit.*, II, p. 111.
161. T.S. WILLAN, *The Inland Trade, op. cit.*
162. J.H. CLAPHAM, *op. cit.*, pp. 381-2.
163. C. DUPIN, *op. cit.*, pp. 148 ff.
164. P. MATHIAS, *op. cit.*, p. 277.
165. C. DUPIN, *op. cit.*, p. 149.
166. *Ibid.*, p. 144.
167. *Ibid.*, p. 157.
168. M. CUCHETET, *Voyage de Manchester à Liverpool par le Rail Way et la voiture à vapeur*, 1833, p. 6.
169. *Ibid.*, p. 11.
170. *Ibid.*, p. 9.
171. *Ibid.*, p. 8.
172. Charles P. KINDLEBERGER, *Economic Development*, 1958, p. 96.
173. J.R. HARRIS, in: *L'Industrialisation de l'Europe au XIXe siècle, op. cit.*, p. 230.
174. M. RUBICHON, *op. cit.*, I, pp. 529-30.
175. See above, section on international trade.
176. *Op. cit.*
177. D. DEFOE, *Tour . . ., op. cit.*, 1927 ed., I, p. 2
178. P. ADAM, typescript, p. 92.
179. D.C. NORTH, R.P. THOMAS, *The Rise of the Western World*, 1973, p. 157.
180. John HICKS, *Value and Capital*, 1939, p. 302, quoted by R.M. HARTWELL, *op. cit.*, p. 114.
181. Jean ROMEUF, *Dictionnaire . . .*, I, p. 354.
182. My italics; Y. BERNARD, J.-C. COLLI, D. LEWANDOWSKI, *Dictionnaire . . . op. cit.*, p. 401.
183. *Op. cit.*, pp. 185 ff.
184. S. KUZNETS, *op. cit., Economic growth of nations*.
185. 'Prise de vues sur la croissance de l'économie française . . .', art. cit., pp. 46-7.
186. P. BAIROCH, *op. cit.*, p. 44, table IV.
187. Gaston IMBERT, *Des mouvements de longue durée Kondratieff*, 1959.
188. E.H. PHELPS BROWN, Sheila V. HOPKINS, ' Seven Centuries of Building Wages', in: *Economica*, August 1955, p. 197.
189. R.M. HARTWELL, *op. cit.*, p. XVII.
190. S. KUZNETS, *op. cit.*, pp. 303 ff.
191. Quoted by Raymond ARON, *Les Étapes de la pensée sociologique*, 1967, p. 321.
192. See above, Vol. II.
193. J. HICKS, *op. cit.*, p. 155 ' . . . It was casual labour that was the typical

194. See above, Vol II.
195. Neil J. SMELSER, *Social Change in the Industrial Revolution. An application of Theory to the Lancashire Cotton Industry 1770-1840*, 1967, p. 147.
196. P. MATHIAS, *op. cit.*, p. 202.
197. *Ibid.*, p. 203.
198. A.E., C.C. London, fos 146-51, 13 March 1817.
199. Neil J. SMELSER, *op. cit.*, pp. 129 ff.
200. *Ibid.*, p. 165.
201. L. SIMOND, *op. cit.*, II, p. 103.
202. E. HOBSBAWM, *Industry and Empire, op. cit.*, p. 51.
203. *Ibid.*, p. 55.
204. P. MATHIAS, *op. cit.*, p. 170.
205. *Ibid.*, p. 151.
206. *Ibid.*, p. 152.
207. *Ibid.*, pp. 152-3.
208. The residue from malt after brewing.
209. L. SIMOND, *op. cit.*, pp. 193-4.
210. P. MATHIAS, *op. cit.*, p. 153.
211. *Ibid.*, p. 154.
212. R.M. HARTWELL, 'The Tertiary Sector in English Economy during the Industrial Revolution', in: *L'Industrialisation de l'Europe . . ., op. cit.*, pp. 213-27.
213. P. MATHIAS, *op. cit.*, p. 263.
214. R.-M. PILLET, *op. cit.*
215. Cf. the debates at the Lyon conference, *L'Industrialisation de L'Europe*, esp. p. 228.
216. See above, chapter 4.
217. H.C. DARBY, *op. cit.*
218. Cf among others, the classic studies by A.N. DODD, *The Industrial Revolution in North Wales*, 1933; H. HAMILTON, *The Industrial Revolution in Scotland*, 1932; J.D. CHAMBERS, *Nottinghamshire in the Eighteenth Century*, 1932; W.H.B. COURT, *The Rise of the Midland Industries*, 1938; T.C. SMOUT, *A History of the Scottish People 1560-1830, op. cit.*
219. E.L. JONES, 'The constraints of Economic Growth in Southern England 1660-1840 in Munich Conference of Economic History*, 1965.
220. *England in the Reign of Charles II*, 1934.
221. *English Social History*, 1942, p. 298.
222. Albert DEMANGEON, 'Iles Britanniques', in: *Géographie universelle*, I, 1927, p. 219.

223. *Ibid.*, p. 149.
224. G.M. TREVELYAN, *op. cit.*, p. 298 et note 1. These figures indicate a per capita income higher in the north than the south (£10 as against £7) which may mean that ordinary people were better off north of Gloucester.
225. A. DEMANGEON, *op. cit.*, p. 149.
226. T.S. SMOUT, paper given at Prato, 1978.
227. Rudolf HILFERDING, *Das Finanzkapital*, 1910, French edition of 1970.
228. *Ibid.*, pp. 311–12.
229. See above, chapters 2 and 3.
230. R. HILFERDING, *op. cit.*, pp. 175–7.
231. François CROUZET, *L'Economie de la Grande-Bretagne victorienne*, 1978, p. 280.
232. P. MATHIAS, *op. cit.*, p. 169.
233. In 1826 out of 552 banks, 49 had one director, 157 had 2, 108 had 4, 43 had 5, and 26 had 6. A.E. C.C. London, 21, f°s 168–77, 22 March 1826.
234. The French diplomatic reports often translate 'Country Bank' slightly misleadingly as *banque de comté*.
235. P. MATHIAS, *op. cit.*, p. 170.
236. *Ibid.*, p. 171.
237. *Ibid.*, p. 176.
238. *Ibid.*, pp. 172–3.
239. *Ibid.*, pp. 171–2.
240. A.E., C.C., London, 27, 319–51, 12, 1837.
241. M. RUBICHON, *op. cit.*, II, p. 259.
242. Chevalier Séguier, London, 5 August 1818; A.E., C.C. London, 13, f° 274.
243. W. BAGEHOT, *Lombard Street, a description of the money market*, 1873, p. 21.
244. A.E., C.C., London, 22, f° 275, London, 24 July 1828.
245. A.E., C.C., London, 12, f° 38 v°.
246. T.S. ASHTON, 'The Bill of Exchange and Private Banks in Lancashire 1790–1830' in *Papers and English Monetary History*, ed. T.S. ASHTON et R.S. SAYERS, 1953, pp. 37–49.

247. A.E., C.C. London, 20, f[o] 29, London, 10 February 1825.
248. T.S. ASHTON, *The Industrial Revolution*, 1948, p. 108.
249. P. DEANE and W.A. COLE, *op. cit.*, p. 296.
250. *Ibid.*, p. 305.
251. S. POLLARD and D.W. CROSSLEY, *Wealth ... op. cit.*, p. 199.
252. P. DEANE and W.A. COLE, *op. cit.*, pp. 166 et 175.
253. *Ibid.*, pp. 304–5.
254. A.E., C.C. London, 13, f[o] 357, 6 September 1818.
255. W. BAGEHOT, *Lombard Street*, 1873, p. 31.
256. *Economic Fluctuations in England 1700–1800*, 1959.
257. P. MATHIAS, *op. cit.*, pp. 227 ff.
258. The terminology now familiar to French historians from the work of E. LABROUSSE.
259. A.E., C.C. London, 101, 14 November 1829.
260. See above, chapter 3.
261. P. MATHIAS, *op. cit.*, p. 404.
262. *Ibid.*, p. 144.
263. P. BAIROCH, *Révolution industrielle, op. cit.*, p. 271, table n° 28.
264. E.H. PHELPS BROWN and S. HOPKINS, art. cit., pp. 195–206.
265. S. POLLARD and D.W. CROSSLEY, *op. cit.*, p. 185.
266. *Ibid.*
267. R.-M. PILLET, *op. cit.*
268. *Ibid.*, p. 30.
269. *Ibid.*, p. 24.
270. L. SIMOND, *op. cit.*, I, p. 223.
271. *Ibid.*, II, p. 285.
272. R.-M. PILLET, *op. cit.*, p. 31.
273. *Ibid.*, p. 350.
274. *Ibid.*, p. 337.
275. *Ibid.*, p. 345.
276. W. ABEL, *Agrarkrisen und Agrarkonjunktur op. cit.*
277. R. BAEHREL, *Une Croissance: la Basse-Provence rurale (fin du XVIe-1789)*, 1961.

NOTES TO CONCLUSION

1. Émile CALLOT, *Ambiguïtés et antinomies de l'histoire et de sa philosophie*, 1962, p. 107, quoting Marc BLOCH, *Apologie pour l'histoire ou métier d'historien*, 5th ed., 1964, p. 10.
2. Theodor MOMMSEN, *Römische*

Geschichte, (many times quoted critically by Marx in *Capital*, always referred to as *Herr* i.e. *Mr* Mommsen). Cf. Berlin edn. of *Das Kapital*, 1947–1951, II, p. 175, n. 39; III, p. 359, n. 47 and 857, n. 45. The crucial passage is perhaps the following, from the third volume of *Capital*, Ch. XLVII, 'Introductory Remarks': 'Even in the agricultural societies of antiquity, which show the greatest analogy to capitalist agriculture, namely Carthage and Rome, the similarity with plantation management is greater than with that form which really corresponds to the capitalist mode of exploitation. There existed at one time a formal analogy which however appears as a deception in all essential parts to a man familiar with the capitalist mode of production and who does not, like Mr Mommsen, discover a capitalist mode of production in every monetary economy'.

3. See esp. *Storia economia e sociale dell'impero*, 1933, p. 66, challenged by Paul VEYNE, 'Vie de Trimalchion' in *Annales E.S.C.*, 1961, p. 237.

4. Cf. the position he several times takes up, esp. in *Les Etapes sociales du capitalisme*.

5. Theodore ZELDIN, *France 1848–1945*, 1973, I, p. 75.

6. Jacqueline GRAPIN, in: *Le Monde*, 11–12 November 1973.

7. *Découvertes d'histoire sociale*, 1920, p. 58.

8. Marteng BUIST, *At Spes non fracta*, 1974, p. 431.

9. 'Appunti sull'economia contemporanea: il dibattito attorno all'azione dello Stato nel capitalismo maturo', in: *Rassegna Economica*, 1978, pp. 279–88.

10. C. OFFE, *Lo Stato nel capitalismo maturo*, 1977.

11. James R. O'CONNOR, *The Fiscal Crisis of the State*, 1977.

12. *Op. cit.*, p. 13.

13. Quoted by Paul MATTICK, *Marx et Keynes*, 1972, p. 11.

14. François Richard, *Injustice et inégalité*.

15. René RÉMOND, '"Nouvelle droite" ou droite de toujours', in: *Le Monde*, 20 July 1979.

16. See esp.: *The Reputation of the American Businessman*, 1955, and *The Image of the American Entrepreneur: transformation of a Social Symbol*, 1963.

17. *Paris Match*, 23 March 1979.

18. In private conversation and also in an unpublished typescript, translated from the Russian, in my possession.

19. See note 17.

20. *L'Express*, 9–15 June 1979.

21. Alain VERNHOLES, in *Le Monde*, 21 July 1979, but cf. *ibid.*, September 1979 – famine was already threatening again in Uttar Pradesh.

22. O'CONNOR is quoted in CAFFE *art. cit.*, pp. 285–6; cf. J.K. GALBRAITH, *Economics and the Public Purpose*, 1974, *passim*.

23. Jason ERSTEIN, 'The Last Days of New York', in *New York Review of Books*, 19 February 1976.

24. Conference organized at Paris by the Maison des Sciences de l'Homme and the Bocconi University of Milan, 22–3 February 1979, on 'Small businesses in the European economic system'. The paper referred to was given by Professor Francesco BRAMBILLA.

25. Quoted by Basile KERBLAY, *Les Marchés paysans en URSS*, 1968, pp. 113–14. The quotations from Lenin are from the Russian edition of his collected works, vol. 31, pp. 7–8, and vol. 32, pp. 196, 268, 273.

Index

About the Author

FERNAND BRAUDEL (1902–1985) received a degree in history in 1923 and subsequently taught in Algeria, Paris and São Paulo. He spent five years as a prisoner of war in Germany, during which time he wrote his grand thesis, *The Mediterranean and the Mediterranean World in the Age of Philip II*, which was published in 1949. In 1946 he became a member of the editorial board of *Annales*, the famous journal founded by Marc Bloch and Lucian Febvre, whom he succeeded at the Collège de France in 1949. He was a member of the Ecole Pratique des Hautes Etudes, and from 1962 until his death he was chief administrator of the Maison des Sciences de l'Homme. Professor Braudel held honorary doctorates from universities all over the world.